Indian Economic Development and Policy
Essays in Honour of Professor V. L. D'Souza

V. L. D'souza
(Born : 15 June 1896 Mangalore)

Indian Economic Development and Policy
Essays in Honour of Professor V. L. D'Souza

Edited by

P. R. Brahmananda

D. M. Nanjundappa

B. K. Narayan

VIKAS PUBLISHING HOUSE PVT LTD

New Delhi Bombay Bangalore Calcutta Kanpur

VIKAS PUBLISHING HOUSE PVT LTD
5 Ansari Road, New Delhi 110002
Savoy Chambers, 5 Wallace Street, Bombay 400001
10 First Main Road, Gandhi Nagar, Bangalore 560009
8/1-B Chowringhee Lane, Calcutta 700016
80 Canning Road, Kanpur 208004

ISBN 0 7069 0683 7

1V02B5001

Printed at Roopak Printers, K-17, Navin Shahdara, Delhi 110032

Introduction

One of the time-honoured ways of expression of affection and gratitude of scholars to their teacher is the presentation of a bunch of essays in his honour. Such a collection is a symbolic *gurudakshina*. In the case of Professor D'Souza, the compendium has been enriched by some contributions from some of his professional friends and admirers.

We commenced the voyage of this collection with some trepidation. The Professor himself, when he came to know of this enterprise, discouraged us very strongly. But we persisted and are now joyous to have been able to garner such a valuable and wholesome store. The very success of this venture is a tribute to the ample goodwill the Professor's name commands from which many of us have been beneficiaries.

There are very few Professors who have lent so much of a helping hand to so many young scholars. The history of economic analysis in the Indian sub-continent is largely a history of the contributions of students and disciples (if this blessed science can yield disciples to any teacher!) of a host of distinguished professors in different parts of the country. To name a few Professors, C.N. Vakil, M.L. Dantwala, D.T. Lakdawala and S.K. Muranjan at Bombay; V.K.R.V. Rao and B.N. Ganguli at Delhi; D.R. Gadgil and N.V. Sovani at Poona; J.R. Niyogi, S.K. Basu and S.N. Sen at Calcutta; A.K. Das Gupta at Dacca, Benares and Delhi; J.K. Mehta at Allahabad; V.S. Krishna and B.S. Rao at Waltair; V.R. Pillai at Trivandrum; V.L. D'Souza and M.H. Gopal at Mysore; B.R. Shenoy at Ahmedabad; Kolhatakar at Baroda; B.V. Narayan Swami Naidu at Annamalai; P. J. Thomas, P.S. Lokanathan and R. Balkrishna at Madras; P.C. Gyanchand at Patna; S.K. Iyengar and Abdul Quader at Hyderabad; L.C. Jain at Lahore have all significantly and devotedly served the cause of development of economics in this country.

A professor's students fulfil themselves in so many ways. In the case of Professor D'Souza, his students include more than fifteen university professors in economics and a very large number of other teachers, more than three directors of research institutions, one deputy governor of a central bank, several economic advisers to governments and banks, a host of ministers and political leaders, a number of distinguished journalists and civil servants, many entrepreneurs, and a prince who later became a king.

A collection of essays, such as this, must naturally deal with diverse themes reflecting the current interests of the contributors. Issues of development and planning in India including problems of finance find naturally a prominent place. No effort has been made to standardize the different styles of presentation. Some editorial liberties have been, however, taken. The contributors, we hope will forgive us.

We are thankful to the distinguished authors who have allowed us to make use of some of their writings. We must refer, in particular, to the substantial help rendered by Dr T.K. Lakshman, Professor of Economics, Bangalore University. We are much beholden to Vikas Publishing House who have agreed to put this volume in print.

The royalties out of this volume will accrue to the Indian Economic Association. We expect the Association to use the corpus of the funds for holding a public lecture, preferably at the time of its annual conference and preferably by a past president of that august body.

P.R. BRAHMANANDA
D.M. NANJUNDAPPA
B.K. NARAYAN

A Remembered Sketch

Around the thirties and forties of this century, the young University of
Mysore had already built a reputation of being one of the best Universities. In the picturesque town of Mysore, the headquarters of the University, was situated the Maharaja's College of Arts, one of the oldest colleges
in the country, which had acquired the fame of being one of the best
University colleges for Arts subjects. The Department of Economics of this
College, which conducted the B.A. Honours and the M.A. courses in Eco-
nomics in the University, had gathered great renown. It was headed by
Professor V.L.D'Souza who had launched around him an extraordinary,
able and dedicated team of teachers in economics. During the forties and
later, this group included among others, apart from Professor D'Souza,
Dr R. Balakrishna, Professor B. Tirumalachar, Dr M.H. Gopal, Professor
S.L. Ramarao, Professor S.L.N. Simha, Professor G.N. Krishnamurthy,
Dr G.T. Hutchappa, Dr C.M. Veeraraghavachar, Dr G. Ramakrishna
Reddi, Professor A.P. Sreenivasamurthy, Dr D.M. Nanjundappa and Dr
K.V.G. Gowda.

A unique feature of this Department, certainly around mid-forties, was
the bond of affection that knit the teachers and the students together. In
these days of large-sized departments, where the student enrolment cros-
ses easily 100 and more, it is difficult to realize how intimate the teacher-
taught relation could be in those days, particularly in a place like Mysore.
There was nothing which the students did not come to know about the
teachers and vice versa. The two groups mingled at college functions, on
the sports ground, at the restaurant and in the homes of the teachers.

The Department of Economics of the Maharaja's College naturally
attracted an enviable set of students for the Economics Honours course
which used to run for three years. Thanks to the great care which Professor D'Souza had lavished on this course, it was possible for students to
obtain a first-hand acquaintance, at such an early stage itself, with the
contributions of thinkers like Ricardo, Marshall, and Keynes. In fact, there
was a full paper on the first six chapters of Ricardo's *Principles* (Ashley
edition). We were induced to deeply absorb the writings of Gonner,
Mccolouch, Hollander, Cannan and Edelberg. Wicksteed, Bohm-Bawerk,
Hayek, were familiar names to us. Marshall's *Principles* of course, was the
locus classicus supplemented by Tausigg but, fortunately for us, we were
presented the opposite position through Knight, Robbins, Fraser (*Economic
Thought and Language*) and Davenport. The main drift of the principles of
economics was learnt through the texts of Briggs and Jordan, and Cairn-

cross. The Cambridge Handbooks were compulsory reading for us. We picked up the Quantity Theory through Fisher and were willingly and gleefully taken through Robertson; Robertson's *Money* was great fun, but *Banking Policy* was horribly tough. No doubt Keynes was much there, distilled—inadequately, we learnt later—by Crowther (*Theory of Money*), and we imbibed doses of the practical implications of Keynesianism through the Beveridge Reports. Sayers, DeKock and Muranjan were our banking experts. We surveyed economic history through Knowles, Birnic, Cogg and Sharp, Arndt and Lewis. We thought on *Economic Thought* through the gay irreverential pages of Alexander Grey; lest we have too much of fun, and also have a one-sided view on Marx, the Professor made us pore over Roll. The great thoughts of the great economists were dinned into our minds through Whittaker's *History of Economic Ideas*. We learnt public finance through Dalton, Seligman and Stamp; we certainly did not escape the "excessivity" canon of Dr Gopal. "Indian Economics," we picked up largely through Professor D'Souza's lectures supplemented by Jathar and Beri, ("never merry") Anstey ("Veeramma's *Purana*" as Professor D'Souza would refer to it) and the series of Oxford pamphlets.

Professor D'Souza took care to bring the students in touch with the Journal literature on leading economic issues (fortunately, the journals were not many). Unlike in many other departments then and now, the Maharaja's College Department encouraged students to debate high topics of abstract theory in the class and outside. One of our classmates had read a rather serious paper to our "Eco Club" on the *Karma* Theory of the Trade Cycle; we then were not aware of Micawber's explanation ("Something will always turn up. . .") of the lower turning point. To give a sample of the level of intensity with which the courses were conducted, at the first Honours course class itself (the mean age of students in the class was around 17-19), Professor D'Souza would expose to the students arguments in the articles like that of Robbins on Stationery Equilibrium and of Davenport on Opportunity Costs. ("Opportunity lost is Davenport's Cost" so went a jingle). He would expect each student to study in detail the portions directly from the different texts. Fortunately, the library of the Maharaja's College contained one of the best collections of that period in economics. Besides the nearby University library was also well-stocked with journals. Students in economics certainly thought that they had an edge over other students and used to walk with their noses in the air. In fact, we were better off (at least we thought so) than students in many celebrated foreign universities; in some of the latter places, one would have probably learnt more about the works of one's own teachers than of others. In our case, we learnt from all, the near and far, the living and the dead. Just imagine the effects of exposure to several, conflicting schools of economics at such a young age when one can pick up everything, and so quickly. We were immunized, once and for all, against getting indoctrinated by any one school of thought as such. When the writer went in 1946 to the famous Bombay School for further studies, he found that most of the portions for the then M.A. course in economics had already been covered by him in Mysore. Fortunately at Bombay there was then a provision for a student to register for M.A course by thesis and after two years to directly proceed for the Ph.D. on the recommendation of the guide that the candidate's work could be carried forward for the Ph.D. Thanks to the high reputation in Economic Theory of two former pupils of Professor D'Souza, who were then teachers at the Bombay School, K.S. Krishnaswami and B.V. Krishnamurthi, students from Mysore were highly valued and warmly welcomed.

I have referred to the atmosphere of intimacy and affectionate goodwill that prevailed in the Department. To a great extent, the high status of the Department of Economics was due to the motherly care which Professor D'Souza lavished on its development. He was a trustee to each student and the latter's problems, all of them, were his own. Like the true Christian he has been he would never pass a harsh judgement on any of us. He stood by us, sure and benevolent. We knew he would forgive us for our lapses. The middle forties were a period of great unrest in the country with its repercussions in our college life. This writer cannot forget the steadfast support which the Professor gave to us in our struggles against the authority.

A remarkable trait in Professor D'Souza which none can forget is his rich humour which he generously and infectiously transmits to his students. He is a master of gentle wit and one cannot spend even five minutes with him without being engulfed in bouts of laughter. No thought is too grave to be reduced to earthly dimensions and no bubble so huge that his sense of fun cannot prick. Our contact with Professor D'Souza made us feel that while economics was important, life and living were much more important and here the most proper attitude or angle should be that of objective good humour. No issue in life should down us; nothing should make one feel depressed. One can always perceive, or discover, a humorous angle in and on everything. We must not merely live, but "laugh to live." Isn't it true that "a man is relieved and gay when he has put his heart into his work and done his best." It was one of Professor D'Souza's great achievements, the measure of which only students of economics can appreciate, that he could extract humour even from Alfred Marshall's *Principles*. (Certainly the book is a profound classic, but why should it have been so ponderous?)

One cannot fail to recollect that Professor D'Souza's friendship with the students has always been considered by the latter to be among their most treasured possessions; and years after the students left the college, both the students and the teacher still continue to cherish the memory of the bond that was forged years ago. An uncanny knack of Professor D'Souza was his ability to spot out the special talent and aptitude of each student. Many students have benefited from this.

Life for us under Professor D'Souza's tutelage was a rich and full affair. There was ample teaching, a great deal of learning in and outside the class room, plenty of fun and laughter, and to cap it all, at the end of each year, there would be a special dinner, which the three "Chiefs" (Mr Chief D'Souza himself, Mrs Chief, Mrs D'Souza and Miss Chief, their little daughter), and the larger household of the Professor's colleagues, would be host to the students (and this good deed would always be on a moonlit night).

While we were students at the college, we knew that a host of eminent students had gone through the Department. Years later we realize that the process has continued. A sobering thought for us—*we* were not unique to Professor D'Souza and his team. After we left the college, Professor D'Souza obtained positions of high honour like that of the Vice-Chancellorship of the University of Mysore and several membership positions in many Government of India committees and tribunals. The Indian Economics Association honoured Professor D'Souza by inviting him to preside over the 1951 Aligarh Conference.

An abiding characteristic of his love for students is his habit of lecturing even unto this day to some batch of students or the other. We teach captive audiences; but Professor D'Souza becomes a captive teacher to his students. This is what makes Professor D'Souza one of the greatest teachers. He is like a perennially flowing river. He continues to give more of his time to the students than for anything else. After all, in the long run, not only we are all dead, but even books and ideas disappear. Everyone lives only in the memories of those with whom one has come into contact; and the memory of these memories gets passed on as a treasure from one generation to another. It is said that no one can ever visibly capture what exactly is the type of knowledge that a student receives from a teacher. Knowledge, say our ancient scriptures, passes on from teachers to students as the *nyagrodha* seed, so minute that it is hardly visible. In the case of a great teacher like Professor D'Souza, it is not knowledge alone that is transmitted but also an attitude of striving and a cheerful outlook on life. The secret of laughter, it is said, is one's love for his neighbour. Besides, only the truly humble can perceive the commonness between the giant and the pigmy, the tower and the plain.

Learning, love, laughter, humility are the gifts which Professor D'Souza had passed on to generations of his pupils, and admirers. This volume of essays is a small, very minute, token of the gratitude and love in which Professor D'Souza has been held by a sample of those who were fortunate to come in contact with him. May he live for a hundred years and may the memory of his humour and compassion linger on and on till the end of time.

P.R.B.

Contributors

C. N. VAKIL
  Former Director, and Founder of Bombay School of Economics, Kalpana, Marine Drive, Bombay.

V. K. R. V. RAO
  Chairman, Institute for Social and Economic Change, Bangalore and Founder of Delhi School of Economics and Institute of Economic Growth, Delhi.

S. L. N. SIMHA
  Director, Institute for Financial Management and Research, Madras.

D. T. LAKDAWALA
  Former Director, Department of Economics, University of Bombay and Deputy Chairman, Planning Commission, New Delhi.

K. S. KRISHNASWAMY
  Deputy Governor, Reserve Bank of India, Bombay.

P. R. BRAHMANANDA
  Professor of Monetary Economics, Department of Economics, Bombay University, Bombay.

D. M. NANJUNDAPPA
  Secretary and Economic Adviser to the Government, Government of Karnataka, Planning Department, Bangalore.

YASHODHA SHANMUGA SUNDARAM
  St Anne's College, Oxford, U. K.

A. P. SRINIVASA MURTHY
  Former Professor of Economics, University of Mysore, Mysore.

T. K. LAKSHMAN
  Professor of Economics, Bangalore University, Bangalore.

N. SRINIVASA IYENGAR
  Professor of Economics, Osmania University, Hyderabad.

LILA RAM JAIN
  Indian Statistical Institute, New Delhi.

M. SEBASTIAN
  Professor of Economics, St. Joesph's College, Tiruchirapalli.

D. L. NARAYANA
  Professor of Economics, Sri Venkateshwara University, Tirupati.

M. H. GOPAL
  Former Professor of Economics, University of Mysore, Mysore.

N. BASKARA RAO
  Senior Fellow, Institute for Social and Economic Change, Bangalore.

R. P. MISRA

Director, Institute for Development Studies, University of Mysore, Mysore.

N. S. P. REBELLO

Director of Evaluation, Planning Department, Karnataka Government, Bangalore.

M. D. CHANDRAKANTH

Department of Agricultural Economics, University of Agricultural Sciences, Bangalore.

B. K. NARAYAN

Senior Fellow, Institute for Social and Economic Change, Bangalore.

S. SUBBARAMAIAH

Professor of Economics, Post-graduate Centre, Anantpur, Andhra Pradesh.

NAGESHWARA RAO

Postgraduate Centre, Anantpur, Andhra Pradesh.

K. PUTTASWAMAIAH

Director of Project Formulation, Planning Department, Government of Karnataka, Bangalore.

C. M. VEERARAGHAVACHAR

Reader in Economics, University of Mysore, Mysore.

Contents

C. N. VAKIL

Growth with Stability*

OBJECT AND SCOPE

My object in this paper is to refer briefly to the work that Dr P. R. Brahmanand and I have done in connection with the techniques of planning. We advocated the Wage Goods Model in 1956 and have continued to do so on several other occasions. I shall try to show that the adoption of the Heavy Industries Model with inflationary finance has resulted in unfortunate consequences for the country with increase in poverty and unemployment, as well as a continuous state of inflation which has added to the misery of the poor. I have drawn freely upon some of our work published on different occasions, though those interested will have to go to the original sources which are indicated. Though enough material on the subject has been published from time to time, I hope it will be possible for Dr Brahmanand to find time to evolve a scientific exposition of the Wage Goods Model as the most suited for countries like ours for economic development so that the concept can be studied in one volume by all concerned.

After pointing out the mistake in the technique adopted for planning, I propose to deal with the problem of rural development to which the Janata Government is rightly giving due emphasis. I shall attempt in the first place a rapid review of the agencies and methods so far used for rural development and draw lessons from the same for the future. This will take me to a tentative scheme for involving the rural people themselves in the effort, because any progress in rural areas imposed from above or done by others is not likely to have lasting effects. The people themselves should feel the urge; they should be willing to change and work for it; and simultaneously they should be provided with facilities and training for such a conscious transformation. Such a change will help improve existing methods, revitalize them and make new schemes fruitful. Consistent with my limited objective. I am concentrating on the most important aspect of rural development namely, the human factor, which has been generally neglected. This is most important for the development to be autonomous and permanent, and at the same time cheaper and effective.

*The first Dr D. R. Gadgil Memorial Lecture, Indian Institute of Socio-Economic Studies, Dharwad, 9 October 1977.

Any effort at rural development involving change in the planning technique, will, if properly carried out, in the light of the experience of the past, lead to the adoption of the Wage Goods Model and create a balanced economy. We shall then have development with stability, as inflation will have no place in such a transformation.

INFLATION AND TECHNIQUES OF PLANNING

CONTINUOUS STATE OF INFLATION

We have been living in a state of continuous inflation since 1942-43. Though inflation has not been noticed on occasions, such as the years of plentiful harvest or the period of PL 480 grain supplies from the USA, our economic policy has remained inflationary both during the period before Independence (1942-43 onwards) as well as after Independence and particularly since we adopted planning as the method for economic development. The entire story of this unfortunate situation has been told, based on contemporary contributions in my forthcoming publication *War Against Inflation or the Story of the Falling Rupee, 1943-77* (Macmillan & Co.).

CAUSES OF INFLATION

Though there have been special occasions like wars and famines leading to inflationary situations, it is necessary to find the real causes underlying this situation continuously for such a long period. The explanation lies in the fact that we adopted techniques of planning since 1951 which were not suited to the conditions of the country. Though the planning techniques were not fully developed during the First Plan period, from 1956 we adopted the Heavy Industries Model based on the plan frame evolved by Professor Mahalanobis with the help of Russian technicians. Planning in Russia was dominated by the desire to have a strong defence equipment as Russia feared that there would be an attack and her independence would be in danger. In other words, the attention in Russian planning was more towards heavy industries required for defence purposes, and not for raising the standard of living of the ordinary citizens, who were required to work hard under military discipline for the security of the state. It was such objectives dominating the Russian plan, which Russian technicians transferred without understanding our requirements to the plan frame adopted by Professor Mahalanobis which became the basis of the Second Plan.[1] The problem of financing such a heavy plan arose, as we did not

[1] A panel of economists was convened by the Planning Commission to discuss the plan frame and other aspects of the Second Plan in March 1956. Several papers were submitted by about 20 leading economists from different universities in the country. Among them were (*a*) "Investment Pattern in the Second Five Year Plan" and (*b*) 'Institutional Implications of a Bolder Plan." Both were jointly done by me and Dr,

have the necessary resources for the purpose. It was not realized by those concerned that the Indian economy does not conform to those background conditions which are true of developed countries. Because of this, policies based on western economic thought, particularly Keynesian theories, did not apply to our conditions. Under our conditions, the scale of real income in each short period is decided by the stock of capital and the supply conditions of wage goods. This happens because of the consumption-real income multiplier.[2] The price level under our conditions is determined mainly by the quantity of money which the authorities decide to maintain in the economy. The volume of savings is determined by the interest rate and fiscal incentives to those who are in a position to save. The distribution of incomes between owners of property and enterprise, and household and wage earners, and the state of expectations concerning the price level, have also their effect on the volume of savings. Savings would be maintained, if there is any reduction in population and its growth. The rate of growth of real income is determined by the proportion of savings to income and the portion of such savings devoted to the expansion of the wage goods sector. If the right set of economic models is adopted for planning on these lines, both employment and real income can grow at a faster rate.

Having overlooked this fundamental characteristic of the Indian economy, we drifted into a technique of economic planning which has not solved our essential problems for a generation. The mistakes that we committed were that we adopted a process of financing of investments for planning which were dependent on a ratio of credit expansion which was faster than that warranted by the growth of the ratio of supplies of wage goods. We went rather slow on the growth of production of wage goods which are common necessities of the average citizens, so much so that the ratio of wage goods to captital went down very heavily. This will be evident from the following figures.[3]

Money supply per unit of capital went up at a compound rate of 0.70 per cent per annum from 1950-51 to 1971-72 and at a rate of 6.25 per cent p.a. from 1962-63 to 1973-74. If we take the entire period of 1950-51 to 1973-74, money supply per unit of capital went up at a compound rate of 2.90 per cent p.a. At the same time, the rate of wage goods to capital went up only at the rate of 0.10 per cent from 1950-51 to 1961-62 and it declin-

P. R. Brahmanand. The Wage Goods Model was propounded in these papers as the most suitable for our country. This was ignored. The same ideas were elaborated in "Planning for an Expanding Economy" which was published in July 1956. Leading international economists who met in Rome in September 1956 for the First World Congress of Economists were impressed by the argument of the book, and some of them wrote appreciative reviews of the book, particularly Professor Ranger Nurkse.

[2]These observations are based on an elaborate econometric study made by Dr P. R. Brahmanand entitled *Determinants of Real National Income and Price Level in India* published by the University of Bombay, 1977.

[3]*Ibid.*

ed at an annual rate of 3.46 per cent during the period 1962-63 to 1973-74. If we take the entire period 1950-51 to 1973-74 the decline in the rate of wage goods to capital is 2.96 per cent p.a. In a large country like ours, where the majority of the people are poor living on the poverty line, unless planning takes care of the essential goods required by such a large population, it is bound to create an unbalanced situation in which we may have heavy industries producing goods for the upper class or for exports, but not within the reach of the ordinary citizen, who would be starved even of essentials. Because by the very definition, such industrial growth would mean a relatively small increase in employment, we would have an increase also in unemployment with our growing population. In consequence, we see a spectacle of one-sided economic growth of industries and of an increase in wealth of certain sections of the people, who live in a different style in western fashion, while the majority of the people continue in poverty, which seems to be on the increase. The inevitable consequence of this sort of planning was the continuous increase in money supply for financing the type of development that we have, with inadequate supplies of wage goods, which was bound to create the endemic phenomenon of continuous inflation in the country.

The way in which we drifted towards economic planning techniques under the influence of Keynesian ideas inevitably led us to heavy deficit financing though, on many occasions the Government desired to avoid such deficit financing. This was so because we went about undertaking ambitious plans without being able to mobilize adequate resources by taxation. The organized industrial firms who were able to lobby for heavy expansion of credit with success, instead of ploughing back their own resources for further investment, adopted the policy of depending on credit from financial institutions. The ratio of savings to income gradually went down which caused widespread distress among the working class. This describes in brief the underlying economic situation in the country on which was superimposed the heavy expansion of money supply due to the conflict with Pakistan over the independence of Bangladesh, and widespread famines during the same period. The inflation which was inherent in our economy because of the above factors grew therefore to large proportions in 1973-74. When economists[4] pointed out the mischief of the monetary factor and the situation in 1973-74, efforts were made in some quarters to emphasize other factors which however important had relatively marginal effect on the price situation.

PRESENT ECONOMIC POSITION AND THE EMERGENCE OF
NEW INFLATION

The anti-inflationary measures taken by the Government from July 1974

---

[4]Memorandum on a Policy to contain inflation signed by 140 economists, submitted to the Prime Minister in February 1974.

along with the administrative measures to deal with smuggling, black-marketing and other economic offences had considerable effect on the economy during the period September 1974 to March 1975. It may be pointed out that the agricultural season in 1974-75 was not very satisfactory. Inspite of this, we noticed that there was a tendency for a fall in prices from September 1974 which continued till April 1976. The bumper harvest of 1975-76 may have helped this tendency from December 1974 when the kharif crop began coming into the market. This means that for the period September 1974 to November 1975 there could be no effect of the bumper harvest of 1975-76. We find that during this period money supply increased only by 0.7 per cent. The impounding of 50 per cent of additional dearness allowance rose to Rs 1400 crores by the end of July 1976. The Government did not take any credit from the Reserve Bank; the commercial sector also did not have the usual loans from the commercial banks. In consequence, we find that the currency was actually declining during the period. It is the combination of these factors which led to the decline in monetary growth and consequent fall in prices during the period referred to above. The bumper harvest of 1975-76 helped the process and the fall continued further. But the Government of India became complacent thereafter, and the budget of 1976-77 again started having inflationary potential. The policy of credit expansion during the busy season of 1975-76 also had inflationary tendencies. The plan outlay for 1976-77 was stepped up, and there was a provision for a large amount of deficit financing in the budget, as well as for large-scale borrowings from the banking system. The impounded dearness allowance and compulsory deposits were due to be repaid in part during the year. Due to all these factors monetary expansion was growing at more than 10 per cent during 1975-76 and was bound to increase further in 1976-77. The Economists' Memorandum had suggested that there should be a ceiling on the annual growth rate of money supply of about 5 per cent as our growth rate had not exceeded 5 per cent in the preceding years. This idea was entirely overlooked with the consequence that the monetary factor had worsened again leading to a rise in prices from March-April 1976.

Money Supply—The Dominant Factor

The effect of money supply on the price level may be further illustrated by the behaviour of the price level during the Fifth Plan period. In the Fifth Plan period the Planning Commission has provided for an increase in money supply of about Rs 6700 crores. Taking into account the price changes since the above calculations were made, it may be estimated that during the entire period of the Fifth Plan,[5] money supply is expected to rise by about 60 per cent. During the same period the real national income may not increase by more than 18 per cent on the basis of past ex-

[5]The Fifth Plan as originally approved during the tenure of the Congress Government.

perience. It shows that there is a high inflationary potential in the Plan. In view of the experience that we have had since planning started in the country, it is safe to lay down certain propositions regarding the behaviour of the price level in our country:

(*i*) Money supply as well as aggregate supplies of wage goods determine completely the level of prices in the Indian economy;

(*ii*) The volume of real savings is negative to the level of wholesale prices or of wage goods prices;

(*iii*) The rate of interest, deflated or undeflated, is positively related to the quantity of money;

(*iv*) Money wages do not have a significant statistical effect upon prices in general and industrial prices in particular;

(*v*) There is a stable multiplier of about 3 between supplies of wage goods and real national income. This means that Rs 100 worth of wage goods generate about Rs 300 worth of national income. By concentrating upon a faster rate of growth of wage goods supply, the economy can obtain each year a higher growth rate in real income than now. In our conditions, the Keynesian multiplier relation between investment and income is statistically insignificant; and

(*vi*) Public distribution not merely has no negative effect upon food-grain prices but is associated with higher prices. The public distribution system, which is necessary for better distribution, does not have the price dampening effect.

The above conclusions which are based on carefully calculated sophisticated econometric technique[6] necessitate an entirely new look in the problem of economic policy formulation in the country.

Unfortunately for the country since March 1976 prices have been rising again—from 283 in March 1976, it crossed the 330 limit by the end of the year. That was the peak which was reached in September 1974. It is not possible that this rise in prices is due to relative scarcity in supply. It is well-known that both agricultural and industrial supplies are satisfactory and that the position except in edible oils has not become worse. The conclusion is obvious that just as the price decline from September 1974 to June 1975 has to be attributed wholly to monetary factors; the price rise since March 1976 must also be attributed wholly to monetary factors. This tendency was noticed by the authorities in December 1976 and certain credit restrictions were imposed on 14 January 1977. But after the announcement of the elections to the Lok Sabha suddenly made on 18 January, oral instructions were given by the Ministers of Finance and Industry to the Chairman of Commercial Banks and Financial Institutions on 21 January to be soft in giving credit. These were followed up by

[6]Dr P.R. Brahmanand, *Determinants of Real National Income and Price Level in India.*

written instructions by the new Deputy Governor of the Reserve Bank in the beginning of February 1977. In other words, we have a sudden shift towards increase in money supply and indifference to inflationary conditions from the authorities during the period. The consequence has been that the Janata Government has been given the legacy of a price level which is higher than the peak level reached in 1974.

The Government and the Reserve Bank have tried to explain the recent increase in money supply by two factors: (*i*) credit given by commercial banks to the Food Corporation of India for purchase of foodgrains and (*ii*) increase in the foreign exchange assets mainly due to remittances by Indians settled abroad which now come in increasing numbers because of certain incentives which have been offered and also because of the fact that smuggling has been controlled.

Regarding the monetary expansion due to the purchase of grains by the Food Corporation of India, if the authorities had overall money supply target, it would have been possible for them to see that the sellers of grains made available monetary resources to those who were denied access to banks.

Regarding the growing foreign exchange reserve, it can be prevented from having an effect on money supply by a variety of methods such as blocked deposits, selectively higher conversion rates for those portions of remittances which are held in the form of blocked accounts. These are adopted in some western countries. At the same time, higher rates of interest may be offered to time deposits in foreign currency. Another important step that can be suggested to remove the monetary effect of the growing exchange reserve would be to lift the ban on gold imports. In the past, it is well-known that gold imports have been a convenient way by means of which the Indian economy utilized its export surpluses with no effects on the monetary process. It would be possible to make arrangements with the nationalized banks to import gold and make it available to those who wish to purchase the same. We have also issued gold bonds some years ago for which the Government has undertaken to repay in gold to the parties concerned. If the gold bonds are cashed in gold, it would withdraw currency to that extent from the economy. Of course, some part of the reserves can be utilized to import essential goods of which there is scarcity in the country. At the same time, the export of essential goods from the country should be stopped, as we can do without the foreign exchange.

ECONOMIC PROGRESS ANALYZED—KEY INDICATORS[7]

We may try to examine more closely the fallacy underlying the trend in our planning effort in order to establish the need for a complete change in our outlook and method of planning. Table 1 gives in a nutshell an idea

[7]Based on "The Future of Planning and the Planning of Future" by Dr P.R. Brahmanand.

of the progress, of key indicators in the Indian economy over the period
1950-51 to 1973-74 and over two sub-periods. As the dividing line 1962-63
is chosen because that was the year of the Chinese invasion. The second
period encompasses one invasion and two wars, events not of our
choice. It is admitted in all quarters that in contrast with the Chinese
economy, China's performance was less than ours in the first period,
whereas theirs was a bit better than ours in the second period.

A look at the table reveals that during the second period, the growth-
rates per annum, total and per capita, of real domestic product, supplies
of wage goods, and supplies of basic goods have been lower than in the
first. Per capita wage goods supply has been going down. Factory-employ-
ment, industrial output, net real investment and savings also have grown
at a lower rate. Real savings and even real government expenditure have
moved up in the second period at a rate slower than real national income.
Population growth rate has risen. Though real capital stock has grown at
a faster rate in the second period, the capital-output ratio has risen. The

TABLE 1

Trends in Economic Indicators: 1950-51 to 1973-74

(*Long-linear rates per annum*)

	1950-51 to 1973-74	1950-51 to 1961-62	1962-63 to 1973-74
1 Population	2.8	1.95	2.18
2 Real domestic product	3.56	3.76	3.22
3 Real capital stock	4.75	3.88	5.33
4 Real income per capita	1.47	1.81	1.03
5 Wage goods supply	2.49	3.47	1.87
6 Wage goods supply per capita	0.04	1.52	−0.31
7 Employment in factories	2.64	2.11	1.78
8 Industrial output	6.09	6.63	4.42
9 Basic goods supply	2.18	2.97	0.31
10 Net real investment	7.19	8.05	4.53
11 Net real savings	5.16	8.58	2.59
12 Money supply	7.52	4.50	10.11
13 Money per unit of capital	2.90	0.70	6.25
14 Ratio of wage goods per unit of capital	-2.02	0.10	-3.46
15 Real government expenditure	6.51	11.04	2.92
16 Wholesale prices	4.74	1.29	7.18
17 Foodgrains prices	5.59	1.04	7.97
18 Manufacturer's prices	3.81	1.40	5.96
19 Wage goods prices	5.04	0·95	7.60
20 Basic goods prices	4.88	0.98	7.82
21 Quantum of imports	3.26	4.52	-0.33
22 Quantum of exports	2.57	1.09	3.37
23 External terms of trade	1.06	1.52	0.83

growth rate of imports has become negative in the second period whereas that of exports has gone up. The terms of trade have been in India's favour (this position is changing since the oil crisis). Money supply has grown at a higher rate in the second period. *Money per unit of real capital* has been going up all through and at a steeply higer rate in the second period. The wage-goods productivity of capital has been going down, rather steeply in the second period. Naturally all sets of prices have risen, and at a higher rate in the second period. The development process has led to an increase in the overall consumption-well-being of the community at a very modest rate.

The general impression of a deceleration in the beneficial results of growth process is obvious. It appears that like Alice, India has been running faster and faster; but unlike Alice she has not been able to remain at the same position.

Somehow the Planners have missed the perspective of the Indian Economy. What are the major economic problems of the country? Most would agree that poverty and unemployment are the two most pressing problems. What is poverty? Most would agree that those households which are not able to obtain a measure of real income which can yield a decent level of subsistence are poor. What is a decent level of subsistence? In India, society has deemed it equal to about Rs 240 per annum per person at 1960-61 prices, or about Rs 750 at 1975-76 prices.

Wage Goods Gap

Hence poverty in 1975-76 could have been eliminated if the macrosupply position in regard to basic wage goods was higher; let us say, by about 25 to 30 per cent. And poverty would not raise its ugly head, if from 1975-76 onwards each year our aggregate supplies of wage goods would be growing at the same rate as population would be growing. Thus there is a basic *wage goods gap* in the economy, which explains poverty. Of course, this gap exists because our capacity to produce wage goods is deficient. The capacity is deficient because the total capital stock designed and directed to produce wage goods is inadequate. Note that total capital stock may be adequate, but capital stock in the specific form of wage goods production capacity may be deficient.

A question may be asked at this stage as to whether, in whatever form capital stocks exist, they cannot be utilized for the production of whatever goods we require; for example, it is not possible for steel mills, machinery making plants etc. to be directed for the manufacture of wage goods. Unfortunately, specific capacities to produce particular goods are not tantamount to capacity to produce whatever goods we require. So long as capital is in a putty, all-purpose fitted form, it can be directed towards creation of any sort of specific capacity, but when once putty-capital becomes capital goods in the form of factories, projects like steel mills, machinery plants, mining and power stations and transport networks, it partakes the nature of clay for a particular purpose. Generalized capital is simply the capacity to produce all sorts of capital goods. Except the stocks of wage goods and the raw materials and accessories involved in their production, the rest of specific stocks cannot be brought under the category of generalized capital. Wage goods enter here because, if stocks of wage goods exist, labour-power can be purchased and deployed for whatever specific capacities are needed in the country.

A group of goods known as inter-connected heavy industry products can have a capacity to generate mutual demands such that, if the workers engaged in this sector are supplied from outside with wage goods, it can go on expanding limitlessly, subject to the constraint of metal and mineral resources in the community.

A considerable portion of an economy can be organized in such a manner and the production inter-relationships so determined that the country may become richer and richer in terms of some types of capacity, but its capacity to produce wage goods may be woefully deficient. In the Fifth Plan, it has been stated that for items like coal, crude oil, iron ore and cement, which form independent sectors in the input-output model, the targets have been derived directly from the sectoral growth rates. The profound meaning of this statement is that the network of heavy industry products in an economy get their growth rates determined independently of the rest of the economy. When the planners tried to obtain a higher rate of growth of production of wage goods within a given growth rate in order to implement a portion of the goal of poverty eradication, they found that the growth rates of a number of heavy industry items got reduced. In other words, the technical proof that certain industrial sectors are not required for wage goods expansion was mathematically demonstrated.

High growth rates in certain sectors can go on endlessly with low growth rates in other sectors. Take the case of the Indian economy during the past 25 years or so. The total real capital stock appears to have increased at a compound rate of 5 per cent per annum. Particularly since the Second Plan, we have built quite substantial production capacities in a number of heavy industries and related lines. On the other hand, all evidence indicates that real capital stock in and for agriculture which produces the dominant wage goods has proceeded at a rate not exceeding that of population growth. The growth rate in production has been rather meagre. Naturally, the proportion of people below the poverty line has tended to be constant over the years. In almost each year we could have stated that if only the wage goods supply were larger by, say, 25-30 per cent, there would have been no macro-poverty in the economy.

The way out of poverty is, therefore, to pay immediate attention to making good the capital gap in respect of wage goods capacity. This, in its turn, would imply a drastic alteration in the pattern of investment in the economy.

Unemployment

The second major problem is that of unemployment. The bulk of the unemployment in the Indian economy, it is conceded, is in the rural areas. Such unemployment does not get reflected in any conventional market signals. According to the studies made by the Jawaharlal Nehru University, 30 per cent of the districts in India had an annual average growth of about 3 per cent in agricultural production (and 12 per cent of the districts had a growth rate of 5 per cent and above). It is interesting to observe that these districts had a share of 36 per cent in aggregate output, of 30 per cent in gross cropped area, of 45 per cent in irrigation facilities, of 39 per cent in fertilizer consumption and of 68 per cent in tractors. If we make the assumption that these areas had about 29-30 per cent of population in the economy, and the growth rate in population in these areas was about the same as in the general economy, we arrive at an important conclusion that production in excess of population growth rate occurred in these parts *and there was no conspicuous incidence of labour shortage.* In other words, the additional supply of labour has been made available from within the surplus labour pool concealed on the existing farms. This evidence is sufficient to demonstrate the existence of disguised unemployment in Indian agriculture. It also points out that further growth in agriculture itself is one of the prominent ways of absorbing the disguisedly unemployed. The same study points out that in 25 per cent of the districts, growth rate was negative. Thus the pressure of disguised unemployment would have increased here.

Granted the existence of disguised unemployment, its eradication becomes conditional upon supplies of wage goods; for, their employment in full-bodied productive capacity would create additional demand for wage goods. Unless the system is able to procure these wage goods, additional employment will not be stabilized. Additional supply of wage goods leading to an improvement in per capita on real income in terms of wage goods and/or in the real wage rate is the mechanism by means of which unemployment gets eradicated. Poverty in terms of inadequate supplies of wage goods is the barrier to full employment or fuller employment. In fact, there are no two problems like poverty and unemployment; there is only one problem—inadequate supply of wage goods.

CONCLUSION

A remarkable factor in India's development experience over the past 25 years is the stability of the relation between supplies of wage goods and total real domestic products. As already pointed out according to a regression exercise carried out at the Bombay University, it has been found that 100 rupee worth of increase in wage goods leads to an increase in real domestic product equivalent to more than Rs 300. There is a stable multiplier of about 3. On the other hand, we find that the Keynesian investment-income multiplier is statistically insignificant in the Indian economy. In our economic policies in the past, we have utilized Keynesian techniques with disastrous effects on social justice and the saving ratio. The Indian economy is a peculiar animal which does not adapt itself to conventional economic models.

RURAL DEVELOPMENT

Though the plan allocations for rural development were not adequate, we have spent fairly large amounts for the development of agriculture and allied activities since planning started. The expenditure on agriculture and allied activities was Rs 332 crores in 1969-70; it rose to Rs 896 crores in 1976-77. The complaint however is that we have not realized the fruits of even this limited investment in rural development. It would be of intetest from this point of view, for future guidance, to have a rapid review of the way in which rural development was organized, so that we can plan the pro- posed additional investment for rural development in the light of such experience, and avoid mistakes which have crept into the system in the past. It will not be possible to go into all details, but an attempt is made to refer to several agencies in brief, which have been charged with rural development, which in the aggregate will give us a coordinated idea of the problem to enable us to devise methods which will not be subject to loopholes of the past.

Community Development. Launched in October 1952, this programme was intended to bring about an integrated development of rural India covering the social, agricultural and economic aspects of community life. We have more than 5,000 Community Development Blocks and about 500 Tribal Development Blocks. Each block has an average area of more than 600 sq. km. and comprises of about 110 villages with a population of more than 90,000 people. In the beginning, the Central Government supplied the funds; considerable assistance was also received from the Ford Foundation. From the Fourth Plan the finances are found by the State Governments, though the Central Government lays down the policy and tries to coordinate the work. A Development Commissioner is in charge of the programme in each state; he coordinates the work of different depart- ments of the state connected with rural development.

Panchayati Raj. This was introduced in 1959 for the purpose of local self-government in 3 stages, namely, village, block and district levels. It is functioning now in most of the states except Meghalaya and Nagaland. Elected representatives carry out the programme of decentralization of power. Some of the Rural Development activities are carried out through the Panchayati Raj. It is well-known that this experiment has not succeeded.

Drought Prone Areas Programme (DPAP). This programme was initiated in 1970-71 to deal with areas which were liable to drought. Steps are taken to develop activities which enable people in these areas to face conditions of drought, if any, such as irrigation, soil conservation and afforestation, road-building and drinking water.

The Prime Minister's Drought Relief Fund. This was set up in 1966 with the object of mobilizing resources for undertaking relief operations in drought-stricken areas. It is estimated that so far about Rs 2 crores have been disbursed out of this fund.

Crash Scheme, 1971. This was introduced for rural development for a period of 3 years. Projects such as road-building, reclamation and development of land, flood protection, minor irrigation and so on were undertaken to give employment to the unemployed.

Applied Nutrition Programme. Undertaken in collaboration with UNICEF, FAO and WHO, this is primarily an education-oriented scheme to help the nutrition of children under 5 years and expectant and nursing mothers.

Tribal Area Development. Several pilot projects have been undertaken for developing tribal areas. More than 2 lakh persons have been dealt with; about 3 lakh acres of land have been brought under improved agricultural practices. Minor irrigation, animal husbandry programme and road construction works are also contemplated.

Indo-German Assistance Programme. With the cooperation of this agency, hill areas are being developed in certain districts of Himachal Pradesh, Uttar Pradesh and Tamil Nadu.

National Institute of Rural Development. The National Institute of Rural Development was established in 1966 as an autonomous institution to (*i*) act as an apex institute for providing orientation and training in the philosophy and aims of community development and Panchayati Raj to key personnel, both official and non-official; (*ii*) undertake programme of study and research in social sciences with particular emphasis on planned social change through community development; (*iii*) provide academic guidance to the training centres in different parts of the country and to impart training to their instructional staff; and (*iv*) function as a clearing house for information on community development and Panchayati Raj.

The Institute has been conducting a number of courses to train personnel—both official and non-official—engaged in rural and community development activities. Besides publishing a number of papers, the Institute is engaged in research projects relating to rural development.

The Whole Village Development Programme. This new programme is being implemented in the Fifth Plan period in some states. The object is consolidation of holdings, overall land development planning through irrigation support and restructuring of the cropping pattern.

Small Farmers and Marginal Farmers Development Agencies. These agencies were set up to provide financial assistance to weaker farmers in the Fourth Plan. More than Rs 100 crores was provided in the Fourth Plan to help farmers with credit for various rural activities. The progress of these schemes was rather halting due mainly to operational deficiencies. In some cases the original project reports were not prepared in detail and had to be revised. Some of the State Departments failed to realize their responsibility in these central projects and hence there was no dovetailing of the State Plans and resources with those of the agencies implementing such programmes. Some progress has been achieved because more than 10 lakh farmers have benefited by this scheme in various ways. The National Commission on Agriculture recommended several changes in these schemes. They have therefore been made composite covering small and marginal farmers and agricultural labourers.

Co-op. Credit and Rural Devlopment. Co-op. Credit is provided mainly for (*i*) seasonal agricultural operations, (*ii*) investment credit for improvement of land, and (*iii*) for conversion of short-term agricultural production loans into medium-term loans.

Marketing. Co-operative marketing is intended to secure the best price for the produce of the agriculturists and to release them from exploitation by private traders, and to help recovery of production finance provided by the credit societies by introducing the system of linking of credit with marketing.

Medium-Term Credit. Credit under this scheme is given for those projects which need comparatievely smaller outlay and include such activities as repairs to wells, installation of pump sets, purchase of agricultural machinery, etc.

Stabilization Credit. In times of calamities like floods and droughts the production loans which cannot be repaid would be allowed to be converted into medium-term loans and fresh production loans would be allowed to the cultivators.

Long-Term Credit. Land Development Banks deal with this type of credit which is given for land development, irrigation and mechanization. The ARDC, the Commercial Banks, the LIC, the State and Central Governments are all actively involved in the development of long-term cooperative credit.

Farmers' Service Societies. These societies are formed to help the weaker sections of the rural people. Such a society undertakes financing of agriculture and allied activities, artisans, craftsmen. It may also supply agricultural inputs as well as consumer goods and also help in marketing facilities. Such a society would also help in mobilizing small savings.

Regional Rural Banks. From July 1975 a chain of Regional Rural Banks have been created. They are similar to commercial banks but with limited objective. The area of their operation would be limited to one or more districts. They would grant loans to small and marginal farmers at rates not higher than those of co-op. societies. The salary structure of the staff of these banks would be fixed with due regard to local conditions. By March 1977, 47 regional Rural Banks were started covering 1 lakh small and marginal farmers.

Financing of Agriculture by Commercial Banks. It was found that cooperative societies could not satisfy the credit needs of agriculture beyond

30 per cent. Besides, they have their shortcomings which vary from State to State. They relate to (*i*) problems of overdues, (*ii*) indifferent management, (*iii*) lack of resources, (*iv*) absence of link between credit and marketing aspects in the coopertive structure of most of the States and so on. Further, cooperative societies are not developed in all States of the country, To make up for this gap the State Bank of India began helping agriculture through cooperatives in 1956. With the nationalization of banks, commercial banks entered the field in a big way for financing agriculture. All types of agriculture and allied activities are financed by providing crop loans (short-term loans) and medium-term loans.

It was found that the approach of banks to achieve certain targets was not satisfactory because of (*i*) unsound lending due to imperfect appraisal, (*ii*) difficulties of scattered lending over a large area, (*iii*) inadequate machinery for supervision of financing (*iv*) disparity in coverage of farmers. It was realized that provision of credit alone was not sufficient because farmers require all-round assistance. The banks have therefore now adopted the area approach. The State Bank started the Agricultural Development Branches (ADBs) with special staff suited to the purpose including some technical personel. Other Commercial Banks are also adopting the same approach of looking beyond the credit aspects in financing agriculture.

Village Adoption. The area approach has, in some cases, taken the form of Village Adoption Scheme. The bank concerned undertakes all-round activities of the villages, including marketing and work of existing agencies.

Selection of Growth Centres. The Lead Bank Scheme introduced in 1969 assigns special responsibility to commercial banks in the respective lead districts. They have to identify growth centres and have economically viable area development schemes for the same.

Problems faced by the Banks in Financing Agriculture (*i*) While implementing area development schemes, the banks are playing the role of prime or sponsored agencies and the Government Development Agencies or machinery are playing a secondary role. This brings in problems of coordination between the various agencies. If the banks are sponsoring agencies, in some areas, Governmental agencies tend to view things with apathy. But wherever there has been co-operation between the banks and the Government agencies, the schemes have borne fruits. (*ii*) Support facilities for marketing the products of village populatian remain inadequate. (*iii*) Presence of two or more financing agencies in an adopted village—lack of co-ordination between the various agencies leads to wastage of resources. (*iv*) Non-availability of up-to-date revenue documents or records. Though the bank's schemes of lending are very liberal and do not insist on security, a few documents like title deeds are required to grant advances. This hinders the successful implementation of credit schemes by the banks.

Conclusion. Despite the rapid strides made by the commercial banks in financing agriculture, certain limitations that commercial banks face have to be acknowledged. Branches of commercial banks are not present in all the 6 lakhs villages in India. Also attitudinal constraints of the bank's staff and high costs of operating funds in financing agriculture are there. The Regional Rural Banks set up to overcome the above two deficiencies may not be able to cope with the credit gaps in the agricultural sector.

Ultimately, one has to admit that co-operatives which have the feel of the rural economy will serve best the agricultural sector. But the many ills from which they suffer have to be removed and the co-operatives have to be organized on scientific lines.

It is only by strengthening the financial institutions at the grass-roots level with a better coordination between commercial banks, cooperatives and governmental agencies that the credit flow to agriculture can be accelerated.

Agricultural Refinance and Development Corporation. This was created by an Act of Parliament in order to help the resources available for agricultural finances. It finances various large institutions through whom the finance is given for rural areas. It gives re-finance facilities. The assistance from World Bank for certain agricultural projects is channelled through this Corporation.

Development of Rural Industries. The Small Scale Industries Development Organizations, National Small Industries Corporation and commercial banks are trying to help the smaller industries. Units which require less than Rs 1 lakh of investment are grouped as the tiny sector. Many rural industries, handloom units, coir, sericulture and silk industries and handicrafts are receiving attention.

Handloom industries is the most important as about 90 lakh persons depend for their livelihood on this industry. The coir industry originated in Kerala as a cottage industry; the Coir Board was formed in 1954. But the mechanization of the coir industry and the advent of man-made fibres has made the work of the Coir Board difficult. It is a cottage industry employing about 5 lakh people. For sericulture, there is a Central Silk Board with 4 research institutions. Handicrafts include a large number of crafts which are backed by centuries of experienec and skill, such as diamonds and jewellery, woollen carpets, rugs, art metal wares, woodwares and printed textiles, shawls, zari, ivory products and embroiderʎ goods, etc. All India Handicrafts Board set up in 1962 helps in developing handicrafts.

The Khadi and Village Industries Commission was formed to encourage the development of cottage industries especially *khadi*. The Commission provides assistance to Khadi and other village industries through co-operative societies.

Rural Electrification Corporation was established in 1969. Some progress has been made in this connection though there is considerable room for improvement.

Central and State Warehousing Corporation. This Corporation encourages various efforts, particularly of co-operative societies for construction of godowns and storage facilities for various agricultural products.

Committees for Rural Development. There are a large number of committees formed by banks and the government functioning at the district and state levels.

The Department of Rural Development, in the Ministry of Agriculture coordinates the activities of the various agencies we have referred to.

IMPLEMENTATION OF RURAL DEVELOPMENT SCHEMES

As we have seen that financial provision made for schemes of rural development was not small, it was not adequate for our requirements. What is of interest is that the multiplicity of agencies referred to above and the administrative staff employed by them absorbed about 60 per cent of the Plan Budget for rural development. It is not clear whether even the remaining 40 per cent reached the rural folk or whether there was leakage, to which, reference will be made later.

It may be noted that the officer who is charged with the work usually works in the red tape fashion. He is an urbanite invariably and does not mix with the rural people. He does not understand their real problems as there is very little direct communication between the officer and the rural folk who usually hesitate to approach him because of the way in which he works and behaves. We have inherited this tradition from the British regime. The Collector of the District under the British was the representative of the King-Emperor, he was not approachable; people were afraid of him; his word was law in most cases. His subordinates imitated him and behaved as the overlords of the people over whom they ruled. The other departments and agencies of the Government which grew in course of time adopted the same official attitude and followed the same method of dealing with the people. The people have to approach them; they have not to approach the people. For each type of help under the Plan Schemes, the person entitled to it has to fill in a form and go through a procedure, which he does not understand. In some cases, middlemen have come into existence who act as intermediaries and help in getting the benefits to which the farmer is entitled, in the process he gets his commission which varies according to the state of ignorance of the farmer. The officer reports that he has distributed the help; the statistics show the same; in reality the amount of help received is less than officially shown. There are cases in which some local influential people (known as goondas or dadas) make a job of this work; the farmers approach them; no help will be available without them; their share will be considerable. Besides they will be able to wield political power in getting votes for candidates to the Assembly or the Parliament.

The Human Factor in Rural Development

For the purpose of more effective results of rapid rural development which is now the objective, some fundamental changes in the personnel that will handle the work is required if success is to be achieved. The following suggestions are made, some for long-term and others for short-term or immediate purposes:

Centres for Rural Development

A Centre for Rural Development must be established in each district. This should be for all-round development of the area, both economic and social. Though ultimately each district should have such a centre, a beginning may be made with a few selected districts in each State to gain experience and establish other Centres as soon as possible. Some districts may have more centres.

It should have a good size farm at its disposal for agricultural work as well as other facilities which may develop as required. The object should be to train young boys and girls of the area in appropriate rural work—agricultural operations; animal husbandry; dairy work; cottage industries; sanitation and health and so on. The trainees would have some basic education in their own language in rural schools and would be in the age group 15 to 16. As far as possible, they should live in the centre in a simple rural style, though with the necessary improvements. Each trainee may specialize in one or more branches of work according to his or her aptitude, though there should be some basic common training to all. The training should be mainly practical, though they should be encouraged to read some simple literature suited to their work. The courses will have to be properly worked out; there may be some differences in different districts, as each district may have some special problems. The training should extend over a period of 2 years; in some special cases it may be longer.

Those in charge of the centre should be devoted workers, who can identify themselves with the life and problems of the area, mix freely with the people, understand their problems and inspire confidence among the people in their work and outlook. They would thus be a type of missionaries or sarvodaya workers, not anxious to have an official career with the usual official emoluments, but satisfied with a reasonable standard of life suited to the area, making it easy for the rural folk to approach them and deal with them.

The persons so trained will go back to their villages and work on their own fields, if any, or those of others, and be able to effect improvements by spreading ideas and practices which they may have learnt. They will thus be centres of rural change in a wide sense, economic, social, health, education, etc. They are not expected to get jobs as employees of others, but work independently and set an example of such self-help to others. They will thus be modern farmers, self-reliant and progressive, willing to learn new methods and adapt them to their requirements. They will have acquired self-respect and be able to stand on their own in relation to any one including officers or local goondas.

The existing agencies and authorities charged with rural development work, such as Block Development Offices, Panchayats, Collectors' Offices and those of his subordinates, and so on should actively cooperate with the newly trained young farmers who go out of such centres, and help them in every way making their work smooth. It may be possible to reduce such Government staff, if they are superfluous; but if they adjust to the new spirit and take to rural development work with enthusiasm, there will be always room for them. Suitable orientation should be given to them so that they may realize their responsibilities.

The cost of establishing such centres of rural development may appear heavy. They will however be cheap in the long run, as they will pay their own way in due course. They can be made self-sufficient; the products of their farms can be sold to yield income to support their expenditure. Besides, the centres will grow in number gradually, their establishment can be enouraged by suggesting to large industrial houses to invest in them by sponsoring them in different parts of the country. Some industrial houses are already doing some rural work by adopting villages; once they go out, the work may flop. If they however establish such centres, they will help in creating a permanent source of improvement in the rural area. Serious thought should be given to this form of investment by industry, as it will have long-term benefits instead of the scattered efforts of some industrial houses, which do some good work in enlightened self-interest.

The above scheme will appear to be a long-term affair. It may be possible however to utilize some of the existing schemes run either by Government or by private parties towards this objective by suitable changes. This will cost less and the work will be quicker.

Intensive Short-period Training for Adults

In order however that we may have a band of devoted workers to help in rural work in time for the proposed new shemes of the Sixth Plan, we may also consider the following method:

In each Taluka, batch of 10 to 20 young persons should be selected. Their selection should be based on their rural background; their intelligence and capacity to work. No hard and fast educational standard need be laid down, though some minimum basic education should be expected with a willingness on their part to make up for their deficiency in this respect. Such a group should be given intensive practical training in rural development work for six to nine months for which suitable arrangements can be made at short notice at one or more places in each district. Officers of the existing agencies, some university and college teachers, some retired persons of the area having appropriate experience—all could be suitably included for this training. Each of them can then be attached to a village in the area for helping the people in effecting improvements or in carrying out the Sixth Plan Schemes in the area. Each will be supported by the village in which he lives and works; he should not be treated as an officer, but a worker from among the people themselves. The details can be worked out. As the work progresses, in due course, such workers will be able to undertake some useful work on their own, particularly when the rural people have adapted themselves to the new environment.

Both the methods of training should be on a continuing basis. Improvements can be made in the light of experience. Varieties of method in different areas should be encouraged; it may be possible to learn from the experience of one another. The object is to create self-consciousness among the people themselves for their welfare; they will realize their capacity and strength in this way. The two types of trainees will be the nucleus to change the rural environment. Unless the desire to change for the better is thus created and spread and unless the necessary effort for the same is coming forward from the people themselves, the work of rural development will not succeed and will only mean a repetition of the blunders of the last thirty years.

Higher Education and Research in Agriculture

For the success of the two types of training referred to above, as well as for developing the necessary consciousness for rural development, other changes in the existing system of education in rural areas and of higher education and research in agriculture and allied subjects which should be made at the same time are briefly noted below:

For the purpose of introduction of modern agricultural techniques and methods, we have the institution of agricultural college in most States of the country affiliated to universities in the area. More recently, agricultural universities have been started in several parts of the country and the tendency is to have at least one agricultural university in each State. Some of these institutions do good work and provide high level training in modern agricultural methods. But the products of these colleges and universities are urban-oriented people, who try to obtain jobs in urban areas in Government or private offices and avoid working on the field. Their knowledge therefore does not reach the farmer.

The Indian Council of Agricultural Research is a high level body with large resources. This Council encourages agricultural research in various parts of the country. The Indian Agricultural Research Institute formerly known as the Pusa Institute, now located at Delhi, is a large organization with several important departments giving training and doing research in different agricultural subjects. Barring exceptions, the results of such research do not reach the farmer. Most of the results are published in journals in English and most of the persons who are familiar with this research are employed in Government or other offices in urban areas. The work of these institutions therefore is divorced from reality and though large amounts spent on them would be shown as spent for rural development, in effect it has very little impact on rural life.

Primary Schools and Poly-technics

What is necessary is that we have to reorient our educational effort in a manner by which people in the rural area who have an aptitude for rural work, get the necessary education to adopt modern methods. Just as for industry, besides high level engineering graduates in different subjects, we have poly-technics which train middle-level technicians who can introduce the work on the spot in the factories, train, guide and help workers by working themselves, we required agricultural poly-technics to train similar people. Unless this link is provided all the high-level work done in colleges and universities will remain in paper as hitherto.

In the primary school in the rural area, a distinct agricultural bias should be given to the courses of studies and the students should be made familiar with agricultural techniques in the rural areas. When some of them grow up, they should be encouraged to join agricultural poly-technics. This can be established immediately without any delay in the agricultural universities and colleges where the necessary facilities would be available. Expansion of this activity may follow in course of time, but immediate results can be obtained in this way. It would be possible by such methods to see that the rural people themselves learn modern methods and use them in their own areas and be not drawn away to the cities.

CONSCIOUSNESS FOR DEVELOPMENT

The above suggestions are made on the assumption that rural development should be rooted in the soil; it should come from within; the people should have an urge for it and take to it willingly and be ready to work for it. The above methods are intended to create such psychology of development which cannot be created by the present method of officials doing rural development work. In the proposed scheme, the officials will have a place. But they will have to work because there is a demand for the work from the people; they will because otherwise they will be found out; they will work because their red tape dilatory method will not be tolerated by the people any more, if the arrangements of self-help as indicated above are made in the proper spirit. At the same time, the official agencies should be rationalized; overlapping avoided and responsibility assigned. The merit of the officers should be judged by results and not by the type of window dressing which now prevails in official reports.

The institutions of higher learning and research such as agricultural universities, Indian Council of Agricultural Research, social science institutes or departments of universities and so on will then have plenty of material to work on as well as increasing demand for utilizing their advice and suggestions or the fruits of their research. It will be possible under the above scheme to utilize the work of such institutions effectively as intelligent persons from the people themselves will be able to carry the results of research to the farmer and enthuse him to adopt the same with effect. In fact, instead of most of such work which is now divorced from life, will be closely linked to the actual realities of the situation in the country; thus utilizing existing facilities to a much better extent.

Industrial Base

There are many other aspects of rural development such as land reforms, which I have not dealt with, as my main concern is to illustrate the technique of the wage goods model for planning. Though we have criticized the technique of planning during the last 30 years, it must be pointed out that we have made some distinctive progress in several directions. Our industrial progress is now considered substantial though there is room for considerable improvement. We are in a position to export industrial technology and consultancy services to countries which are still in the early stages of development. Though other industries have been developed, industries likely to help agriculture such as fertilizers have also been developed. In other words, it is possible to utilize the industrial base that we have now got for the development of agriculture. It is possible to point out that with the same resources which we have invested in development so far, we could have done much better because of wastage, inefficiency and corruption, but we have got to start from what we have, and make good the deficiencies in the situation.

This means that the change in the planning technique more towards rural development should not mean the starving or neglect of industries which we have already got. In fact, it would be desirable to see that the deficiencies in the existing industries, large and small, are removed and their capacity is fully utilized, so that the large investment made in them and the skill obtained can be utilized to the fullest extent in the interest of the country. The only thing that could be said is that because of the need for diverting a greater portion of our resources for rural development, there may not be any substantial new investment for industrial development in the Plan. In fact, it should be laid down as a guideline that the large public sector undertakings should now be made so efficient that they may yield enough surplus partly for their own development and partly for contribution to the Plan effort in other directions. In other words, having pumped large resources in industry so far, it should now be the turn of industry to return such resources for development of the country in other sectors which have been neglected.

Balanced Economy

Whereas the technique adopted so far resulted in an unbalanced economy, the object of the wage goods model is to evolve a balanced economy. If the production of wage goods in increasing proportions in line with the basic requirements of the people as well as with the growth in population is carried out and adequate resources set apart for the same, we shall have a nucleus around which other activities can be organized. The effort to produce wage goods, not only for the consumption of the rural people but also for a marketable surplus, would create employment and purchasing power, which in turn will help industries in urban areas, because they will then have a ready market and will not be affected with a surplus which cannot be sold, leading to unutilized capacity. This means that in order to bring about a balanced economy, the production of increasing quantities of wage goods as suggested above, should be the basic consideration; other ancillary activities which support such production should be looked after next, such as fertilizers, irrigation, roads and so on, and other industries may have a low priority. If such a balance is produced, it should be possible to finance such activities from our own genuine resources without having to have recourse to inflationary finance. If at the same time, the rural people are persuaded to change their psychology and be conscious of their privileges and responsibilities and show willingness to work for the same with initiative and self-respect we shall have the necessary background for success. The efforts of the Government for rural development will then bear fruit instead of the waste of resources as hitherto. The proposed change would therefore surely lead to growth with stability as well as balanced economy and full employment in course of time.

REFERENCES

C. N. Vakil and P. R. Brahmanand, *Planning for a Shortage Economy*, Vora & Co., 3 Round Building, Princess Street, Bombay 2, 1952.

C. N. Vakil and P. R. Brahmanand, *Planning for an Expanding Economy*, Vora & Co., 1956.

C. N. Vakil and P. R. Brahmanand, "Investment Pattern in the Second Five Year Plan," Working Paper submitted to the Panel of Economists, Planning Commission in March 1956 in connection with the preparation for Second Five Year Plan.

C. N. Vakil and P. R. Brahmanand, "Institutional Implications of a Bolder Plan," Working Paper submitted to the Panel of Economists, Planning Commission in March 1956 in connection with the preparation for Second Five Year Plan.

P. R. Brahmanand, "Perspective Planning," *Industrial March*, May 1962.

P. R. Brahmanand, "The Future of Planning and the Planning of Future." An abridged version of this was published in *the Illustrated Weekly of India*, 24 October 1976.

P. R. Brahmanand, *Determinants of Real National Income and Price Level in India*, University of Bombay, 1977.

C. N. Vakil, *War Against Inflation or the Story of the Falling Rupee 1943-1977* (forthcoming), Macmillan Co. of India.

C. N. Vakil, *Memorandum on a Policy to Contain Inflation*—signed by 140 economists from 50 Indian universities with a supplement (known as Semibombla) submitted to the Prime Minister in February 1974.

C. N. Vakil and P. R. Brahmanand, *Memorandum on Inflation Reversal and Guaranteed Price Stability* (submitted to the Prime Minister in April 1977), Vora & Co.

Some material relating to the Implementation of Rural Development Scheme was first published as an article in the *Free Press Journal* on 14 August 1977.

I am indebted to L. D'Mello, Economic Adviser, State Bank of India, for the material on existing agencies for and methods of rural development.

(Items 3-6 above have been included in *Poverty and Planning*, forthcoming publication by C. N. Vakil, Allied Publishers; due November 1977.)

V.K.R.V. RAO

The Public Sector in Indian Socialism

A progressive enlargement of the public sector and its assumption of what are called the commanding heights in the economy has been the major strategy adopted by the Planning Commission and the Indian Government in their attempt to build up a democratic socialist society with a mixed economy in this country. While in statistical terms, this strategy has been pursued with a considerable amount of vigour and success, there has been grave public dissatisfaction at the working of the public sector in India and the opinion has been freely expressed that as a strategy for socialist development, it has been a signal failure. And yet there is no doubt that the public sector should form the kingpin of socialist development in a mixed economy. In this paper, therefore, I propose to deal with the role of the public sector in the mixed economy of a socialist and, more specifi-cally, with the practical policies and expedients required for the successful implementation of this role.

I would like to start my discussion of this subject with a reference to fundamentals. Why do we lay so much stress on the public sector in a mixed economy? What is its role in bringing about a socialist society? Unless we answer these questions clearly and categorically, we will have no defined criteria for evaluating the work of public enterprises from the point of view of their contribution to socialism; and we would fall back on a meaningless ideology of public sector for the sake of having a public sector, as if socialism just means the expansion of the public sector irrespective of how it functions and what contribution it makes to the realization of the values and aspirations that lie behind our espousal of the socialist creed. When I read some of the writings on the subject or more rarely hear some of the speeches which are made on the subject, I am constrained to believe that concepts like "nationalization" and "public sector," which are essentially functional instruments for the attainment of socialism, have become values in themselves. The means are mistaken for the ends, and the trees for the forest. Enthusiasts for socialism loudly demand more and more of nationalization and want a wider and larger extension of the public sector without caring to link their demand with the fulfilment of the objectives they have in view and without specifying or asking for the conditions that alone can make these concepts successful instruments for bringing about a socialist society. Destruction of public property, and lack of identification of either the public or the workers with nationalized or public sector enterprises seems to worry them much less than the slow pace of the extension of the public sector. It is not surprising therefore that during the near three decades that our Parliament has functioned under a republican government committed to a planned economy, not even twenty days have been found for a discussion in depth either on the efficiency or the socialist functioning of our public sector enterprises. The same—and perhaps more understandable—lack of appreciation of the socialist implications of public sector enterprises is shown by other critics of the public sector who hail from the private sector and seek to apply to the public sector the criteria of performance and profits they find in their own sector. These critics quite often indulge in *suppressio veri suggestio falsi* in their treatment of the public sector and in fact seem to be mainly actuated by an ideological disbelief in the very existence of the public sector except in the fields where they do not find it possible for the private sector to function or where the existence of a public sector is of crucial relevance to the very success of the private sector, as for example, in the case of transport and communication. I am afraid that both these types of critics, those who want an indefinite expansion of the public sector irrespective of how it functions and those who want a severe curtailment of the public sector of their ideological preference for the private sector irrespective of the social failings in its functioning, have both missed the real import of public sector enterprises in a mixed economy. Hence the necessity for dealing with first principles in regard to the *raison-d'-etre* of public sector enterprise.

A public sector enterprise is, by definition, an enterprise where there is no private ownership, where its functions are not merely confined to the maximization of profits or the promotion of the private interest of the enterprise, but are governed by the public or social interest, and where the management is responsible to the government either directly as in a departmental undertaking or indirectly as in government companies and corporations. Among the more important functions of the public sector are the following:

1. Building up the infrastructure of the economy or the economic overheads without which it is not possible to bring about an optimum utilization of the country's economic resources.

2. Contributing either wholly or in part to the production of the basic goods and services which constitute material and human capital formations for the production of both capital and consumer goods and services.

Both (1) and (2), taken together determine the rate of economic growth and emphasize the role of the public sector in determining and accelerating this rate.

3. Taking charge of all kinds of economic enterprises that are of a monopolist and semi-monopolist character so that the anti-social practices and profits associated with monopolies do not arise and, more positively the monopolist or semi-monopolist position is used to make the industry serve the social interest and be regulated by public policy in regard to its

prices, profits, and utilization of its products.

4. Occupy the commanding heights and strategic points in the economy in order to use this position for regulating the functioning of the private sector in the social interest and in accordance with public policy.

5. Take charge of all large undertakings involving either large amount of capital or large number of workers with a view to avoid exploitation or the accrual of large profits or concentration of economic power in private hands. Exception, if any, to this policy should be confined to the private corporate sector and be clearly indicated in the government's statement of industrial policy.

6. Demonstrate the superiority of socialist ideology over capitalist ideology by its performance in terms of minimization of costs of production, maintenance and improvement of quality of the output, and in general, by the degree of consumer satisfaction that it generates.

7. Demonstrate its socialist identity by the extent to which it secures worker identification with the enterprise and worker participation, initiative, and enterprise in the operation, improvement, and increased productivity of the enterprise.

8. Arrange for worker education and opportunities for improvement in their skills.

9. Give opportunities for preferential employment to members of socially backward and otherwise handicapped sections of the community, simultaneously arranging for such training they may need so that their efficiency becomes comparable with that of the other workers in the enterprise.

10. Pay special attention to activities that require a long-term investment and, in particular, to the development of the backward regions of the country which, in spite of having natural resources, have remained backward.

11. Locate or otherwise promote industrial or other enterprises in areas of low levels of income and surplus labour to the maximum possible extent, consistently of course with economic considerations pertinent to the overall interest of the national economy.

12. Prepare and implement a programme of planned profits for each enterprise so that each enterprise can make its maximum contribution to the funds available for reinvestment in the same enterprise or investment in other enterprises in the public sector. In fact, in due course, the public sector should become the most important financing source for its further expansion and increasingly shed its reliance on the public exchequer, whether through loans or taxes, for its requirement of capital funds.

These twelve functions sum up in effect the socialist function of the public sector in a mixed economy.

This means in truth that sectors of economic activity which involve either monopoly conditions or strategic economic power or possession of large resources in private hands should be publicly owned and operated as public enterprises. It also means that public enterprise should make itself responsible for the building of the economic overheads on the external economies like transport, power, fuel, and basic capital goods without which increase in the production of consumption goods and services either on the required scale or necessary economic basis will not be possible, irrespective of whether it is to be in the private or public sector. It also means that the extension of the public sector in economic enterprise will be followed by a substantial growth in the volume of national savings and investment as well as the fund available for governmental outlay on social services. Finally, it implies the acceptance and demonstration of the principle of efficiency, namely, maximization of output with minimization of costs consistent with quality of output, living standards of labour, and retention of funds needed for re-investment and contribution to national welfare programmes. Without public enterprise, there can be no private enterprise. In fact, it is the former that enables the full growth of the latter. At the same time, merely having a large field of economic activity in the public sector does not necessarily mean either increase in efficiency or in savings or in equality of opportunity. Everything depends upon the manner in which the public enterprise is operated and the policy it follows in regard to the pricing of its products and the distribution of its profits between wages and salaries, savings, and contribution to the national exchequer. The overall test of the success of public enterprise in the economic field is the extent to which it brings about increase in national income and savings in both the public and the private sectors; while in the social field the overall test is the extent to which it brings about a sense of identity of labour with the enterprise and promotes equality of opportunity. Now let us see what practical implications these first principles of public enterprise have in terms of pricing, operational and admininistrative policies.

To begin with, all types of economic activity cannot be run by public enterprise even in a socialist society. In a country like India where the working population is so large and agriculture and small enterprise have to play such an important role in the national economy, the bulk of economic activities, which give people an occupation and means of livelihood, has to be outside the field of public enterprise. And a major task of public enterprise has to be the creation of conditions and facilities that will enable the desired increase in the number and efficiency of units of private economic activity in terms of small enterprise. Hence the importance of economic overheads as a major field of public enterprise. Hence, also the need for confining public enterprise activity to fields where the nature of commodity or service produced is such as to give rise to monopolistic conditions or the possession of strategic economic power over either small enterprise or the community at large, or is a crucial determinant of growth, or is not likely to be produced in the private sector. The second choice should be in those fields of production where the economic units are large and their operation involves the use of large economic resources and gives rise to large profits in absolute, though not necessarily in percentage terms. In no case, however, should units be chosen for the public sector which require constant and careful personal attention and the success of which depends upon the extent to which identity is established between the entrepreneur and the enterprise. The success of public enterprise thus depends on the choice of units or sectors of economic activity for its application.

Another important factor that determines the success of public enterprises is the extent to which it performs the socialist function of superiority in productive efficiency. The biggest complaint against the working of public enterprises in India has been that its efficiency is much less than that of private enterprises, that far from making contributions to the public exchequer for financing investment and social expenditure, it is making huge losses, and that it is ridden with bureaucracy and unable to show the initiative and the adaptability that is required of modern business undertakings. These complaints ignore the gestation period required for a large undertaking to reach the high profitability stage when comparing public enterprises of recent existence with private enterprise that have been in existence for a long enough time to get over their teething troubles and their pre-profitability gestation period. The last two years have also shown that, given time, public sector enterprises can also give a good account of themselves. The fact remains, however, that, even after making allowances for the factors which the critics of the public sector have ignored, the performance of many of the public sector undertakings has not been satisfactory from the point of view of their productive efficiency. There is also no doubt that in comparison with private undertakings, they do suffer in respect of initiative and flexibility; and decision-making is restricted by bureaucratic functioning. Under the circumstances, it is necessary to ensure real autonomy for public sector undertakings if we want them to prove a match and in fact demonstrate their superiority over private sector enterprises; and yet this autonomy cannot be of the same character as that of the private sector because they have primarily to function in the public interest and are accountable to Parliament for their policies and performances.

For ensuring autonomy for public sector enterprises, it is necessary that there should be no bureaucratic control from the central secretariat and that decisions are decentralized and responsibility placed fairly and squarely on the managements for their operational policies and performance. Once the broad guidelines of policy regarding production, investment and prices, are formulated by the central authority—and this must be done in consultation and due regard for the opinions of the public sector managements concerned—it should be left to the managements concerned to implement the policies and take all the other decisions necessary in their judgment for the successful functioning of their enterprises. Of course, there must be adequate provision for periodic reports on performance and progress and evaluation; and appreciation of success and reproof for failure; but subject to these, the managements must be given a real feeling of responsibility for their actions. Unless this autonomy is assured, public sector undertakings will find it difficult to fulfil their socialistic role of maximum economic efficiency.

S.L.N. SIMHA

Four Decades of International Monetary Co-operation

The year 1936 in which I became the student of Professor V. L. D' Souza in the B.A. (Hons) Course in Economics, at the University of Mysore, saw the conclusion of what was then regarded as an outstanding event of international monetary co-operation, namely, the conclusion of the Tripartite Monetary Agreement between the U.S.A., France and Great Britain. The progress of international monetary co-operation in the four decades since the conclusion of the above agreement has been of a magnitude and character that would have been inconceivable in the years prior to the Second World War. True, much more remains to be done in the realm of international economic co-operation but what has been accomplished is spectacular and hence an account of the evolution of the international monetary co-operation in the last three to four decades is worthy of record.

The Tripartite Agreement figured much in lectures on international economics and in newspaper and magazine articles in the country. Another subject that created widespread interest in India, during the greater part of my Honours Course, was the exchange rate of the Rupee. The bulk of Indian national opinion was that at 1s. 6d. the Rupee was very much overvalued, leading to deflationary pressures on the economy. If I remember right, Professor D'Souza also entered the controversy, on the side of maintenance of the 1s. 6d. ratio. I am mentioning this not so much to defend or criticize the particular stand which Professor D'Souza took on the question of the external value of the Rupee as to say that the exchange rate question was one of the subjects which interested the Professor a great deal. I also remember very well his lucid exposition of the Purchasing Power Parity theory.

In the course of my professional career, it fell to my lot to take a great deal of interest in the subject of international finance, as a member of the Research Staff of the Reserve Bank of India, as a staff member of the International Monetary Fund and later as a member of the Board of Directors of this great international body. Based on the rich experience I gained while working in these two institutions, rather than by virtue of any academic eminence, I have ventured to write this paper by way of a humble tribute to one from whom I received much guidance, encouragement and affection. Professor D'Souza belongs to that generation of teachers, who took a deep and abiding interest in the welfare of their students, even to the point of assuming responsibility for finding brides and bridegrooms for them, and in particular of bringing about matches between students.

In dealing with the subject of international monetary co-operation, and economic co-operation generally, I recall to my mind the remarks made by an eminent British Philosopher and Statesman, Lord Samuel, in a lecture delivered at the University of Mysore, over which, if my memory is right, Professor D'Souza presided, that there is a tendency to exaggerate the few unpleasant and unfortunate developments in national and international life that occur and to ignore the enormity of co-operation, fellow-feeling and righteousness that prevailed.

For over six years now, the international monetary system has been passing through severe stresses and strains, with floating exchange rates, phenomenal balance of payments surpluses and deficits, especially on account of a meteoric rise in price of oil, a sky-rocketing of the price of gold, high rates of inflation, severe recession and stagflation. More than once, it seemed as if the international monetary system would collapse and the world would return to an area of economic isolationism, trade war and beggar-thy-neighbour policies. Fortunately, this did not happen though anxiety over the future of international economic co-operation has not quite abated. While the international monetary system built at Bretton Woods in July 1944 has cracked quite a bit, the fabric of international financial co-operation has remained strong, with continued efforts towards further progress.

PRE-WAR AND WAR YEARS

The major part of the period between World Wars I and II was characterized by import restrictions, competitive depreciation of currencies, bilateralism in trade and exchange matters and utter inadequacy of arrangements for short-term and long-term international borrowing. Germany was unable and unwilling to meet the onerous obligation for reparations and other debts and German economic policy moved rapidly in the direction of autarky.

The Pound Sterling, the premier reserve currency, got into serious difficulties, the return to pre-War parity, at the time of the restoration of the Gold Standard in 1925, proving to be a serious error. Finally, in September 1931, Britain went off the Gold Standard, the Pound depreciating in relation to the Dollar. France had its own quota of economic and currency troubles. Between 1929 and 1934, the world was also plunged into a severe economic depression.

In those years, generally speaking, comprehensive and consistent anti-cyclical fiscal and monetary policies were not applied. Also, the role of Government in the matter of reviving investment expenditure and consumer demand was comparatively of small dimensions.

Likewise, arrangements for international borrowing were hopelessly inadequate. London was still the international centre for short-term and long-term money, but in a situation when the British economy was passing through a difficult period and the Pound Sterling was weak and unstable, there was not much scope for large-scale international borrowing and lending in or through London. The New York money market was growing in importance, but, for a number of reasons which need not be gone into here, the American money and capital markets had not developed to a stage that New York could become the primary centre for international lending. Moreover, on account of the interconnection of economic and political factors, the uneasy peace that prevailed among nations in the post-War years also stood in the way of any major expansion in international banking activity. The tendency was for small groups of countries to try to align their monetary and exchange policies and preserve a modicum of financial stability. The Tripartite Monetary Agreement, concluded in 1936, between the U.S.A., France and Great Britain, was an example of such efforts. It laid down the broad principles of exchange management by the three countries.

During the years 1936-39, there was marked economic recovery in most countries, partly due to the operation of cyclical factors and partly as a result of the stimulus provided by intensive re-armament. During the War years, there was very close monetary and financial co-operation between the U.S.A. and the U.K. In the first two years of the War, the U.K. had to draw heavily on its foreign exchange assets for meeting its external expenditure. Later, the United States gave substantial assistance under Lend-Lease Programme. Throughout the War period, after an initial depreciation of about 20 per cent, the exchange value of the Pound was held steady at $4 to the Pound.

The early post-War years also witnessed considerable stress and strain of the international monetary system. Although the International Monetary Fund was established within six months of the cessation of the hostilities, massive assistance from the United States had to be provided to the U.K. under the Anglo-American Loan Agreement of 1946 and later to the U.K. and Europe, under the Marshall Aid Programme. During the War and early post-War years, the United States also took the lead to work for the establishment of an international economic and monetary framework, characterized by absence of restrictions on trade and exchange, consultation among countries in the matter of economic and monetary policies and arrangements for short-term and long-term international lending for meeting temporary difficulties in balance of payments and for investment purposes. These efforts began even as early as 1943 and bore concrete results, so far as international financial co-operation was concerned, in the establishment of the International Monetary Fund (IMF) and the International Bank for Reconstruction and Development (now called the World Bank), in July 1944, as a result of an international monetary conference held at Bretton Woods, U.S.A. For purposes of this article, the IMF is of greater interest and we shall now turn to its features and functioning, as this would epitomize the functioning of the international monetary system in the last thirty years.

INTERNATIONAL MONETARY FUND—OBJECTIVES AND OPERATIONS

The statute or the "Articles of Agreement" of the International Monetary Fund came into force on the 27 December 1945. As of that date, 30 countries (including India) were members of the IMF. The present membership is 130. With the exception of Switzerland, the Soviet Union and the East European countries (other than Rumania), nearly every country in the world is a member of the IMF. There have been indications from time to time that Switzerland might become a member. Recently, hopes have been expressed that U.S.S.R might also join the IMF and the World Bank. Incidentally, the U.S.S.R took part in the Bretton Woods Conference and was a signatory to the Articles of Agreement.

The IMF has a two-fold function. In the first place, it is a club, which prescribes a high code of conduct for its members and also ensures that members comply with the code. The second aspects of the IMF is that it is a financial institution, standing ready to provide loan assistance to member countries, for relatively short periods and under proper safeguards, to assist the countries to tide over their balance of payments difficulties pending the formulation of appropriate measures for correcting the disequilibrium in balance of payments. The two functions are very much inter-related. Without its financing role, member countries would not have bothered much to follow the code of conduct prescribed by the IMF. On the other hand, without a code, the financing operations of the IMF would have been arbitrary and haphazard in character, failing to serve effectively the cause of international monetary co-operation.

International monetary co-operation as conceived by the IMF has 2-3 fundamental aspects, namely, harmonization of the national economic interests with those of other members of the international community, provision of financial assistance on a temporary basis so that countries may restore balance of payments equilibrium without hurting the economies of other member countries, and the promotion of economic growth and high employment. The corner-stone of the IMF edifice is a fixed par value system, with provision for exchange rate changes to correct a "fundamental disequilibrium," not only through consultation with the IMF but by its approval. Equally important is the emphasis on freedom from exchange control on current transactions. Where, either for a transitional period or otherwise for a temporary period, restrictions on these transactions have to be placed, the approval of the IMF has to be obtained. In the IMF system, there was also till recently, a fairly important role for gold.

The IMF is like a co-operative society in regard to its resources and operations. The member countries provide the IMF with some gold and their own currencies, according to their respective "quotas." Roughly, quotas can be compared to the shareholding of an individual or any other entity in a joint-stock company. They also determine a member country's voting strength and its borrowing rights. The economic criteria for determining a country's quota are its national income, holdings of international reserves, level of imports and fluctuations in its exports. But, quotas are not fixed wholly on economic considerations. It is a politico-economic matter.

At Bretton Woods, a total quota of $8,80 million was fixed, which included a $400 million for undivided India and $2,750 million (the largest) for the United States. The Soviet Union did not join the IMF. Quotas have been increased thrice, by 50 per cent, 25 per cent and 25 per cent, in 1959, 1966 and 1970, respectively (Table 1). It has been decided to raise the quotas further, by fractionally over one-third, from the present aggregate level of approximately $35 billion or 29.2 billion of international money, that is, Special Drawing Rights (SDRs), to SDR 39 billion (or $47 billion). The increase for individual countries is generally one-third of their respective quotas, but there are substantial increases for the oil-exporting countries. As a result, the share of the major oil exporters in the aggregate quota is to double, from 5 to 10 per cent. The combined quota of the 87 non-oil producing developing countries is to be maintained at 20.85 per cent of the total. As a result, there is to be some reduction in the share of the developed industrial countries as a whole.

Till recently, member countries were required to pay 25 per cent of their quotas in gold and the balance in their respective currencies. The gold subscription was intended to enable the IMF to obtain currencies which may be in great demand by member countries but of which the IMF may not have adequate holdings. In addition to the amounts provided by quotas of member countries, the IMF has also arrangements to borrow currencies of individual member countries or groups of them. In this connection, reference should be made to an important borrowing arrangement made with effect from January 1962, under which a group of ten countries undertook to provide to the IMF their respective currencies, for a total of $6 billion. This is known as the General Arrangements to Borrow (GAB) and the ten countries are known as the Group of Ten. Very recently, a further borrowing arrangement was made by the IMF for a total of about $ 10 billion.

Reference has already been made to the co-operative character of the IMF's working. Its resources are utilized to provide loan assistance to member countries to tide over balance of payments difficulties and restore equilibrium. The loan facilities provided by the IMF correspond to short- and medium-term lending of commercial banks, for general purposes. Amounts loaned by the IMF have to be repaid not later than three to five years, though recently the period of payment has been raised to four to eight years, in certain cases of hardship.

The language of the IMF's financial transactions is different from the one we are accustomed to in the ordinary banking transactions. The borrowing of member countries from the IMF and the repayment of borrowing are called by different names in the IMF, namely, "purchases" and "repurchases" of currencies. When a country borrows, it is supposed to be purchasing other currencies or making a "drawing." Likewise, when it makes a repayment, it is supposed to be "repurchasing" its currency from

TABLE 1

Quotas of Member Countries of IMF

(As of 30 June 1977. Amounts Expressed in Millions of SDRs)

Indstrial countries		18,365
United States	6,700	
Canada	1,100	
Japan	1,200	
Denmark	260	
France	1,500	
Germany	1,600	
United Kingdom	2,800	
Other European countries		1,548
Australia, New Zealand, South Africa		1,187
Oil exporting countries		1,421
Algeria	130	
Indonesia	260	
Saudi Arbia	134	
United Arab Emirates	15	
Other less developed areas		6,697
Other's in Western Hemisphere		2,270
Argentina	440	
Bolivia	37	
Chile	158	
Hounduras	25	
Other's in the Middle East		475
Egypt	188	
Asian countries		2,784
India	940	
Pakistan	235	
African countries		1,167
Morocco	113	
Sudan	72	
Zambia	76	
All countries		29,218
Aggregate quotas	1958	9,088
prior to increase in	1965	15,977
	1969	21,231

the IMF. "Borrowers" have to pay interest, though it is called a charge "lenders" also receive interest.

Assistance is provided by the IMF under a number of heads of account, namely, general operations, compensatory financing for shortfalls in export proceeds and the financing of international buffer stocks of primary products. In addition, during the years 1975-77, the IMF gave special facilities of an *ad hoc* character, to finance balance of payments deficits on account of the sharp rise in the price of oil.

It should be emphasized that the assistance provided by the IMF is a loan facility and it also carries like all other loans, a rate of interest. Further, the lending operations of the IMF, like those of a commercial bank, combine automaticity with conditionality. That is to say, modest borrowings are permitted automatically but larger borrowings (in relation to the quotas of the individual member countries) are based upon a careful review of the fiscal, monetary and exchange policies of the country and the assistance is conditional upon the member country's undertaking measures for restoring equilibrium in balance of payments within a reasonable time. The idea is that the restoration process should be such as not to cause hardship to the economies of other member countries. But, definite steps must be initiated to restore external equilibrium.

In laying down conditions for the grant of assistance, the IMF is sympathetic, and pragmatic. Rarely has there been a case when a member country has considered the conditions imposed by the IMF as onerous and unreasonable. This is an example of the remarkable manner in which sovereign countries have agreed to be guided by an international organization in regard to their fiscal, monetary and economic policies.

There are also some broad limits to the quantum of assistance which member countries can receive from the IMF. Under present arrangements, a member country could have an outstanding borrowing of as much as 250 per cent of its quota. Rarely, of course, does borrowing go to such levels, but the theoretical possibility of assistance being available on this scale does provide confidence to member countries and restrains them from taking drastic steps to correct their balance of payments disequilibria.

In addition to an immediate request for loan assistance, a member country can also avail of the "stand-by" arrangement, in terms of which the IMF agrees to provide credit, up to a specified amount, over a period of a year. This arrangement was introduced in 1952, when the IMF's lending policies had not crystallized. In the view of the writer, stand-by arrangements are wholly unnecessary and totally inconsistent with the IMF's philosophy of liberal extension of credit to member countries, up to the limits prescribed in the Articles of Agreement. The IMF itself is a source of stand-by credit and a formal stand-by arrangement appears to be unnecessary. Be this as it may, member countries, developed and developing, have liked the system of stand-by arrangement.

The quantum of assistance provided by the IMF has varied a great deal from year to year, depending upon the balance of payments position of member countries and the IMF's own philosophy in regard to provision of assistance. In the early years, the IMF was rather strict, but in the last twenty years or so, policies have been rather liberal. The resort to the IMF increased considerably in recent years, largely on account of the sharp rise in the price of oil, though in relation to the magnitude of deficits of individual countries, the IMF's assistance should be regarded as modest. The figures of the IMF's operations for selected years is given below, in terms of international money, that is to say, Special Drawing Rights, or the same

as pre-1972 U.S. Dollar. At present, one SDR is equivalent to approximately $ 1. 2.

TABLE 2

IMF's Operations

(In millions of SDRs)

	Lending by IMF (purchases by members)	Repayment to IMF (repurchases by members)
1948	606	—
1952	46	37
1957	1,114	75
1962	2,243	1,260
1967	1,061	340
1972	2,028	3,122
1973	1,175	540
1974	1,058	672
1975	5,102	518
1976	6,591	960
1977	4,910	868
Total 1948-77	42,463	19,216

However, the importance of the assistance provided by the IMF should
not be judged mainly by its quantum. The essential thing to note is that
here is a source of assistance available to member countries readily, sometimes within a matter of days. This is a remarkable thing when one recalls
that in the pre-War days, even the mighty Britain, on whose empire the sun
never set, as it was said, found it extremely difficult even to raise modest
sums of money and for this purpose it had to approach Wall Street bankers
on bended knees! So far as the developing countries are concerned, without
an agency like the IMF, borrowing would have been most difficult and
such borrowing as they would have obtained would have been onerous, in
terms of strings and cost.

EXCHANGE RATE SYSTEM IN THE IMF REGIME

Perhaps no other aspect of the IMF's functioning is as important as that
relating to the exchange rate policies prescribed for member countries. It
is also an aspect that has come in for the most severe criticism, though a
good part of the criticism arises from a misunderstanding of the statutory
position and the manner in which the system has actually worked.

The exchange regime established by the Articles of Agreement is one of
what has been known as the "per value system" or a system of fixed exchange rates. One of the important purposes of the IMF is "to promote
exchange stability, to maintain orderly exchange arrangements among
members and to avoid competitive exchange depreciation." The founding
fathers of the IMF had before them the unhappy experience of the inter-

War period during which there was a marked tendency for exchange rates to fluctuate and also for countries to resort rather freely to competitive depreciation as a way of promoting exports. Except for understanding for relatively short period among 3-4 countries such as the U.S.A., the U.K. and France, countries felt completely independent in the matter of fixing exchange rates of their currencies vis-a-vis other currencies. In other words, it was a period of exchange autarchy at the national level and disorder at the international level. Consequently, those who worked out the principles of international monetary co-operation in the post-War years, attached the greatest importance to the stability of exchange rates and the limitation of the freedom of member countries in the matter of fixing and varying exchange rates. In other words sovereign nations agreed to fix the exchange rates of their currencies in consultation with the international community, so that there may be harmonization of the interests of all member countries and the purposes of the IMF could be fully achieved.

In terms of the Articles of Agreement, each member of the IMF was required to express the par value of its currency "in terms of gold as a common denominator or in terms of the United States dollar of the weight and fineness in effect on July 1, 1944," that is to say, on the basis of $ 35 per ounce of fine gold. The day-to-day fluctuations in the exchange rates were to be confined to a narrow range of one per cent of either side of par value.

A procedure was also laid down in the Articles of Agreement for changing the par value of any currency, since it was obvious that exchange rates had to be changed from time to time, in response to economic changes and balance of payments movements. The *initiative* for a change in par value had to come from member country but the change required the *concurrence* of the Board of Directors of the IMF. This preserved national sovereignty in the matter of the exchange rate but provided a safeguard against an unreasonable change in the rate, as a result of the unilateral action of a country.

Further, with a view to ensuring that exchange rate changes were made only in response to real need, it was laid down that exchange rate changes should not be proposed by a member country "except to correct a fundamental disequilibrium," though this was not defined in the Articles. In practice, the IMF has had no difficulty in dealing with requests for exchange rate changes on the score of difficulty in identifying a fundamental disequilibrium. Rather, the problem has been one of passivity on the part of the IMF even when a currency was developing a fundamental disequilibrium.

The exchange rate system established by the IMF's Articles of Agreement cannot be appreciated in isolation without taking into account the multilateral character of the exchange system and freedom from exchange restrictions in respect of current transactions, leading to a system of "convertibility" of each member's currency, which the Articles prescribed. For exchange rates can be held at unrealistic levels through an elaborate network of exchange controls over current transactions and practices such as "bilateralism." The obligations for avoidance of restrictions on current payments, avoidance of discriminatory currency practices and convertibility of currencies were stipulated in Article VIII. If members have to accept this obligation, they have to have realistic exchange rates and pursue appropriate fiscal and monetary policies in order to achieve balance of payments equilibrium, while at the same time fulfilling the objectives of economic growth and full employment. If the exchange rate becomes unrealistic, then in terms of the IMF's philosophy it is better to change the exchange rates rather than persist in maintaining an unrealistic rate through controls of various sorts on imports, exchange, etc. In other words, the system which was envisaged at Bretton Woods was an integrated one and on the whole one that was on the right lines.

However, it was recognized that there would be problems of post-War transition before members would accept fully the obligations of avoidance of restrictions on current payments and the obligations of convertibility of currencies. So, in Article XIV provision was made for a "transitional period." The Article provides that "in the post-War transitional period members may, notwithstanding provisions of any other Articles of this Agreement, maintain and adapt to changing circumstances . . . restrictions on payments and transfers for current international transactions." Members were enjoined to do their best to remove the restrictions as early as possible. Provision was also made for the member countries having restrictions inconsistent with Article VIII to consult the Fund as to their further retention; naturally it is the Fund's policy not only to encourage members but even to put pressure on them to eliminate exchange restrictions and implement the convertibility obligation.

It should be noted that the exchange system envisaged at Bretton Woods was not merely one of fixed exchange rates but of unitary rates. That is to say, for each country there was to be only one exchange rate, applicable to all kinds of transactions. In the inter-War years, a system of multiple exchange rates had become widespread, in particular in the Latin American countries. There is a wide variety of multiple exchange rates, applying to not only imports and exports but also the different types of commodities and transactions. Basically, a multiple exchange rate system is one of taxes and subsidies.

In the long run, a multiple exchange rate system has a tendency to grow in range and intensity, leading to all kinds of distortions in cost and output. Consequently, one of the important policy efforts of the IMF has been to bring about a simplification and an eventual elimination of multiple currency practices. Let us now study how the exchange rate system worked in practice till mid-August 1971, when the Bretton Woods principles received a rude shock with the suspension of the convertibility of the U.S. Dollar.

The general comment that can be made is that the objective of exchange rate stability worked too well. In other words, whereas the pre-War experience was one of competitive depreciation and exchange instability, under the aegis of the IMF there was the opposite tendency of a general reluctance to vary exchange rates. This was true of countries which were in serious balance of payments difficulties and needed devaluation as a corrective step as much as of countries whose currencies were exceptionally strong and which required to be appreciated.

This is not to say that exchange rate adjustments were few and far between. There have been a number of exchange rate changes, but these have not been as frequent as the economic circumstances seem to justify. Exchange rate changes occurred infrequently and for this reason the extent of change was also considerable. Thus, in the case of even major currencies, the extent of change was as much as 20 to 30 per cent, on some occasions. This meant that the adjustments in the exchange rate was rather abrupt, thus giving considerable support to the system of floating exchanges that became widespread since the middle of 1973.

Another aspect of the functioning of the exchange rate system during the period 1946-71, was that the exchange rate adjustments came mostly from the deficit countries. Germany was the only major surplus country, which turned to the expedient of currency appreciation but this was a token measure rather than a carefully calculated step, on the basis of intrinsic strength of the currency. In other words, the burden of adjustment fell primarily on the deficit countries, whereas what was envisaged at the Bretton Woods was that the chronic surplus and deficit countries should both make efforts to bring about equilibrium.

In other words, whereas the Founders of the IMF desired a system of exchange stability, in actual practice, there has been a certain amount of exchange rigidity. This is not the fault of the Founding Fathers, but that of those who administer the system. In this connection, it is necessary to remove a misunderstanding that has arisen that the IMF has been very passive in the matter of exchange rate adjustments, in blind allegiance to the Articles of Agreement. The fact of the matter is that the IMF has taken much initiative, though behind the scenes, in bringing about exchange rate adjustments. Thus, to give a striking example, when the string of devaluations that took place in September 1949, with the Pound Sterling and several leading currencies being devalued by over 30 per cent, the initiative came from the IMF Management which itself might have been influenced to a considerable extent by the thinking of the U.S. Government. On occasions when member countries came to the IMF for substantial drawings or stand-by arrangements, the IMF Management utilized the opportunity to mention discreetly about the need for exchange rate adjustments. It is no secret that the World Bank has also played a not insignificant role in the matter of bringing about exchange rate adjustments.

At the same time, it must be mentioned that such influence as the IMF has exercised on member countries in this matter has been only on countries experiencing serious balance of payments difficulties and therefore being in need of devaluation. The Fund has not at all used its influence, at least in a firm manner, in cases where an appreciation of a currency was called for. Thus, in the case of West Germany, while two formal appreciations took place prior to August 1971, they were both small and considerably delayed, thus partly contributing to later international currency turmoil. In the case of Japan, the IMF took no initiative; the Japanese Yen should have been appreciated 8-9 years back.

The one major exception to the above proposition is that of the United States. The IMF failed in its duty in not putting pressure on the U.S. Government to bring about a depreciation of the Dollar in view of the prolonged state of U.S. balance of payments difficulties from the mid-1950s. This aspect will be discussed in some detail, in a later section of the paper.

In regard to the system of multiple exchange rates, the IMF did not succeed in its elimination, but, considerable progress was made to simplify the system in most countries. The multiple exchange rate system has been prevalent mostly in the developing countries, to whose problems the IMF has shown considerable sympathy. Consequently, the IMF has handled this matter also in a flexible and tolerant way. The IMF has not also raised objection to the introduction of a multiple currency system by a number of countries, though always on the assumption that the arrangement is a temporary one.

As already mentioned, a multiple exchange rate system is one of taxes and subsidies and there is a tendency for any arrangement to get entrenched itself. Any radical change would mean not only economic disturbance but political trouble. All the same, in retrospect, the comment should be made that the IMF authorities have been unduly tolerant in the matter.

An integral aspect of the fixed change rate system is, as already mentioned, the absence of restrictions on current transactions and the availability of convertibility in respect of current transactions. In this matter too, the performance of the IMF has been modest. Over the years, a number of countries have removed restrictions on current transactions and have accepted the convertibility obligations enunciated in Article VIII. Still, the majority of the countries have exchange restrictions under the provisions of Article XIV.

The post-War transitional period has turned out to be much longer than the Founding Fathers of the IMF visualized. This is also in part due to the fact that quite a number of countries are pursuing inflationary fiscal and monetary policies and supporting unrealistic exchange rates through a paraphernalia of import and exchange controls on current and capital transactions. The system of exchange control which was instituted in most countries during World War II was not only not dismantled but in fact made more comprehensive and stringent, as part of an overall economic planning to achieve economic growth and social justice. In this matter also the IMF has been quite tolerant and adopted what one might call a pragmatic approach.

Even in the case of the developed countries, the progress towards elimination of restrictions on current transactions and the fulfilment of convertibility obligations was a somewhat long-drawn-out process. With the exception of the U.S.A. and Canada which assumed the obligations at a very early date, most of the countries formally accepted these obligations only from 1961 onwards, that is to say, 15 years after the IMF started functioning; informally these obligations had been accepted about three years earlier. Japan accepted the obligations only in 1964.

The functioning of the exchange rate system should also be considered in relation to movements of capital, in particular short-term capital. An exchange rate that is reasonably good for keeping current transactions in equilibrium may become unstable if there are large-scale capital movements. In the pre-War years, large-scale international movements of short-term capital, often referred to as "hot" money, constituted a serious disequilibrating factor. These movements largely reflected the political instability that prevailed in those years.

In the years since the close of World War II also, short-term capital movements have been fairly large, though the motivation has been less political than economic. The Articles of the IMF envisaged control over capital transactions. In fact, at a very early stage in the IMF's functioning, namely September 1946, the IMF Board took a decision that its resources were to be limited to financing current account deficits. However, in practice, there has been substantial freedom in capital movements, largely under the influence of the U.S. authorities. In fact, in July 1961, the IMF Board reversed its September 1946 decision and permitted the use of its resources for meeting deficits on capital account. In retrospect, this approach, contrary to what was envisaged at Bretton Woods, led to many difficulties, in particular for the U.S. Dollar. If capital movements had been kept under check, the world would have been spared much of the disturbance to international financial system that occurred in the 1960s and the 1970s.

At this stage, it would be useful to make an interim assessment of the functioning of the IMF during its first 15 years or so. It is clear that the basic principles of an international monetary system as conceived at Bretton Woods were sound. Obviously, even the wisest people cannot anticipate *everything*. It is satisfactory that the framers of the Articles of Agreement provided remarkable flexibility, so that the policies and procedures of the organization might be adapted to new situations. A lot of adaptation was in fact done, though much of it was by way of giving relief to what has become the World's most important currency, namely the U.S. Dollar. A detailed account of these adaptations and innovations will be given in a later section.

As regards the extent to which those in charge of the IMF's affairs, that is to say principally the Managing Directors and the members of the Executive Board, implemented the objectives enshrined in the Articles of

Agreement, the performance of the IMF seems to be definitely good, though not exceptionally good. International monetary co-operation has been promoted to an extent that has not only no parallel in history but is even better than what the Founding Fathers had envisaged. International trade expanded a great deal and on the whole rates of growth of the economy and employment have been quite high. The post-War world has not known what an economic depression is though there have been recessions. In fact, the Articles of Agreement definitely ruled out deflation as a means of correcting balance of payments deficits. It is quite true that the rates of growth of the economy have been uneven and the gap between the developed and the developing countries has widened. But even the developing countries have done much better than what would have been possible without the international financial co-operation and development assistance that the post-War world has witnessed.

Apart from achieving, to a substantial extent, the objectives of exchange stability, avoidance of competitive depreciation and promotion of multilateralism in payments, the IMF has given plenty of confidence to member countries by standing ready to give loan assistance to correct balance of payments disequilibria. There has been a progressive liberalization in the matter of permitting member countries to use the IMF's credit. Efforts have been made to provide special assistance to primary producing countries.

However, gradually the weaknesses and deficiencies of the IMF system came to be noticed. As already mentioned, a certain amount of rigidity had crept in so far as the exchange rate mechanism was concerned. Further, the burden of adjustment had fallen too much on deficit countries. Also, there was a pronounced tendency, in particular on the part of the U.S.A., to finance deficits through an increase in liabilities rather than through transfer of assets.

Another serious deficiency was that the assistance provided by the IMF was conditional. It was necessary to devise some source of unconditional assistance to member countries in general, as a means of expanding international liquidity, or in other words international reserves. The IMF's attitude to the role of gold as an element of international liquidity was also far from pragmatic. By freezing the price of gold at $35 an ounce, such contribution as gold might have made to expanding international liquidity, of course with safeguards, was denied.

These aspects of the functioning of the international monetary system under the aegis of the IMF came into prominence by the prolonged and serious troubles of the U.S. Dollar, on whose strength the smooth working of the IMF system largely depended. It is, therefore, time to turn to the functioning of the IMF in the 1960s, giving an account of the U.S. Dollar's difficulties and the adaptations made to meet this new situation.

THE TROUBLES OF THE U.S. DOLLAR

In the early post-War years, the United States was the main source of aid for the war-ravaged world. The U.S. Dollar became a stronger-than-ever-before currency, leading to what looked like a permanent Dollar shortage. However, even the mighty Dollar became less mighty and it was not long before it became a weak currency. In other words, the shortage of Dollar had given place to a situation of overabundance of Dollar. This is one of the extraordinary features of the international monetary system of the last 25 years.

There is a view that the Dollar's weakness is of a comparatively recent origin. It is true that the Dollar has been passing through exceptional difficulties in the last 6-7 years. However, the decline of the Dollar's position began as far back as 1950. In retrospect, it is clear that the extent of devaluation of major currencies, which took place in 1949, was too large in relation to the strength of the U.S. Dollar. In other words, the Dollar's competitive position was weakened. From 1950 onwards, beginning with the Korean War, many developments occurred to create balance of payments difficulties for the U.S.A.

Large-scale foreign investment by U.S. companies, large-scale military aid by the U.S. economic aid to the developing countries and expansionary fiscal and monetary policies to achieve full employment and high rates of growth, all combined to create balance of payments deficits. Further, with the establishment of the Common Market, the European economy became much more competitive. In the Far East, Japan recorded phenomenal industrial expansion and the efficiency of the Japanese economy was such as to make Japanese goods very competitive all over the world, especially in the U.S.A. Finally, the prolonged military involvement of the U.S.A. in the Far East added substantially to fiscal imbalance and disequilibria in the U.S. balance of payments. In such a situation, large-scale movements of capital from and to the U.S.A. became endemic, all contributing to serious disturbances to the U.S. external account.

It would be useful to indicate the magnitude of the U.S. balance of payments deficits. In this connection, it should be mentioned that there are various concepts of balance of payment deficit, varying from country to country and for the same country from time to time. Definitions of surplus and deficit are changed, partly out of the desire to redefine concepts and definitions and partly by way of window-dressing.

The three measures of balance of payments which are relevant are those relating to (*a*) merchandise accounts, (*b*) current account and (*c*) overall account, referring to the settlement of balances through official reserves. The overall balance is also the sum of balances on current and capital accounts. The overall balance is in a sense of the most important magnitude, since ultimately the residual financing is the responsibility of Government and governmental agencies, including the central bank of the country.

During the 20-year period 1950-69, the United States had an aggregate overall deficit of about $ 24 billion. In 1970 the deficit was very large at about $ 10 billion. The deficit shot up to about $ 30 billion in 1971. No wonder that in such a situation the U. S. President suspended, in August 1971, the convertibility of the Dollar into gold. In other words, in the 22-year period 1950-71, the aggregate deficit was of the order of $ 63.5 billion.

Turning to other elements of the U. S. balance of payments, it is observed that except in 1971, the U. S. had a surplus on merchandise account. But this surplus tended to become small, in relation to the U. S. transactions under other heads. For a highly developed country like the U.S. and for fulfilment of the role of the U. S. Dollar as the primary reserve currency of the world, it must have a substantial surplus in its merchandise account.

The current account of U.S. balance of payments has had ups and downs but on the whole during the period covered above, there was a net surplus. But this surplus was offset by deficits on capital account. So that in the aggregate there was deficit to be financed by official reserve transactions.

1971 was a very bad year on all accounts. There were deficits of $ 2.9 billion on merchandise account, $ 2.8 billion on current account, $ 16.8 billion on capital account and $ 10.9 billion under "errors and omissions."

The United States met about 25 per cent of its overall deficit in the above period through draft on its gold reserves. The balance was met primarily by an increase in the U.S. liquid liabilities to foreigners, thus adding enormously to the world's reserves of Dollars.

The United States resorted to several expedients to tackle its balance of payments difficulties. The other trading partners, in particular the European countries and Japan, were urged to remove various kinds of restrictions on imports of U.S. goods. Secondly, to prevent a further drain of its gold reserve and keep down the price of gold at $ 35 an ounce, with a view to publicizing that the Dollar was still a strong currency, a Gold Pool was set up in 1961 by the U.S., with the co-operation of the central banks of seven European countries. The Pool was to buy gold whenever the price tended to go below $ 35 an ounce and sell gold when the price showed a tendency to go significantly above $ 35. The Gold Pool was a failure; central banks of the Pool countries lost enormous gold holdings, particularly in 1967. Consequently, the Gold Pool was abandoned in March 1968 and its place was taken by a two-tier system of prices, an official market at $ 35 and a free market. It is needless to say that the free market for gold went on rising.

The U. S. authorities also tried to regulate, but in a very feeble way, movements of capital from the United States. For this purpose, among other steps, an *Interest Equalization Tax* was also levied, with effect from August 1963, in order to raise the cost of U.S. capital to foreign borrowers other than from Canada and the developing countries, roughly by 1 per cent. The U. S. has not at all been enthusiastic about restricting capital outflows. The U. S. investments abroad have risen phenomenally, also bringing substantial income.

Yet another step which the U. S. authorities took was to conclude, beginning in 1962, a series of bilateral arrangements between the Federal Reserve System on the one hand and several foreign central banks and the Bank for International Settlements, on the other. These are known as Reciprocal Currency Arrangements or Swap Facilities. It is a reciprocal credit facility in terms of which a central bank agrees to exchange, on the request of the other central bank, its own currency for the currency of the other country, with which the agreement is entered into; the exchange is up to the maximum amount specified in the agreement and is valid for 3-6 months. These arrangements were invoked now and then, not only by the United States but also by other countries, such as the United Kingdom and Italy. These Swap facilities were raised from time to time. The total was almost $ 12 billion in 1972.

The Reciprocal Currency Arrangements constitute an excellent example of international monetary co-operation. No criticism need be made of the fact that these arrangements were outside the purview of the IMF. It is good that there is a wide variety of credit arrangements. Having some arrangements outside the IMF makes for flexibility.

Further, the U.S. Treasury made arrangements to raise medium-term credit from foreign central banks and the Bank for International Settlements, these loans being designated in foreign currencies. These Bonds are referred to as Roosa Bonds or Roosa Paper, after the then Under-Secretary of the U. S. Treasury, Mr Robert V. Roosa.

However, the various measures proved to be of little avail. It had become clear that the exchange rate of the Dollar vis-a-vis other major currencies was no longer tenable. There was too much of dollar floating around and the holders began to lose confidence in the dollar and convert their holdings into gold and other currencies. The outflow of the Dollar assumed alarming dimensions in the Spring and Summer of 1971.

During the years 1958-71, when many defences were being put up for the U. S. Dollar, the International Monetary Fund was also active, adapting itself to the situation of U. S. Dollar's problems and the need for expansion of international liquidity, conditional as well as unconditional. These matters are discussed briefly in the next section.

IMF'S ADAPTATIONS—SDRs

The IMF took several steps to provide larger assistance to member countries, by liberalizing the policies for obtaining assistance and by expanding its resources. Until about 1956, the IMF was unduly strict in the matter of assistance to the member countries. Later, the policy was liberalized. It is not necessary to go into the details of liberalization.

The resources of the IMF were increased mainly in the form of increases in quotas of member countries. The quotas were raised, as already mentioned, by 50 per cent, 25 per cent, 25 per cent respectively, in 1952, 1966 and 1970. The aggregate of the quotas of the member countries now stands at something like $35 billion. In addition to general increases, special increases were approved for a number of countries such as West Germany, Japan and Italy. As a result of these increases, the IMF's holdings of gold as well as currencies of members increased.

Even with quota increases, the IMF could not get enough supplies of leading currencies, particularly in the context of the difficulties of the U.S. Dollar, making that currency not quite suitable for large-scale lending. As a matter of fact, the United States itself became a borrower from the IMF. To meet this situation, the IMF entered into a general arrangement to borrow from ten leading countries. A reference has already been made to this arrangement, known as the General Arrangements to Borrow (GAB). The GAB came into effect in January 1962 and has been renewed from time to time.

The outstanding development in the adaptation of the IMF's functioning is the decision to establish the facility of Special Drawing Rights (SDRs) or international money. A decision in this regard was taken, in principle, in September 1967, and the first issue of Special Drawing Rights was made on 1 January, 1970.

Before proceeding to describe the features of SDRs, it is necessary to indicate briefly the rationale for the creation of SDRs. Corresponding to the growth in the volume of international trade, there is need for an increase in international liquidity or reserves. Till 1970, the three forms of international reserves were (a) gold, (b) foreign exchange, and (c) reserve positions in the IMF. The reserve position of a member is the total of gold subscription to IMF quotas and credit extended by the member through the IMF. The comparative importance, during selected years between 1937 and 1969, of the different types of reserves is given in Table 3.

TABLE 3

International Reserves

(*Billions of U. S. Dollars*)

		End of Period		
	1937	1950	1958	1969
Gold	25.3	33.8	38.0	39.1
Foreign exchange	2.4	14.6	16.9	32.3
IMF reserve positions	...	1.7	2.6	6.7
Total	25.7	50.1	57.5	78.2

It will be seen that in the eleven years 1958-69, the quantum of gold remained more or less unchanged, the principal increase in reserves being in the form of foreign exchange holdings.

There were problems in the matter of bringing about expansion in international reserves through the above forms. Gold production was concentrated in a few countries and the price of gold was also pegged at an artificially low level of $ 35 per ounce, for almost 38 years from 1934. It was considered that it was wrong to base the international monetary system on the vagaries of gold production. The main snag as regards foreign exchange reserves, mainly U. S. Dollars, was that any substantial increase in this form meant corresponding balance of payments deficits on the part of reserve currency countries, which meant really the United States. The U.S. authorities were very keen that the Dollar should cease to be an important reserve currency. Other countries, such as West Germany and Japan, were also unwilling to shoulder, even to a modest extent, the responsibility of being reserve currency centres.

The third type of reserves, namely, reserve positions in the IMF, also has limitations. Such liquidity, which is created by the IMF's lending operations, is a temporary one. When debtor countries repay their borrowings, there is a contraction of international liquidity to that extent. Moreover, the liquidity created by the IMF in its general transactions is of a conditional character. Member countries can obtain funds from the IMF subject only to the fulfilment of certain conditions.

For all these reasons, it was considered desirable to create a new form of international reserves which had all the favourable aspects of the other types of reserves and free from their shortcomings. After prolonged discussions, it was agreed that the new form of reserve must possess the following characteristics:

(*i*) It must be an asset, owned by the participating countries rather than a credit facility; that is to say, it must be unconditional in character.

(*ii*) The participation in the new reserve arrangements must be on an international basis, covering the developed and the developing countries rather than being confined to a small number of developed countries. The logical arrangement is for the new system to be established under the aegis of the IMF, so that the two types of reserve creation, conditional and unconditional, are regulated by the same agency.

(*iii*) The reserve asset must represent a deliberate creation of the international community, taking into account the needs of a growing world economy.

(*iv*) While the new reserve should be unconditional in character, there must be some built-in safeguards against its excessive creation.

(*v*) There should be a certain amount of long-range planning in the creation of the new reserve asset, so that the participating countries may have confidence about the availability of reserves to a reasonable extent.

The SDRs satisfy these features eminently. Hence, not only was there fairly speedy action in amending the statute of the IMF for this purpose and making three issues of SDRs but also the SDRs became quite popular as international reserves, with a lot of transactions taking place in the new reserve asset.

We may now turn briefly to the main features of SDRs. In this connection, it should be noted that in regard to several matters such as the name of the new asset and the manner of its use, there was a desire to provide the semblance of a continuity between the ordinary facilities of the IMF and the new facility. However, the SDRs are a totally different form of reserve asset available for use at the will of the holder, in a practically unconditional manner.

The features, the creation and the use of SDRs may be put down in a series of points.

(*i*) A unit of Special Drawing Rights was declared to be equivalent to 0.888671 gram of fine gold, which was the same as the gold equivalent of the pre-Smithsonian Dollar. Or, an SDR equals one-thirty-fifth of an ounce of fine gold. However, SDRs cannot be exchanged for gold nor could SDRs be obtained by giving gold.

(*ii*) Participation in the SDR arrangements is open only to the members of the IMF. However, membership in the SDR system is not obligatory.

(*iii*) SDRs can only be held by official agencies, that is to say, Government or any agency of the Government such as the central bank. The SDRs are not issued in the form of certificates. The initial allocations and the transactions are recorded in the books of the IMF.

(*iv*) While SDRs are an asset to the holders, they do not represent the liability of the IMF or any other agency. There is no "backing" for SDRs, in the form of other assets. The real backing is the undertaking given by sovereign member countries to abide by the regulations concerning the SDRs.

(*v*) The heart of the SDR system is the unconditional right of a holder to receive from other holders convertible currencies, in exchange for SDRs. This right is matched by an even larger obligation on the part of member countries, namely, to accept from other members SDRs, up to a maximum of 200 per cent of the allocation of the country, and give in exchange convertible currencies, including its own currency if it is convertible and so desired by the country which is transferring SDRs.

(*vi*) Although a member can use up all the SDRs allotted to it, it is required to maintain an average holding of 30 per cent of the initial allocation, during a five-year period. This is to restrain member countries from rushing into using up SDRs without drawing upon their other types of reserves.

(*vii*) The issue of SDRs to member countries is strictly in proportion to their quotas in the IMF.

(*viii*) Those who make use of SDRs to acquire other currencies (debtors) have to pay interest rate and those who receive SDRs from others (creditors) would receive the same rate of interest, originally both being 1.5 per cent per annum.

(*ix*) There is a complex procedure for the issue of SDRs, so that it represents a near unanimous decision of the participating members. A proposal for issuing SDRs requires an 85 per cent majority of votes of the Board of Governors.

(*x*) In order to provide some long-range planning, the Managing Director is expected to propose the allocation of SDRs for a basic period of five years generally, the aggregate amount being issued in instalments. But, this period, like some other features, including the rate of interest, can be varied. So far as the first allocation was concerned, the basic period was conceived in terms of three years.

The Amendments to the Articles of Agreement of the IMF for the establishment of the SDRs facility became effective on 28 July 1969. In September, the Managing Director of the IMF made a proposal for an aggregate isssue of approximately 9.5 billion units of SDRs, over a three-year period 1970-72. The proposal was approved by the Board of Directors and allocations were made on 1 January 1970, 1971 and 1972, for 3,414 million, 2,949 million and 2,952 million units, respectively, or a total of 9,315 million.

It is interesting to note that contrary to earlier doubts, the SDRs proved very popular among the members. A lot of transactions have taken place between members directly as well as through the process of designation by the IMF. The IMF itself became a holder of SDRs. Transactions in SDRs have taken place with remarkable smoothness. The whole thing speaks volumes of international monetary co-operation.

There have been no further issues of SDRs since 1 January 1972. The situation concerning international liquidity became markedly different on account of the sharp increase in world oil prices since the last quarter of 1973. Besides the question of further allocations, there has been a lot of criticism and suggestions concerning the principles governing the distribn-tion of SDRs among individual member countries, the link with gold and the reconstitution provision. The developing countries have also expressed a strong desire for establishing a "link" between the issue of SDRs and provision of developmental aid. These matters cannot be discusssed in any detail here. Immediately, we will turn our attention to the developments in international finance since mid-August 1971 when the U.S. President suspended the convertibility of the Dollar. Before normalcy could be restored following this development of far-reaching importance, the oil crisis came and it was a question of adding fuel to the fire, though the analogy may not be quite appropriate since fuel itself was the cause of much trouble!

THE YEARS OF CRISES, SHOCKS AND AD HOCISM

In an earlier section, a fairly detailed account has been given of the troubles of the U.S. Dollar and the various steps that were taken by the U.S. authorities to preserve the Dollar's international strength. However, the various measures proved to be of little avail. It had become clear that the exchange rate of the Dollar vis-a-vis other major currencies was no longer tenable. There were too many Dollars floating around and the holders began to lose confidence in the Dollar and convert their holdings into gold and other currencies. The outflow of the Dollar assumed alarming dimensions in the Spring and Summer of 1971.

In the circumstances, on 15 August 1971, the United States suspended convertibility of official Dollar holdings into gold, besides imposing a 10 per cent surcharge on all dutiable goods imported into the United States, a 90-day wage, price and dividend freeze and a 10 per cent cut in US foreign aid. This upset the fixed exchange rate system of the world and there was widespread floating of exchange rates—currencies like the German Mark and the Japanese Yen appreciating substantially. There was a threat of return to the pre-War system of currency instability, if not chaos.

Fortunately, this did not happen and there was an earnest endeavour to return to a system of fixed exchange rates, with some devaluations and appreciation of major currencies. These arrangements were concluded at a meeting of the leading powers in Washington DC, on 18 December 1971, in a building of the Smithsonian Institution. Hence, the agreement is popularly known as the Smithsonian Agreement.

In terms of the Agreement, the U.S. Dollar was devalued by a modest 7.9 per cent and the leading currencies realigned. The new official price of gold was $38 per ounce. Some exchange flexibility was also provided, by permitting exchange rates to move within margins of 2.25 per cent on either side instead of just one per cent hitherto.

But, the Smithsonian Agreement was only in the nature of a "truce"; one major currency after another began to weaken. The Pound Sterling was the first one to suffer; the British Government put the pound on a floating basis from June 1972. The Italian Lira and Dollar also came under severe pressure while the Swiss Frank and the D-Mark appreciated. The U.S. Dollar was devalued a second time, in February 1973, by 10 per cent, the corresponding new price of gold being $42.22 per ounce.

The second devaluation of the Dollar did not help much to restore confidence in that currency or in the system of fixed exchange rates. The world moved on to a system of floating (that is to say, fluctuating) exchange rates, so far as the major currencies were concerned. The currencies of most developing countries have been pegged to some currency or the other, and, consequently, they have been fluctuating along with the currencies to which they have been pegged. There is now a wide variety of exchange rate practices. In the 1975 Annual Report of the IMF, the prevalent exchange rate practices have been very well summarized in Table 4.

TABLE 4

**Exchange Rate Practices of Fund Members,
30 June 1975**

	Number of currencies	*Percentage share of trade of fund members*
(*i*) Currencies that float independently	11	46.4
(*ii*) Currencies pegged to a single currency of which:	81	14.4
(*a*) Pegged to U.S. Dollar	54	12.4
(*b*) Pegged to French Franc	13	0.4
(*c*) Pegged to Pound Sterling	10	1.6
(*d*) Pegged to Spanish Peseta	1	—
(*e*) Pegged to South African Rand	3	—
(*iii*) Currencies pegged to a composite of other currencies of which:	19	12.4
(*a*) SDR	5	5.0
(*b*) Other	14	7.4
(*iv*) Currencies pegged to others but that change the peg frequently in light of some formula	4	2.0
(*v*) Currencies that are floating jointly	7	23.2
Total	122	98.4

It will be seen that as of June 1975, the Dollar was the most important currency to which other currencies were pegged. The decline in the importance of the Pound Sterling is also evident from the Table.

Exchange rates have fluctuated a great deal. So far as the U.S. Dollar is concerned, there have been alternating periods of strength and weakness, reflecting the fiscal and monetary policies of the U.S. and the other major countries and the cyclical movements of the various economies. So far as the Pound Sterling is concerned, the troubles have been more serious than those of the U.S. Dollar. On the whole, the Pound Sterling has declined considerably in relation to the U.S. Dollar.

During the above years of currency confusion and worldwide inflationary trend, the price of gold in the free market rose more or less continuously, and sharply too. Thus, between December 1970 and July 1973, the average price of gold in the London market went up from $37.44 per ounce to $ 120.36, or about three times the official price of $ 42.22. The price rose even to higher levels in 1974, of almost $ 200, reflecting the oil crisis and the subsequent sharp increase in oil prices. It would be convenient to turn to a brief account of the impact of the new oil situation on international payments and the measures that were taken to finance the phenomenal deficits that started emerging.

Between the third quarter of 1973 and the first quarter of 1974, the price of oil went up by about 250 per cent. Later, there was a further rise. The impact of the new oil price was felt particularly in the year 1974, as may be seen from Table 4.

TABLE 4

Global Structure of Current Account Balance

(*In billions of U.S. Dollars*)

Groupings	1967-72 Average	1973	1974	1975	1976
Major oil exporting countries	0.7	6	67	35	41
Industrial countries	10.2	12	—10	19	— 1
Other non-oil countries					
More developed	—1.7	1	—14	—15	—14
Less developed	—8.1	—11	—30	—38	—26

The major oil exporting countries which had an aggregate surplus of $6 billion in 1973, saw the surplus shoot up to $67 billion in 1974! All the other groups of countries had deficits in the aggregate. In 1975, there was a marked improvement so far as the industrial countries as a group were concerned. But, in 1976, there was a setback.

It must be mentioned that the net figures given against various groups of countries do not bring out the true magnitude of the deficits/surpluses that required to be finished. Thus, in 1974, for the industrial countries as a whole, the deficit was $10 billion. However, the aggregate of the deficits of countries having deficits was over $25 billion. Likewise, in 1976, for the industrial countries as a whole there was a current account deficit, of only about $1 billion. But the aggregate of the deficits of countries having deficits was $15 billion.

Imbalances of the above magnitude have somehow been financed. Financing has taken several forms, namely. lending by the IMF, extention of Governmental credits and aid, and financing through the banking chan-nels, in particular through the "Euro" markets. Actually, the Euro-markets got extended to what has been called Petro-Dollar markets.

So far as the IMF is concerned, in addition to larger lending under its General Account, it took the initiative of creating a special oil Facility Fund, in 1974 and 1975. Contributions to this Fund were made primarily by the oil exporting countries. Between the two Facilities created in 1974 and 1975, there was some increase in the interest rates. Thus in respect of the 1974 Facility, the IMF was to pay an interest of 7 per cent per annum and in respect of the 1975 Facility, the rate was increased to 7.25 per cent. Likewise, the lending rates by the IMF under the Oil Facility, were also put up. Borrowings under the Oil Facility are repayable in sixteen quarter-ly instalments, to be completed not later than seven years after the borrowing. A large number of developing countries and a number of developed countries have made use of the two Oil Facilities, for an aggregate amount of SDRs 6.9 billion; the developed countries accounted for about two-thirds, namely SDRs 4.4 billion. With a view to providing relief to the "Most Seriously Affected" (MSA) countries, in respect of payment of interest under the Oil Facility, a Subsidy Account was created in August 1975. The Subsidy Account is financed by developed countries and oil exporting countries. A total contribution of about SDRs 160 million is anticipated, of which about SDRs 65 million has been received. A number of countries have received the Subsidy, for a total of SDRs 41 million, till the end of April 1977. India has been the largest receiver of the Subsidy.

The loan assistance provided by the IMF, highly useful while it has been, has constituted a comparatively small portion of the total financing of balance of payments deficits. The major portion has been financed through banking channels. It is beyond the scope of this paper to describe the functioning of international money and capital markets, as represented in particular by what are known as the Euro-currency, the Euro-bond and the Euro-medium-term finance markets. The operations in these markets run into scorses of billions of Dollars. Thus, in the year 1976, it has been estimated that the international financial markets provided as much as $95 billion of new credit. The gross external claims of banks operating in the Euro-markets are of the order of $500-600 billion!

The participants in the Euro-currency markets are commercial banks, central banks, multinationals, Governments and international financial institutions such as the Bank for International Settlements.

The vast size of the international currency markets is a matter for both satisfaction and worry. The satisfaction is that the banking system has risen to the occasion of financing surpluses and deficits of what should be considered as astronomical magnitude. On the other hand, there is also cause for anxiety, inasmuch as the standards of lending are going down and the risk element is growing, with the result that there is the danger of the international credit system receiving a rude shock, like the banking crises witnessed in several individual countries. There is now clear recognition of the need for regulating these Euro-markets, but unfortunately there is no consensus regarding the principles and techniques of regulation. Some countries, in particular the U.S.A., are not enthusiastic about imposing controls. So far as the U.S.A. is concerned, the present system is a boon in that its balance of payments deficits are automatically financed as it were. To the extent that the focus of this paper is on international monetary co-operation, the vast growth of the Euro-markets should be held as an outstanding development.

REFORM OF THE INTERNATIONAL MONETARY SYSTEM

It is now time to turn to the efforts that have been made to reform the international monetary system, in particular to amending the objectives, procedures and set-up of the International Monetary Fund which was badly bruised from August 1971 onwards. In essence, the reform of the IMF has been going on for several years. Yet, after the Dollar crisis of August 1971, efforts had to be made in a demonstrative way to reform the international monetary system. The general view appeared to be "the IMF is dead; let us have a new IMF and wish it long life."

With a view to having meaningful as well as broad-based discussions, the task of reform was entrusted to a Committee, officially known as "The Ad hoc Committee of the Board of Governors on the Reform of the International Monetary System and Related Issues," popularly known as the *Committee of Twenty*.

The Committee's main task was to submit proposals regarding what is known as the "adjustment process," that is to say, ways and means of preventing balance of payments disequilibria and of restoring equilibria, especially through the instrument of exchange rates. Naturally, the Committee considered a wide variety of matters such as the role of gold, the character and use of SDRs and greater contribution of the IMF to the rapid growth of the economies of the developing countries. The *Committee of Twenty* made its interim report in September 1973 and its final report in June 1974, the latter not differing in material respects from the proposals contained in the interim report. It should be noted that between the interim report and the final report, the oil crisis occurred, followed by a sharp increase in oil prices. Consequently, the matter of long-term reform of the IMF lost some of its importance and immediate attention had to be given to ways and means of financing the phenomenal balance of payments deficits that had started occurring.

The main features of the final report may now be referred to briefly. Whatever may be one's comments on these recommendations, the important thing to note is that the work of the Committee of Twenty represents yet another outstanding example of international monetary co-operation. The fact that the Committee's Report was unanimous is also a matter of satisfaction. This is not to say that every country was happy with the Report of the Committee. Undoubtedly, every country has had its complaints and reservations, but what should be taken note of is the general satisfaction regarding the Report as a whole.

On the important question of the exchange rate mechanism, the Committee recommended the golden mean of "stable but adjustable par values." Further, the IMF was to have a positive role in the matter of bringing about exchange rate adjustments promptly. Some indications were also given of the cirteria to be employed in bringing about exchange rate adjustments. An indirect blessing was also given to the system of floating exchange rates, as being useful in "particular situations." Further, the responsibility of surplus countries in bringing about balance of payments equilibrium was emphasized.

The SDR was to become the principal reserve asset and the role of gold and of reserve currencies was to be reduced. The use of SDRs was to be expanded and several steps were to be taken towards this end, including the abolition of the reconstitution provision. On the question of providing a link between the issue of SDRs and developmental aid, the Committee seemed to be sympathetic and indicated the lines on which such a link could be provided. The Committee also made a number of proposals by way of "immediate steps," pending action to implement the Committee's recommendations contained in the first part called "Outline of Reform."

Since the submission of the Committee's Report in June 1974, a number of important developments have taken place. These can only be referred to very briefly, for lack of space. The dethronement of gold from the IMF system is taking place much sooner than was anticipated by the Committee of Twenty. No longer need gold subscription be paid towards quotas of member countries. Actually, the IMF decided to return to the member countries a part of the gold (25 million ounces) at the official rate and has decided to sell another 25 Million ounces, over a 4-year period, through a series of auctions, the profits of these sales going to a Trust Fund, for the benefit of the developing countries. The first such auction was held on 2 June 1976.

An interim solution has also been found to the question of the valuation of SDRs. It may be recalled that in terms of the IMF statute, the SDR was defined as being equivalent to one-thirtyfifth of an ounce of gold. In view of the fact that the price of gold went on rising to what should be regarded as giddy levels (reaching almost $200 towards the end of 1974, as compared to the official price of $ 42.22 per ounce), the link between the the SDRs and the gold became untenable. It was, therefore, decided to express a unit of Special Drawing Rights in terms of a basket of currencies of sixteen countries "that had a share in world exports of goods and services in excess of one per cent on average over the 5-year period 1968-72." This came into effect in July 1974 and as of that date one SDR was equivalent to 1.206 U.S. Dollars or approximately the same rate that prevailed on the basis of $ 42.22 per ounce of gold. In terms of the basket arrangement, the value of the SDR in terms of Dollars has fluctuated a great deal, between $ 1.155 to $ 1.236. At present, the quotation is something like $ 1.176, which means that the Dollar has on the whole appreciated, as compared to July 1974.

Reference has already been made to the decision to enlarge the quotas of member countries further from the present level of about SDRs 29 billion to SDRs 39 billion. A further increase looks likely before long. Meanwhile, to augment its resources, the IMF has made arrangements to obtain "supplementary credit" from 13 member countries and Switzerland, for a total of the equivalent of SDRs 8.43 billion. It should be noted that this supplementary facility is in addition to the General Arrangements to Borrow which has been in operation from the beginning of 1962. The supplementary credit will be somewhat costly, the IMF initially paying a rate of 7 per cent per annum until 30 June 1978, and later a rate equivalent to the average yield of short-term U.S. Government securities. Incidentally, it may be mentioned at this stage that in recent years the com-

plex of the interest rates of the IMF has gone up substantially, for transactions in the General Account and also for SDR transactions. Thus, for
SDR transactions, as against the original rate of 1.5 per cent per annum,
the present rate is in the range of 3.5-4 per cent.

So far as the exchange rates are concerned, they continue to fluctuate
considerably, both ways. At the same time, it must be said that considering the extraordinary magnitude of balance of payments surpluses and
deficits, the sharp swings of cyclical activity on the whole, and a period
of high inflation, the exchange rate fluctuations should be regarded as
modest. This is so because very few leading countries have left exchange
rates completely to the freeplay of market forces. There have been varying
degrees of intervention, with a view to keeping exchange rate fluctuations
within modest limits. In other words, to an extent, the new policy of
stable but adjustable exchange rates has been in operation. All this again
speaks volumes of the extent of international monetary co-operation that
prevails and anxiety not to let exchange rate movements of one currency
lead to acute problems for the other trading partners.

The experience of the last four years provides plenty of material for
scholars to speculate on the question of fixed versus floating exchange
rates as an integral aspect of the adjustment process. The Annual Reports
of the Executive Directors of the IMF are naturally somewhat equivocal
on the subject and there is also a certain tendency to justify the
system of floating exchange rates that has prevailed in recent years. At
the same time, happily, there is also recognition of the possibility of
a system of floating exchange rates having aggravated inflationary forces,
through lack of disciplining effect on domestic fiscal and monetary
policies.

It is the author's view that on the whole, the world stands to gain more
by the system of fixed exchange rates than that of fluctuating exchange
rates. As already mentioned, no country can afford to allow exchange rates
to be left wholly to market forces. In particular, in the absence of adequate
controls over capital transactions, movements of capital funds may distort
the exchange rates. This means that the monetary authorities have to
intervene actively in the exchange market. It is better to go back to the
system of fixed exchange rates but bring about adjustments more
frequently than earlier. This principle was implicit even in the earlier IMF
statute; only the member countries and the IMF authorities did not administer the system properly.

Happily, the IMF's formal role in the matter of exchange rate adjustments has been recognized. Much has been made of the difficulty of having
objective indicators for bringing about exchange rate changes. The level
of international reserves of a country and movement in reserves are both
important. Nor should one ignore the Purchasing Power Parity principle.
If, in the past, exchange rate adjustments were not brought about promptly,
it was not on account of any great difficulty in identifying moments for
action or the extent of exchange rate change that was required. Rather,

it was a case of false prestige in the matter of bringing about exchange rate adjustments so far as the deficit countries were concerned and fear of loss of competitiveness on the part of the chronically surplus countries.

In this connection, it is imperative to have a broad system of controls over capital movements. Whereas the Bretton Woods system provided for control over capital transactions, the IMF has been operating a system relatively free from such controls, largely under the influence of the United States, which has genuinely believed in free movement of capital, private and public. This has also led to the creation of the Euro-markets. The Euro-markets need to be controlled as also the operations of multi-nationals. Without a measure of control over market transactions, there is bound to be distortion of exchange rates, affecting trade patterns adversely.

An area where there has been stagnation in recent years is in regard to further issue of Special Drawing Rights. There has, of course been, a phenomenal increase in international reserves in recent years. From a total of about SDRs 72 billion at the end of 1969, the international reserves rose to SDRs 152 billion in 1973 and further to 240 billion in July 1977, as may be seen from Table 5.

TABLE 5

International Reserves

(In billions of SDRs)

End of year/month	1969	1973	1977 (July)
Gold	39.1	35.6	35.5
SDRs	—	8.8	8.4
Reserve positions in the IMF	6.7	6.2	18.4
Foreign exchange	32.3	101.7	178.0
Total	78.1	152.3	240.4

The enormous increase in foreign exchange reserves is not an unmixed blessing, since it reflects the enormous short-term liabilities of reserve currency countries, in particular the U.S.A. It is time that the issue of SDRs was resumed. It should be possible to work out agreements whereby the allocations to the developing countries are larger than their quotas in the IMF. It should be hoped that from 1978 the issue of SDRs will be resumed.

CONCLUDING OBSERVATIONS

The foregoing survey has brought out vividly the extraordinary progress in the field of international monetary co-operation in the last four decades. In the above paragraphs, the full story of international economic co-operation has not been given, for lack of space. The narrative primarily relates to co-operation under the aegis of the IMF. Monetary co-operation has been taking place, in a big way, outside the IMF too. No mention has been made in the above paragraphs of the extraordinary role which the IMF's twin, the World Bank has been playing, in providing development finance. The World Bank's lending now runs into billions of Dollars per annum, a good part of which represents soft assistance under the World Bank's affiliate, the International Development Association. In trade matters too, there is a fair amount of international co-operation.

This author believes that what has been achieved in the field of international monetary co-operation is truly extraordinary. Naturally, a lot more needs to be done and will be done. Those who are dissatisfied if not cynical with the progress in international financial co-operation have only to look back to the pre-War years and see for themselves the contrast.

In 1936, a loose form of monetary co-operation among just three countries was hailed as an extraordinary event. Today there is even closer co-operation among 130 countries, belonging to the IMF family. In 1937, there was no IMF, no club to prescribe a code of conduct and no assured source of help to countries for meeting their balance of payment deficits. What a contrast today!

In the pre-War years, there was no international money like what we have today. What was then international money, subject to the vagaries of production, namely gold, is fast going out of the international monetary system, as a result of understanding among the international community.

Again, the pre-War years were characterized by large movements of hot money, which caused much economic havoc and political instability too. While even now there are vast movements of capital, their impact has been made rather smooth through international financial co-operation.

The most remarkable change is the willingness of scores of sovereign nations to surrender a part of their economic sovereignty in the interest of the good of the world community. The indications are that there will be further progress in this direction. There is no other alternative for enduring progress if not for the very survival of people on this planet.

Concerning our own Rupee, it is interesting to note that the exchange rate of ls. 6 d. remained unchanged till June 1966. Even in a free India, the reluctance to devalue the Rupee has been rather marked. However, the Indian monetary authorities are now a little bolder in the matter of experimenting with the exchange rate of the Rupee as compared to the pre-War years. While it is hard to say that the Rupee is now a much stronger currency than in the pre-War Years, undoubtedly the Indian economy is much more diversified and far stronger than it was in the pre-War Years.

D. T. LAKDAWALA

Value-Added Tax

The last two decades have been characterized by the spread of the value-added tax in Europe and Latin America which has been as rapid as that of the general sales tax between the two world wars. It owes its quick popularity to its being recognized as an instrument of tax harmonization in the European Economic Community, which was anxious to ensure that the powers of its member States to levy commodity taxation should be reconciled with the principle of free trade within the Community. According to the principle of destination which had been recognized by the member countries, exports to other States within the Community were entirely tax-free, and imports from the member countries had to be treated in the same manner as domestic production destined for internal consumption. This ruled out a tax on exports qua exports, but export goods were likely to have been taxed at earlier stages in their production or distribution. To observe the rule, this tax had to be refunded, which made it necessary to ascertain precisely the amounts of taxes paid on them before they were identified as exports. A method had also to be devised by which imports (on which taxes paid in their State of origin had been refunded and which had escaped earlier taxation of the importing State) could be taxed in the same manner as goods domestically produced. A value-added tax levied according to the voucher[1] method is almost a tailor-made devise to meet

---

[1]Value-added in the gross income concept (we take this to avoid complications) in a process may be determined either by the base income approach—addition procedure (wages+interest on borrowed capital+gross profits) or the product approach—substraction method (gross sales—gross purchases excluding those of capital goods). The invoice or "tax-from-tax" method is an improved variant of the latter; the tax instead of being levied on the difference between gross sales and purchases (making adjustments for the use of capital goods) is levied on gross sales, and credit given for the tax already paid on purchases. This makes a difference when the tax rate of output is different from that of inputs; if a producer purchases Rs 66,000 worth of materials (including tax) and adds Rs 14,000 worth to sell his goods at Rs 80,000 (excluding tax) and if the inputs are taxed at 10 per cent and the output at 15 per cent in former case (accounts method), the total tax paid on the product would be Rs 6,000+Rs 2,100 i.e., Rs 8,100 in the voucher method, it would be Rs 12,000 and the producer would be taxed Rs 12,000-Rs 6,000. In the latter method, it is only the rate of the final consumers' goods that matters; the rates on inputs and intermediate goods, if, different from this rate, would lead to administrative complications (including sometimes refunds if rates on inputs are markedly more than those on output) but do not matter in the final instance. Unlike the sales less purchases or accounts method, this is neutral to the break-up of the process in various stages.

these two requirements and, therefore, endears itself to the EEC.

There is, however, another important reason which has made for its easy acceptance. In the free market economics, the principle of neutral commodity taxation has an instantaneous appeal. Non-discrimination between goods and services on the one hand and among different goods and different services on the other alone can ensure prevention of distortion of consumers' tastes and preferences. To achieve this objective, the tax should be levied at or up to the final stage of sales to consumers, as otherwise commodities which gather proportionately less of their values at post-tax stages will bear a greater tax burden. A general retail sales tax, levied at a uniform rate on consumption goods, will serve the purpose, but it suffers from some severe limitations. In the first place, in case of goods which can be used as both intermediate goods and final consumption goods, exemption for the former use becomes difficult. Secondly, the proceeds have to be collected from a very large number of small dealers, who find systematic book-keeping and dealing with assessing authorities difficult. Widespread evasion and harrassment are likely to result. The higher the tax rate, the greater the incentives to evasion; and one-stage tax rates are likely to be high. The logic of a sales tax is based on the assumption of its being shifted to the consumer. But economic theory recognizes occasions and situations, when the whole or a part of the sales tax has to be borne by the producer or trade who may also not find it possible to pass it on backwards. In order that in such contingencies the tax may not become oppressive on the dealer, the rate must bear a reasonable relationship to his trade margin. A single-stage tax cannot fulfil this requirement, as the rate has to be high to fetch the same revenue. Being uniform, it cannot be adjusted to different trade margins prevalent in different trades or lines of production. An equally productive turnover tax will be levied at a low rate, but its commodity-wise incidence will be uneven and it will encourage integration to reduce the number of taxable stages.

A value-added tax combines in many ways the advantages of both the final-stage retail sales tax and turnover tax. Compared with the former, it only alters the method of collecting the tax, not its base. It is levied at all stages from the first to the last, but only on the value added at each stage, so that even at a high rate, it bears a more reasonable relationship to the trade margin.[2] Its incidence is certain (especially when levied on the voucher-method) and independent of the stages through which a commodity passes before reaching the final consumer. According to the concept adopted—gross income, net income and net consumption—it can be used to discourage or encourage capital—intensive methods. It is collected from producers of various inputs, producers of final outputs, wholesalers, retailers, etc., and a very substantial percentage will be gathered from those who are persons of substance, keep proper accounts and know how to deal

---

[2]If a V.A.T. can be shifted backwards, it has the effect of a proportional tax on factor incomes.

with officers on equal terms. Except at the stage of sale to final consumers checking is easy, as sales of a person are purchases of another and the tax on sales that a dealer gives is counteracted by the refund that the purchaser obtains. The latter is interested in obtaining a proper receipt showing the tax paid on his purchases unless he also wants to evade. A chain of evasion is difficult. Besides, a value-added tax necessitates uniformity in rates, if the voucher-method is followed, as the rates on inputs do not matter, and the only rate variations of consequence are at the final stage. Wide variations in final output rates will be possible without necessitating large refunds or large tax payments, only if the inputs are distinct. For all these reasons, a value-added tax works better than a final-stage retail sales tax or a turnover tax from the viewpoint of neutrality.

CORPORATE TAXATION

Earlier a question was often raised whether in the gamut of taxes a value-added tax that could replace the corporation tax should be included.[3] The base of the value-added tax is much wider than that of the corporation tax, even if the former is confined to only corporations. In its net-income concept, the base of the value-added tax will include in addition to profits before tax, interest payments on borrowed capital and wages and salaries, so that the equivalent rate for a value-added tax on companies will be much less than the effective corporation income tax. This is amply borne out by the calculations made by the late Dr Saravane[4] for replacing the corporation income tax by a value-added tax for 1969-70. The latter could have been levied at 13 per cent while the effective rate of the former was 46 per cent (Table 1). The calculation is on the assumption that many tax reliefs and concessions which make the effective tax rate on corporations much less than the formal one would not be attempted in the value-added tax. There is no logical reason why the value-added tax should only be confined to companies and not extended to firms at least the larger firms in which case the equivalent tax rate will be much smaller—less than half.

TABLE 1

Corporation Tax and Value-Added Tax on Companies: 1969-70

(Rs crores)

Company profit before tax	...	443
Tax provisions	...	203
Tax provisions as % of comany incomes	...	45.8%
Value added (net income concept)	...	1548
Tax provisions as % of value added	...	13.1%

Source: Reserve Bank of India Bulletin, March 1976, p. 14.

[3]See J.F. Due, "Should the C.I.T be replaced by the V.A.T?" and Smith, D.T., "The V.A.T. as an Alternative to the C.I.T" in *Proceedings of the National Tax Association*, September 1964.

[4]"Tax on Value Added for India: Issues and Alternatives," *Reserve Bank of India Bulletin*, March 1976, p. 14.

A considerable part of the corporation income tax is derived from commerce, transport and communication, finance, construction and utilities and profession. In 1972-73, these fetched nearly half of the tax revenues from corporations (Table 2). The experience of other countries with value-added tax reveals that several services are not amenable to the same tax rate as commodities, or that they need some special form of treatment. The general tax rate may need some adjustment on this ground, but insofar as many of these are business services in the nature of inputs, the general rate adjustment will not be substantial.

TABLE 2

Company tax Receipts by Trade-wise Classification: 1972-73

Classification		Income surcharge (in lakhs of rupees)	as per cent
Commerce, transport & communication		192.42	35.20
Metals & chemicals		139.53	52.25
Cement, rubber & other minerals		59.09	10.81
Finance	...	49.81	9.11
Textile & leather processing	...	45.52	8.32
Primary food processing		34.52	6.31
Construction & utilities		10.89	1.99
Professions		10.33	1.88
Forestry, mining & quarrying		4.50	0.82
		546.62	100.00

Source: All India Income Tax Statistics, Central Board of Direct Taxes, Directorate of Inspection, Research Statistics and Publication, 1972-73, pp. 9-17.

In comparing the value-added tax with the corporation income tax, it is not so much the wider basis and the lower rate of the former that are of importance as the varying relationships between profits before tax and the value added of different companies. There are, for instance, companies which make no profits and, therefore, pay no tax by way of company income tax. In 1970-71, of the 1501 Public Limited Companies, 365, i.e. nearly one-fourth, made negative pre-tax profits.[5] There would only be a few out of these which added no value in the course of their operations; they would, therefore, have to pay something by way of a value-added tax. On the other hand, companies making high profits in relation to value added and paying surtax may be called upon to pay much less in a value-added tax system. The industry-wise tax provisions as a percentage of value added give some idea of the amplitude of variations that the replacement of company taxation by value-added tax would imply. For 1970-71, the former varied from negligible for aluminium and 2.7 per cent for jute textiles to 46.4 per cent for mineral oils (Table 3). The large change

[5] *Reserve Bank of India Bulletin*, March 1976, p. 12.

TABLE 3

Tax Provisions as Percentage of Profit before tax and Value-Added by Industry Classification: 1970-71

(Amt. in lakhs of rupees)

| | Profits before tax | Value-added (gross sales-gross value of inputs inc. depreciation provisions) | Col. I as percentage of col. 2 | Tax provision | Tax provision as per cent of | |
					Col. 1	Col. 2
	1	2	3	4	5	6
Tea plantation	1109	3511	31.6	591	53.3	16.8
Coffee	124	247	19.9	63	50.8	25.5
Rubber	104	308	29.6	66	63.5	21.4
Coal mining	289	4434	6.5	158	54.7	3.6
Grains & pulses	60	174	34.5	41	68.3	23.6
Edible vegetables and hydrogenated oils	393	645	60.9	242	61.6	37.5
Sugar	277	1151	—	293	105.8	—
Tobacco	1161	2864	40.5	655	56.4	22.9
Cotton textiles	3034	27600	11.0	1700	56.0	6.2
Jute textiles	268	5713	4.7	154	57.9	2.7
Silk & rayon textiles	3567	5954	59.9	1815	50.9	30.5
Woollen textiles	277	944	29.3	87	31.4	9.2
Iron & steel	1785	6476	27.6	716	40.1	11.1
Aluminium	1598	2781	57.5	1	ng.	ng.
Other non-ferrous metals	279	723	38.6	63	22.6	8.7
Engineering	9733	31922	30.5	4749	48.8	14.9
Chemicals	7619	16054	47.5	3907	51.3	24.3
Matches	258	664	38.9	150	58.1	22.6
Mineral oils	1527	1699	89.9	785	51.6	46.4
Cement	1683	4076	41.3	343	20.4	8.4
Pottery clay, earthenware & clay products	238	903	26.4	144	60.5	15.9
Rubber & rubber products	1159	3363	34.5	543	46.9	16.1
Paper & paper products	1759	4430	39.7	531	30.2	12.0
Constructions	129	2006	6.4	81	62.8	4.0
Electricity generation and supply	1032	2321	44.5	342	33.1	14.7
Trading	1308	4923	26.6	741	56.7	15.1
Land & estate	39	79	49.4	25	64.1	31.6
Shipping	708	1877	37.7	71	10.0	3.8
Hotels, restaurants & eating houses	95	412	23.1	20	21.1	4.9

Source: Reserve Bank of India Bulletin, March 1976, p. 10.

implied in going over to the value-added tax is regarded as a stimulant to greater efficiency; more profitable companies will be enabled to distribute greater dividends and invest more.

The choice of a V.A.T. in place of C.I.T. has however to be decided on a view of the rationale of the corporation income tax, and its likely incidence. The case for replacement is strong, if the tax on companies is shifted to the consumers of its products. Its commodity-wise incidence is then very uneven, and it weights heavily on companies with a low turn-over in relation to profits. If, however, the company income tax is regarded as a direct tax, the case for substituting it becomes debatable. It has then to be decided whether the company income tax can be regarded as a tax on ability of companies or as a fair charge for the special benefits that are conferred on companies and/or a substitute for an undistributed profits tax. Only if this view is rejected outright, the need for its substitution will arise. In view, however, of the uncertainties about the shifting of the corporation tax and its being generally classed as a direct tax, there has been no recent revivals of attempts to replace C.I.T. by a V.A.T.

COMMODITY TAXATION

The more recent discussions in India and elsewhere in this direction have been confined to the replacement of some forms of commodity taxation by the V.A.T. The discussion in the Indian context gets restricted to the "general excise duty" if one confines oneself to alternatives within the Constitution which empowers the States to levy taxation on sales of goods.[6] But if the possibility of amending the Constitution in desired direction is not ruled out, this opens a wider vista. Since the terms of reference of the Jha Committee[7] concede the possibility of changing the tax powers of the two layers of the Government, if need be, it may be better to discuss the V.A.T. in this wider context.

Taxes on commodities and service fetched Rs 5,636 crores in 1973-74, i.e. more than three-fourths of the total central and state tax revenues of Rs 7,400 crores. The two major sources of revenue of the Union Government were customs revenue—Rs 996 crores, and excise duties—Rs 2,602 crores. The remaining sources of commodity taxation, mainly from Union Territories, brought only Rs 80 crores. The States obtained Rs 1,143 crores from sales taxation and Rs 815 crores in other ways. Of the latter, State Excises fetched Rs 354 crores and motor vehicles taxation Rs 148 crores. Both these were specific taxes levied on special principles. The excises were meant to restrict consumption of intoxicating drinks. Motor vehicles taxa-tion was meant partly to cover the cost of wear and tear of roads. The

[6]*Final Report on Rationalization and Simplification of Tax Structure*, Government of India, Ministry of Finance, 1969, p. 6.

[7]*Indirect Taxation Enquiry Committee*, Government of India, Department of Revenue and Banking, para 2 (viii)-Terms of Reference, 1976.

rest was largely obtained from taxes on services. The discussion of replacement by value-added tax is mainly confined to customs duties, central excises, and general sales taxation which are in the nature of general commodity taxation, and to octroi which is a source of local revenue and, therefore, not reflected in the table here (Table 4).

TABLE 4

Revenue for Taxes on Commodities and Services:
1973-74

	Revenue (Rs crores)	Percentage
Central government		
Imports	832.00	
Exports	88.00	
Other revenue	17.00	
Refunds	41.00	
Customs: net receipts	996.00	17.67
Excise duties	2602.00	46.17
States' share	631.00	
Excise, net receipts	1971.00	
Sales tax	43.00	0.76
State excise	12.00	0.21
Tax on vehicles	4.00	0.07
Other taxes & duties	21.00	0.38
Total: Central government (including States' share)	3678.00	65.26
State Government		
Central sales tax*	1142.80	20.28
Motor vehicles tax	148.40	2.63
Tax on passengers & goods	114.20	2.03
Entertainment tax	99.60	1.77
State excise	353.70	6.28
Electricity duties	81.30	1.44
Other taxes and duties	17.70	0.31
Total: State government	1957.70	34.74
Total: Central & States	5635.70	100.00

*Includes central sales tax and sales tax on motor spirit.

CUSTOMS DUTIES

Of the four types of commodity taxation mentioned above, two—customs duties and octroi—can be easily disposed of. For many years to come, India is likely to continue to feel the need for resorting to customs duties for protecting domestic production or giving it a differential advantage over imports in a wide range of commodities. It will also be in need of resorting to extensive exchange control, and may like to use import duties as a second line of defence to fill the substantial difference between the world prices of certain commodities and their domestic prices. It may also occasionally resort to export duties or subsidies. There is no idea of treating foreign goods on par with domestic goods, not even domestic goods meant for export. All that can be asked for is reasonable and purposive discrimination and this can be better achieved by rationalization of customs duties. V.A.T being based on a different philosophy is not suited for this discrimination. There can, therefore, be no question of replacing customs duties on imports and exports by a V.A.T.

OCTROI DUTIES

Octroi is an import duty levied on goods entering local boundaries for use, sale or consumption therein. It has to be refunded if goods go out of the borders of the local body in the same form in which they entered. Octroi is an antiquated tax with no counterpart in the developed world. It frequently necessitates long holdup of transport and thus leads to great delay and waste. This has raised strong protests from transport authorities, industrial and trade interests, and official committees. Fortunately today some of the States levy no octroi and in the States allowing them, many local bodies have not utilized their right to impose them. For instance, in Gujarat, while octroi was levied by all corporations and municipalities and 49 Nagar Panchayats out of 59, of 11,968 Gram Panchayats, only 279 levied it.[8] Imagination shudders at the physical obstacles to commodity movements if the right to impose octroi were more fully used; and there is a great temptation to do so. It has not been adequately recognized that the imposition of octroi creates artificial tariff barriers between one small locality and the rest of India, which are alien to the integration of the national economy. In the new context of rural industrialization, it has the great danger of obstructing free access of products of small areas to the prosperous urban markets. There is, therefore, a strong case for abolishing the octroi duty which has so far survived only because of its revenue productivity. More recently, there have been some high level discussions of replacing them by a local sales tax, a supplementary local sales tax, or a state surcharge on the existing state sales tax, or a state turnover tax at uniform on differential rates.[9] There can be no theoretical objection to the suggested course. Its further replacement by the value-added tax will depend on whether it is deemed advisable to replace the sales tax by the value-added tax.

CENTRAL EXCISE DUTIES

The remaining two types of commodity taxation viz., central excises and sales taxation, present important debatable fields for possible substitution.

[8] *Report of the Octroi Enquiry Committee, 1970*, Gujarat, p. 34.
[9] *Ibid.*, pp. 82-89; *Report of the Study Group on Octroi*, Maharashtra, pp. 47-58.

Revenue-wise, they occupy a very important position, accounting for 46 per cent and 20 per cent of commodity taxation respectively. In discussing their major features, we shall naturally confine ourselves to those aspects where the introduction of the value-added tax will mean considerable differences. We shall begin our discussion with a brief comment on the administrative practicability of a value-added tax.

It must be immediately agreed that being in many respects novel, the value-added tax will have to be sold to the tax-payers, and will need a vigorous training programme for tax-administrators. But this is a transi- tional problem which can be tackled, and need not influence our views on the long-term desirability. It has been argued that the V.A.T may make unreasonable demands on the tax payers and greatly add to the burden of tax-compliance. It may be acknowledged that gross sales returns are much easier to file than the value-added tax returns which need in addition accounts of taxes paid on past purchases. Even in the present sales tax systems, however, much greater information than turnover accounts is required, and the records to be kept for excise taxation are elaborate. Besides, most of the excise and sales tax payers are also income tax payers.[10] Excise duties are largely collected (95 per cent) from firms with gross production of more than Rs 5 lakhs (vide Table 5). In such diverse States as Maharashtra and U.P dealers with a turnover of more than Rs 1 lakh contribute more than nine-tenths of the sales tax revenue (Table 6). If these are any indication, the V.A.T accounts requirements will present no particular difficulties, provided a more ambitious coverage is not attempted.

We may now pass on to consider the relevant aspects of central excise taxation.

Preponderance of Specific Duties

A substantial part of our excise revenue is derived from specific duties. In 1973-74, Rs 863 crores were derived from *ad valorem* duties, while Rs 1,450 crores (63 per cent) were obtained from specific and mixed duties (Table 7). Specific duties have the administrative advantage of being easily ascertainable as they raise no valuation problems. On the other hand, a specific duty on a commodity with wide varieties and qualities tends to be regressive on higher varieties and qualities. To remedy this, the commodity is so subdivided and the varieties so defined that the price of a unit belong- ing to one classification does not vary significantly. The identification of the sub-variety however often becomes a substantial problem. A specific duty is price-inelastic. While frequent revisions can give it a buoyancy experience has revealed that revisions in pace with constantly rising prices

[10]"In a country where every business has to compute its net income for tax purpose, it is hard to imagine that a value-added tax could present any really significant pro- blems." Dan Throup Smith. "The Case for VAT," *Harvard Business Review*, November-December 1970, p. 79.

TABLE 5
Distribution of Excise Duty Revenue by Gross Production of Firms: 1971-72

Production	Dealers		Revenue	
	Percentage	Cumulative percentage	Percentage	Cumulative percentage
More than Rs 10 crs	0.13	0.13	28.43	28.43
More than Rs 5 crs but not more than Rs 10 crs	0.17	0.30	13.95	42.38
More than Rs 2 crs but not more than Rs 5 crs	0.38	0.68	13.99	56.37
More than Rs 1 crore but not more than Rs 2 crs	0.81	1.49	13.51	69.88
More than Rs 50 lakhs but not more than Rs 1 crore	1.22	2.71	10.48	80.36
More than Rs 25 lakhs but not more than Rs 50 lakhs	1.60	4.31	6.72	87.08
More than Rs 5 lakhs but not more than Rs 25 lakhs	6.39	10.70	8.38	95.46
More than Rs 1 lakh but not more than Rs 5 lakhs	11.28	21.98	3.26	98.72
Rs 1 lakh and below	78.02	100.00	1.28	190.00
	100.00		100.00	

Report of Central Excise (self-removal procedure) Review Committee, Government of India, Ministry of Finance (Department of Revenue and Insurance), 1971, pp. 35-42.

TABLE 6
Collection of Sales Tax Revenue by Turnover of Dealers

Turnover Rs	Dealers		Revenue	
	Percentage	Cumulative percentage	Percentage	Cumulative percentage
(a) Maharashtra 1964-65				
1 crore and above	0.68	0.68	40.90	40.90
50 lakhs ... 99.99 lakhs	0.92	1.60	11.50	52.40
20 lakhs ... 49.99 ,,	2.80	4.40	13.08	65.48
10 lakhs ... 19.99 ,,	4.57	8.97	9.90	75.38
5 lakhs ... 9.99 ,,	7.68	16.65	8.69	84.07
1 lakh ... 4.99 ,,	31.51	48.16	12.51	96.58
Below 1 lakh	51.84	100.00	3.42	100.00
	100.00		100.00	
(b) Uttar Pradesh 1972-73				
2 lakhs and above			82.3	82.3
1.25 lakhs to 2 lakhs			5.7	88.0
Below 1.24 lakhs			12.0	100.00

Source: Report of the Maharashtra Sales Tax Enquiry Committee, 1975-76, Table 10, Government of Maharashtra, 1976, p. 178.
Report of the U.P. Taxation Enquiry Committee, 1974, p. 216.

TABLE 7

**Distribution of Excise Revenue, Ad valorem & Specific:
1973-74**

	Revenue (*in crores of rupees*)	Percentage
Ad valorem duties	863	37.31
Specific & mixed duties	1450	62.69
	2313	100.00

Calculated from Indian Customs & Excise Tariff, 1973-74 and Central Government Budget, Government of India, Ministry of Finance, 1975-76.

are difficult to carry out and prove vexatious.[11] Since India has experienced sharp price rise since the Second Plan, this aspect is likely to make a powerful impact. V.A.T is based on accounts and not physical inspection and has, therefore, to be *ad valorem*. This makes it price-elastic and proportional to price on all varieties and qualities. The potential manoeuvrability of the V.A.T to yield much higher revenues by a change in the rate or a few rates imparts it a much greater buoyancy.

The important question to answer is why a large part of the excise duties has remained specific, in spite of the earnest efforts of the Ministry of Finance to turn as many of them into *ad valorem* duties as possible over the last few years. The value-added tax will have to tackle the same obstacles which have hitherto hindered the introduction of *ad valorem* excises, and there seems nothing peculiar in its character which will make its chances of success much greater. In this connection, it is interesting to note that the Venkatappaiah Committee, after a detailed examination of the excise revenue system, regarded only 29 commodities produced almost entirely in the organized sector accounting for 60 per cent of revenue as amenable to account-based control, 92 commodities contributing 38 per cent revenue as suitable for production-based control and the rest for clearance-based control.[12] It is only the former that easily lend themselves to a value-added tax.

Coverage

The Bhootalingam Committee stressed another lacuna in Excise Duties viz. its failure to automatically cover at least all factory production. New commodities had to be identified and duties levied on them.[13] This was not

[11] *D. T. Lakdawala and K. V. Nambiar, Commodity Taxation in India,* Sardar Patel Institute of Economic and Social Research, Ahmedabad, 1972, pp. 56-57.

[12] *Report of the Central Excise (Self-Removal Procedure) Review Committee,* 1971, pp. 72-73, Government of India, Ministry of Finance, Department of Revenue and Insurance.

[13] *Final Report on Rationalisation of Tax Structure,* Government of India, Ministry of Finance, 1969, p. 5.

a great difficulty as new lines of factory production could be easily located. Even this minor difficulty has been got over by a defined rate of tax, now low, on all residuary factory-produced commodities.

While universal coverage has a certain spontaneous appeal, extension of coverage beyond a point may be attended with diminishing returns, and it needs close scrutiny to find out up to what point the operation is worth-while. A commodity-wise analysis of the excise duties reveals that in 1973-74 the first 23 items fetched 84 per cent of revenue, and the first 40 items 93 per cent; the remaining 77 items out of 117 brought only 7 per cent (Table 8). The Venkatappaiah Committee felt[14]—and many others have voiced the same feeling—that the question of continuing the duties on items which fetched small amounts needed consideration as it might be more paying to divert attention to items yielding much more. A value-added tax or sales tax does not easily admit of such exemptions, but this does not automatically get rid of the problems of optimum coverage.

TABLE 8

Distribution of Excise Revenue by Commodities Ranked According to Revenue: 1973-74

No. of commodities (ranked according to revenue contribution)	Revenue in course (of Rs)	Percentage
23 (more than Rs 20 crores each)	2,229	84
40	2,464	93
Remaining 77	188	7
117	2,652	100

Report of the Central Excise (Self Removal Procedure) Revenue Committee, Government of India, Department of Revenue and Insurance, Ministry of Finance 1971, p. 27.

Double Taxation

Manufactured intermediate products and capital goods as well as final consumption goods have to pay excises. While it is difficult to neatly classify all excised commodities into final consumption goods and inter-mediate and capital goods, the commodity-wise sources of excise revenue show that about half of the central excise duties is derived from intermediate and capital goods. This means that in the absence of specific refund provisions, factory goods made by means of other factory goods pay excise duties both on their outputs and on some or all of their inputs. The departmental rules provide, to some extent, more than is often realized, for re-

[14]"We fully subscribe to this view [of the Public Accounts Committee] and consider that all existing levies with a yield of less than Rs 50 lakhs should be reviewed." *Report of the Central Excise (Self-Removal Procedure) Review Committee*, 1976, p. 99. See also *Report of the Central Excise Reorganization Committee*, 1964, p. 15.

funds of duties paid at previous stages, but the refunds do not cover all cases. The best way to realize the double taxation involved is to prepare an input-output table for final consumption goods in terms of commodities taxed at different rates, but the data are difficult to get. More easily available data are according to the Planning Commission's 66-Sector Table, which gives the effective excise duty paid by each sector directly, from which the indirect tax burden on each sector can also be worked out. Working upon it, several striking conclusions emerge: (*i*) of the 66 sectors, only 2 sectors pay no excise duty, directly or indirectly (*ii*) 64 sectors pay duties indirectly through inputs, but only 46 sectors pay directly; (*iii*) of these 46 sectors, 11 pay more indirectly than directly; and (*iv*) the 20 sectors, which do not pay excise duties directly, account for more than half of the total output (Table 9 and 10).

TABLE 9

Prevalence of Direct and Indirect Excise Duties: 1973-74

	No. of sectors
No direct and indirect excise duty	2
No direct, only indirect, excise duty	18
Indirect tax greater than direct tax	11
Indirect tax smaller than direct tax	35
	66

Computed from (*i*) Total Coefficient Table, pp. 37-47, and (*ii*) from Excise Duty per Rupee of Output for 66 sectors, p. 60, *A Technical Note on Approach to the Fifth Plan of India (1974-79)*, Government of India, Planning Commission, 1973.

TABLE 10

Sector not Directly Taxed Through Excise

Sector	*(Gross output Rs millions)*
Foodgrains	107,104.4
Animal husbandry	40,650.0
Forestry	6,863.0
Coal	2,960.5
Crude oil	770.0
Other minerals	1,270.0
Refractory	540.0
Agricultural implements	1,600.0
Machine tools	1,020.4
Other machinery	5,330.0
Electricals	596.0
Telephone, telegraph, etc.	536.0
Ships and boats	437.3
Aircrafts	405.0
Watches & clocks	118.3
Misc. scientific equipment	373.0
Printing	1,761.1
Construction	48,567.0
Railways	12,030.0
Other services	1,24,543.0
	3,57,475.0

It may be argued that the double taxation can be easily avoided if excise duties are confined to final consumption goods; the revenue loss can be more conveniently made up through higher rates on final consumption goods. Apart from the difficulty of classifying goods, in many cases, final consumption goods are less easily amenable to taxation than intermediate and capital goods due to the greater role of organized sector in the latter. It is easier to tax steel than steel manufactures or cement rather than building construction. Rubber tyres are used for new cars as well as for repair and renewal work, and the latter use may evade tax more easily, compared with the former, unless tyre manuactures are taxed. Aluminium utensils are more difficult to tax than aluminium itself. It is , therefore, difficult to eliminate taxation of inputs, all of which may not amount to double taxation.[15] It is not possible to replace the inputs tax by a tax on final outputs. A refund system, however well devised, cannot be satisfactory unless it takes its clue from the V.A.T. which will tackle satisfactorily the problem of taxed inputs being used both in taxed and non-taxed outputs.

Multiplicity of and Variations in Rates

The excise duty in India has another special characteristic viz. multiplicity of rates. Besides a number of rates mentioned in the excise enactments, a large number of notifications are issued from time to time, and these substantially modify the effective rates. In 1973-74, 66 commodities, more than 2500 rates (2593 rates to be exact) could be counted—40 rates on an average—and one commodity, cotton fabrics, had as many as 300 rates. Along with the multiplicity of rates, their burden may also be touched upon here. The levels of and variations in effective tax burdens are more important than the formal tax rates, and because of the multiplicity of

TABLE 11

Incidence of Excise Duties—Direct and Indirect Sector-wise: 1973-74

Incidence	No. of sectors
0-5	28
5-10	11
10-15	6
15-20	3
20-25	3
25-50	11
50-100	1
Above 100	3
	66

Technical Note on the Approach to the Fifth Plan of India (1974-79), Planning Commission, Government of India, 1973.

[15]If final outputs can be efficiently taxed at appropriate rates, there is no general case for taxing inputs. If they cannot be taxed, input taxation is the only sensible method of commodity taxation. But in India we have the problem of the same inputs being used both in organized and unorganized sectors. This makes the problem difficult to tackle.

rates these are bound to vary greatly. From the Planning Commission source quoted earlier, it is possible to make an analysis of the sector-wise variations in rates, which are given in Table 11. Since a sector often includes both factory-produced goods and others, the sector-wise excise duty burden seems much lighter than a more detailed division of excisable articles would show.

The only other place where we have information regarding effective rates is the *Statistical Year book of Central Excise, 1973-74* where we can get the production value and revenue collected for 30 commodities. Of these commodities 13 paid more than 20 per cent and 5 above 50 per cent (Table 12).

TABLE 12
Effective Direct Excise Rates: 1973-74

Item no.	Serial no.	Commodity	Effective rate ad valorem
1	(1)	Sugar	14.72
2	(2)	Coffee	11.72
7	(3)	Kerosene	52.54
6	(4)	Motor spirit	71.24
14	(5)	Paints and varnishes	16.29
34	(6)	Motor vehicles	8.20
38	(7)	Matches	48.43
4	(8)	Tobacco raw	33.43
14A	(9)	Soda ash	27.38
14B	(10)	Caustic soda	9.24
14D	(11)	Syn. org. dyestuffs	2.32
14G	(12)	Acids	7.10
16	(13)	Tyres	66.89
	(14)	Tyres	66.66
23	(15)	Cement	17.10
26B	(16)	Zinc	5.60
27A	(17)	Lead	6.88
29	(18)	I.C. Engines	3.51
30	(19)	Electric Motors	6.66
15B	(20)	Cellophane	23.25
37A	(21)	Gramophones	13.80
33	(22)	Electric Fans	7.49
29A	(23)	Refrigerators	18.90
8	(24)	Refined diesel oil	63.64
9	(25)	Diesel oil N.O.S.	32.13
11	(26)	Asphalt & Biloman	22.13
16A	(27)	Rubber products	27.00
12*	(28)	Vegetable N.E.S. oils	0.79
14HH	(29)	Fertilizers	8.07
11A	(30)	Petroleum products	25.75

Computed from the information available in the *Statistical Year Book of Central Excise, 1973-74,* Vol. I and II.

A wider coverage is possible for formal *ad valorem* rates where we can get details regarding 151 commodities. The rates vary from 10 per cent to 200 per cent; additional excise duties increase the maximum rate to 20 per cent. To form an idea of the incidence of excise revenue, one should know, besides the number of commodities subject to certain rates, also how much they contribute to the revenue. Table 14 gives this picture, as far as *ad valorem* rates are concerned. It will be seen that only 9 per cent of the revenues was obtained from commodities subject to 10 per cent duty.

TABLE 13

Frequency of Ad Valorem Excise Duties by Number of Commodities

Rate (Per cent)	No. of commodities & sub-commodities
10	49
15	21
20	42
25	13
30	15
40	3
50	3
75	2
100	1
200	2
	151

Computed from *Indian Customs and Central Excise Tariff, 1973-74*, Vol. I and II, Government of India, Department of Publication, Ministry of Works and Housing.

TABLE 14

Excise Duty Collections from Commodities Subject to Ad Valorem Rates: 1973-74

Rate (Per cent)	Revenue (Rs crores)	Percentage	No. of commodities
10	77	9.0	30
15	86	9.9	8
20	72	8.3	15
25	55	6.3	3
30	35	4.1	2
10— 15	23	2.7	4
10— 20	29	3.4	5
10— 25	28	3.3	3
10— 30	170	19.7	6
10— 50	103	11.9	5
75—100	21	2.4	1
100—200	164	19.0	1
	863	100.0	83

Computed from *Indian Customs and Central Excise Tariff, 1973-74*, Vol. I & II, Government of India, Department of Publicity (Ministry of Works and Housing); Central Government Budget, Government of India, Ministry of Finance, 1975-76.

About two-fifths of the revenues accrued from commodities subject to 15 per cent and more. As compared with the manifold rates of our excises, the value-added tax is levied at one or a few rates. The transition from a large multiplicity of rates with wide variations to a few rates with comparatively small differences will raise adjustment problems of changes in demand and production for quite some time. Ignoring them, the major question that should be considered is: "Is the Indian situation more propitious for a very small number of commodity rates, or is a large number called for?"

It must be admitted at once that the large tax rates prevalent at present cannot be justified and their complexity needs to be considerably cut down. A great number of motives like conservation of foreign exchange, increase in export earnings, conservation of scarce resources, incentives to new industries, development of backward areas, making commodity tax burden more progressive, etc., enter into the determination of excise duties. Some of them are not always helped by the system of prevalent excise duties, and for others more effective devices can be found. But the question is: "Can we drastically reduce the number of rates to three or four without hampering any of the basic legitimate objectives of excise duties?"

Commodity taxation has, besides yielding revenue, to serve at least one major purpose in India. In the planned economic development of the country, in fixing production targets, while the likely trend of demand for a commodity is taken into account, it is not always thought essential to provide enough supplies to meet it fully. This is a deliberate device to restrain increases in consumption and to discriminate commodity-wise. Apart from the sudden shortages which would arise in the case of unanticipated increases in demand or decreases in demand or decreases in anticipated supply, a gap between demand and supply is planned in the case of some commodities, the gap being decided by many circumstances like the nature of the commodity, the import dependence, the scarce resource use, etc. One of the effective ways to meet demand-supply gap would be an appropriate increase in the excise duty rates on such commodities. These tax rates are likely to be different depending on the difference between demand and supply prices at planned supply levels. It follows that India needs differential tax rates as a part of its basic planning technique which is entirely at variance with the logic of a value-added tax. It has also been our experience that with fast rising prices, setting up of a new unit or substantial expansion of an old one requires much greater capital per unit of production. In order to exist and compete on fair terms, such units need favourable treatment. Since excise duties are high, they offer one easy way of discrimination. In a labour-surplus economy like India, it becomes necessary to encourage labour-intensive methods of production. Small units generally use less capital-intensive methods of production and excise duty concessions linked to production can be used to help them. The Venkatappaiah Committee Report, critical of the system of present excise concessions to industry, recommended an exemption to units with a production level of less than 5 lakhs a year. Such exemptions give rise to a host of problems in value-added tax, as these smaller producers are in no position to keep account of the taxes paid by them on purchases; tax exemption does not therefore imply in their case zero rate of tax, since taxes will have been paid at earlier stages. Further, if this small industry output is bought by purchasers who are not final consumers, the latter will have to pay the full tax on their output, but will not be entitled to a refund of the tax previously paid in the absence of special devices.[16] It is thus obvious that if commodity-wise and production-wise distinction are needed in tax measures, V.A.T is not designed to achieve them. While one may believe that we have at present too many of them, we cannot dispense with them entirely.

Evasion

The Venkatappaiah Committee was painfully surprised at the range, diversity and, in certain segments of production, at almost the universality of evasion.[17] A number of commodities were being sold in the market at less than their cost plus the tax rate. They ascribed this both to the machinery of implementation and its substance. More than slack, non-existent or dishonest supervision, unnecessary complications in tariff items and unrealistically designed exemptions provided in-built incentives for evasion. The commodities were subdivided on the basis of their physical and chemical properties, some of which could not be identified on the basis of even laboratory tests; exemptions and reliefs were given according

TABLE 15

Excise Duties in Relation to Factory Output: 1969-70

	Rs Crores	
Excies duties	1425	
Factory output—gross	12,055	
Value added in factory sector—gross	3,326	
Excise duties as percentage of gross output of factory sector		12%
Excise duties as percentage of value added in factory sector (1969-70)		43%

[16]This has created special problems in the treatment of agriculture and many services, which are exempt from value-added tax. T e EEC regards these problems as legitimate pressures on these two sectors to fall in line with the rest of the economy. A temporary respite has been given to agriculture by the concepts of zero tax rate (which entitles agriculture to claim tax refunds) but this has not been extended to services. The result is a tendency to the integration of some services like those of architects with their customers producing goods. See National Development Office, *Value-Added Tax*, H.M.S.O., London, 1971, p. 18 and A.A. Tait, *Value-Added Tax*, McGraw Hill Book Co., London, 1972, pp. 20-24.

[17]*Report of the Central Excise (Self-Removal Procedure) Review Committee*, 1971, p. 55.

to employment, size, use of power, etc., which could be concealed or mis-reported or formally complied with without changes in substance.

There is no doubt that a simpler system of uniform rates or few rates will reduce evasion, and a value-added tax is such a system. But other similar alternatives are also possible.

Equivalent Value-Added Tax

For ascertaining the equivalent value-added tax rate or rates, it is essential to know the base of the value-added tax. We may take this to be the same as that of value added by factory production; according to the Industrial Census of Production and the SISS, the base was Rs 3330 crores for 1969-70. Since the revenue realized by excises was Rs 1400 crores in the same year, an average rate of 43 per cent would be indicated (Table 15). The voucher method would, however, also tax non-factory inputs entering into factory outputs. The gross output of the factory sector in the same year was Rs 12,000 crores. If this whole output, which comprised double counting of some factory output, was considered as the base, the rate would be 12 per cent.[18] In practice, the rate would be somewhere in between, which would be a fairly heavy average rate. If the coverage could be extended to non-factory production and some part of distribution, the rate would be lower, but in that case, the tax burden on non-factory production would be much steeper than now.

Summing up, one may say that apart from transitional problems of adjustment, which would be severe, the choice between retention of central excise duties, and their substitution by a value-added tax will largely depend on whether we take the view that commodity taxation should be universal or selective, and whether commodity-wise rate discrimination is essential.[19]

SALES TAXATION

The value-added tax may replace general sales taxation as a state tax, as in the Brazilian case, or as a national tax. The case is very different for the two variants. We shall begin with the value-added tax of the sub-national type.

General sales taxation is *ad valorem* and is based on the accounting method rather than on physical description method. The rates of taxation have not the same variance or diversity as excise taxation. In a single-point

[18]Similar figures for factory production in 1973-74 are not available. Allowing for an increase in industrial production index of 16 per cent and of a price increase in manufactured products of 57 per cent, the gross factory output could be estimated at Rs 22,000 crores. The revenue from excises in the same year was Rs 2617 crores, broadly 12 per cent.

[19]"It would be much better to persevere with our excise duties and reform them at least so long as we levy many of them for regulatory purpose and so long as rates have to be very different." Lakdawala and Nambiar, p. 69.

tax system, the rate will generally vary from 3-4 per cent to 15 per cent and in a multi-point system from 0.5 per cent to 3 per cent. From the viewpoint of avoiding double taxation, a state value-added tax has no special advantage in those States which have a single-point sales tax in respect of final consumption goods. Even in States which adopt multi-point sales taxation, the tendency is towards single-point sales taxation in case of commodities with recognized channels of distribution,[20] and this accounts for three-fourths of State revenues, so that the advantage is only regarding the rest. In both these types of States, sales taxes are levied on raw materials, and intermediate and capital goods which contribute substantially to State sales tax proceeds.[21] The double tax element in this is, however, partly counteracted by relief provisions for manufacturers who use these commodities in production for sale in the domestic market. A large amount of sales taxation (93 per cent) is collected at the first point from wholesalers of various types, and a very small amount from retailers for reasons of convenience of collection (Table 16). Breaking up of tax collections by processes implied in the value-added tax will present a grave problem, or tax authorities will have to stop short much earlier than the final distribution stage. The replacement of State sales taxes by a value-added tax presents no great advantage.

The real advantage of a value-added tax would be realized if it was substituted for the sales tax on a national scale. State sales taxation in one State overlaps with that in another and with Central excise taxation. The taxation Enquiry Committee had gone into the first question at some length, and laid down local consumption as a criterion, but in order to avoid the vexatious need of various big dealers complying with the sales tax requirements of different States, it suggested levying a Central sales tax on exports from one State to another,[22] and limiting the tax rate on commodities of inter-state importance like jute, coal, cotton, hides and skins, oilseeds, iron and steel, etc. A commodity exported from one State to another may already have paid (besides the central sales tax) a sales tax earlier depending on State law and whether the producer was the exporter. It would be subject to a tax in the importing State if it underwent another transaction there before its use or consumption. As the central sales tax rate has been increased, ways have been developed to sending goods outside State borders on a consignment basis. This has reached such a level that the States are now fighting a hard battle to get powers to tax consignments through constitutional changes which, if enacted, would violate the fundamental principle of no trade barriers from one State to another and no discrimination according to the

[20]For instance in U.P., the revenue from commodities subject to single-point tax was less than 50 per cent of sales tax revenue in 1960-61. It increased to 78 per cent in 1972-73. *U.P. Taxation Enquiry Committee Report*, p. 210.

[21]*Ibid.*, p. 224. In U.P., more than one- third of the sales tax revenue was derived from this source.

[22]For a brief summary see D.T. Lakdawala, *Taxation and the Plan*, pp. 12-14.

TABLE 16

Sales Taxes Paid by Types of Dealers in Maharashtra
1964-65

	Type of dealers	per cent of dealers	per cent of sales	per cent of taxes
I	Wholesalers			
	1. Manufacturers and exporters	8.36	36.22	51.34
	2. Manufacturers but not exporters	4.76	6.77	5.71
	3. Wholesalers who were exporters	10.66	22.98	23.14
	4. Wholesalers who were commissio agents	1.60	5.86	2.59
	5. Wholesalers other than those mentioned in 3 and 4	12.37	19.40	9.95
	Total (items 1 to 5)	37.75	91.23	92.73
II	Other than wholesalers			
	1. Jobbers	1.44	0.38	0.68
	2. Restaurants, hotels, bars, etc. and other eating places	6.07	0.77	0.51
	3. Petty manufacturers	18.50	2.24	2.79
	4. Other retailers	35.69	5.32	3.18
	5. Contractors, etc.,	0.75	0.07	0.13
	Total (items 1 to 5)	62.45	8.77	7.28
	Grand Total	100.00	100.00	1100.00

Source: *Report of the Maharastra Sales Tax Enquiry Committee,* 1975-76, pp. 176-77, Table 9.

State of origin.[23] A national value-added tax will radically change this situation, but a relevant amendment in the Central Sales Tax Act could do the same.

The largely unencumbered power of the State to levy a local sales tax has met obstacles in the rights of producers, dealers or consumers to freely move commodities on own account throughout the country. We have already dealt with the consignment device of the former two, but even consumers may systematically purchase durable consumption goods outside, if the rate variations are large. Zonal meetings have been held to arrive at some common understanding, but in the absence of a coordinating agency, they have not achieved notable success. The vigilant States have in self-interest adjusted tax rates so as not to lose revenue and divert trade and production to neighbouring States. This has meant tax rates being kept lower, which can be seen by comparing the excise duties and sales tax rates on the same commodities. A central value-added tax will achieve this end, but a central coordination of sales tax rates can do the same.

[23]For a clear enunciation of problems in this connection, see Lakdawala, "Problems in Indian Public Finance," a speech delivered at the M.P. Economic Association, October 1976, para. 20, pp. 13-14.

Apart from being an independent source of revenue to the State, the technical reason for seperating sales tax from excise duty was that a large part of Indian production was outside the factory sector and therefore not amenable to excise duties. On the other hand, distribution being centralized in the case of many commodities, they were liable to sales taxation. It, however, has so happened that because of our many considerations in sales tax imposition like exemption of cottage industries, exemption of necessaries, etc., and the inefficiency of sales taxation, the basis of sales taxation seems to greatly overlap with that of Central Excises. As commodity-wise collection figures are available only for a few States, and it is difficult to know how much of each of them is factory-produced and how much otherwise, only a rough classification of sales tax proceeds according to which commodity is factory-produced or otherwise can be attempted. In the case of Maharashtra, it is estimated that 60 per cent of the sales tax revenue is derived from commodities which are also liable to central excises.[24] For India as a whole, the percentage would be smaller, implying that sales taxation covers in value terms as much of non-excised commodities as excised commodities. An all-India value-added tax will achieve uniform taxation of both factory-produced and non-factory-produced goods distributed through organized channels if it replaces both central excises and sales taxation. Both the taxes will then be integrated. Under it, uniformly high tax rate will be levied both at production and distribution stages, but only on value added at each stage. Goods which have not been subjected to excises will have to pay the combined rate on both at the first point of distribution. This will mean deprivation of the differential favourable tax treatment of the non-factory production. Inter-State transaction will automatically fall into this pattern and consignments will furnish no advantage.

There is, however, one great difficulty to the course suggested. The States are greatly dependent on sales taxes and they greatly value their power to vary the tax rates to suit their revenue needs. The States can only be reconciled to a surrender of this power if they can be assured of an adequate share in the tax proceeds which will more than compensate them for not only their immediate revenue loss but also for the potential loss. The experience of sharing additional excise proceeds furnishes the lessons to be borne in mind.[25] A value-added tax of this sort will even then be worthwhile experimenting with if it can replace both central excises and sales taxation together, but the desirability of the former course is doubtful. If this is ruled out, the necessary coordination of sales taxation can more simply be brought about through an all-India sales tax system.

[24]*Report of the Sales Tax Enquiry Committee,* 1975-76, Maharashtra, p. 21. An idea of the existing cumulative tax burden of excise and sales taxation on some select commodities is given in Table I of the Report, p. 187.

[25]For a brief account see D.T. Lakdawala, and K. V. Nambiar, *Commodity Taxation in India,* Sardar Patel Institute of Economic and Social Research, Ahmedabad, 1972, pp. 50-55.

K. S. KRISHNASWAMY

Thoughts on Inflation and Distribution

Over the last twenty-five years during which I have worked as an economist in the public sector, I have been associated mainly with matters
connected with development planning and monetary policy. In both these
areas, these past two decades have witnessed a great deal of development in
the Indian economy—significant growth in the national product, diversifica-
tion of economic activity, creation of national markets, adoption of modern
technology over wide areas, attainment of higher standards of public health
and technical skills, and many more notable achievements. In the immediate
past, much success has been achieved in combating inflation and in developing exports. Yet despite all this, one cannot help feeling that, while
many battles may have been won, the war is far from having been won.
Poverty, unemployment and malnutrition have yet to be banished—a
long way to go before we can even speak of full employment at a reasonable
standard of living. We have yet to find a way of maintaining continuous
development without domestic inflation, payments imbalance and social
or political instability. These are challenges not only to the politician and
the administrator, but equally to the economist and the social scientist.

In pondering over these matters, the economist has to recognize that
the problems to be solved are related to particular historical contexts. I
make this obvious point for the reason that, in the process of evolving
workable solutions, it is inevitable that we should make many simplifica-
tions and assumptions. While doing so, we create schemes or models which
need not necessarily reflect the existing reality fully. And having evolved
model solutions, we are apt to overlook the difficulties of clearly establishing the identity between the logical scheme and the specific problem on
hand. Even when care is taken to avoid oversimplification of the real
world, the solutions we evolve cannot always be given a clear-cut time
profile or a precise quantitative measure. Admittedly, more or less of such
divergence from reality is inevitable for the reason that not all facts can be
known at once or measured with equal facility; and even if that were so,
not all of them are necessarily reconcilable. While economists may be
aware of these limitations when recommending prescriptions or policies,
those who implement such policies often fail to appreciate the reservations
if the results indicated are broadly acceptable to them. The risk of such

*Presidential address delivered to the 59th annual conference of Indian Economic
Association, held at Mysore in December 1977.

blind acceptance is often enhanced by the fact that both the policy-maker and the economist are likely to view things from their particular cultural standpoint. They are then liable to minimize or ignore the limitations readily. It is also possible that they act without any knowledge of the enormity of institutional or motivational change which a solution subsumes. These risks are particularly great when change, no matter what it is or what it is for, becomes in itself a desired objective of policy. Under such conditions, the economist who seeks to advise the policy-maker has to exercise great care and forbearance in suggesting solutions to the nation's problems. If they do not do so, they may end up as apologists and pro-pagandists for some group rather than as scientists concerned with the interests of society as a whole.

Lest there be any misunderstanding, I should add that there are many in such positions who have tendered honest advice, maintained fully their intellectual integrity and earned the respect of the laity and the professional alike. My intention is essentially to bring out the need for greater objecti-vity and caution in providing solutions to the many economic problems that we face. If I have been more explicit in the case of the economist, it is only because I am one of them and, therefore, am better aware of the pressures to which they are subject.

Since, as I said earlier, my own involvements in the past have been in the areas of development planning and monetary policy, I have had the opportunity to watch closely the conflicting elements that have to be re-conciled in the process of decision-making in these areas. It is not possible— nor would it be interesting—to comment on all of them. However, during the rest of my paper, I should like to dwell on two elements which have recurred over the years, viz., the questions of price inflation and of distri-butive justice. I should like to offer some random thoughts on these for the further reason that, in my judgement, they have become as much matters of political friction as of economic analysis.

II

There is perhaps more public debate on the question of prices than on any other issue these days, not only in India but the world over. This is not surprising, since, depending on what side of transactions he is on, every-body finds his welfare adversely or beneficially affected by a movement in one or more prices. When groups of people are so involved, there is ob-viously a conflict of mutual interests arising from the effect of price changes on money incomes, output, distribution of real income, balance of payments and so forth. It becomes inevitable for each social group and for the Government to take a position on this issue, and economists are naturally drawn into the fray.

There is of course no question but that a large and continuous rise in the general price level is injurious to the social interest, both in terms of current welfare and future development. However, it is not always clear at what point price movements cease to curb demand or elicit the additional supplies desired by the community. In principle, output becomes inelastic to price or demand increase at the point of full employment of one or the other of the factors of production. This of course is tautological, since there is often no way of identifying the point of full employment except in terms of price increases accompanying demand increases. There is implicit in all this the assumption that commodity or factor substitution at the margin has ceased to be a possibility for technological or structural reasons. Consequently the position one takes on price changes in particular context depends on a variety of judgments not only on the prevailing technological and structural factors, but also on the desirability of a change in them.

Since in reality prices do not change all at once, a series of adjustments in relative prices will have occurred before the overall price index shows a perceptible rise. Such changes in relative prices are generally likely to be accepted as useful, unless the distributive effects are socially disruptive and there is little or no evidence of increase in output or employment. Indeed, under conditions of administered prices, relative price changes are effected for achieving these very objectives; price increases of particular commodities are viewed as incentives to additional production or investment and hence to additional employment. That in the meantime the terms of trade between two groups alter for the worse for one of them is either ignored or considered worthwhile. If relative price changes caused resource and demand shifts to occur in such a way that no bottle-necks arose, no particular group need be affected seriously or for long. On the basis of an increased real product, countervailing measures in the shape of fiscal transfers could, if necessary, be adopted to modify the aggrieved sections. But if bottle-necks in production or supply intervene and there is a cumulation of prices and costs, efforts to counter this situation through fiscal measures may lead to further price increases. Lags in the adjustment of output and expenditure to higher prices further complicate the matter.

I have referred to these commonplaces in economics because they get blurred in public debate, especially when such debate is between interested groups. As we all know, in the last few years when there has been a great upsurge in prices, there have also been significant shifts in terms of trade— between food and non-food articles, between agricultural products and manufactured goods, between wage goods and investment goods. In each of these phases, there have simultaneously been demands for curbing inflation, providing price incentives for additional production and neutralizing the price changes through compensatory policies. In general, wage-earners and fixed-income earners have pressed for anti-inflationary policies—particularly in terms of over-all monetary and fiscal measures—while the agricultural, trading and manufacturing sectors have sought specific price and profit incentives in the name of additional production and employment. Both arguments have been plausible; the dispute has been about the measure in which each of them is right in any particular context.

When price increases were very large, it became the fashion to focus on the demand factors of the economy as the leading factor in inflation. This is true not only of economists but of politicians and businessmen as well. They all campaigned for measures to curb money supply through cuts in monetary spending by one or the other sectors of the economy. Reduction in Government expenditure, curbs on spending by the upper income earners, taxation of agricultural incomes, wage, salary and profit freezes—all these were advocated with greater or less emphasis by different interested groups. Despite many differences, there seemed to be, however, general agreement that, unless increases in money supply were strictly limited, other anti-inflationary policies would have little or no effect. This had of course the appeal of simplicity and perhaps of equity in a superficial sense, in that the cuts in expenditure were mooted in terms of aggregates and in terms of rates of increase. It was only when those who had to implement policies probed into operational details that the remedies lost their appeal or even became unpalatable because of their impact on other objectives of economic policy.

Let me elaborate a little on this. Leaving aside eccentric remedies, the most common prescription recommended to the Government and the monetary authorities has been to assign the primary role in price variations to money supply with the public. Typically, the argument has taken the form of identifying a "safe" rate of increase in money supply or in deficit financing by the Government or in credit expansion by the banking system. This would naturally be based on assumptions regarding expected growth in the national product, likely amount of import surplus and constancy over a period of economic parameters defining the behaviour patterns in the systems. Occasionally the ceteris paribus conditions would refer explicitly to patterns of distribution or consumption. But these aspects were brought up either separately or as an after-thought rather than as an integral part of the argument.

In the kind of monetary analysis that we have pursued, we have tended to postulate categories broadly corresponding to economic sectors or social groups identified in national accounts or plan programmes. Changes in money supply with the public are related to (*i*) net borrowing by the Government sector, (*ii*) gross lending to the commercial sector, (*iii*) net increase in foreign assets (that is to say, net lending to the rest of the world), and finally (*iv*) net variations in the non-monetary liabilities of the banking system. Each of these sectors, namely, Government, the commercial entities and the rest of the world is believed to be motivated differently; and if the accommodation each of them seeks from the monetary system is to be adjusted upwards or downwards, different types of instruments will have to be used. It is of course possible to argue that this approach leaves out the motivations and reactions of banking institutions in the economic milieu and bring in a little bit of money multiplier analysis. But the fact remains that, whether we talk of net bank credit to some sector or increase in high powered money as a source of monetary expansion, we are still talking in generalities. Before they become meaningful in an operational sense, they have to be dissected into their components and this is when the trouble arises.

Take the Government sector. The component associated with it, viz., net bank credit to the government, is a conglomerate of several items. It includes long-term borrowing by the Central and State Government from the banking system, absorption of treasury bills by the RBI and commercial banks, and net advances to the Central and State governments. Since loans to and investments in public sector corporations are excluded, this element consists of borrowing by "general government"—that is to say, that part of government concerned with the administrative functions of the governmental system. These functions are not, in principle, related to market operations. In terms of categories, however, it is not exclusively consumption expenditure that belongs here, but also some investment.

Now, each of these elements—viz., market borrowing, floatation of treasury bills, and net advances to government—derives from a different set of judgements or commitments. Long-term borrowing is treated as a non-inflationary source of finance for plan-purpose, on the argument that ultimately it amounts to absorption of the saving of households via the financial institutions. Consequently, it is accepted that the objective of policy should be to maximize it. When this course is followed, there will formally be an increase in the accounting measure of net credit to the government sector and one is then apt to argue that a major factor causing increases in money supply is government borrowing from the banking system.

This pitfall has been well-recognized and attempts are made now-a-days to segregate what may be called "pure" deficit financing by the Government. This is defined generally as the increase in governments' floating debt (i. e. treasury bills) plus net loans and advances to "general government." Since commercial banks do not provide short-term credit facilities to the Central or State governments, and since generally treasury bill holdings of commercial banks are limited, it is also the practice to judge "pure" deficit financing by the extent of net RBI credit to the Government. This includes, however, the additions to RBI's holdings of rupee securities attributable to its open market operations. In other words, its size as now measured depends not only on a variety of decisions taken within the Government proper, but also in the Reserve Bank on macro-economic considerations. It is apparent that a different kind of judgement than that pertaining to purely governmental functions could operate here.

Allowing for minor adjustments, it seems legitimate to focus on RBI credit to the Government as indicative of the additional liquidity generated to enable the Government to carry out its commitments within any given period. On the plea that it is injurious to price stability, many economists have argued for minimization, if not elimination, of this element from the Government budget. Virtually all businessmen have endorsed it more with a view to limiting the scope of the public sector than for any other consideration. There have of course been occasions on which those in the private sector have favoured deficit spending by the Government as a means of creating additional demand for industries faced with sluggish markets. That apart, the general view at this point of time is that the less deficit financing there is, the better it is for the economy; and this tenet has been strongly adopted by the expenditure controllers in the Government. However, as against the expenditure controllers, those in charge of the Government programmes of various kinds will be focussing on the real objectives which they are enjoined to achieve, and their pull will understandably be in the direction of over-achieving the targets. When these interests collide, the outcome depends on the distribution of political power within the Government rather than on any economic logic. When it appears politically expedient to press ahead with certain programmes of investment of mass welfare, the expenditure controllers' first gambit will usually be to try to impose cuts on non-priority or non-productive items of expenditure in the Government budget, or to seek a transfer of resources from the non-governmental sector to the budget. Trimming non-productive expenditure often involves having to dispense with transfer payments, cut-back on interest paid on government borrowing, reduced expenditures on defence and administrative services, and so forth. In all these areas there may undeniably be room for economizing in various ways. But since these economies are required to be attained without affecting employment, reducing subsidies, curtailing the services and so forth, the budget-makers may have little scope to operate. In other words, the curtailment of any part of government expenditure will be resisted on the ground that it leads to deprivation of income or benefit in some part of the community or another. And depending on their social or political backing these cuts become or cease to be practicable propositions.

Since no ministry or department in the Government will accept that any part of its spending is wasteful, the attempts at cutting non-productive expenditure in the past have usually ended in minor changes in provisions for stationery and printing, travelling allowances and such inconsequential items. Not unexpectedly, those in charge of budget operations have sought to impose their cuts elsewhere, and this has inevitably been in the shape of reducing development outlays. They have been able to do so for two reasons; firstly, these are expenditures which have yet to be incurred and, therefore, it can be argued that there is no obvious denial of jobs or income to any of those who may be presently occupied. It is in respect of future jobs and future benefits that the decisions have to be taken; and these are more easily taken, since future costs and problems may be highlighted sufficiently to make the cuts appear on balance socially beneficial. The second and perhaps more important reason is that, as budget deficits become large and prices rise, the development lobby finds itself weakened by the onslaughts of middle and higher income groups which have vested interests in the status quo and in limiting public sector involvement in investment and trading activities. The conflict between these elements is as real and potent within the Government as it is among academicians or politicians. Projects or programmes yielding benefit over a period, as well as those that contribute to an improvement in the quality of life—such as education, health and environmental improvements—are postponed if not abandoned. While this may be a smart thing to do in terms of demand management, it has clearly the effect of perpetuating patterns of production and demand in their existing moulds. It protects, in other words, the prevailing power structure in society from having to yield place or accept unpalatable adjustments. Indian experience of the last two decades is replete with "remedies" of this kind.

There is of course a point beyond which this cannot be pushed in a development-hungry country like India. When this point is reached, and the budget controllers discover that the "saving" in expenditure is also prospective, they have sought to cover their flanks by seeking additional resources for the Government, particularly in the form of shifting budgetary items of expenditure to financial institutions and/or appropriating a larger part of commercial bank resources through sale of more long-term securities to them. As is well-known, the statutory obligation of commercial banks to hold government securities has steadily gone up over the last few years—this has not always been with a view to reducing the RBI's holding of such securities, in which case it would have been a pure and simple monetary operation. The objective has rather been to put the Government in possession of more funds for expenditure during the year.

It will thus be seen that, because of the multiplicity of governmental objectives—and the diversity of interests within the Government—there is or can be no precise relationship between economic achievement and the budgetary outcome. Much the same type of problem arises in the area of credit to the commercial sector. This is a grab-bag including mammoth public enterprises, large and medium-sized productive units in the private sector, small-scale industries, wholesale and retail trade, agriculture, professions, so on and so forth. Furthermore, the needs of these are met by a large number of independent institutions, each of which has its own ethos and interests to satisfy. Much more relevantly, each of the banks—or banks' management—has to take cognizance of the social and political impact of their decisions on the community in which they live and work. It would be unrealistic to expect them to take a completely objective view of things, or stand up to pressures of all sorts regardless of consequences. Indeed, they have to be more or less than human to be totally impervious to anything but a formula or a guideline. Within the policy framework set by the Reserve Bank, the management of any individual bank has to apply it to each case, and assign weights to each of the elements entering into the assessment. Even when the guidelines are clear-cut and simple, it is inevitable that individual decisions should deviate from the norm. And when this happens to run counter to the interests of a politically powerful section, the bank runs the risk of being adjudged unfairly.

The trouble is compounded by the fact that, with monetary policy having to serve a multiplicity of ends, the guidelines are never simple and few. When credit expansion in the economy is to be limited, there is always a proviso attached viz., that credit control or restraint should operate in such a way as not to inhibit additional production or additional investment in this or that essential sector. Food procurement, exports, agriculture, small industries, vulnerable sections, core industries—all these become, each on its own logic, a priority claimant on the banks' resources. On top of it all, on grounds of preventing sickness in industry or avoiding displacement of labour or alleviating deprivation under scarcity or drought conditions, further demands are made on the banking system. Individually, none of these items can be considered unworthy of support in our conditions—but in the aggregate they leave the banker with no choice but to deviate from one or more of the directives that may have been issued on the basis of macro-economic balance.

This inherent difficulty in applying scarce credit to alternative uses is complicated by two further elements. As I have already mentioned, when they are hard pressed, budget-makers find it advantageous to shift the pressure on to the banking system. One way of doing it, as already mentioned, is to seek direct support for government spending from banks' investment portfolio. When this indirect pressure is fully exploited, additional spending by the Government is sought to be countervailed by requiring a curtailment of bank credit to the private sector. However, since big industry, small-scale industry, agriculture and so forth claim immunity as productive sectors there is again a search for dispensable borrowers. For the most part, the candidate elected for this purpose is the trading sector on the ground that this sector is unproductive and given to rigging the market at the slightest provocation.

There has undoubtedly been considerable exploitation of scarcity conditions by traders in India as elsewhere. Hence it is both legitimate and attractive to require that commercial bank credit be not made available to traders who are prone to use it for speculative stock-building. However, if speculative stock-building is to be obstructed, it is not enough to leave the task to be accomplished through denial of bank credit. Every other monetary asset which can be used to hoard goods at a time of rising prices will have to be controlled, or, alternatively, all trade—especially wholesale trade—should be taken over into the public sector. As long as either of these is not done, trading transactions injurious to the community will be possible and pursued. As has been demonstrated in the last two years, the most effective means of combating speculative trading are partly monetary but mainly administrative. Moreover, it would not be logical to act as if commercial bank lending to the trading sector can be reduced to zero. No matter how production is organized, goods have to be held in the distributive pipelines by somebody or the other. If private trade is abolished, this function has to be performed either by the producers or by the government trading units. In either case, the means of stock-holding have to be found and credit provided in some measure by the banking system. Similarly, under conditions of normal trade, provision of bank credit to the private traders will in some measure be necessary. It is not legitimate to turn a blind eye to this social requirement. When therefore pressure is exerted by the budget-makers to withhold credit facilities from some part of the private sector, the reactions tend to be similar to those that are generated in the wake of attempts to reduce non-productive expenditures in the Government. The outcome in either case tends to be incommensurate with the effort.

III

Let me turn briefly to another matter, viz., that concerning distributive justice. It is now generally accepted that, unless the benefits of economic growth are more equitably shared, there will be neither social progress nor political stability. The programmes of banishment of poverty, ensuring minimum standard of living and employment, dispersal of economic power, the habitat movement—all these are manifestations of this desire. Because of their obvious appeal, virtually everybody extends his or her allegiance to such programmes regardless of social or political status. However, it is again not always obvious that the means adopted are consistent with the general objective of social justice; and the reason for this is often the same, an unwillingness to grapple with the dynamics of institutional change.

One of the policies which has been evolved as conducive to both larger output and better distribution is that of price support and procurement operations for farm products. Given the low levels of income of the large mass of agriculturists, there is a palpable case for offering higher support or procurement prices when the crops come to the market. Simultaneously with providing additional income to the farmers, these policies have been favoured on the ground that they prevent food and essential article prices from rising steeply and affecting the agricultural labourers and urban poor adversely. To be consistent with these objectives, the operational arrangements have to be such that they ensure maximum procurement both when the so-called free market prices threaten to rise sharply on account of inadequate supplies, and also when the crop is bountiful and the farmers face very low prices in the primary markets. In actual practice, procurement has been low just when there is a shortfall in production and the need was for maximizing regulated distribution, whereas in times of bumper harvests farm prices have been allowed to fall below the procurement prices. In consequence it is hard to avoid the impression that the benefits from this policy have not accrued fully to the poorer sections of the agricultural or the urban sectors. Taken along with the fiscal and monetary strains imposed on the economic system as a result of food subsidies, low agricultural taxation and limitless credit for food procurement, one is puzzled as to what net benefit has actually been sought and derived. Procurement and buffer-stock policies have a role to play in the achievement of growth and distribution objectives; but it is unlikely that this role will be performed effectively without the establishment of an enduring public distribution network. For known and unknown reasons, implementation in this regard has been far from adequate; and one can only surmise why.

Similarly, during the past decade or so, sustantial investments in the private sector have been financed with loans and other assistance provided through public financial institutions. In the more recent past much thought and many policies have been directed towards giving larger incentives to private industrial investment. However, this has not showed up materially in large employment or larger supplies of essential consumer articles. Nor has there been any reduction in the demand for aid to sick units; there are many which have resorted heavily to borrowing from bank for meeting cash losses. Altogether there is no saying at this point of time as to what the distributional effects of these measures have been or will be, and it is difficult to show that the vulnerable sections in the community have benefited in a relative sense. There is, however, some evidence that in the process some of the resources which might have been mobilized for stepping up development outlays in the public sector have not been so utilized. Otherwise, there is no reason why there should be such accumulation of unsold stocks of steel, coal, fertilizer and so forth. Like the building of foodstocks this also has inflated commercial bank lending, with attendant consequences on money supply and current and expected prices in several markets. The question once again arises; what precisely has caused such a combination of ill-assorted consequences?

I have referred to these because in my judgment the lack of resolution of such problems is not due to non-availability of relevant or sophisticated economic analysis. Rather, it is because of implicit and explicit value judgments. Hence it is necessary that the economist keeps in mind a variety of para-economic elements that impinge on operational decisions. At the present juncture there is some danger that an unusually large expansion in money supply with the public or aggregate monetary resources accompanied by a general increase in prices will either be unduly played down or unduly played up, depending on one's role in the economic system and one's political or economic ideology. There is undoubtedly need for exercising great restraint but not, in my view, for panic or scare-mongering. While the general policy of avoiding cheap credit and moving towards better planning of its use are part of the desiderata, the basic solution to the problem of concurrent price increases and demand inadequacies has to be found elsewhere, namely, in the resolution of conflicts on the plane of objectives and sectional interests. Inflation, in other words, is not so much a monetary as a social phenomenon; and its nemesis has to be sought at a fundamental level, that is, in changes reflected in the socio-economic structure.

P. R. BRAHMANANDA

Essential Propositions of the New-Classical Dynamic Economics

I

I was a student at the Maharaja's College, Mysore for Economics Honours when I was first exposed to the locus classicus of Classical Economics. We had the first six chapters of Ricardo's *Principles of Political Economy* as the text for a whole paper. Exposure to Ricardo's highly conceptualized and abstract thinking at that impressionable age had profound effects on me. Much of my later work, I consider, is a continuation of the lines of thought bequeathed by Ricardo. Professor D'Souza gave me tremendous encouragement to pursue this path which was not generally popular in India at that time.

In this paper an attempt has been made at codifying certain important propositions or theorems thrown up by the New-Classical Economics, which is presented as an evolving alternative to the mainstream (or ortho-dox) Economics which is sometimes identified as Neo-classical economics, or Neo-classicized Keynesian economics. I had made a similar effort nearly fifteen years ago at the wake of the "Sraffa Revolution," a term which had been used by me in connection with the profound and far-reaching implications to economic science of Sraffa's *Production of Commodities by Means of Commodities—Prelude to a Critique of Economic Theory*, (Cambridge, U. K., 1960). I have written rather extensively since, on the constituents of a New Classical "System" (or "Paradigm") of Economics. (Please see *Explorations in the New Classical Economic Theory of Political Economy—A Connected Critique of Economic Theory*, Bombay, Allied Publishers, 1974.)

The great advantage of the New-Classical Paradigm is that it is able to look at Economics from a very fundamental angle; one can go to the causes of economic phenomena. Since the physiocratic and classical econo-mics concerned itself intimately with problems of economic development and these problems are essentially dynamic in nature, and further the New-Classical Economics is deemed as a continuation of the physiocratic and classical (and relevant Marxian) lines of thinking, the present exercise is also concerned with tracing the lines of continuity. There are a number of ways in which classical economics, as modified and expanded under our present empirical conditions and sets of economic theory, has a great deal of contemporary relevance. In fact, it is only the classical apparatus that is error-proof. The propositions are specially adjusted to suit the requirements of a dynamic analysis of Indian development processes and the issues thereof.

*   *   *

I want to work out first the essential features in the classical school's paradigm of the working of an economy. I shall seek to contrast these features with those in the generalized version of the neo-classical school's paradigm, *the* paradigm of mainstream economics. The statement of the contrasting features enables us to understand why the mainstream growth models have not, and could not have, delivered the goods. The alternative economics, had it served as the basis for the growth models actually adopted, could have yielded the desired results. There *are* two systems of economics, two contending schools, two different worlds of analytical thought. In the public mind neo-classical economics, of one sort or the other, is identified as the only economics. In India it is the neo-Keynesian brand of neo-classical economics with shades of neo-classicized Marxism, that was the dominant part of our establishment economics. In recent years the neo-classical brand has become more prominent particularly in the planning circles. Though our policy goals are changing by and large the economists in and close to the Government and to the planning process continue to be neo-classicist in their thinking. In what follows, I state and explain first the classical position. The neo-classical position is stated next and contrasted with the former.

> *The fundamental motive in the classical paradigm for carrying on production in a growth-oriented economy is that of obtaining a positive rate of return on the values of capitals advanced for and used in production.*

As contrasted with the classical stand-point, the neo-classicists emphasize the goal of maximization of the level of satisfactions, given initial endowments of resources, technology and the pattern of wants. Even a producer is deemed to maximize the utility measure of the surplus, i.e. the difference between costs and returns. The neo-classical surplus or profits, with its utility counterpart is an *absolute* magnitude. The neo-classical theory postulates that all production has a direct or indirect end in consumption, which yields utility. Directly or indirectly, each producer is deemed to be interested in the consumption counterpart of the profits which he is expected to earn. Such consumption counterpart may accrue in the current period and/or may be deferred for a later period. Saving is deferred consumption. In the classical theory, consumption occurs because of (*a*) the need to consume wage-goods with a view to enabling one to work, and (*b*) the inability to provide for accumulation because of constraints on the rate of growth of labour. The system is deemed most efficient which economizes on aggregate input requirements and related consumption advances for obtaining any given aggregate *flow* of production; such an economy is subject to constraints in the form of a conventionally determined real wage-rate. Absolute profits are derived after applying the prevalent rate of profits to given values of capitals. Since profits are a ratio, there is no utility significance to the absolute amount of profits. In the classical scheme, there is no necessary result that growth must culminate itself in the form of an improved level of consumption per capita. There is no requirement that full-employability conditions must obtain in each and every period as a result of production operations, or eventually in some period during a sequence. Full employment, and a tolerable and rising level of per capita consumption, are sometimes the by-products of growth, and under no conditions are they the necessary results of growth. The producers and entrepreneurs have no causally intrinsic concern with the end-product of their activities.

Each individual firm or production unit conducts its operation such that given the prices of inputs purchased and used in production, the conventional real wage-rate and the exogenously given standard or normal rate of profits, its expenses of production per unit of commodity are the lowest for given quantities of output or alternatively, the values of the quantities of outputs produced for given values of quantities of inputs are maximum that can be obtained.

At the micro-level, the motive force of profit-maximization leads to an economy of input, for manufacture of given outputs. The principle of economy is derived from the framework of competition, implying thereby (a) full mobility, (b) full information, and (c) capacity to absorb information. Monopoly in any form is not conducive to the operation of the principle of economy. In the classical paradigm the economy principle refers to the minimization of stock and flow inputs for given stock and flow outputs. Production processes are always conditiond by lags. In the neo-classical paradigm, the economy principle very often refers to production processes in which inputs and outputs are instantaneous or almost so.

There exists a standard rate of profits which is exogenous to each firm or undertaking or even each industry.

There is an important difference between neo-classical theory and classical theory in regard to the above position. In neo-classical theory, absolute profits (=interest amounts) are explained on the ground of the principle of marginal productivity. The Marginal Productivity principle is applicable at a micro-level to individual firms; the macro-result, in the form of global profit amounts (=interest amounts), is applied as the numerator to the denominator of the macro-notion of the value of capital. Thus is obtained interest or the rate of profit relevant for the economy. The implication here is that that if there could be a small increase in the quantity of capital, appropriately distributed among different firms, there would be some increment in the net product, again appropriately distributed among diffe-

rent firms. This increment in net product at the macro-level is the global
amount of profits. Hypothetically, each producer may be deemed as a
consumer and the incremental inputs may be reduced to the measure of
consumption foregone, and the increment in net product to the measure of
increment in consumption. Thus, there can emerge a ratio between consumption goods or between measures of pure utility sums.

I need not mention here that there are a number of formidable difficulties
in proceeding along with the neo-classical practice in this respect. Since, in
classical theory, the standard rate of profits, which is a norm to different
enterprises, is exogenously determined and is not deemed to be a result of
the actual or hypothetical operations of the different firms at their micro-
levels, there is a world of difference between the classical and the neo-
classical practices. To the classicists, profits are wholly a social affair in
origin and distribution. The level of the rate of profits *is* affected by
factors like the rate of population growth, the conditions of productivity
in basic goods, the real and expected rate of technological change in
basic goods,the distribution of incomes among social classes as well as the
propensities to save out of the income shares accruing to different classes.
Why are profits so important? Because they are the source of the bulk of
savings. But more important than profits is the physiocratic net product
after deduction of rents. For this net product is the source of profits.

*There is free mobility of labour and/or versatile means of production as also
of finance. Such mobility, actual or potential, enables the real wage-rate to
be uniformly the same for similar types of work and the rate of profits to
be equalized in all fields.*
The tendency to equalization of the rate of profits is an important requirement for the proper allocation of investible resources in the classical paradigm. It is not necessary that there must be immediate adjustment whenever there are deviations in the particular lines from the standard rate. But
such adjustments do tend to occur over some length of time. Note that the
standard rate itself is undisturbed by the differences and variation in relative profit rates in different lines. The classical theory does *not* hold that
every production line must obtain the same rate of profits; it permits scope
for some differences on account of risk etc. Similarly, the classical
theory also does *not* require that every unit of labour must obtain the
same wage-rate; it permits some measure of wage differentials which arises
on account of the differences in social conventions regarding the methods
of payment for higher grades of labour etc. As Cairnes pointed out,
equalizing tendency can hold true even if there are non-competing groups,
provided the size within each group is quite large. Each class will itself throw
up sufficient men in each grades to see that the equalizing tendency works.

In neo-classical theory, there is no notion of a standard rate given from
outside to enterprises. Marshall who may not be included among the neo-
classicals uses the term normal profit very frequently. But we are not clear
whether this is a rate or an absolute amount. The notion of a rate of pro-

fits does not fit well in the neo-classical paradigm. One may not understand how absolute amounts in different lines tend to be equalized.

The relative prices of commodities are flexible both upwards and downwards. The level of the real wage-rate within limits, also is flexible downwards and upwards in the short period.

The level of the real wage-rate is fixed by convention. Such convention permits of considerable differences in the composition of the wage-basket. The theory of utility can be helpful in understanding the composition of the wage-basket in different countries and in different regions in the same country. There is always room for giving some weightage to utility as against sheer maximization of the profits ratio, or rather of the surplus ratio. The classical theory *does* require that the adjustment process is most efficient when there is scope for upward and downward movement in the level of the real wage-rate. This is the basis for the classical difference between the *normal-conventional commodity wage* and *the market commodity wage*. When the market wage exceeds the conventional wage, there is a tendency for population to expand; the opposite holds true when the market wage falls below the *normal-conventional* wage. There is considerable ambiguity in regard to some of these matters, and I have to return to the implications thereof at a later stage. For example, I may mention that the classicists were beautifully vague about whether the normal-conventional wage maintains population intact or permits some normal growth rate in population, nor were they very clear about the difference between the wage-rate which enables subsistence for a unit of labour and that which makes labour-yield the normal quota of work hours expected of it. The latter obviously will require a higher real-wage-rate than sheer subsistence requirements would warrant. Again, if population is to grow and the worker has to provide for a growing population, the level of the normal-conventional wage-rate will have to be adjusted upwards in the same direction as is the rate of population growth. These are refinements to which the classicists did not pay any attention; nor was Malthus very clear on these matters.

The neo-classicists make the wage-rate depend upon the marginal product of labour. At separate micro-levels, each industry is appropriately equipped with a small increment in labour; the capital assisting each industry is deemed to be so malleable as to transform itself into such form in each line as would accommodate the increment in labour. Adjustment is also assumed regarding overhead expenses like those for coordination, supervision, etc. Given malleability and divisibility in regard to capital and overhead costs, the increment in labour is expected to lead to appropriate increments in net products in different lines. The aggregate of such net products is the marginal product of labour. This procedure involves again formidable assumptions. Suffice to note that the scope for downward and upward flexibility in real wage-rates *with the same equipment* etc. does *not* obtain in the neo-classical theory. Keynes, for example, permits variations

in the real wage-rates to occur as a result of the variations in the volume
of employment and in the degree of utilization of equipments. From a
long-run angle, the measure of capital-intensity per worker has to change
in the economy, if the real wage-rate is to change. Hence, the notion of a
difference between the market and normal wage-rate does not obtain in
neo-classical theory, whereas such a difference is fundamental to the dynamic process in the classical model.

In both the classical and the neo-classical models, the relative prices of
commodities have to be deemed to be flexible. In the classical theory, they
are flexible on three scores: (a) changes in productivity, and (b) changes in
the scale of output in agriculture (basic goods) and (c) changes in the rate
of profit, and in the relative shares of wages. The neo-classical theory
accepts (a) and (b), but does not provide scope for (c). Besides, the neo-
classical theory permits relative prices to vary consequent upon relative
demand variations under conditions where non-constant costs obtain.
This role of demand, particularly in regard to basic goods, is absent in
classical theory.

*The commodities produced in the economy are classified under a dichoto-
mous scheme of necessities or basic goods or luxuries or non-basic goods.
The level of the standard rate of profit tends to be determined by, and is
capable of variation as a result of, conditions of productivity in the necessities
or basic goods.*

In neo-classical theory, there is no distinction between basic and non-basic
goods or between necessities and luxuries. In fact, the entire discussion
regarding productive and unproductive labour is devoid of any content in
neo-classical theory. In classical theory, wage-goods and the necessary
materials involved in their production, are basic goods, and since no commodity can be produced without labour, directly or indirectly, and all or
most capital equipments can be deemed to be a joint result of the application of labour with basic commodities, there is room for emphasizing,
in a special sense, the productivity conditions in wage-goods as the ultimate determinant of the rate of profits. For, such productivity alone can
determine the ratio of surplus to capitals, and surplus is the source of
profits. Non-basic goods do not enter into the process of determination of
surplus as these are a result of of the pattern of utilization of surplus. The
classicists, therefore, sharply distinguish between those technological
changes which lead to improvements in productivity conditions of basic
goods and those which lead to such improvements only in non-basic
goods. The former alone are of significance in the determination of the
surplus ratio and the rate of profits.

The classical standpoint stems from, and is a development of, the
physiocratic standpoint that agriculture, and agriculture alone, is the sole
source of surplus whereas all other activities are surplus-fed since the
latter do not enter in any vital manner in the production processes of the
former. Note that neo-classical theory considers utility as the end-product

of activity and not as an element in the absolute cost of production of commodities. In neo-classical theory, as wages are paid at the end of the period of production, there are no necessary requirements of a wage-fund as an input for labour in order that it may work. Either the input-output processes are instantaneous, or, the wage-goods stocks are deemed to carry a zero price, if such stocks exist.

I may mention here that Marx is an important spokesman for the basicness of agriculture. In fact, conditions of productivity in wage-goods were deemed as crucial in the determination of the technical surplus ratio. In this respect, Marx was as staunch a supporter for agricultural commodity development as Ricardo and George Ramsay had earlier been.

The neo-classical theorists deem every commodity at the margin as similar to every other commodity. Every improvement in productivity is expected to help in the augmentation of measure of consumer satisfaction. The neo-classical theorists would not raise their eyebrows if a viable and satisfactory allocation can occur among goods even though the outputs of basic goods, as also their growth-rate, are minimal. It is possible in the neo-classical world for the whole portions of the economy to be starving and/or to be underfed at the same time that some portions are having a high measure of consumer affluence. The neo-classical theorists would not interfere with the order of investments; for example, they would not emphasize the prior allocation of investment in wage-goods on the score that the latter goods are basic to an economy, unless the given income distribution warrants such an allocation according to the free market principles. We know that the income distribution at any point of time is governed, among others, by the past order of investments and the past priorities. If that sequence do not lead to a higher realized market demand for wage-goods, why should the pattern be altered? In fact, any alteration would lead to non-optimalities, according to neo-classical theory.

In this respect, I submit that the Soviet development pattern can be deemed to be eminently neo-classical though individual neo-classicists would protest against the results of such a pattern. The latter do not notice that what was wrong was the theory that was applied. A similar sequence of events, as in the Soviet Union has taken place in India since 1955-56. Here also, it is the neo-classical theory which somehow turned our minds and plans away from the poor. Since laymen and even politicians who were applauding the Second Plan strategy knew only popular versions of neo-classical economists from all parts of the world, we should not blame them if they concluded that the *whole* of economics was with the framers of the Second Plan. But we know that there were dissents—at least there was one major dissent.

> *The wage-goods and inputs going in the production of wage-goods come under the category of necessities or basic goods.*

There is an evolution of thinking on this issue starting from Quesnay and culminating in Sraffa. Quesnay, the leader of the physiocratic school, treated the activity of agriculture and closely related lines like foresting and animal husbandry, as the sole productive or basic activity. Agriculture supplied commodities to feed labour, and raw materials to enable manufactures to work upon. Services had to be assisted by advances of food and related goods. Agriculture had the property of its own output serving also as its own all-inclusive input. Surplus in agriculture could be perceived as a lagged net output to input ratio between the same kinds of commodities. A notion of a physical rate of profits could exist without a reference to values. However, the physiocrats did not distinguish between the rental component in net product and the pure profits component. It is the razor-sharp intellect of Ricardo that separates these two notions. Ricardo introduced the hypothesis of a commodity wage-rate as the determinant of the flow of supply of a unit of population and of labour. Since commodities could be produced only with the aid of labour and since labour required advances of wage-goods during the naturally and otherwise lagged period of production, the notion of profits could be conceived as a ratio between the composite of wage-goods as advanced input-stocks, and a similar composite as a technical surplus connected as profits. The notion of a commodity wage-rate included primarily consumption necessities, the mix and the amounts conventionally determined. Ricardo noted that at the point of the final dose of production of the composite of wage-goods, the expenses of production would consist solely of wage-reimbursements. There would be no differential rental component in the expenses of production of the final dose of wage-goods—specifically the agricultural portions of the wage-goods. Thus did Ricardo sift between differential rents and pure profits. Ricardo's wage-goods included some components of manufactured commodities also as consumption necessities. Though Ricardo made provision for tools and implements to be used in the production of wage-goods, he adopted the practice of reducing the values of such equipments to a measure of dated labour years allowing for the play of compound interest.

George Ramsay (1838) criticized Ricardo for treating wage-goods as necessary costs of production. Ramsay's point was that only components of fixed capital employed in the production of wage-goods could be deemed as necessary inputs and could thus emerge as the components of costs of production of wage-goods. Ramsay distinguished between the notion of cost from the micro-angle and the same notion from a macro-angle; from the latter standpoint, wage-goods could not be treated as necessary elements in the costs of production of wage-goods.

Marx treated wage-goods and commodities necessarily involved in their production as sole basics. At an earlier stage, in his enquiries, Marx adopted the practice of Ricardo of reducing the value of every commodity to the sum of direct and indirect labour years. At a later stage, he found that the price of fixed capital cannot be reduced to a sum of direct and indirect labour years for there would always be some commodity residue at the back. It was always a question of constant capital plus labour even under the hypothesis of zero wages.

However, in a capitalist system, wage-goods also have to be advanced. We, therefore, get production during any year as a result of the input of constant plus variable capitals both assisting labour. The crucial issue is whether the wage-goods advanced can be deemed to be basics and/or whether fixed capitals entering into wage-goods alone be deemed as basics, or whether wage-goods and fixed capitals together be deemed as basics.

Sraffa's practice is, in some respects, at variance with all the above three alternatives. For most of his book, Sraffa avoids treating wage-goods as basic goods. He defines basic goods as those commodities which enter directly and indirectly into the production of themselves and of other commodities. Sraffa thus places himself in the company of George Ramsay. Since the conditions of productivity in basic goods alone determine profits, Sraffa's appears to rule out the influence of exclusive conditions of production in wage-goods as entering into the determination of profits.

In my view, Sraffa has placed himself in a position here which is rather untenable. Natural lags are inherent in the production of most of the wage-goods. So long as there are lags and so long as even in a non-capitalistic portion of society wage-goods have to be held in advance before production during the subsequent year can ensue, wage-goods *are* basics in the same manner as other production inputs which have to be advanced in production because of lags. It is possible at the opposite extreme to treat all machinery and plant as being the result of the application of labour, advance wage-goods. Even if there are some components of wage-goods which are lagged for more than one agricultural year, it would follow that the whole process of accumulation may be deemed to have begun historically at one stage or the other with the shortest production period wage-goods as being employed along with labour. Anyway, it is theoretically possible to include both wage-goods and fixed capitals involved in their production as basic goods. It may be possible to abstract from the treatment of *most* of machinery and plant as basic goods in this connection.

In my own treatment, at an earlier stage, in "Planning for an Expanding Economy" I had considered wage-goods as the sole basics. From the point of view of developing economies, I do not think this is a serious lapse, but it would be proper in my view to include short-gestation period fixed capital components along with wage-goods, but involved in their production as basics. It is the approach which I would like to adopt for subsequent discussions. I would however, like to state that my practice is perhaps closer to that of Marx and of Ricardo than is the practice of Sraffa. However, Sraffa categorically state that he would like to treat a portion of real wages as basic and the luxury portion as non-basic. As his book is designed as a prelude to a critique of economic theory, we might be permitted to state that Sraffa's own approach to positive economics should not be much different from the approach adopted by me. However, there is a big distinction between the approaches together of the physiocrats, Ricardo, George Ramsay, Marx, Sraffa and myself and of the bulk of the economists, who swear by the name of Marx, and almost all the neo-classicals. It is well-known that in the models of Feldman, Mahalanobis, Joan Robinson ("Accumulation of Capital"), and of Gautam Mathur ("Planning for Steady Growth"), there is a tendency to treat machinery and plants and the conditions in their productivity as the sole ultimate determinants of production and growth. Even in the Joan-Robinson-John Eatwel book, *Introduction to Economics*, the important distinction between Quesnay, Ricardo, Ramsay, Marx, Sraffa and myself, and the standard neo-classical approach is completely blurred. This is very unfortunate inasmuch as often the development of socialism is identified, and erroneously so, with the development of heavy industries. Such a line of reasoning is violently anti-classical and Marx *is* a great figure among the classical economists. It is unfortunate that Marx's works are allegedly supposed to give prestige to an entirely erroneous standpoint.

> *The relationship between the level of the wage-rate and the rate of population growth is such that when wage-rates exceed the conventional level, there tends to be an expansion in the size of population. When the wage-rate moves below the conventional level, there tends to be a contraction of population. Hence, the rate of population growth varies depending upon excess or deficiency in the prevailing wage-rate, compared to the conventional level.*

Neo-classical theory treats the population growth rate as an autonomous variable. Also any given size of population, has no relation with the level of production of subsistence goods. A category is postulated known as *pure* population and *pure* labour which, in theory, is deemed to maintain itself intact, whatever the available level of subsistence goods. In standard neo-classical theory, wages, as pointed out earlier, are paid at the end of the production period and the same theory is applied irrespective of whether the input-output processes are simultaneous or not. Theoretically, any size of population can be fitted in a malleable capital—and malleable consumption-mix model. There always exists some measure of the marginal productivity of labour yielding a real wage-rate sufficient for the population to subsist. Nor does neo-classical theory recognize that population growth-rate must be linked to the growth-rate of stocks of wage-goods.

It is true that within limits variations in the actual growth-rate of population are subsequentially determined. The hypothesis that population growth-rate has no relation at all to the long-run prospective real wage-rate, and trends thereof, appear to be empirically unrealistic. Variations in per capita consumption levels and prospects thereof may leave the population growth-rate unaffected only within a narrow range. If such variations cross this range and expectations too are affected, population growth-rates cannot but be affected though the full effects are seen secularly. In this respect, the classicists' hypothesis has great empirical validity.

At one extreme in the modern neo-classical theory there is a viewpoint that for any autonomously given trend in population growth, corresponding adjustments in the savings to income ratio occur such that the consumption prospects that the households' desire can always tend to be fulfilled. In the famous Modigliani-Brumberg life-cycle theory of savings, it is the growth-rate in consumption level that accommodates positively through adjustments in the savings ratio to any changes in the prospective population growth-rates. The thesis is almost the opposite of that of Malthus, Ricardo and Marx. Lest eyebrows be raised on my clubbing of Marx with Malthus and Ricardo on the population issue, I may mention in his interpretation of the course of capitalism in Vol. 3 of *Capital* Marx did expound a positive link between the wage-rate and the population growth rate. Since *Capital* Vol. 3 was written at a mature stage of Marx's own thinking, we may consider these observations as support to the Ricardo and Malthus wage-population link. It is true that Marx also stated that the essay of Malthus was a libel on human race. What Marx meant here is that, under mature socialism, human beings would tend to consider population growth in terms of its exact impact on society. Unlike Malthus who believed that the population pressures would destroy socialism, Marx held the view that it is only under socialism that social control over population can become understandingly feasible. It is only the later followers of Marx who unfortunately advanced the thesis that Marxian theory does not recognize, under all conditions, the problem of surplus population. This is yet another respect in which the more well-known disciples of Marx have done a great injury to the doctrine of their supposed fountain-head of ideas. In passing, may I mention that Marx is too deep and too conscientious a scholar to be treated so casually as his disciples have done. No wonder that Marx is supposed to have exclaimed at a later stage in his life, "Thank God, I am not a Marxist!" Marx's writings and standpoints have to be understood in the light of his own reading and, I may add, only in that light.

The secular prospect of the standard rate of profits in the production of basic goods is one of a tendency to a decline. This is because of the law of diminishing returns which applies in regard to agricultural commodities and commodities depending directly or indirectly, upon them.

The law of diminishing returns is different from the law of variable proportions which has to be truly deemed as a bastard offspring of the classical law. It is extremely difficult to empirically verify the law of variable proportions. The law of diminishing returns is empirically verifiable. It applies to the operations of the complex of certain group of activities coming under agriculture and related sectors. The law of diminishing returns is nothing else than the law of the falling rate of profits in a world of constant relative share of wages. Alternatively, it is the law of the falling maximum rate of profits, with the growth of accumulation in basic stock.

The late Professor Svennilson, in his famous report on early post-war

Europe, had noted this tendency in the economy of most European countries. I have tried to point out elsewhere that the growth process of the Soviet Union manifests a clear tendency for long-run diminishing returns. I have also drawn attention to a similar empirical tendency in India. It is true that in some countries like the U.S., this tendency is kept in abeyance by continuous technological progress in agriculture. In a general sense, if we include *all* activities associated with scarce natural resources, and not simply agriculture, the tendency of diminishing returns still continues to be manifest in most countries. Standard neo-classical theory has no notion of a commodity rate of profits. The hypothesis of secular decline in the rate of interest with increasing capital-intensity per worker or with increased capital-deepening cannot be substantiated either theoretically or empirically. This is because the very notion of a marginal productivity of capital, as applicable to the whole of society, is not logically tenable. I shall have more to say later about the notion of the social rate of return which the neo-classicists have substituted as a macro-proxy for the old notion of the social marginal productivity of capital.

In a short period, unemployment can be caused by the exogenous disturbances reducing the volume of production of basic goods. Unemployment can also occur because of excesses in the rate of population above the growth-rate of the wage-goods or of the fund of circulating capitals.

The classical school permitted the existence of unemployment in the short-period, but did not allow it to be carried over to the long period. The classical economists were writing at a time when capitalism was becoming stronger and stronger, and trade unions had not yet developed sufficient countervailing power; besides, the concept of a welfare state with the provision of arrangements for dole almost equal to a minimum real wage had not taken roots during the latter half of the eighteenth and over the nineteenth centuries, even up to the time of the Second World War. Unemployment could, therefore, be treated as a result of an imbalance between the stock of circulating capitals and the size of population. From a dynamic angle, such a state of affairs could be accounted by a rate of growth of circulating capitals lower than the rate of growth of labour force. The institution of work houses for the unemployed, with the financing of such work houses based on local rates, introduced a direct relation between the physical pressure on the employed and the expenses of maintenance of the unemployed. Social hostility would tend to emerge against the notion of unemployment itself. Let us also note that most of the Western countries did not have a system of joint families, common in the agricultural sector in most of the underdeveloped economies today. An important difference is made to the analysis when once we introduce the notions of joint-family maintenance and work-spreading. This permits the accumulation of unemployment as a hidden or invisible phenomenon. It also tends to affect adversely the level of efficiency in production operations and to reduce the proportion of agricultural surpluses that become available in exchange for other goods and for reinvestments. These are important respects in which classical theory needs to be modified. I drew attention to this limitation of classical theory in my early work on the "Studies in Economics of Welfare Maximization." Later we tried to incorporate disguised unemployment, which can be a long-period phenomenon, by means of the notion of *wage-goods gap* as potentially inhibiting an equilibrium of a larger volume of employment.

As has been pointed out earlier, the neo-classical theory cannot take in long-period unemployment, disguised or otherwise. This is because of the assumptions of (*a*) alternative consumption-mixes yielding the same level of utility in a context of fixed but differing coefficients of production and (*b*) of a spectrum of production techniques. Unemployment can be empirically permitted in neo-classical theory only in a transition.

There is one additional reason for unemployment. This is due to the disproportion between fixed and circulating capitals. I shall come to this later on.

It may be noted that what is relevant in explaining unemployment is the juxtaposition between circulating capitals, *not* total capitals, and the size of the labour force. In this respect also, the neo-classical theory proceeds in a different direction. Readers of Marx's recently published *Grundrisse'* may recollect that Marx conducts the analysis of mechanization in a framework of a constant capital-output ratio! This in itself is sufficient to show up the difference between pristine-Marxian theory and the bastard version which has been unfortunately made popular in the writings of some of his so-called disciples, may I say not excluding the venerable Joan Robinson.

Balanced productions, mathematically balanced with respect to mutual production requirements and income elasticity of demand considerations, would tend to be bought by productions. There could be no general glut of production capacity.

Readers might recollect that the above proposition is none other than Say's Law. Say's Law is a theorem about exchange-interdependence in production operations. Since investment is in anticipation of demand, or of requirements, there can tend to be some errors, but because of technical inter-dependence and the necessity of a fund of basic goods serving as capitals, a deficiency in one line has to be compensated by an excess in another. By and large, the activities concerning basic goods *are* not affected by errors. This is because the relationship among many basic goods is largely one of complementarity.

There are two types of exchanges in classical theory. There is first of all the exchange embedded in production, including the production inter-connections among different wage-goods; secondly, there is the exchange which arises as a result of consumption out of differential rents, capitalist consumption, wage-earners' consumption above their necessary wages and government consumption. The last three categories cannot have a place in early classical thinking, for capitalists are prone to save almost all their incomes, the workers' real wage does not exceed the conventional level and the role of the government is minimal. Consumption out of differential rents can occur. There could be general upsets like climatic excesses and failures, famines, adverse balance of payments, wars which could cause general upsets in the continuity of production, and there could be some unemployment, sectoral under-utilization and excess demands. These can be taken in classical theory. What the classical theory denies would be the phenomenon of a general glut which plays such an important role in the writings of Keynes.

There can be no co-existence between Keynesian Economics and Classical Economics. I have to refer to this issue at a later stage. For the present, my statement may be accepted as an assertion requiring further elucidation. I have mentioned this because some of Sraffa's colleagues, particularly the Cambridge colleagues, have tried to mix up Keynesian contribution with the implications of the Sraffa revolution. It is very clear from the beginning that there can be no reconciliation between so great a Ricardian as Sraffa and so Keynesian as say Keynes! May I express my strong protest at the implications, which are so naively drawn, that since Joan Robinson, Luigo Passinetti, Kregel, Harcourt and others are Keynesians and also call themselves as disciples of Sraffa, the Ricardo-Sraffa universe can contain Keynesian theory as a subset. This implication is wholly mistaken and is causing the greatest possible damage to the correct understanding of Sraffa's ideas. If at all Sraffa is close to any Cambridge economist other than George Ramsay, it is to Pigou who, in his *Employment and Equilibrium* categorically states in the preface that Sraffa, whom he expected to demolish his draft, instead gave him continuous encouragement! This was pointed out to Joan Robinson, but the vested interest in Keynesianism in Cambridge circles has been so great that they have not able to shake off the Keynesian roots of intellectual development. Did not Keynes himself warn against the power of vested ideas? May I mention a thought here. Is it not possible that Joan Robinson, Ricard Kahn, L. Passinetti and others *are* aware that Sraffa's work *is* a shattering critique of the Keynesians themselves? Perhaps these eminent scholars want to hide this aspect from the view of their students and admirers by propagating the impression that Samuelson and Solow are the persons whose writings alone are adversely affected by Sraffa?

> *The quantity of money in relation to the stock of circulating capitals determines the level of prices. The monetary value of stocks would tend to be a mirror image of the stipulated part of the quantity of money. The demand for money would be governed on the principle of economy, nobody holding a quantity of money more than what is strictly required for transactions and precautionary purposes.*

Here again, the classical theory emphasizes the relation between the *stock* of production inputs in the form of circulating capitals and the quantity of money. Quantity of money itself is the counterpart of the volume of credit. The classical theory has implicitly a constancy assumption regarding income velocity. Such a constancy is a result of the operation of the motive of economy. Real money balances can be deemed to be a constant fraction of gross value of the exchanges embedded in the matrix of production operations and relations. It is wrong to treat the holding of real balances as an aspect of behaviouristic demand. The notion of real money balances is akin to the notion of production inputs in a model of fixed coefficients. In this respect, the classical practice is close to that of Irving Fisher though the latter tended to relate money to national income whereas in classical theory the relation is one between two stocks.

The long-term level of the rate of interest is based upon the long-term course of the normal rate of profits. In general, there can be a stable relation between the two rates.

The classical economists, particularly Ricardo, tended to treat the rate of interest as a proxy for the rate of profits. Bond yields were not affected much at that time by budgetary deficits as a normal phenomenon. The quantity of money in each country would largely be governed by international circumstances. The rate of interest itself would tend to be governed by the rate of profits. The standard of normal rate of profits would, of course, make some allowance for risk, or rather the *entrepreneurial incentive differential*, as one would like to call it. George Ramsay was among the first of the economists to differentiate between interest and the rate of profit. It was he who first brought in the notion of risk-taking as a characteristic function of the entrepreneur. The time-horizon in respect of the long-term rate of interest is rather long, whereas that in respect of the rate of profits would tend to be shorter. Naturally, entrepreneurial activities would tend to come to a stop, long before the rate of interest actually became zero. Accumulation would cease before the stationary state is actually reached. I shall dwell later upon the nature of the difference between interest and the rate of profits. This issue requires greater attention than what the classical economists could give during the time of their writings.

The variations in the quantity of money would not be in a position to affect the level of long-term interest rates.

The classical economists used to treat savings and investment as almost identical. There could be short-period effects of an excess issue of currency as a result of which the short-term rate of interest might come down, but there would tend to be repercussions such as export of gold, an adverse balance of payments, which would tend to lead to a contraction of currency, since the authorities could continue to maintain the exchange and yet keep gold reserves intact. At a later stage, Alfred Marshall introduced a different mechanism of explanation. An increase in bank reserves and in the facility of credit expansion would lead to a fall in discount. This would lead to an expansion in borrowing, which would lead to a higher level of prices. This, in turn, would lead to an expansion in the demand for loans, which, however, could not be satisfied without a running down of reserves. Hence, the discount rate would now move up. Variations in the quantity of money could not, therefore, lead to any permanent and enduring effect upon the rate of interest.

But, both early classicists and Marshall do permit the short-term rates to move up and down consequent upon the variations in the quantity of money. I might also mention here the important contribution of Hawtrey who brings in the effect of an internal drain as a result of the redistribution of income in favour of wage-earners flowing from increased borrowings and the rise in prices. Wicksell brings in the external drain which also is taken in Hawtrey. Wicksell of course permits room for an internal drain particularly because of payments made to agriculturists, who had a propensity to hold more of their money in the form of currency. I refer to these contributions because there is an incorrect view that the classical theory treats the short-term rate as incapable of being affected by variations in the quantity of money. This, I am afraid, is a gross injustice to the classical line of thinking.

In neo-classical monetary theory, the rate of interest is determined by the interconnections between forces of savings and of productivity i.e. by the interconnection between the supply and demand schedule of savings. In the standard Keynesian theory, the quantity of money reappears as an important determinant of the rate of interest in conjunction with the liquidity preference schedule. The Hicksian generalization of Keynes permits a sort of a room for savings, investment, quantity of money and liquidity preference. In both Keynes and Hicks, there is room for a permanent effect upon the long-term rate of interest caused by variations in the quantity of money. This standpoint is foreign to the classical line of thinking, and cannot be reconciled with it. It is true that in standard neo-classical theory, as in the writings of Patinkin, or even in that of Robertson, there is some room for effects of variations in the quantity of money upon the short-term rate of interest. But somehow there is no close integration between movements in the short rates and the movements in the long rates. In the classical theory, the long rate cannot under any circumstances be affected by monetary factors.

There is, however, some room for a quarrel with the classical theory on some of its positions in regard to the interest theory. I shall deal with the needed refinements later. Suffice to state here that I do not consider the classical treatment on this issue to be evolved in this respect for when once you permit room for distribution changes consequent upon quantity of money variations, in a context of constant or almost constant money wage-rates and money rental rates, there is room for changes in the volume of real savings and of real investment, and this can lead *via* diminishing returns to some fall in the long-term rate of interest. If we permit room for quantity of money variations, and through this to distribution alteration, we *have* to permit some room for interest variations as a possible enduring effect. It is in neo-classical theory that the above sort of an effect may not be noticeable. For example, take the Patinkin position wherein the long-term rate of interest is unaffected by the variations in the quantity of money. Not also a similar position in Fisher.

The rate of population growth can be controlled by social action culminating in moral restraint on the part of the labour force. Such social action leading to moral restraint would be a function of the level of education particularly in the sphere of economics and of the development of the attitude of moral restraint.

This significant standpoint of the classical economists is well understood now-a-days particularly in less developed countries, where the authorities have come to recognize the importance of public education in regard to population control. The standard neo-classical treatment would be to emphasize the significance of material incentives at the micro-level. This approach is not valid when group action or mass action is called forth. In the case of such action, a large number of people must feel themselves sure and secure that everyone else is adopting a similar course of action. For otherwise, at the microlevel, there may tend to be uncertainties in regard to supporting action by others; as a result, no individual will undertake the required action because he is not sure whether, if, others do not follow a similar action, his position itself might not become worse off, or might not improve. This is a point to which I drew attention in my *Studies on Welfare Maximization*. In recent years, the point of view which I maintained in those years is becoming more important in Welfare Economics as the "isolation paradox" or the "assurance paradox." I may modestly mention that innumerable such paradoxes are outlined in the *Studies in the Economics of Welfare Maximization*; in fact it was the aim of that book to draw attention to mass action as contrasted with an aggregate of independently and isolatedly governed micro (or individualistic) actions. In fact, I developed that standpoint as a critique of some naive positions taken by early classicals regarding the population issue and such other matters.

However, one might note that standard neo-classical theory treats of community behaviour as an aggregate of individual behaviours ,each governed by motives affecting micro-level action. In fact, the bulk of welfare economics is cast in this type of a tradition. The notion of the market as an aggregate of individual responses of households and of firms is still a dominant concept in neo-classical theory. I may mention that it is only in the writings of Haavelmo, among the Western economists, that a realization of alternative possibilities of social action, as potentially acceptable to individuals, has been emphasized.

A greater employment of machinery, or the substitution of fixed capitals in place of circulating capitals, can occur within the framework of a given capital to net output ratio and even of a given standard or normal rate of profits. Hence the ratio of fixed capitals to circulating capitals can go up leading to unemployment with some rise in the share of profits.

In the classical theory at any point of time there can exist, on the same rate of profits and the same capital to net output ratio, two processes of production for the same commodity with different proportions of fixed capitals to circulating capitals in each process. For the manufacture of a given quantity of net output of say, some components of wage-goods, one process might imply less of advances of circulating capital and less of labour assisting fixed capitals. Whereas another process might imply more of circulating capitals and hence, more of labour assisting a reduced component of fixed capitals. Suppose now because of diminishing returns in wage-goods production the rate of profits is reduced; it would be so on both the processes, but the reduction would be less in respect of the process which has a greater component of fixed capitals and a smaller component of circulating capitals. The latter process will now be adopted in the place of the process in which the circulating capitals component is relatively larger. There will then ensue some unemployment. Since the level of real wage-rate is equal to the conventional limit, the unemployed may have gradually to disappear from the system, or they may have been absorbed through the long-drawn process of a higher rate of growth. It is possible that because of a reduction in the actual output of goods consisting of circulating capital, the share of wages in net output would tend to be lower and the relative share of profits would be higher. This might lead to more of savings out of a given net output than in the other case. With the same overall capital to net output ratio, the growth-rate may now tend to be higher. So some of the unemployed may be re-absorbed over some length of future time. *However, there has to be some unemployment.* The ratio of the unemployed to labour force will go up.

In the neo-classical body of analysis, the substitution process is expected to occur directly between labour and capitals. There is a rise in the capital-intensity of labour and possibly in the capital-intensity of net output. With given total capitals, this causes unemployment. In the neo-classical theory, wages are paid at the end of the period of production and unemployment will be further reflected in a fall in the real wage-rate. This will help to restore the previous method of production, with a lower capital-intensity and lower capital to net output ratio. *Hence the neo-classical system would rule out the possibility of unemployment at any point of time.* This is because of the assumption of the existence of a spectrum of techniques and of alternative consumption-mixes.

As Sraffa has shown in his *Production of Commodities*, there is no reason why with a lower real wage-rate and a higher profit rate, there should tend to be a lower capital-intensity to labour and a lower capital-intensity in net output. Similarly, there is no reason why for a higher commodity wage-rate and a lower rate of profits, there should be a higher capital-intensity of labour and a higher capital to net output ratio. If we include the implications of Sraffa's possibilities in the neo-classical analysis, it would appear that we cannot be definite about the direction of employment with changes in the commodity wage-rate and in the rate of profits. *In the classical theory, however, even at a given-commodity wage-rate or profits mix, there can be arbitrarily a shift in favour af machinery against circulating capitals.* Note that the overall capital-intensity of output does not necessarily go up or go down. What happens is a variation in the proportion of circulating capitals to fixed capital. The automatic readjustment, consequent upon unemployment, etc. is a problematic affair. *Anyway there is nothing in the behaviour of prices to lead to restoration of full employment.* Hence in the classical theory, unemployment can emerge independent of whatever is happening to the growth-rate. Unemployment is essentially a result of an inappropriate quantity of circulating capitals in relation to the labour force. The use of machinery reduces the former component in a total of given capitals. That is why unemployment is inevitable, with the large-scale introduction of machinery.

I may submit that the classical approach has great relevance in the context of the experience of countries like India. The problem of choice of techniques has to be looked at not in terms of substitution process between labour and capital, but as one involving alternative proportions between fixed and circulating capitals within the framework of a largely unchanged capital to net output ratio. The classical theory makes it clear that even within a frame of unchanged relative prices, the commodity wage-rate and rate of profits, there can be a shift in favour of processes with more fixed capitals and less of circulating capitals. Even with some fall in the commodity wage-rate, it would not follow that the original proportions would tend to be restored. This is because there is a sequential process involved. It is not easy for an economy whose circulating capitals-fixed capital proportions have been disturbed to regain the original proportions, except through a long-period of readjustment. Anyway, there is no automatic restoration of full employment. Much depends on what happens to the savings-income ratio and the nature of emergent technological changes.

Technological progress leading to an improvement in the conditions of productivity in necessities would tend to raise the standard rate of profit and the rate of interest. The continuous occurrence of such improvements and such prospects thereof enable the level of rates of profits to be higher than what would have been the case otherwise.

The classical theory distinguishes between basic and non-basic technological changes. Basic technological changes are those which affect conditions of productivity in basic goods. Non-basic technological changes are those which affect conditions of productivity in non-basic goods. Non-basic technological changes have no effects upon the ratio of surplus to capitals and the rate of profits. It is true that technological changes are largely autonomous but to the extent that the research and development expenditure can stimulate basic technological changes, these would be helpful to the economy. In general, organizational innovations which improve the conditions of productivity in the basic sector are of greater importance than those which affect non-basic goods.

In the neo-classical theory, even in Schumpeter's development theory, there are no distinctions between basic and non-basic goods and all technological changes are supposed to be similar in their general effect upon the rate of profits. One consequence of the distinction between basic and non-basic technology is that the less developed countries are bound to waste their funds, especially foreign exchange, if they blindly adopt Western technology, for Western countries have reached a higher level of development. Improvement in non-basic goods is rather very important in these countries. In fact, basic goods are so much taken for granted that all attention is on non-basic goods, except in emergencies as for example, in the wake of the oil cut-back.

One consequence of the absence of a distinction between basic and non-basic technological changes is that the less developed countries are confronted with a rapid rate of technological change in the machinery sector, particularly when they take the technology from the Western countries. It follows that for any given net output, the conditions favouring more of fixed to circulating capitals are greater now than in the earlier stages of industrial revolution. Not merely is the volume of employment for a given component of total capital less because of a smaller circulating capitals component, but also the chances of autonomously maintaining a higher ratio of employment of labour force are dimmer because of the rapid improvement in the conditions of productivity in machinery. One alternative is to concentrate on improving the conditions of productivity in such a manner as not to adversely affect the proportion of circulating to fixed capitals. Conditions of relative productivity in circulating capitals-dominant methods of production are of great importance in less developed countries. Note that this conclusion is not the same as that which favours vaguely an intermediate technology, for the later term belongs to neo-classical theory which is most unclear in regard to development matters.

Given a secular tendency to a decline in the rate of profits, a higher rate of accumulation caused by, let us say, higher savings propensity, can only bring the stationary state nearer.

This proposition cannot be derived in this form from a neo-classical theory. It points out that accumulation *per se* is not a matter of great benefit to a society. What is important is whether a higher real wage-rate can be sustained thus improving the conditions of well-being of the mass of the people. The latter result is possible if, and only if, basic technological changes are initiated and kept up continuously and the forces making for population growth rate are kept under heavy check. For a less developed economy, savings are a boon in a context in which the pattern of technology in basic goods has improved continuously. In the neo-classical theory, savings are a boon even under conditions in which technological changes are wholly in the non-basic sector.

Under all conditions, a higher real wage-rate can be obtained by a reduction in population size or in its rate of growth.
This of course is a very important result. Its implications ore obvious.

D. M. NANJUNDAPPA

Taxation of Urban Land

THE PROBLEM

Preventing concentration of wealth and economic power in the hands of a few and bringing about a reduction in income inequalities is one of the avowed objectives of planned development. For too long, the income redistribution objective did not get integrated with the production promoting objective. With the recognition of the need to achieve rapid growth with social justice the income redistribution issue has rightly come to the forefront. Among others, real estate, viz., land and buildings, has been one major source of speculative and windfall accruals of wealth and incomes. Since investment in real estate provides a hedge against inflation, the attraction has been all the more and this was further egged on by the devastating role which black money played in the parallel economy. With the implementation of stringent monetary, fiscal and non-economic measures inflation can be arrested and the parallel economy subdued, if not completely eliminated, as in the case of India. Along with monetary and fiscal policies, there ought to be a set of non-budgetary regulatory measures to match them to plug any opportunities that may exist for such sources to thrive. Among these, legislative measures to restrict the holdings of real estate namely land and buildings are an important instrument for achieving the objective of reducing income inequalities.

The year 1976 witnessed two policy measures in India, sought to be implemented through appropriate legislation on this subject. One related to the imposition of a ceiling on urban land under the Urban Land (Ceiling and Regulation) Act of the Government of India. The other related to the levy of tax on urban land under the Urban Land Taxation Act in some of the States. The former is intended to prevent concentration of urban land in the hands of a few persons, speculation and profiteering and bringing about an equitable distribution of land in urban agglomerations. To achieve its objective, the Urban Land (Ceiling and Regulation) Act imposes a ceiling on vacant land. The Urban Land Tax Act provides for the levy by the State Government of a tax on urban land. The ostensible objective is to make the owner of the urban land realize that an unproductive holding of the land is socially undesirable and that he should either fully use it for construction purposes or must pay for reserving for himself the right to hold such vacant land for a purpose of his choice.

With the enactment of these two Acts, one imposing a ceiling on the urban vacant landholdings and the other imposing a tax on vacant urban land, several questions seem to arise: What is the cumulative impact of these two Acts? Is it necessary for an urban land tax when there already exists a ceiling on urban land? What is the effect of these two Acts on housing supply? Since these are in addition to the wealth tax, property tax (levied and collected by the Municipal Corporations) and the capital gains tax which are levied on the same tax base will not the introduction of an urban land tax amount to multiplication or unjustifiable additional taxation? How will the exemptions and taxable base get through the tests of equity? Is it not possible to rationalize property taxation as a whole in an attempt to eliminate multiple levies and introduce a single simple levy? These and other host of questions are of a complicated nature. This paper tries to examine them in a brief canvas. Since the Urban Land Ceilings Act and the Urban Land Taxation Act have come into force only recently, there is not much of experience on which our analysis could draw. Therefore, to a very large extent, the analysis is to be done in a theoretical framework and further research may become necessary to get at the most precise answers. For our analysis, wherever necessary, illustrations are taken from the legislation in a State like Karnataka to develop the points that arise in respect of the above enumerated questions.

THE THEORY

Economic development accelerates urbanization which together with growing population and trade have led to many issues of rising land values. The soaring urban land prices and their sale and purchase at fantastically high prices lay bare the extent to which urban land is being sought as the principal vehicle for investment of idle cash besides being a hedge against inflation. Speculative gains resulting from the rise in land values are suppressed and they escape assessment both under capital gains taxation and stamp duties on transactions of immovable property. The rising values represent unearned incomes and wealth insofar as they arise from general development and not individual effort. The unearned increments should be mopped up and appropriated to the public fisc and the source of such unearned increments should be subjected to regulation.

This problem has attracted attention in the past in one form or the other. The Zakaria Committee, which reported to the Government of India in 1963 on the "augmentation of financial resources of urban local bodies" has discussed the issues arising from unearned increments of land values and strongly advocated taxation based on the market value of a particular piece of land on the assumption that it would be developed with permission from the concerned authorities to its optimum use, disregarding the value of the building, if any, which are at present standing on it.

In the Town and Country Planning Acts, several State Governments have proposed a levy on the value of urban land arising from the prospects of material development but this has not been effectively pursued.

Against this background, we discuss here briefly the nature of urban land values.

In growing urban areas, land values (i. e. values of parcels of land that can be used for commercial and residential purposes) tend normally to rise. Sizable land is held as curtilage for luxurious living and outlaying areas, which give promise of early development, are snatched by speculators who hold them as long as their speculative hopes are realized.

The value of a particular parcel of land or site can comprise of two parts: (i) its value in the current use to which it is put and (ii) its development value which is the value with the right to develop or the likely value with the prospects of material development minus the existing use value.

Value of land in current use may also rise due to natural advantages and activities of those around it. The building of a house on a site does not add to the situation value of the land as such. After the house is built, there is a greater real estate value by the value of the house, but the land, separately considered, is worth the same as before. If, however, some persons build attractive houses in the neighbourhood of such a site, it may come to have a higher situation value, whether sold with or without a building on it, than it would otherwise command. Thus unforeseen tastes and consequent building of houses by some people may increase the sale value of vacant land of others. Vacant lands are not put to their optimum use and this may inhibit proper land use in a growing city.

Vacant lands are sometimes held back without being developed thereby creating an artificial scarcity of land within the city. It is also conceivable that if such vacant land is assessed to reflect their most productive use, such a measure can be employed to encourage the use of idle land and to put unutilized land to more effective use.

Where the general property tax is levied on the annual rental of land and buildings and is supposed to be a charge on the owner or the occupier, the rent in question and hence valuation is closely tied to the existing use. When a town or urban agglomeration is improving rapidly in a developing country, people would like to buy urban land so much for its existing use as for what they could put there instead. For this reason, its true value may far exceed the capitalized value of the land and the true value will go on rising as the town develops although the rent may be fixed. Thus, there accrues a surplus to the owner which gets realized when he sells it. Otherwise, the surplus accrual will continue. Where there is a slight increase in the market value of land for its existing use, this increment is subject to ordinary capital gains tax with concessions in rate for gains from real estate in some countries.

If instead of annual rental being the base for property taxation, we start with a tax on capital values which are kept current with changing price level, such an assessment would take the rising value into consideration. Thus, one part of the advantage which is supposed to be got from urban land value taxation can in theory be obtained by property taxation based on capital values.

The development of a town or a city or its business centre is always attended by a rise in value of surrounding land or properties. This rise takes place before the land or property in question is built on or rebuilt. It is due to the expectation that such property will be able to find a use in future that will be worth more than the use to which it is put at present. As development comes into sight as a practicable possibility, because of town planning schemes even though the time horizon and their materialization may be far away—speculators begin to buy sites in that area with the expectation of making profit later on when development takes place. Even urban land or sites that are not sold to speculators will be retained by the existing owners for making speculative gains. Present owners of vacant land who would otherwise have been willing to sell at a fairly low price retain them in the hope that they can sell them later on at a higher price. Of course, until development actually takes place, such land continues to be used in the old manner. Developers who would be willing to improve them, if they were available at their existing use value, will not be able to buy them as speculators—professional as well as owner-speculators —hold such land off the market.

The difference between the current use value and prospective potential use value is commonly referred to as unearned increment which is actually appreciation in the value of any urban land which is not caused by the efforts of the individual urban land owners but of the community as a whole. The benefits of such appreciation should be shared by the owner with the entire community. Under site value rating, such beneficiaries will have to pay a tax or rate which is proportionate to the value, including development value, they themselves set upon the land and not one proportional to the value of the land in its present (less valuable) use. Therefore, a tax on land value in such a case will act as a tax on unearned increment and on speculation so that it will siphon off the surplus into the Government fisc and at the same time tend to reduce the period for which owners or speculators may hold back land from full utilization or development.

When land value is interpreted as value of an improved land and the latter is made the base of the tax involving derating of improvements both visible and invisible, the distributive effects in a growing economy would cause much concern. In the urban areas, there is undoubtedly a strong tendency for the more expensive buildings to be put up on more expensive sites/lands. There is also a tendency for the value of buildings relatively to their sites to be higher in the case of the wealthiest property owners so that derating of building would reduce tax of those who are more able to pay and raise it on those who are less able to pay. Thus, the effect of the distribution of the rate burden would be regressive. Graduated and limited derating for a short period together with defining site value as including invisible improvements and as the sum which the title to land may be expected to bring in a bona fide scale can reduce regressiveness and also serve as an incentive to construction activity.

Two policy instruments, one fiscal and the other non-fiscal, have been deployed to tackle the problems arising from rising urban land values. Although the wielding of the tax weapon was done in some Sates a few years ago, the non-fiscal instrument of imposing a ceiling on urban land in select areas has been wielded only recently.

The fiscal approach takes the form of taxation or urban vacant land. The main object is to reduce the incidence of capitalizing on urban lands owing to the rise in values not from the efforts of the owners. The value of the completely virgin land increases highly with the provision of public services, flats, buildings and other services through public money or as a result of investment by private parties on housing or construction. But usually, the private parties enter into the scene only when the public utilities are provided by the Government. Therefore, the unearned increments in land values of owners in these areas require to be taxed. The importance of urban land tax gains gets enhanced because the existing property tax concentrates only on the improvement (i.e. building).

Interest in urban land or site value taxation has been increasing in recent years particularly on the part of many who are concerned with the problems of urban development and redevelopment. In simple terms, it means imposition of a tax on the value of land only and not on the collective value of land. This form of taxation is in vogue on a substantial scale in Australia, New Zealand, Denmark and some parts of Canada. Its justification is on grounds of equity and socio-economic considerations.

On equity ground, it is being levied on land as most of its value is a consequence not of actions by individual owners but of collective investment, community development, population growth and urbanization. Therefore, it is entirely appropriate for the community to recapture the unearned increments of these individual landowners by taxation and use them for community services.

On economic ground, it is a tax which is independent of the improvement on the site and will not effect the use of the site for the most profitable purposes. In other words, the best use before tax remains the best use after the imposition of the tax. In technical terms, the tax is neutral with regard to land use decision. Therefore, such neutrality on the part of site value taxation encourages construction activities, but discourages keeping it idle expecting further rise in land values. Because, within the individual urban jurisdiction, taxes on vacant land would tend to rise thereby increasing the holding costs of vacant land and making the speculative withholding of land from development a less attractive proposition. Such land value taxation, has two types of impacts: one is that in metropolitan or central areas, it would encourage more investment in buildings; and in the outlying areas, it would tend to discourage land speculation. The second one is that it stimulates redevelopment of slum areas. The tax on urban land would fall on the owners of the slum properties and keeping them in the same conditions would turn out to be uneconomic for them.

The main argument against urban land value taxation is that it can be valid only when levied on realization basis but not on accrual basis. Another point made out in this connection is that it may not be easy to administer such a levy.

It is argued that separate valuation of land may pose problems. This, however, is no longer unsurmountable. Land valuation techniques have been developed and all that is required is the setting up of an independent central valuation agency with land valuation experts as has been done in U.K. and U.S.A. Such an agency can be used for valuation of all other property for the assessment of which, urban local bodies, have no suitable machinery. It is also beyond the means of urban local bodies which impose and collect property tax to have a separate agency of their own. In fact, due to a lack of such an independent valuation agency, serious under-reporting of property values is resorted to, depriving the local bodies of their legitimate revenues. A study in one of the urban agglomerations in Karnataka State that was done sometime ago showed that variation between the assessed rateable value and the actual property income ranged from 15 per cent to as much as 154 per cent.

As regards the argument that the tax should be levied only on realization basis (when land is sold in order to reap the benefits of the incremental value) but not on accrual concept, it should be noted that it fails to take note of the complexities of an equitable taxable base. Instead of income, spending power has been very rightly argued by Professor Nicholas Kaldor as the appropriate base of taxation. The spending power depends upon not merely the actual accrual of income but also the prospective accruals inherent in the wealth held by individuals. The only way in which an individual can reduce his numerous sources of income into a common yardstick of his own choice is his spending power which manifests itself in actual expenditures. Therefore, taxing on an accrual basis commends itself in equity. Moreover, imposition of a tax on the realization basis has the other disadvantage of "locking in" of the land in its less efficient use. It is on account of this that the introduction of the Capital Gains Tax an on accrual basis is being advocated by several economists.[1]

Under a pure system of land value (site value) taxation, the building value is irrelevant. Therefore, it is suggested that if building activity is to be encouraged, that part of increase or improvement in the value of property over the value of unimproved land, which is due to only or mainly to building can be exempted from taxation. Perhaps in the early stages of a city's development "unimproved value rating" may be considered appropriate subject to considerations discussed in the earlier section.

[1]See D.M. Nanjundappa, *Studies in Public Finance*, Asia Publishing House, 1976, Chapter 3: "Capital Gains Tax and Development Finance."

Where only land value is assessed by an expert technical body, there arises no problem of derating of buildings. If the total value of land and building is taken into consideration for tax purposes it will only discourage holding more urban property than encouraging any construction on the land/vacant portion of the land. Such a land value base tax amounts to land value increment tax and strikes directly at the unearned increments that accrue to individual owners without penalizing any enrichment of the land through buildings.

KARNATAKA URBAN LAND TAX ACT: AN ILLUSTRATION

In Karnataka, urban land tax was introduced in the Budget of 1976-79. Until that time, there was no tax exclusively on land in urban areas. Only municipalities were collecting property tax on the ratable value of the property as per Section 94 of Karnataka Municipalities Act, 1964. Actually, under this tax, the rate on land is very little. As Scheduled I to Section 94 prescribes, the tax on vacant land is Rs 2 per 100 sq metres. But the continuous rising values of urban land requires a suitable fiscal measure from the viewpoint of socio-economic objectives apart from revenue motive. It can have direct impact on the holdings of urban property, by way of discouraging or preventing concentration of wealth in the hands of a few.

It has come to force since April 1976 in the Bangalore Urban Agglomeration, the city of Hubli-Dharwar and the City Municipalities of Mysore, Mangalore, Belgaum, Gulbarga, Bellary, Davangere, Bijapur, Shimoga and Bhadravathi. It may also come into force in such other cities or other urban areas on such date as the State Government notifies.

According to the Karnataka Urban Land Tax Act, there shall be levied and collected by the State Government for every financial year commencing from the appointed date a tax on each urban land from the owner of such urban land.

For the purpose of this Act, the market value of any urban land shall be estimated to be the price which such urban land will fetch if sold in the open markets on the appointed date. While determining the price, it may be the price obtained at the relevant time for urban land more or less similarly situated in the neighbourhood or with certain other relative factors.

Another important feature of this Act is that the owner has freedom to give particulars about his land and the amount which in his opinion is a market value of that urban land. The duration of market value determined above can remain for a period of 5 years or for a further period not exceeding 5 years as the State Government may notify. The urban land tax shall be first charged upon the urban land and upon the immovable property of a person liable to pay such tax. Urban land tax will be levied in lieu of land revenue, ground rent, *jodi* or quit rent and such other amount as the State Government may specify.

The urban land tax shall be payable in respect of any land, the extent of which exceeds 223 sq. metres (2,400 sq. ft) and the rates are as given below:

(*i*) While the market value of the urban land does not exceed Rs 5,000	Nil
(*ii*) While the market value of urban land exceeds Rs 15,000 but does not exceed Rs 5,000	0.5 per cent amonut by which market value exceeds Rs 5,000
(*iii*) While market value of the urban land exceeds Rs 15,000 but does not exceed Rs 25,000	Rs 50+0.75 per cent of the amount by which the market value exceeds Rs 15,000
(*iv*) Where market value of the urban land exceeds Rs 25,000	Rs 125+1 per cent of the amount by which the market value exceeds Rs 25,000

There are also appropriate provisions for assessment of urban land held by an owner in different urban areas separately.

URBAN LAND (CEILING AND REGULATION) ACT

Urban landholdings contribute much to the concentration of economic power. Any restrictions on acquiring such a power are to be welcomed. The Government of India has introduced the Urban Land (Ceiling and Regulation) Act, 1976 which specify limits to urban land that could be held by a person and these limits vary depending on the size of urban agglomerations. Implementation of this legislation is viewed as a solution to the problem of concentration of urban property.

A ceiling has been imposed on urban vacant landholding with a view to checking the excess holding of urban sites which are vacant and reduce the possibility of speculation and profiteering therein and also preventing luxurious construction of houses. The surplus lands acquired are to be used for redistribution. The Act lays down the ceiling on vacant land that could be held by a person as 500 sq. metres in the four main metropolitan cities of Delhi, Bombay, Calcutta and Madras and a ceiling going up to 2,000 sq. metres in smaller cities.

In Karnataka, Bangalore has been categorized as 'B' City for the above purpose with 1,000 sq. meters, Hubli-Dharwar and Mysore as 'C' category with 1,500 sq. meters and Mangalore and Belgaum as 'D' category with 2,000 sq. meters, as the ceiling limit. This Act also empowers the State Government with the previous approval of the Central Government to notify any area other than the urban agglomerations specified in the Schedule to the Act. As an urban agglomeration, the Act applies having regard to its location, population (being more than 1 lakh) and other relevant factors. However, it is not the intention of the Central Government to apply the discipline of the Act to every urban area of which population is more than 1 lakh. General criteria to be considered are the location of the city, the rate of the growth of population, occupational pattern, workers population etc. Therefore, considering urban areas with a population above 1 lakh in Karnataka, there are 12 cities, out of which 5 cities only have now been specified in the relevant schedule for purposes of applying the Act. The remaining 7 cities are Gulbarga, Belgaum, Davangere, KGF City, Bijapur, Shimoga and Bhadravathi and these cities are now not covered under the Urban Ceilings Act.

This Act restricts itself for the immediate purpose to taking over of surplus vacant urban land. Vacant land for this purpose is defined as "any land with or without building owned by a person along with other vacant land." Obviously, urban land which is now utilized for construction or making other improvements is clearly untouched *whatever is the extent of such urban land*. To this extent, the Act can have a very limited fulfilment of the objective of redistributive justice.

EMERGING ISSUES

The joint development of the two policy instruments, namely, the Urban Land Ceilings and the Urban Land Tax seems to give rise to some issues. The major issues may be enumerated as follows:

(*i*) Is the Urban Land Tax necessarily a supplement to the Urban Land Ceilings? Can the objectives in view be achieved or not by any one of the instruments?

(*ii*) What is the combined incidence of the Wealth Tax, Property Tax and Urban Land Tax?

(*iii*) How valid is the point that the Urban Land Tax leads to double taxation?

(*iv*) Is the shifting of the tax, which is permitted in the Act desirable?

(*v*) Is the exemption prescribed in terms of a particular size of the holding satisfactory in terms of equity?

(*vi*) Is the definition of urban land clear about the intended coverage of the Urban Land Tax Act? and

(*vii*) Will the cost of administering the Urban Land Tax too high?

We will briefly examine each one of these issues in the same sequence.

Coverage of the Two Instruments

The Urban Land Ceiling Act is in force only in five cities/urban agglomeration in Karnataka State, viz., (*i*) Bangalore Urban Agglomeration (*ii*) Mysore, (*iii*) Mangalore Urban Agglomeration (*iv*) Belgaum Agglomeration and (*v*) Hubli-Dharwar. The coverage may get extended in future. The Karnataka Urban Land Tax Act is in operation in 11 centres viz., Bangalore Urban Agglomeration, the City of Hubli-Dharwar, the City

Municipalities of Mysore, Mangalore, Belgaum, Bellary, Davangere, Bijapur, Shimoga and Bhadravathi. The State Government may extend the application of this Act to other cities in future.

As it stands now, the cities of Gulbarga, Bellary, Davangere, Bijapur, Shimoga and Bhadravathi are not covered by the Urban Land Ceiling Act. Insofar as only the Urban Land Tax is applicable to these cities, the question of finding the total impact of the Urban Land Ceilings and the Urban Land Tax Act at present does not arise. The hypothetical question that can be posed now is what will be the situation in these cities in case the Government extends application of the Urban Land Ceilings Act to them also, in which case the general answers which emerge from our analysis should be valid for these centres also.

The coverage of the two Acts is somewhat different and this provides opportunities for the owner of Urban Land to defeat the purpose of the legislation. Under the Urban Land Ceilings Act in Karnataka, Bangalore has a ceiling of 1000 sq. metres and Hubli-Dharwar and Mysore has a ceiling of 1500 sq. metres, Mangalore and Belgaum a ceiling of 2000 sq. metres. Under the Urban Land Ceilings Act, exemption is given for about 223 sq. metres of Land. This implies that even within the Urban Land Ceilings Act, owners of land (eligible for exemption) will not be obliged to pay anything and remain untouched by law. Nearly 5 to 8 times the land exempted under the Urban Land Tax Act would be with such owners. If the Urban Land Tax is not imposed, they would continue to enjoy the benefits of incremental values of the property they hold. Again, it is possible for them, physical conditions permitting, to divide the urban land into sites of $60' \times 40'$ and show them in the names of distant relatives in order to claim exemption from the payment of Urban Land Tax. Thus, while the ceiling puts a limit for the prospective accruals of sources of income, which in itself is leading to an accentuation in the holdings of wealth and consequently of economic power, there is nothing in the Urban Land Ceiling to reduce the inherent potential for concentrations of wealth through surplus value accruals. Therefore, the Urban Land Tax cannot be said to be redundant merely because there is a ceiling on urban land.

Incidence of the Tax

In the absence of field data, we are presenting here the probable combined incidence for illustrative purposes taking some annual rental incomes. The rateable value, the value of wealth and the value of urban land have been deduced from the expected rental income in consultation with the concerned authorities. In this computation, capital gains tax does not figure because at present the capital gains tax is levied on realization but not on accrual basis. The combined incidence of the wealth tax, property tax and urban land tax is shown in Table 1. From this it will be seen that the combined incidence is about 15.7 per cent at a rental income of about Rs 6,000 and increases to 27.6 per cent at a rental income of about Rs 60,000. The urban land tax as such will come to Rs 35 where the value of

TABLE 1

Illustration of Combined Incidence of Wealth Tax, Property Tax and Urban Land Tax : Karnataka

(Columns 1 to 8 in Rupees)

Rental income per year (Rs)	Rateable value (83.33% of col.1)	Wealth*	Urban land value	Wealth tax	Property tax	Urban land tax	Combined incidence of taxes	Incidence as per cent of rental income	Incidence as per cent of rateable value
1	2	3	4	5	6	7	8	9	10
6,000	5,000	72,000	12,000	—	750	35	785	13.08	15.70
9,000	7,500	1,08,000	18,000	40	1125	73	1238	13.75	16.50
18,000	15,000	2,16,000	36,000	580	2250	235	3065	17.02	20.43
24,000	20,000	2,88,000	48,000	940	3000	355	4295	17.89	21.47
30,000	25,000	3,60,000	60,000	1300	3750	475	5525	18.41	22.10
45,000	37,500	5,40,000	90,000	3100	5550	775	9425	20.94	25.13
60,000	50,000	7,20,000	1,20,000	5800	7000	1075	13875	23.12	27.75

*8.33 per cent annual yield.

the urban land is Rs 12,000 and reaches about Rs 1075 for urban land value at Rs 1.2 lakhs. When wealth tax is also taken into consideration, there is no doubt that urban land tax will increase the total tax. But, the addition is not so high as to make the urban land tax very oppressive. This is especially so when it is recalled that the wealth tax rates have been slashed down in the 1976 Budget. For net wealth of Rs 5 lakhs, the tax is only half a per cent and for wealth exceeding Rs 15 lakhs, the tax liability would be Rs 20,000 plus 25 per cent of the amount exceeding Rs 15 lakhs.

The present rates structure of the urban land tax seems to be somewhat regressive. In order to examine this aspect, we have worked out the incidence of urban land tax for lands with varying market values with reference to income ranges which are presently followed by the income authorities. The illustration of this incidence is shown in Table 2. From this, it can be seen that the urban land tax as per cent to the mid-point of the income range of less than Rs 8,000 will be 0.63 and declines to 0.01 per cent at more than Rs 2 lakhs. Where the market value of land ranges from Rs 15,000 to Rs 25,000, the incidence declines from 3.13 per cent to 0.8 per cent. Where the market value of land exceeds Rs 25,000, incidence declines from 21.8 per cent to 0.35 per cent. This suggests that the rate structure should be reconsidered and proper progression built into it in order to ensure that the tax becomes more equitable.

Double Taxation

It is voiced in some circles that urban land tax leads to double taxation insofar as there exists already a property tax, which is levied and collected by the Municipal bodies. This argument is rather weak. Firstly, the rateable value on the basis of which property tax is collected, is grossly underestimated due to the weaknesses of the local bodies of administration. Secondly, property tax is a tax which is given in return for some of the direct benefits/services which the local bodies provide to owners/occupiers of the house. In other words this tax is a *quid pro quo* one and is based on the benefit principle and not the ability-to-pay principle of taxation. The urban land tax, however, is intended to capture a part of the incremental surplus value which accrues as a result of urbanization and other public investments. Thirdly, the rateable value which is the basis of property taxation is not the appropriate method for assessing vacant land values. Even in the case of improvements also (buildings, etc.) the rateable value is an unsatisfactory measure. It is only the capital value assessed at current market price which reflects the true values. Thirdly, urban land tax is intended to be a tax on the unimproved value of the land and such land has developmental potential which carries with it the surplus accrual potential which cannot be captured in rateable value.

Shifting of the Tax

According to the existing provisions, in Karnataka urban land tax is an

Table 2 A

Incidence of Urban Land Tax with Varying Market Values of Land and Various Income Ranges
Illustration : Karnataka

Sl. No.	Income range	Urban land tax with the market value of land				
		Does not exceed Rs 5,000	From Rs 5,000 to Rs 15,000			
			Minimum		Maximum	
			In Rs	As percentage*	In Rs	As percentage*
1	2	3	4	5	6	7
1.	Less than 8000	—	—	—	25	0.63
2.	8000-15000	—	—	—	25	0.22
3.	15000-20000	—	—	—	25	0.14
4.	20000-25000	—	—	—	25	0.11
5.	25000-30000	—	—	—	25	0.09
6.	3000-500000	—	—	—	25	0.07
7.	50000-70000	—	—	—	25	0.04
8.	70000-1,00,000	—	—	—	25	0.03
9.	1,00,000-2,00,000	—	—	—	25	0.02
10.	More than 2,00,000	—	—	—	25	0.01

*Represents the percentage of Urban Land Tax to mid-point of the income range in Col. No. 2.

TALLE 2 B

Incidence of Urban Land Tax with Varying Market Values of Land and Various Income Ranges
Illustration : Karnataka

Sl. No,	Income range	Urban land tax with the market value of land							
		From Rs 15,000 to 25,000				Exceeds Rs 25,000			
		Minimum		Maximum		(Say Rs 50,000)		(Say Rs 1,00,00)	
		In Rs	As percentage*	In Rs	As percentage*	In Rs	As percentage*	In Rs	As percentage*
1	2	8	9	10	11	12	13	14	15
1.	Less than 8000	50	1.25	125	3.13	375	9.38	875	21.88
2.	8000-15000	50	0.43	125	1.09	375	9.26	875	7.61
3.	15000-20000	50	0.29	125	0.71	375	2.14	875	5.00
4.	20000-25000	50	0.22	125	0.56	375	1.67	875	3.89
5.	25000-30000	50	0.18	125	0.45	375	1.36	875	3.18
6.	30000-50000	50	0.13	125	0.31	375	0.94	875	2.19
7.	50000-70000	50	0.08	125	0.21	375	0.63	875	1.46
8.	70000-1,00,000	50	0.06	125	0.15	375	0.44	875	1.03
9.	1,00,000-2,00,000	50	0.03	125	0.08	375	0.25	875	0.58
10.	More than 2,00,000	50	0.02	125	0.08	375	0.15	875	0.35

*Represents the percentage of Urban Land Tax to mid-point of the income range in Col. No. 2.

indirect tax in the sense the Act permits the owner to pass on the burden of the tax to the occupier. Where the owner himself is the resident, the incidence of the tax is on himself and this incidence gets reduced because of the 50 per cent rebate given in such cases. One may, therefore, question the validity of this provision in the Act. If the basic justification for the urban land tax is that it is meant to capture a portion of the capital gains which accrue to the owner, in theory it may be unsound to provide for shifting the burden of the tax to the occupier in the form of higher rent by the amount of the tax. But, it may be administratively difficult to make the incidence rest with the owner himself, even if the Act specifically states that the burden should not be shifted. This weakness need not be blown up beyond its life size, because even a major direct tax like the Corporation tax is being shifted and recent researches have shown that shifting is even more than 100 per cent.[2]

Exemptions

Market value has been adopted as the basis for taxation. However, exemption is given in respect of urban land the extent of which does not exceed 2400 sq. ft. and such land is used solely for residential purpose. It is to be presumed that 2400 sq. ft. of urban land everywhere has the same market value irrespective of its location which will necessarily not be so. In a highly developed and posh locality, market value would be more when compared with the same size land in a far-off and undeveloped area. Moreover, exemption in terms of the size of land has nothing in it to make the owner use the land which is less than 223 sq. meters for construction purposes quickly instead of holding it idle. For speculative purposes, even this size of urban land should be considered substantial, especially viewed in the context of the locality where it is situated. Under the existing provisions, a land which has a lower value now because of its location and present use may have a higher potential speculative value in future. These possibilities have not been taken care of in the rates structure. It may, therefore, become necessary to determine exemption in terms of the value of the land rather than in terms of the size of the land. This will have the advantage of applying the same principle of market value both for purposes of taxation as well as for purposes of exemption.

Cause for Confusion

Some confusion seems to arise about the tax base from the definition of urban land and the related aspects like the owner or occupier of such land and the rebates.

For example in Karnataka Urban Land Tax Act, each urban land is defined as land comprised in any lot of land whether built upon or not, and includes the areas in which a city survey has been made, a survey

[2]See D.M. Nanjundappa, *Studies in Public Finance*, *op. cit.*, chapter on Incidence of Taxation.

number or a subdivision number.

The "occupier" is defined as (*a*) any person for the time being paying or liable to pay to the owner rent or any portion of the rent of the urban land or of the building constructed on the urban land or part of such land or building in respect of which the word is used or the damages on account of the occupation of such land, building of part; and (*b*) a rent free occupant.

The "owner" is defined as any person in possession of urban land with or without a building constructed thereon which has been granted, allotted, or leased by an Improvement Trust Board, the Karnataka Housing Board or any local authority subject to the condition that the tax in respect of such land or building shall be payable by the grantee, allottee or lessee concerned.

While the professed objective of the Act is to lay a tax on vacant urban land only, these definitions do not make such a point clear. The scope for such an assertion is all the more when we take note of the clauses regarding rebates.

By way of a concession in respect of owner resident buildings, the Act stipulates that where any building is occupied by the owner thereof solely for residential purposes, he will be given the rebate of 50 per cent in the urban land tax payable on the urban land on which the building has been constructed and on the urban land appurtenant to such building.

These seem to call for clarifications. If the intention is to tax only unimproved land, it should be stated so in clear terms. However, while doing so, the need to introduce derating of buildings in an attempt to encourage housing construction must not be conceded at the cost of income redistribution objective.

Cost of Administration

There is also the issue regarding the cost of administering the urban land tax. For example, in Karnataka, it is estimated that about Rs 50 lakhs may be the revenue expected in the first instance and it may gradually rise to about Rs 75 lakhs. For collecting such a small revenue, the expenditure to be incurred on the staff is feared to be very high and therefore on balance, the collection of the urban land may become unremunerative. In the absence of precise details about the number of assessees, the value of the urban land, etc., it is extremely difficult to pronounce any views on this aspect. However, it is to be noted that the proportion of expenditure to total revenue would go down once the staff is put to optimal use and the coverage is complete both in respect of the levy and enforcement.

The position is likely to vary from one city/town to another. If the experience of another State is any guide, it appears that in Tamil Nadu, the percentage of expenditure to receipts in 1975-76 is about 9.2 per cent; in Madras, 6.4 per cent; in Madurai, 6 per cent, in Coimbatore, 4.4 per cent; in Salem 14.4 per cent and in Trichi 28.1 per cent. In Coimbatore, for example, this proportion has come down from about 26 per cent in 1972-

73 to 6 per cent in 1975-76. In Salem, it has come down from about 40 per cent to 14.4 per cent within three years. In Trichi, it has declined from 72 per cent to 28 per cent within the same period. This shows that the costs of administration will decline once the efficiency in terms of coverage, and the deployment of the staff is maximized.

It is also important to note that the cost of administration can be very much reduced if a Central Valuation Agency is set up and its services are made available not only for the urban land tax administration but also for all urban local bodies like the Corporations and Municipalities. This can be extended to rural local bodies also. Then it will have the advantage of contributing to improving the property tax assessment which, at present, is somewhat hopeless. It is therefore, felt that the cost of administration need not be a red herring.

Conclusion

The foregoing suggests that an urban land tax is a supplement to the urban land ceilings and it has a legitimate place in the tax armoury of the State, especially to siphon off a part of the capital gains accruing from real estates into Government fisc for public investment. The combined incidence of the wealth tax, property tax and urban land tax may not be that much oppressive. The fear that the cost of administering the tax is likely to be too high is also to be discounted. The rate structure can become somewhat repressive and therefore, it has to be carefully worked out to make it more equitable. Definitions are likely to cause some confusion about the intended coverage of the tax and clear-cut definitions have to be attempted confining the levy of the tax on the unimproved value only. Exemptions, unless carefully worked out and based on market value and not area will clash with equity test. Laxity in the enforcement of urban land tax limits the income redistribution objective of the urban land ceilings.

YASODHA SHANMUGA SUNDARAM

The Genesis of Welfare Economics

BEGINNINGS

The beginnings of the science of economics can be traced to the writings of "philosophers, theologians, pamphleteers, special pleaders and reformers."[1] Thenceforth it had always been concerned with problems of public policy and welfare. Specifically from the time of the physiocrats and Adam Smith there is no instance in the literature to show the lack of awareness to this problem. In some sense perfect competition represented an optimal situation even though this doctrine underwent modifications and diverse proofs over time.

A brief survey of classical economic thought would reveal that Political Economy, "in its origin and for the greater part of its history" has been "Welfare Economics."[2] Broadly it was quite directly related to policy or principles, objectives and criteria of the art of legislation. The utilitarian calculus was concerned mainly with the establishment of principles to guide policy. Political economy was considered as dealing with "the happiness and improvement of political society."[3] Following Adam Smith, Jeremy Bentham and Henri Storch broadened economics to deal with the "prosperity" of nations and not with the "wealth of nations." Herein civilization is also included as wealth.

In the applied economics of scholastic doctors of the classical period, the pivotal concept of "public good" dominated their economic sociology. The public good was conceived in "a distinctly utilitarian spirit" and referred to the satisfaction of economic wants of individuals as discerned by the observed reasons. Barring technique, Schumpeter observes, it was exactly the same thing as the welfare concept of modern Welfare Economics[4] (e.g. Pigouvian Welfare Economics).

The inception of economic thinking, positive economics and welfare economics were intimately associated with one another until the later part

---

[1]P.A. Samuelson, *Foundations of Economic Analysis,* Harvard University Press, 1948, pp. 203-4.

[2]T.W. Hutchinson, *A Review of Economic Doctrines*, Clarendon Press, Oxford, 1953, p. 280.

[3]Dugold Steward, *Political Economy*, edited by Hamilton, 1885. Quoted in I.M. Kirzner, *The Economic Point of View,* Princeton, 1960, p. 46.

[4]J.A. Schumpeter, *History of Economic Analysis,* Oxford University Press, 1952, p. 97.

of 19th century when the economic treatises "combined advocacy with analysis in a quite uncritical manner."[5] More often the analysis was to subserve the policies advocated. But in the later nineteenth century the economists were faced with a twofold task. Firstly to clearly distinguish between normative maxims implied in welfare economics and neutral positive analysis and to evolve positive science devoid of political maxims and principles. Secondly, to meet the social challenge by re-examining the role of the state in economic life in a "more detached, systematic and detailed way."[6] The examination of welfare proposals was taken up under the latter.

FROM CLASSICAL DOCTRINES TO MODERN WELFARE ECONOMICS

Applying traditional methods and pursuing stereos-typed objectives, the classical economists emphasized production, supply and cost in their approach to economic science. Referring to the classical theory of Production Welfare Economics, Myint concludes that even in its most sensitive version, it was a pure problem of technology with special attention to "dynamic changes in the supply of factors with a dash of belief in Laissez Faire as a practical rule of them, the then true significance of which is all but forgotten."[7] Criticism of classical thought has resulted in revolutionary changes in the method of solution to economic questions. Modern theory of welfare economics stresses on consumption, demand and utility. Welfare and not wealth is the direct objective.[8] As the early classicism passed into late classicism and then into marginalism the "felicific" calculus became more explicit. The economists who focussed on the theory of value shifted their emphasis from production to distribution. In the language of the neoclassicists, the vocabulary of liberal hedonism is altered.[9] The modern approach differs from the classical approach by better techniques and consequently better results. However, classical welfare propositions including those of Bentham displayed a "remarkable awareness of the qualifications to which consideration of instantaneous welfare maxims become subject as soon as we take account of the future."[10]

Economic theorists from the earlier days have dealt with systems of living. Adam Smith did not discuss consumption directly but held it as the end of production. J.S. Mill reversed this. For him production and not consumption was the key to national wealth. Improving upon Adam Smith,

[5] W.M. Reder, *Studies in the Theory of Welfare Economics*, Columbia University Press, 1947, p. 13.

[6] T.W. Hutchinson, *A Review of Economic Doctrines*, Oxford Clarendon Press, 1953, p. 281.

[7] See H.L.A. Myint, "Welfare Significance of Productive Labour," *Review of Economic Studies*, 1943-44, p. 27.

[8] Neff Frank, *Economic Doctrines*, McGraw Hill Book Company, Incorporated (1950), p. 425.

[9] H.K. Girvetz, *Wealth to Welfare*, Stanford University Press, 1950, p. 116.

[10] J.A. Schumpeter, *op cit.*, p. 1073.

Lauderdale emphasized consumption and outlined some of its principles. Wants determine the direction to be taken by the industries. This idea is further developed by Senior with emphasis of the "love of variety and love of distinction."[11] Generally, the classical writers find standard or level of living in *man* and in his collective representations.

The treatment of non-market values by Adam Smith, Mill and others is unique and form rudiments of a new approach for orienting research around specific elements of well being. This seems methodologically more helpfull, in certain respects[12] than modern welfare economics. In the classical writings are found a wide range of value standards, cursory appraisal of economic process in terms of these standards, and consideration of ways to correct market biases. What is missing is an attempt to ascertain whether the value standards are actually prevalent. When we consider the contribution of Marshall and Pigou in detail the unique features of classical writers would emerge clearly.

The Emergence of Welfare Ideals from the Medieval Utopias

The utopian writings of the period from Francis Bacon to Adam Smith are of two types—utopias of escape and utopias of realization. The former assumed plenty as their starting point and the latter, scarcity. The utopias appeared mostly in times of tension—social, political or economic. They were not entirely cultural phenomen a but were results of an increasing belief in "secularization of the spheres of politico-economic life, a belief that the non-religious world and its activities can be so recognized by human action as to be capable of improvement and the attainment of a degree of perfection."[13]

The Medieval Europe in the period of the Renaissance was faced with a constantly widening "breach with moral conceptions of solidarity, stewardship and a *justum pretium*."[14] The power of status, jealously guarded so long by the feudal system as a socially accepted distinction, was abandoned to a great extent. The new bourgeois class after achieving economic success tried to obtain political recognition. The adoption of experimental methods in science opened immense new prospects and naturally economic optimism seemed to justify the most ambitious dream of a golden age.

In this background the welfare proposition of social sympathizers could be followed with interest, in their attempt "to persuade, to help and to seek new ways for the society."[15] Their ultimate aim was to find an economic solution to the problems of poverty and social backwardness. In the 17th century west, all the proposals were for the short run in view of the

---

[11]C.C. Zimmerman, *Consumption and Standard of Living*, p. 479.

[12]H. J., Levia, "Standards of Welfare in Economic Thought," *QJE*, 1956, p, 123.

[13]J. K. Fuz, *Welfare economics in English Utopias, Francis Bacon to Adam Smith*, The Hague, Martinus Nihoff, 1952, p. 4.

[14]*Ibid.*, p. x.

[15]*Ibid.*, p. 8.

urgency of time and distressing circumstances. Between the 17th and 18th centuries the welfare ideas could be grouped under two main groups, viz. a peripheral case of welfare economics under mercantilist influence and the other put forward by Utopian writers belonging to the proper field of welfare economics. The former was concentrated around the unification and strengthening of the newly emancipated national states to make wealth statutory and if possible, to attain self-sufficiency. Mercantilist economic policy was a true reflection of the spirit inherited from Machiavelli.

The mercantilist measures for stimulating production for increasing trade or agriculture were of welfare promoting characteristics but their goal was the state and its wealth, and not that of its members. Here the divergence of opinion between the two schools of thought is the strongest. The welfare of an individual including his education and social security, the elimination of poverty or of unemployment as such, or of some other socio-economic disorder were never subjects of direct enquiry by the mercantilists. But they were only by-products of other activities, which were regarded as important, and only touching upon them when the supposed interests of the state made it unavoidable. The only one common feature between mercantilist doctrines and utopian welfare ideals was this increase in physical output.

In breaking with the traditional way of thinking, Bacon's utopia can be treated as "one of the most important contributions to the history of social science,"[16] and he was rightly called the spiritual father of Industrial Revolution. His *Nova Atlantis* was written in Latin in 1969. Its most important part is the description of the House of Solomon, a prototype of a research centre and of the role of science in promoting material welfare. He held the pragmatic view that the progress of mankind was possible only through science which must produce material conditions necessary for "ever increasing welfare, knowledge and understanding human nature." Commenting on this Macaulay wrote: "Its aim. . . was to provide man with what he requires while he continues to be man. . . ." Baconian society was not static but an ever-moving scientifically directed one with dynamism. It was the first utopia to take such a modern view. Though he gave a large list of projects, only those that are relevant to economic welfare would be mentioned here. The first group of projects concerned man, his wealth, education and work; and the second with plans regarding the improvement of soil, raw material, substances and food. The third group embodies industrial interventions of a mechanical or a chemical character, new sources of energy and material wealth; and the last group includes sport and communication. He even prefigured on aeroplanes, submarines and telephones.

Baconian utopia served as a background for all other utopias of the following period. From the point of view of welfare economies in a strict sense, he had nothing much important to say. He had evaded economic problems. The praise-worthy feature in his work was the scientific atmos-

[16]J. K. Fuz, *op. cit.*

phere, the stress on the necessity of planned research and the idea of the organization of science in the service of mankind, for solving practical questions. His contribution was the substitution of practical aims for metaphysical philosophy. The effect of his writing was to quicken the phase of technological progress. Bacon centred the whole idea of human progress around scientific discovery and interests which hitherto were only slightly touched upon.

Samuel Hartlib of Poland wrote his *Macaria* (In great place of felicity)—a document urging reforms by the New Parliament for the general welfare of the country. *Macaria* had a highly modern touch with its proposals meant for direct application by the Parliament. It is similar to the present-day economic and cultural programme. Under the framework of the existing society Hartlib's work claims originality as a first project of welfare economics in the Utopian writings of this medieval period. "A state, in order to regulate the economic affairs of society, must possess an apparatus functioning well, which should be in touch with the economic position of the country and therefore all the more easy to execute the desired course of policy."[17] The proposed ministry consisted of five departments dealing with national welfare, internal trade, foreign trade, agriculture, fishing and colonies. This idea of ministries embracing the whole national activity was introduced in very many states only after the turn of this century.

He suggested a very dynamic policy with economic welfare of the country as its primary goal. His proposals of national welfare were on the following lines. Public works, improvement of wasteland, and construction of roads and buildings are to be financed by the inheritance tax at the rate of 1/20 part of a property after the death of its owner. A progressive penal taxation and a threat of confiscation of property and even an expulsion from the country were the media through which efficiency of agriculture increases. It is worth noting that precisely similar measures were introduced in Great Britain during the Second World War to stimulate agricultural production.

His approach to the population problem is significant. A governmentally organized and subsidized emigration was the solution to the emigration problem. He was essentially Baconian in his ideas regarding advancement of science. But his was a shorter presentation and more practical in outlook. The basis on which Hartlib's ideals were drawn were political liberty, economic opportunity accessible to all and safeguarded by the state and the physical and moral health of its citizens.

Hartlib differed distinctly from the early mercantilistic practices which were mostly directed towards problems of money and foreign trade. These were on isolated economic questions. The handling of food supplies, regulation of the supply of skilled labour, creation of opportunities for employment, the cultivation of wasteland and lastly, emigration were the means to

[17] J. K. Fuz, *op. cit.*, p. 22.

increase the welfare of the country. Such was the all-embracing national policy put forth by Hartlib, directed towards the elimination of poverty and increasing the wealth of the inhabitants.

His contribution in the background of the contemporary utopian writings of the time is significant in stressing on the point that one must first know the facts before taking action or trying to improve things. Without such a background knowledge and appreciation of existing conditions, the improvement of a country's economic welfare could not be carried out. This deep understanding of the complexity of economic life is important from the historic point of view as well, for he has given a scientifically justified approach to welfare economics.

Another English medieval writer Peter Chamberlin (1649) gave a similar economic plan without the utopian orientation. In fact it was intended for immediate applicatoin to the bad economic situation of the country. The highest degree of economic welfare was to be attained by nationalization of the estates of the king and clergy, of commons, forests, all wastelands, unused lands, mines (which were not worked) as well as treasure found inland or in the sea. Poverty was to be remedied only by increasing the wealth. However, there was no mention on the distribution of the national wealth. The lead to the subsistence theory of wage is to be found in the statement, "demands of the poor are but food and garment and to be disposed into such an order that they and their posterity should not lack the necessaries of life." Restating the core of mercantilistic thought, state was the only agency to secure welfare policy and his significant contribution lies in equating the national wealth to economic welfare. Hence it is on a different level from those of other mercantilist writers like Colbert. The intended goal was to satisfy the demands of the poor, recognized as members of the society and as necessary to it as were all other social groups and to give them means for economic and social rehabilitation.

Another of the medieval writings concerning as to how to advance the trade of nations and employ the poor was by William Goffe. Instead of the irregularly paid charities to the poor, practical proposals for the employment of the poor were suggested and this was to be financed by taxing all the parishes, for three years. This is to be viewed as a reformist ideology against the medieval church. Goffe's proposals regarding the employment of the poor is to be examined in the light of present-day situations. In advocating the prevention of excessive economic mobility of labour he showed keen economic insight. He aimed at setting the unemployed in such a way, that they could learn a trade and earn a decent living. He apparently had in mind the redistribution of labour by persuasion to prevent a situation arising which today has led to "depressed areas." However, the mercantilist in him comes to the surface and his attitude is strongly protectionist when he subscribes in the employment possibilities, shipbuilding and fishing.

The works of Goffee and Chamberlin can be regarded as welfare action within the framework of the existing society. The stress was on the state interference with which the structure of the society would not be affected. This is a contradiction. Pigou later adhered to the same state intervention as a means for the ultimate change in the structure of the society.

Of the later works in the same vein, mention could be made of Robert Wallace's "Various Prospects" in 1761, John Beller's "Proposals for Raising a College of Industry" (1765) and Bernard Mendeville's, "The Fable of the Bees of Private Vices, Public Benefits" (1705-1728). In these writings could be perceived an emphasis on the individualism and self-interest. According to Wallace, "Idleness must be banished, universal industry must be introduced and preserved. Labour must be properly and equitably distributed and everyone must be obliged to do his part. . . ."[18] John Bellers similarly pointed out to profit as a motive for the participation of individuals in industry. His *College of Industry* was the centre where all his proposals operated in several branches, viz. trade and agriculture, education, housing and social service schemes like old-age pensions. Through collective effort each will become self-sufficient. The welfare character can be illustrated in his own words: "These are essays towards making the nation happy, by possessing or restoring them, Wealth, raising their riches . . . ."

Mendeville goes a step ahead and puts the *spiritus moven* of economic action as human egoism. His welfare proposals were thus based upon the free action of the individual in the existing society. Government could only stimulate welfare by creating the necessary atmosphere of toleration, liberty and peace and would not interfere in the economic affairs except procuring employment in the case of the unemployed. He indicates frugality as the main cause of the lack of economic activity, He is very much Keynesian when he emphasized that spending occupied a very important place as a stimulant of employment. To provide a steady stream of demand, "the interest of all rich nations requires that the greatest part of the poor should never be idle and yet continually spend what they get."[19] In this respect, he can be truly regarded as the originator of the idea of modern multiplier approach. The monetary supplement to his primary welfare proposals[20] is very much Keynesian. The money in circulation should closely be aligned with employment, price and wages. Wages in particular follow the cost of living thereby approaching the modern concept of minimum wages.

FROM UTOPIAS TO CLASSICAL THOUGHT

In the medieval literature between Bacon and Smith, we perceive three characteristic strands of welfare action, (*i*) the utopian cravings of dreamers of a welfare land, (*ii*) the mercantilistic "down to the earth"

[18]Quoted from Fuz, p. 66.

[19]Quoted from Fuz, p. 87.

[20]His secondary welfare proposals are a liberal policy for universities to facilitate the exchange of students and scientific works without prejudice to nationality and race.

proposals with the twin goals of economic welfare and national supremacy, and (*iii*) the unorthodox, yet realistic ways and means towards aggregative happiness on the foundations of liberty and individual freedom. Writers during this period offered various solutions under the following three heads: Middleway, Collectivist, and Individualist, and their total contribution can be summarized as primary welfare proposals and secondary welfare proposals. The former includes improvement of agriculture, exploitation of minerals, stimulation of productivity and technological progress as well as the role of money and foreign trade. These are propositions immediately directed towards increase of physical output. The latter includes all action indirectly promoting general welfare, such as education, both general and professional, care of public health, the progress of science and research and the development of the arts and general culture. The central point of all their welfare action was the problem of full employment. Occurrence of unemployment reflected a bad economic structure. It was not a necessary evil. Their achievement also lay in the analysis of relationship between politics and economics especially with regard to economic power and domination and exploitation of labour. In fact these were the early attempts at an economic interpretation of the theory of state and society. Their appreciation of the role of the state as an economic institution, guaranteeing general welfare of the country is noteworthy. Their very important contribution however is the idea of a standard welfare which even in our times is not yet adequately dealt with. Consider the statement "whether a livelihood be not the right and propriety of everyman" which is in correspondence with the economic and social ideal of justice.

It was Bentham[21] who laid the solid foundation on which the whole edifice of welfare economics stands. Identifying happiness with welfare he laid stress on the economic significance of equality. With social inequity an equal sum of utility is of unequal importance to different men. From this fundamental premise he deduces his several axioms:[22] (*i*) Each portion of wealth has a corresponding portion of happiness; (*ii*) Of two individuals with unequal fortunes he who has the most wealth has the most happiness; (*iii*) The excess in happiness of the richer will not be so great as the excess of his wealth; (*iv*) For the same reasons the greater the disproportion between the two masses of wealth, the less is it probable that there exists a disproportion equally great between corresponding masses of happiness and (*v*) The nearer the actual proportion approaches to equality the greater will be the total mass of happiness.

As much as he stressed on the importance of equality so much also was the emphasis on perfect liberty. However, these two are conflicting forces.

---

[21]Though chronologically Adam Smith preceded Bentham, the latter is treated first because of the characteristic ethical mooring of his philosophy.

[22]W. Stark, "Jeremy Bentham as an Economist of Liberty and Equality, "*Economic Journal*, 1941, pp. 73-74.

Hence his improviso: If an "equality maximizing principle cannot be upheld at least an inequality minimizing principle must be proclaimed." In this respect Bentham is a link between capitalism and communism—a mixture of the justice of communism and the efficiency of capitalism—the union of equality in the changes of life with liberty in pursuits of life. A practical synthesis of liberty and equality which corresponds to his theoretical synthesis of the doctrine of empiricism and rationalism and thereby individual and the society are thus reconciled. As Start observes, "a loftier ideal has never been conceived."[23]

The entire Benthamite system is built on feelings. His is a sensational and hedonistic philosophy. "The object or end in view should be the production of the maximum happiness in a given time in the community in question." In his moral arithmatic, feelings of pleasure constitute the positive, and feelings of pain the negative quantities. To his hedonist imperative of maximum happiness of men, State should be subservient.

The Manual of Political Economy (1773) proves that free economy is the most productive and puts forth the demand that State should observe strict passivity in all economic matters. On this fundamental attitude is erected the system of political economy as a science of the means to serve the greatest possible national welfare. All economically relevant action is divided into three groups, viz. *Sponte acta* of the individuals, *agenda* of the Government and *non-agenda* of the Government. All empirically given measures of economic policies are examined and are fitted into either of the categories—agenda or non-agenda.[24] His touchstone is the utilitarian calculus of gain and loss. He thus envisages a "scientifically exact system"[25] of welfare policy and proves that by its very abstaining the Government is contributing to the commonweal than by interfering. Writing two decades after Adam Smith and two decades brfore Ricardo his position in the development of social sciences is very interesting. By means of economic as well as politicoethical arguments, Bentham refutes Adam Smith's thesis that interference in foreign trade and usury is justifiable by rational thinking. While freedom of economic intercourse is only a postulate of opportunity to Adam Smith, it is a matter of principle to Bentham.

In the seemingly irreconcilable thesis of Bentham viz. "there is no true interest but individual interest," "the greatest happiness of the greatest number"—is justified as merely apparent. "As egotism leads to love of his neighbour, individualism leads to societism."[26] Thus there is a "natural and indissoluble" connection. This is the essence of his liberal thought

---

[23]*Ibid.*, p. 76.

[24]In the category of agenda are included (*i*) measures for the removal of obstacles and (*ii*) the measures for the satisfaction of more important before less important needs. The basic idea behind this grouping of non-agenda is that production is limited by capital which cannot be created by action of the Government. Hence the State is incapable of aiding economic life.

[25]*Ibid.*, p. 64.

[26]*Ibid.*, p. 68.

which feels that there is an "automatic harmony"[27] between the self-interest of the individual and welfare of the whole. Hence the preaching for the release of the individual from prohibitive social controls with such missionary zeal by the Liberals.

The contribution of Bentham is immense in that the utilitarian principle has travelled via ethics and gets fused with mathematics thus exorting the great possibilities of welfare economics as a separate branch of study. Happiness of the society is the sum total of the happiness of all the individuals and man's happiness is the sum total of his satisfactions. This is the maximization of utility principle or the Utility Calculus, which is scientific ethics. Welfare economics thus follows from this branch of ethics, from the fact that a maximization of satisfaction is largely due to economic causes. As Little and Edgeworth agree the "maximum happiness principle invited the application of the differential calculus to the problems of ethical economics."[28] Vast areas of development in welfare theory have very largely been the result of the application of mathematics to the quantitative ethical concepts which are made available from Benthamite philosophy.

The impact of Bentham's doctrine has been far-reaching both on the theoretical and practical planes. The recent economic literature is simply a revival of Benthamism in the armour of a better technique such as comparability of satisfaction of different people. With no exception all the countries have the conviction that the greatest good of the greatest number is ultimately the concern of the state which may be rightly attributed to the new political power of the mass vote.[29]

In conclusion it is necessary to inquire into the soundness of an equalitarian standard based on the calculus. The validity of this theory rests entirely on its assumption. Does wealth have the same capacity to confer happiness upon different individuals? Bentham accepts to be so. But Hegal feels otherwise[30] and believes that individuals are naturally unequal. There is nothing in economics to indicate the soundness of either view. This problem which has caused much difficulty to Mill has been grappled by Pigou who makes a conciliation between Bentham and Hegal. Equalizing wealth might not increase economic welfare.[31]

ADAM SMITH, RICARDO AND MALTHUS: CLASSICAL VIEW POINT

The keynote of Smithian economic philosophy is his conviction in Labour Cost Theory. Consider his introduction to *Wealth of Nations*. "The annual labour of every nation is the fund of which originally supplies it with all

---

[27]H.K. Girvetz, *Wealth to Welfare*, Standford University Press, 1950, p. 112.

[28]I.M.D. Little, *A Critique of Welfare Economics*, 2nd edn, 1957, p. 7.

[29]Barbara Ward, *India and the West*, p. 41.

[30]Whittakar, *History of Economic Ideas*, Longman Green & Co., London, 1940, pp. 278-79.

[31]A.C. Pigou, *Economics of Welfare*, pp. 90-91.

the necessaries and conveniences of life which it annually consumes which consists always either in the immediate produce of that labour or in what is purchased with that produce from other nations." The true source of wealth is human activity. Hence behind the "facade of market phenomena"[32] there are Smith's more fundamental ideas regarding the national dividend as the fruits of application of labour to natural resources and that being the source and measure of all value and economic welfare.

His labour cost theory was the dominant influence in his price system and became the fountain-head of all non-allocative elements in English thought. This is essentially a man-against-nature approach to economic problem. The logical conclusion from this is that economic welfare could be increased either by removing the "real" technological obstacles against labour force or by increasing the quantity of labour applied. In this setting a fuller appreciation of his theory of division of labour becomes explicable by which the technological obstacles are sought to be removed and economic welfare increased. Naturally this leads to the policy of free consumption, a typical model of expanding economy. While to the majority of classical economists, competition is an instrument of expansion, to the modern welfare theorist it is primarily a method of intensifying the effectivenes of readjustments. In short it is more tightening and not widening.

Economics meant more than value theory to Ricardo. It is interested in "riches" or economic welfare, as per Chapter 20 in *The Principles of Political Economy and Taxation*, London, 1817. This riches or economic welfare is equal to the physical quantity of social output. From Chapter 20 to 26 he seems to emerge from this value theory to a concept of aggregative value of the social output. This is determined by the total quantity of labour required to produce a given social output with a given margin of cultivation and given capital equipment. Thus it becomes an index of technological obstacles facing social products and varies inversely with economic welfare. The physical quantity of output can be increased only by increasing the "Net Revenue (i.e.) the gap between total social output and the subsistence fund."[33]

Since utilitarianism is behind Malthus' famous Theory of Population, Malthus' humanism cannot be doubted. He was against all legal relief like the poor relief. Not that he objected to the poor being aided but only objected to relief as an illusory thing "which relieves suffering at the cost of creating time." Consider the statement, "It is most desirable that the labouring classes should be well paid for a much more important reason than any that can relate to the wealth, viz. the happiness of nearly 36 millions." No scholar was more anxious to find that truth on the issue with which he dealt. It goes to his credit that he emphasized man before wealth, and wealth was related only to man's well-being. "Had other economists placed greater emphasis upon man than upon wealth . . . economic science might have

---

[32]H.L.A. Myint, *Welfare Significance of Productive Labour*, RES, 1943-44, p. 20.
[33]*Ibid.*, pp. 20-21.

taken a different course."

Compared to Ricardo, and his own contemporaries, Senior's treatment
of value was more original in some respects. Utility was given a more
important place, in the value theory than was done by Ricardo. Jevons
regarded Senior as "one of the many prophets of the marginal utility
theory."[34] However, the extent of his contribution to utility and welfare
analysis depends upon our "symphetic willingness" to attach meaning to
his treatment. Despite his awareness of the relative utility of differing
objectives being different to different persons, and of the difficulty of
measuring utility of various elements of marginal utility theory, Senior
did very little to develop his ideas into a cogent theory.

Of the marginalist school of thought Wicksell's welfare system was one
of the first to contain an explicit development of the set of marginal conditions necessary to attain maximum welfare. He systematized the several
contributions to the marginal conditions individually. His marginal conditions for exchange were not dependent on inter-personal comparisons
of utility. He discussed the difficulty of measuring it and the futility of any
such measure. But the other marginal conditions were on the premise of
inter-personal comparisons. On the basis of identical marginal utilities
for equal income he argues that welfare could be increased by the transfer
of income from the rich to the poor. He advocated consequently minimum
wages and tariffs even though this interferes with marginal conditions of
exchange.[35] In spite of such formulation Wicksell attacked the Benthamite
doctrine of maximum satisfaction. However he held that free competition
is normally a sufficient condition to ensure maximization of production. In
this respect his position was, far ahead of that of Walras.[36]

In the same stream of thought, Weiser's treatment of the problem of
economic calculation in different forms of society along with Sax's work
on public finance, represents the nearest Austrian equivalent to English
Welfare Economics and the Italian Pareto-Barone's formulation of
optimum allocation of economic resources. But the Austrian attempt is
neither "a systematic review like the former, nor an elaboration of pure
and precise theoretical formula like the latter."[37] According to Weiser
the exchange economy maximizes exchange values and the state maximizes
the natural value or social utility. These two aims may be conflicting with
each other. Apart from this Weiser has not carried further his analysis of
how natural and social values are to be calculated to weigh against the
exchange values. The mere calculable exchange values cannot be taken as
criteria for social policy.

[34]J.F. Bell, *History of Economic Thought*, The Ronald Press Company, New York,
1953, p. 258.

[35]Naey Ruggles, *The Welfare Basis of the Marginal Cost Pricing Principle*, RES, 1949-
50, p. 29.

[36]J.A., Schumpeter, *op. cit.* p. 625.

[37]T.W. Hutchinson, *A Review of Economic Doctrine, 1870-1929*, Oxford, Clarendon
Press, 1953, p. 157.

Laundhart had made interesting contribution in this context. He gave something like a pure theory of welfare economics. He showed that there is a sense in which exchange at equilibrium yields a maximum total utility. Laundhart argues that if exchange takes place at a price more favourable to the poorer party than the equilibrium price, not only will the gain for the poor man be greater, but there will be greater total gain. It is striking that he is a vehement critic of a Laissez Faire Policy at this particular juncture of the glorious time of Laissez Faire. He concludes that "principles of Laissez Faire laid down by 'Machesterism' simply means handing over the weaker to the mercies of the stronger.[38] (pp. 38-43, *Mathematische Begiu Udug der volk Swirt Schfafst*, 1885).

The need for governmental intervention is emphasized by another economist of this period. Sismondi agreed with the general principles of the classical economists but disagreed as to the ultimate aim and method. He breaks the orthodoxy and holds Laissez Faire responsible for growing inequalities. Well-being is the ultimate aim and a better distribution of produce for consumption brings ultimate happiness to people. Sismondi is an admixture of Smith's fundamentals and his own brand of liberalism.[39]

Mill leads the utilitarian school of the 19th century. "His philosophy was Bentham's utilitarianism" though his psychology that of his father."[40] (As found in *Principles of Political Economy*, Book IV, Ch. 1.) He lists the following as characterizing progressive economic advances in civilized nations . . ." "a progress in wealth," an advancement of what he called "material prospects," "increase in production and population," "the growth of man's power over nature" . . . "improvement in the business capacities of the general mass of mankind," "mankind's greater capacity of united action," "the capacity of cooperation which led to the formation of joint-stock companies" and "associations of work people either for production or for their common consumption." In short wealth or economic well-being consisted of all useful and agreeable things which possessed value in exchange and in this as evident from the above he included skill and talents as well. Though he is often described as leading the utilitarian bandwagon of his time, his liberal views were often at variance with his economic foundations. Though, a liberal, parliamentarian and in a restricted sense a politician, he was not really in touch with the liberal movement and its leaders except from the "book" approach. He did not foresee the full implication of utilitarianism as it might be applied under a liberal Government. Theoretically it could directly establish economic institutions like the Corporate form of enterprise to make the decisions on behalf of the thousand people they serve the goods and services, rather than the few

[38]*Ibid.*, p. 188.

[39]O.F. Bell, *History of Economic Thought*, The Donald Press and Company, New York, 1953, p. 290.

[40]O.F. Bell, *History of Economic Development*, The Donald Press and Company, New York, 1953, pp. 256-57.

who own the shares.

Mill like Marshall had the capacity of sympathizing with all cases. But Mill seems to have thought unlike Marshall that the term "pleasure" was suited to represent the aspiration of removal of poverty. "He had not Bentham's antipathy to other people's formulae but like Bentham he aimed at increasing the sum total of happiness.[41] He shows that the "hurt" caused by levying taxation on the poor is greater than that levied on the rich for the same amount.[42]

In spite of a lack of comprehension and cogency Mill can be rightly regarded as the forerunner of the Marshall-Pigou idea of national dividend. He pushed the implications of the "labour embodied theory to its logical conclusions and systematized the idea that economic welfare can be calculated in terms of capital, and can be increased with every increase in capital stock.

To find the magnitude of the net addition to wealth more attention has been paid to the distinction between productive and unproductive consumption and not to that between productive and unproductive labour. The net accumulation could come from the capitalist alone according to Smith and Ricardo. But to Mill it could come from anyone including the unproductive labourer who receives an income he might save and thus add to the net addition of wealth assuming wages to be above minimum. This line of thought led him to the logical conclusion of expanding a very interesting idea with regard to the concept of national dividend. In the *Principles* he defines the net produce as "whatever is annually produced beyond what is necessary for maintaining the stock of materials, and implements unimpaired for keeping all the productive labourers alive and in condition for work and just keeping their numbers without increase."[43] This is the logical outcome of treating economic welfare as technological function of given productive stocks irrespective of anticipation.[44]

THE NEO-CLASSICAL REORIENTATION OF WELFARE ECONOMICS

It can be said that the starting points of Marshall's theory are the concepts of utility and the marginal idea.[45] Schumpeter considers Marshall as belonging to the modern utility theory and Keynes credits Marshall as having independently discovered marginal utility. Economics to start with is the science of wealth which is the quantification of "satisfaction."

Marshall made his entry into Economics via ethics. In his *Memoriam* Keynes observes: "Marshall never departed explicitly from the utilitarian ideas which dominated the generation of economists who preceded him."[46]

[41] J.S. Mill, *Lectures on Progres and Poverty*, 1883.

[42] J.S. Mill, *National Taxation after the War*, 1917.

[43] J.S. Mill, *Principles of Political Economy*, p. 89.

[44] H.L.A. Myint, *Welfare Signification of Productive Lobour*, RES, 1943-44, p. 27.

[45] T. Parson, "Wants and Activities in Marshall," QJE, 1931-32, p. 102.

[46] J.M. Keynes, *Memorials of Alfred Marshall*, A.C. Pigou (ed.), Macmillan and Company Ltd., London, 1955, p. 9.

But in his handling of the matter he was more cautious than Sidgwick for there is no passage in his work in which he links economic studies to any ethical doctrine in particular. Economic problems could be solved not by an "an application of the hedonistic calculus" but by "a prior condition of the exercise of man's higher faculties," irrespective almost of what we mean by "higher."[47] In his anxiety to do good he was even inclined to undervalue such intellectual parts of the subject that were not directly connected with human well-being especially that of the working class and the like. An important result of utility analysis of Marshall is the conception of consumer's surplus in consumption and marginal productivity—a derivation of utility—in production which in economic sense consists in the satisfaction of wants. His entire theory is finally generalized in terms of maximum satisfaction doctrine.

In the public spirit of seeking for the maximum happiness Marshall is comparable with Mill. In their aspiration towards the removal of extreme poverty and degrading toil both Mill and Marshall are on equal grounds. But Marshall did not think, as Mill did that the term pleasure represented the incentives to such aspirations. "He had not Bentham's rabid antipathy to other people's formulae—but similar to Bentham he aimed at increasing the sum total of happiness."[48] The "hurt" increased by imposition of taxes on the poor is far greater than that levied on the rich.

While the neo-classical school headed by Marshall built on the superstructure laid by their classical predecessors they differed from them by their rejection of the hedonistic approach and sought to build a theoretical system without it. Marshall attempted to discover a means by which comparison could be made between benefits to individuals from private and governmental action (*Principles*, pp. 492-93) and thus to policy decisions. Exactly the same was the search made by Bentham when he looked for the "moral thermometer." But the difference is that Marshall abandoned the use of the words like pleasure, pain and happiness in favour of others like benefit which had a less hedonistic implication.[49]

As stated earlier Marshall was introduced to economics through Mill's principles. It was Mill who furnished the link between the classical trio—Adam Smith-Malthus-Ricardo and the neo-classical Marshall. Mill's Philosophy has been used by Marshall as the anchorage for his own theories. However Marshall was not a utilitarian in the Benthamite sense nor a liberal political and social reformer in the sense of Mill.

In his inaugural lecture after his election to Professorship at Cambridge in 1885 as a successor to Professor Fawcett, Marshall gave an account of "those intelligent applications of his doctrine of Laissez Faire" which assumed

[47]*Ibid.*, p. 9.

[48]F.Y. Edgeworth, *Memorials to Alfred Marshall*, A.C. Pigou (ed.), p. 17. (Reference to Marshall's *Lectures on Progress and Poverty*, 1883.)

[49]E. Whittaker, *History of Economic Ideas*, Longman Green & Co., London, 1940, p. 166.

whatever increases wealth must necessarily increase well-being. He showed
that the same sum of money measures a greater pleasure for the poor than
for the rich. This helps in determining the relation between the money gain
from any given social or individual change and the total increase in happiness arising from it. This according to Marshall properly belongs to the
"economic organon."[50] The measurement of either desire or satisfaction,
for Marshall, is not impossible. Lack of a direct measure can be made good
by relying on a measurement which "economic supplies of the motive or
the moving force of action, we make it serve with all its faults, both for
the desires which prompt action and for the satisfaction which results from
them."

There are three things implied in the above statement, viz. (*i*) the motive
or the moving force to action, (*ii*) the desire behind this and (*iii*) the satisfaction resulting from this. The first can be measured according to Marshall. Marshall made a significant departure from the classical tenet that
satisfaction is at the maximum under Laissez Faire. He considered the possibility of turning individual action into channels more conducive to general
welfare than those of Laissez Faire. Particularly he proved that with free
competition there would be overinvestment in increasing cost industries and
underinvestment in decreasing cost industries[51] and therefore averred that
the sum total of satisfaction in a society might be increased beyond the
maximum attainable under Laissez Faire in a state of perfect equili
brium in perfect competition, by taxing the commodities produced under
decreasing returns and using the proceeds to subsidize commodities
produced under increasing returns.[52] This was latter amplified by Pigou
and Kahn.

Even though the virtues of the doctrine of maximum satisfaction had been
questioned many times earlier on a variety of standpoints—for the first time
Marshall questioned it "within the range of the pure theory". . . . the first
time on the theoretical plane.[53] This has to be contrasted with Walrasian contention that a State of pure equilibrium all round guarantees a maximum
of satisfaction for all concerned. Even allowing for inequalities of income
Marshall showed by the sum of money that the desirer is just willing to
pay for the desired thing. The force of motive is this sum of money.
Secondly, money could also serve as a measure for desires and satisfaction.
Regarding the marginal utility of money as constant, Marshall gives the
money measure of happiness as "the excess of the price which a man
would be willing to pay rather than go without having a thing over what
he actually pays"[54] for that maximum satisfaction and competitive equilibrium are not conterminus, through the increasing and decreasing cost

---

[50]Marshall, "The Present Position of Economics," Inaugural Lecture at Cambridge,
1885 in A. C. Pigou, (ed.), *Memorials to Alfred Marshall*.

[51]T. Parson, "Wants and activities in Marshall," *QJE*. 1931-32. pp. 25-126.

[52]A. Marshall, *Principles of Economics*, p. 392.

[53]J. A. Schumpeter, *History of Economic Analysis*, E. B. Schumpeter (ed.), New York,
Oxford University Press, 1952, p. 1070.

[54]A. Marshall, *op. cit.*, p. 131.

industries.[55] Therefore the neo-classical economists cannot be all treated as "unconditional eulogists" of pure competition.[56]

The axiom formulated by Marshall to attain a level of satisfaction higher than that realizable under the Laissez Faire is this: "If the producers were as a class very much poorer than the consumers, the aggregate satisfaction might be increased by restricting supply by which demand price will rise (with inelastic demand). If the consumers as a class are very much poorer than the producers, the aggregate satisfaction might be increased by extending production beyond the equilibrium amount and selling the commodities at a loss. Hence Marshall gives a broad proposition that satisfaction can prima facie be increased by a redistribution, voluntary or compulsory.[57] Marshall started out with an enquiry into the science of economics which dealt partly with man and partly with wealth. He placed the emphasis on the latter in order to make it a servant of man, and improve his well-being. The earlier classical school considered economic order merely as a mechanism of want satisfaction. Economic process was the means to the end of want satisfaction and the human qualities involved in such a process was of no importance. This Marshall was unwilling to accept because for him the development of the character is the main issue of human life. In his analysis of wants, he stresses on the "science of activities and not on the science of wants."[58] These two are supplements. One is incomplete without the other.

The doctrine of consumer's surplus, Marshall's significant innovation in the quantitative study of the science of well-being has undergone major improvements. Marshall entertained high hopes originally of making the consumer's surplus principle to subserve as an instrument of social betterment. But he himself eventually lost faith in it. Despite this it is burdened with severe criticism. Little calls this as a mere "theoretical toy." This doctrine has attracted the ingenuity of several eminent economists[59] like Hicks to use it as a practical tool of welfare analysis.

National income or dividend is a better indicator of national prosperity than national wealth. This is because income consists chiefly of commodities in such form as to give pleasure directly. The national income concept is

[55]A. Marshall, *Principles of Economics*, London, 1920, pp. 415-16.

[56]J. A. Schumpeter, *History of Economic Analysis*, Oxford University Press, 1952, p. 985.

[57]A. Marshall, *Principles of Economics,* Macmillan and Company Ltd., London, 1920, 8th edn. (reprint), 1949, p. 391.

[58]*Ibid.*

[59]On the basis of the theory of Consumers' choice, Hotelling presented a formula of consumers surplus in 1938 which was more precisely formulated by Dr Sono in 1942. Ichimura in 1953 gives the same formula in terms of line integral. Ichimura proves that the concepts of consumer's surplus can be derived from this formula when the integral path is properly chosen and that if the standard commodity is additively separable from the other commodities. The formulae derived both from demand functions and in terms of marginal rate of satisfaction are given in S. Ichimura, "On the Concept of Consumer's Sprnlus," *Econometrica*, 1953, p. 484.

the major link between Marshall and Pigou. Marshall's optimism is apparent in his frequent references to the positive relation between the size of
national output and values like the health, strength and vigour of the
people and fullest development of their spiritual, and physical faculties.
Modern industries and commerce stimulate such values while poverty
harms these values, consequently reducing efficiency and output.[60] In the
interests of the community there is a prima facie case for state intervention
directly and indirectly. Marshall thus paved the way for state interference in
economic performance which forms yet another basic link between him and
Pigou. He did not therefore mean unrestricted laissez-faire though a
"rugged individualist" he was. Neither did he defend the social and economic inequalities as did his predecessors. Rather he supported the lessening
of the inequality such that it "would not sap the springs of free initiative
and strength of character."[61] There could be no moral justification for extreme poverty side by side with great wealth. However he was equally
averse to the emergence of socialistic movement as the "greatest present
danger to human well-being"[62] in supporting public in the place of private
management. This would stigmatize private enterprise. For almost the same
reason he distrusted the monopoly.

Marshall's contribution to welfare economics is a landmark, since the
current work in economics as developed by Pigou and Pareto harks back
to his teachings. To mention the two basic contributions, firstly he redis-
covered Dupuit's Consumer's Surplus and presented welfare economics with
an analytical tool and secondly he formulated several propositions of the
kind that are typical of modern welfare economics. Marshall indeed was
the creator of genuine school comprising of Edgeworth, Pigou, Robertson,
and Keynes. They thought in terms of a "well defined scientific organon"[63]
and supplemented this by a bond of personal cohesion. They all started from
his teachings but seemed to have travelled far beyond it.

The Need for Human Valuation—the Gospel of Hobson

Hobson is an important economist to reckon with in the development of
the thought on economic welfare. Writing a decade earlier than Pigou he
almost marks the turning point in the trend of thinking through his down-
right condemnation of all that is traditional theory and putting human
welfare atop the economic barriers. He strongly disbelieved that free competition would any longer be tenable and held that pecuniary standard
of market price was no index to welfare. Economic science could not serve
in the work of human valuation. On the other hand industry ought to be
evaluated in terms of the standard of welfare, good life being its proper

    [60]H. J. Levein, "Standards of Welfare in Economic Thought," *Quarterly Journal of Economics*, 1956. p. 124.

    [61]A. Marshall, *op. cit.*, p. 714.

    [62]A. Marshall, *Ibid.*, p. 714.

    [63]J. A. Schumpeter, *History of Economic Analysis*, Oxford University Press, New York, p. 1070.

test. Later Veblen[64] also joined Hobson in the critical examination of the classical economics as well as Pigouvian welfare theory with reference to these conflicts and convergence of economic and non-economic welfare. They also studied alternative institutional arrangements to narrow the gap between economic and non-economic welfare.

The fundamental question of Hobson is this. What happens to the basic needs of workers, investors, employers and consumers—their chance to realize their potentialities when national output rises? He agrees with Pigou that changes in output probably change economic and general welfare in the same direction "bearing evidence to the contrary." However Hobson is much concerned with such evidence which he believed to be widely neglected.

Hobson proposes to strike a balance between human costs and human happiness. In his welfare philosophy man is more than an organism in the scheme of production of marketable wealth. His needs are objective in the productive process and human costs arising in the productive process are the sacrifices which must be balanced against the utilities created. Hobson's reasoning has a fundamental flaw in concluding that it is the small savers and those engaged in manual labour who bear the cost of production which somehow borders on the outdated sacrifice and abstinence theory of the early economist. For the purpose of human valuation, Hobson attempts to discover and formulate an intellectual procedure. "A human valuation of industry will give equal attention to productive consumption, will express cost and utility in terms of human efforts and satisfaction and will substitute for the monetary standard of wealth, a standard of well-being." The human standard according to him is to be conceived in terms of a good and desirable life. He takes the desirable life as the norm and calls it organic welfare. The provision of standard of valuation in terms of organic welfare has two advantages, viz. it gives a sound method of estimating those physical costs and utilities, with which the major part of industry is associated. Secondly it avoids the grave errors common to the mechanical treatment of economic science based on commercial wealth. Unless society is treated as an organic structure, social interpretation of industry is not possible. This task of devising a method of valuation of industry demands that economic processes shall be considered "not only in their bearing upon individual lives but in the bearing upon the welfare of society." The contradiction of production and consumption, cost and utility—physical and spiritual welfare, individual and social welfare, all find their likeliest mode of reconcilement and harmony in the treatment of society as an organism."

For this purpose Hobson proposes a social control of practically all economic activity to ensure full employment, good wages, health, education and recreation. In giving omnivalence to the State to achieve the greatest human happiness Hobson only falls into the category of "utopian socialism"

---

[64]J. A. Hobson, *Work and Wealth*, second edn, London, 1933, p. 1-3; Veblen, *Theory of Business Enterprise*, New York, 1932; *Place of Science in Modern Civilization*, New York, 1952.

a grouping that cannot be imputed to Pigou."[65] There is striking similarity between him and Pigou in their zeal for state intervention. In view of the mal-production and mal-consumption state intervention is essential to enforce better distribution. Hobson's basis of social reform is "for each in accordance with his needs as consumer."

In evaluating Hobson's contribution to welfare economics one thing that strikes us is that he was mainly engaged in translating the ideals of John Ruskin who desired to "re-enthrone craftsmanship as a substitute for machine age" into the economic system with its essence as human value. At his best Hobson is only the "economic theorist of the middle class reformers"[66] whose concern is welfare and not wealth. The term economic welfare obviously implies that the system of thought is designed to promote welfare in the society. That Hobson's ideas intended the furtherance of social welfare is the distinguishing characteristic of his thought. This is drawn from the individuality of his orientation. His critical writings are sharply heretical. The individuality of Hobson has been aptly described by H. W. Peck who terms his approach as "the expression of a personality who combines the characteristic of a theoretical man, the social man and the artistic man."[67] The theorist in him is shown by his rigid training in economic thought of the Marshallian school—the inability of working the competitive system for the ameliorative principles turned him a social man who felt the necessity for making his economic theory more functional to eliminate the injustices. The artist in him chose the aesthetically satisfying goal of society based on human valuation. This potent directive force he labelled as the "definitely humanist and ethical trend of Ruskinian thought." Probably this conscious humanitarian aim has earned for his economics the apellation of "welfare."

[65]J. F. Bell, *History of Economic Thought*, Sir Ronald Press Company, New York, 1953, p. 625.

[66]F. Neff, *Economic Doctrines*, McGraw Hill Book Company, 1950, p. 425.

[67]M. Lazare, "Welfare Economics—A Misnomer," *American Economic Review*, 1940, p. 347.

A.P. SRINIVASAMURTHY

The Problem of Underutilization of Productive Capacity in Indian Industry

INTRODUCTION

Since the Independence and more specifically since the adoption of economic planning in 1951, India has launched a programme of rapid industrialization of the country. One of the strange and rather unfortunate features of the process of Indian industrialization has been the fact of underutilization in many branches of industry, of the increased industrial productive capacity that is being built up under the programmes of industrial development.

The importance of utilizing the productive capacity created by investment can hardly be overemphasized. Achievement of higher rate of growth of output, employment and income and increasing the supply of industrial products *commensurate* with the investments made in industries depends largely on capacity utilization, which in turn depends on conditions relating to the supply of inputs and the demand for their products. Moreover, the effective utilization of existing capacity would give the necessary impetus to fresh investment, making the process of industrial development proceed smoothly. Allowing unutilized capacity to exist works, in a way, against the objective of self-reliance. For, the loss of potential output may prevent possible import substitution and/or export increase. This may also add to trade deficit and consequent balance of payment difficulties. Another serious matter associated with underutilization is inflation. When large investments are made without commensurate increase in total output, inflationary pressures are generated. Beside, if the productive capacity is not fully utilized, the cost of production and the price of products tend to rise which also add to inflationary forces. In a situation where, on account of several other factors, inflationary pressures tend to gather momentum it is unwise to create new industrial productive capacities which cannot be utilized. The volume of excess capacity also indicates the extent to which the economy is failing to make the best use of its scarce capital resources. It also adversely affects the task of stepping up the saving rate. Maximum production through fuller utilization of the capacities already created would help further capital formation. Thus, from various points of view a full utilization of the productive capacity already created is of very great importance and any great degree of underutilization which also persists over a fairly long period must be regarded as a major problem which needs prompt attention and corrective measures. The situation in Indian industry in this respect demands a clear analysis of the several questions which are involved. What are the trends as regards underutilization of industrial capacity? What exactly has been the degree of underutilization of the industrial productive capacity? Does this situation indicate that there was misallocation of investment in industries whose products did not have commensurate demand? Or, is it that the potential capacity could not be utilized for reasons other than the lack of demand for the products of the industries? What are the more recent trends as regards industrial capacity utilization and what prospects are there of a full (or near full) utilization of this capacity? Answers to these questions are important both in judging the soundness of investment allocation under India's plans and also in evaluating India's development strategy in general. Basic to the analysis of the above questions is the availability of correct estimates of the productive capacity of the several industries in India and the extent of utilization as indicated by actual output. It is widely known that fully dependable data in these respects is not available. The available data on industrial capacity also is based on alternative approaches, viz., the "peak-output approach" and the "installed capacity approach." In section I, we shall examine these alternative approaches made in computing the data on trends in industrial production capacity and in its utilization (and hence also its underutilization) with a view to understanding their limitations and ascertaining their appropriateness in studying the problem of utilization of productive capacity in Indian industry. In section II we shall present a brief picture of trends in the degree of underutilization in Indian industries based on selected available statistical data. In section III, an attempt is made to set forth the various factors which generally contribute to underutilization of industrial capacity. Section IV states the conclusions.

SECTION I: THE AVAILABLE DATA AND ITS LIMITATIONS

The importance of having correct estimates of industrial productive capacity and the extent of underutilization is obvious. But the concepts of *industrial capacity* and its *utilization* do not lend themselves to any simple and unambiguous definition and measuring it in practice also presents difficulties. The conceptual aspects have been discussed in the theoretical literature on the subject[1] but it is not proposed to review these theoretical discussions here. What is relevant here is to note that several studies[2] made

---

[1]See, A. Phillips, "An Appraisal of Measures of Capacity" in *American Economic Review*, May 1963; L.R. Klein, "Some Theoretical Issues in the Measurement of Capacity," in *Econometrica*, April 1960; and Klein and Preston, "Some New Results in the Measurement of Capacity Utilization," in *American Economic Review*, March 1967.

[2]A few of these are: M. Budin and S. Paul, "Utilization of Indian Industrial Capacity, 1949-59," *Indian Economic Journal*, July 1961; R.K. Koti, *Utilization of Industrial Capacity in India, 1967-68*, Gokhale Institute Series No.9, 1968; Ramaswamy and P. Fouts,

in recent years on the problem of underutilization of production potential in Indian industries have been based primarily on *either* the statistics furnished by the Reserve Bank of India *or* the Central Statistical Organization. These two sources of the data may be taken to represent typically the *"peak output method* and *the installed capacity method* respectively of indicating the production potential of an industry.

In the peak output method the capacity of industry is taken to be indicated by the highest level of output actually achieved so far and underutilization is measured as the difference between this level and the actual production. In the installed capacity method, on the other hand, the maximum output that a plant is capable of producing is established on the basis of the number of operable shifts appropriate to the industry concerned. It is assumed that the necessary inputs are all available. The extent of underutilization is then taken to be indicated by the difference between this level of output and the actual output. While there can be little controversy regarding the available data on the actual production in different industries in India, the use of the data relating to industrial capacity as indicated by the above two approaches to assess the extent of underutilization of the industrial capacity raises several points for consideration. In what follows we shall examine critically the limitations and usefulness of the data based on these two approaches for a correct understanding of the problem of underutilization of industrial capacity in India in recent years.

The Reserve Bank of India in its first study[3] on *Recent Recessionary Trends in Organized Industry* (July 1968) used the data on "installed capacity" from the *Monthly Statistics of the Production of Selected Industries of India* published by the C.S.O. On the basis of these, it worked out the capacity-utilization ratios for different industries. In its second study also, on *Excess Capacity and Production Potential in Selected Industries in India*[4] trends in underutilization of industrial capacity were studied for the period 1963-67 on the basis of "installed capacity" data taken from several sources. But in the subsequent studies[5] on the problem of utilization of productive capacity, the Reserve Bank has adopted the "peak output approach" to indicate what it calls "potential production." The earlier

---

Utilization of Industrial Capacity, GOI and USAID, 1965; *Underutilization of Industrial Capacity*, NCAER, New Delhi, 1966; Yogindar K. Alagh, "Utilization of Industrial Capacity in Indian Economy" in J.C. Sandesara (ed.), *The Indian Economy—Performance and Prospects*, University of Bombay; Samuel Paul, Industrial Performance and Government controls" in J.C. Sandesara (ed.), *op. cit*, K.N. Raj, "Growth and Stagnation in Indian Industrial Development," *Economic and Political Weekly*, Annual Number, February 1976 and the studies by Reserve Bank of India, *RBI Bulletin*, July 1968, April 1969, April 1970, March 1972, October 1973 and September 1975.

[3] See *R.B.I. Bulletin*, July 1968, pp. 862-77.

[4] See *R.B.I. Bulletin*, April 1969.

[5] "Index of Potential Production and Potential-Utilization Ratio for the Manufacturing Industries in India," *R.B.I. Bulletin*, April 1970; "Trends in the Index of Potential Production and Potential Utilization Ratio for the Manufacturing Industries during 1970," *R.B.I. Bulletin*, March 1972, October 1973 and September 1975.

approach was stated to suffer from some defects.[6] *First*, it yielded certain figures which showed actual production being in excess of installed capacity which is obviously an unrealistic situation. *Secondly*, capacity for each industry was based on different considerations—some on two shifts, some on three shifts and so on. *Thirdly*, in the case of some industries like cotton and jute textiles, units of measurement of capacity are different from the units in which actual production is expressed. *Fourthly*, installed capacity figures are given for some items only. These reasons are given by the Reserve Bank for giving up the "installed capacity" basis in favour of the "peak output approach" to measure what it labels as "potential production" distinguishing this from "capacity." The Reserve Bank of India quotes the Wharton School in the U.S.A. which has developed capacity measures based on peaks of the seasonally adjusted quarterly output series of the Federal Reserve Board. The Wharton School is also said to have developed indices of capacity based on this peak output approach. Though there are some differences in details of computation, the Reserve Bank seems to find justification for choosing the "peak output approach" to indicate potential production, on the basis of its adoption for the advanced countries like U.S.A., U.K., France, Germany, Italy, Belgium and Netherlands by the Wharton School. We shall comment on these several grounds later in this section. We shall first describe what the Reserve Bank means by the terms "index of potential production" and "potential utilization ratio."

"Potential" for any given industry is defined "as the peak [maximum] level of production attained for that industry at the point of time or prior to it at which potential is measured."[7] Since the official series of index numbers of industrial production are available on a comparable monthly basis for a number of industries, "potential for an industry for a year has been taken as the peak *monthly* level of the production index reached by the industry during the year under consideration."[8] This differs from the Wharton School capacity index which is based on quarterly peaks. Though the question whether the peaks should be considered on the basis of monthly or quarterly production or for some other period is debatable. We need not enter into this discussion here. The monthly peak can be taken to represent the highest level of production reached in the industry concerned. In the case of three highly seasonal industries, viz., tea, salt and sugar, the annual average production index has been considered in choosing the peak production. This seems to be reasonable.

In order to construct the "index of potential production" the peak levels of production indices since 1960 are first obtained for all important manufacturing industries. Index of potential production is then derived by taking monthly peak production for the year 1960 as 100 (the base) and adjusting

[6]*R.B.I. Bulletin*, April 1970, p. 574.
[7]"Index of Potential Production and Potential-Utilization Ratio for Manufacturing Industries in India," *R.B.I. Bulletin*, April 1970, p. 575.
[8]*Ibid.*

the rest of the peak production figures proportionately. In deriving the index of potential production for subgroups, groups and all manufacturing industries appropriate weights are given. In presenting this data industries have been rightly grouped *firstly* into (*a*) all manufacturing industries, (*b*) basic industries, (*c*) capital goods industries, (*d*) intermediate goods industries and (*e*) consumer goods industries and *secondly* into (*a*) agro-based industries, (*b*) metal-based industries and (*c*) chemical-based industries. Trends in index of potential production since 1961 have been worked out in respect of these groups.

Next, in order to assess the level at which the industries are operating compared to the peak level achieved, the Reserve Bank has worked out the "potential-utilization ratio" for an industry (or industry group) which is defined as "the percentage ratio of the average monthly production index to the potential production of the industry (or industry group) during the period of one year."[9] In the case of sugar, tea and salt potential-utilization ratio refers to the average production to the potential production index for the year under reference. Potential-utilization ratio for "all the manufacturing industries" sector is then compiled as the weighted average of the ratios for individual industries. Utilization rates and trends since 1961 are also worked out for the different groups as under the index of potential production.

It is claimed that a measure of industrial potential utilization on the above lines will be helpful for any analysis of current economic development and serve as an important statistical indicator of changes in industrial activity over time.[10] This statement, however, does not indicate the limitations of this measure which needs to be emphasized.

In the first place, the use of the term "potential production" for the realized peak level of output is highly misleading. *Potential* really means what is latent, expressing a possibility which meaning is also what is conveyed by the term *capacity*. So, any attempt to distinguish between these two terms as having different connotation, as is done by the Reserve Bank, is unjustified. It must be noted that where the peak output is generally less than the installed capacity level of output, it would be incorrect to use the former as the basis for estimating the extent of underutilization. The extent of utilization of capacity as compared with the peak production may show a fairly high percentage thereby concealing the gravity of the problem of real underutilization. The use of the term "potential-utilization" ratio in this context is apt to be misleading as it may create an erroneous impression of the real extent of underutilization of industrial capacity. What is suggested here, therefore, is that it would be more appropriate to use the term "index of peak production" instead of "index of potential production" and the term *peak production-utilization ratio* instead of "potential-utilization ratio."

It may be noted here that in the April 1969 study by the Reserve Bank of India (paper prepared by M.V. Raghavachari) the index of *potential*

[9]*Ibid.*, p. 580.
[10]*Ibid.*, p. 575.

production was computed on the basis of installed capacity taking first the then existing shift pattern and then the desirable multi-shift pattern.[11] This meaning of potential production could have been kept up in the subsequent papers on the subject published by the Reserve Bank instead of creating confusion by using the term "potential production" to indicate the peak level of output realized.

Secondly, besides the above terminological aspects of measurement of underutilization of industrial capacity stated above, there are some fundamental grounds on which the "installed capacity" approach is to be preferred to the "peak-output approach." We shall state briefly a few of these arguments.

(*a*) When the level of peak output itself is low in spite of the availability of large installed capacities the peak output cannot be taken to represent the "optimal" output. "Excess capacity" based on this concept of industrial capacity will then be underestimated.

(*b*) Besides, if the earlier peak production level is not exceeded and replaced by new higher levels of peak production even when the installed capacity is increasing, an incorrect impression may be created that new investments are not taking place in these industries.

(*c*) In the case of industries whose production schedules are not on a monthly basis, a monthly peak does not have much significance as representing industrial capacity. It is possible that the finished product may come out in a particular month though it has been in the process for several months. Peak output take account of the finished output of the month. In such cases monthly peak output may not reflect real capacity of the industry and only "installed capacity" approach can be helpful.

Next, we may note that the arguments given by the Reserve Bank of India[12] to give up the installed capacity approach in favour of the peak output approach are not convincing enough.

(*a*) One reason given is that, with the available figures, for several industries actual production exceeded the installed capacity. This position is, indeed, unrealistic. But this argument can only support the need for a more realistic estimate of installed capacity. For, it is illogical to hold that actual production can exceed the installed capacity. In the situation referred to by the Reserve Bank of India, the actual production must have been increased by working the factories for more shifts. So, it becomes important to consider the appropriate number of shifts to be taken into account in estimating the installed capacity. If on the basis of available figures actual production was in excess of installed capacity, it only suggests the need for a more scientific estimate of installed capacity. Switching over to the peak output approach on this ground cannot be justified. Indeed the C.S.O. has revised its method of computing installed capacity on the basis of appropriate number of shifts for different industries.[13]

[11] *R.B.I. Bulletin*, April 1969.
[12] *Ibid.*, April 1970, p. 574.
[13] See, *C.S.O.*, *M.S.P. of Selected Industries in India*, March 1974, 1976.

(*b*) A second argument adduced by the Reserve Bank of India for considering installed capacity as inappropriate is the capacity for different industries would have to be worked out on the basis of different number of shifts, i.e., some on two shifts, some on three and so on. This argument is untenable beacause, given the availability of inputs, the number of operable shifts in industries is a technological factor and whatever is this number for an industry should be taken to determine the optimal output that it is capable of yielding. It may also be noted that in the case of industries like some chemical industries the plant has to be kept in continuous operation and potential in these cases will necessarily have to be worked out on this basis itself. So the adoption of different number of shifts for different industries cannot be taken as a relevant argument against the appropriateness of the installed capacity approach.

(*c*) The third argument against the installed capacity approach to the measurement of capacity is that in the case of some industries like cotton and jute textiles unit of measurement of installed capacity is in looms while production is in yards. This again points to the need for adopting a uniform unit of measurement both for installed capacity and actual production rather than being an argument against the installed capacity approach to the measurement of industrial capacity. For instance, in textiles though the production in terms of yardage may vary according to the count of yarn used, it should be possible to work out some standard relationship between loomage and yardage so that a uniform unit of measurement could be adopted to measure both capacity and actual production.

(*d*) Finally, it is stated that installed capacity is given only for some items. This reason mentioned by the Reserve Bank of India can only point to the need for wider coverage of the data. Indeed, the C.S.O. has been improving from time to time the coverage of the data that is presented in the Monthly Statistics of Production of Selected Industries. It is obvious from the above discussion that the various arguments mentioned by the Reserve Bank of India as having led it to adopt the peak output approach giving up the installed capacity basis adopted at first are not convincing. If the object was to indicate trends in the industrial capacity and the extent of its utilization and underutilization it would have been better for the Reserve Bank to have continued its reliance on the installed capacity approach which it adopted at first.

It may, however, be pointed out that the statistics of peak production and variations from this level in the various industries may have a usefulness of their own. For instances, if in any year, the level of output is much below the peak output achieved earlier, a comparative study of the situations in the two years should enable us to sort out the constraints which have prevented achievement of the peak level. But, a more fundamental consideration relates to the narrowing of the disparity between the maximum output that can be achieved with the existing installed capacity and the peak output actually realized. If this disparity is great and persists over a fairly long period it does become a matter of very great concern.

Presently, our concern is with an analysis of the problem of underutilization of industrial capacity in India. From what has been discussed so far it is clear that for this purpose it is not appropriate to depend on the peak output approach and the data furnished by the Reserve Bank's studies on what it calls "index of potential production" and "potential-utilization ratio." It would be more appropriate to rely on the data for industrial capacity based on the "installed capacity approach." But even this available data has its own peculiar drawbacks which may be set forth here before proceeding to its use in the next section.

As stated earlier, the installed capacity refers to the assessed capacity of the industry concerned based upon the appropriate number of shifts. It represents the "optimum level" of utilization of the plant. But there seems to be some vagueness about the concept of installed capacity as it has been used in India with reference to industries. The main difficulty seems to be that standard definitions appropriate to different industries are yet to be evolved. This appears to be rather strange because industrial licensing system which has been in operation for several years now requires for its precise application a satisfactory method of working out installed capacity and additions thereto.

In estimating installed capacity it should be remembered that there are some difficulties to be overcome. In the first place, the notion of "capacity" is, perhaps, difficult to apply to an industry as a whole. For, the several units in an industry differ in their efficiency besides exhibiting a diversity in respect of products manufactured and the techniques employed. This difficulty will have to be got over by determining for different groups of industries a sample of plants and range of products as a basis for collecting and computing on a continuing basis statistics on capacity and actual output.

A second difficulty relates to the number of operable shifts to be taken into account in estimating installed capacity. Obviously this cannot be the same for all industries. There are some industries like some of the chemical industries where the plant has to be kept in continuous operation and hence these industries will have to work all the shifts. For those which need not be kept in continuous operation the problem is one of deciding the number of operable shifts on which to assess the installed capacity. Even the reporting of installed capacity in the *Monthly Statistics of Production of Selected Industries in India* has not been found satisfactory from this point of view. In the analysis of utilization of installed capacity made by the Reserve Bank of India in July 1968 on the basis of the C.S.O. data it was found that for several industries actual production exceeded the installed capacity,[14] which is, indeed, an illogical situation. This situation arose because for most of the product groups the C.S.O. data on installed capacity was based on a single shift basis. The M. V. Raghavachari

[14]See Appendix I on page 596 of the *R. B. I. Bulletin*, April 1970.

Paper[15] pointed out cases where the M. S. P. shift basis was incorrect. He states that sixteen stated chemical industries were working on a three-shift basis while M. S. P. showed single shift working for these industries. So also, seven stated metal and engineering industries were found to be working on a two-shift basis while M. S. P. showed single shift operation. In another study[16] by Professor Samuel Paul of the Ahmedabad Institute of Management, the shift pattern adopted by the C.S.O. in estimating installed capacities has been criticized. He has pointed out that the category of 275 industries which the C.S.O. takes as operable for only single shift is really capable of being worked on a two-shift basis; that for the second category of seven product groups 2.5 shifts would be more realistic than the two-shift basis as assumed by the C. S. O. The chief point to note is that the data on installed capacity reported in the *M.S.P. of Selected Industries in India of the C.S.O.* has its own limitations chiefly because of the fact that its reckoning of the number of operable shifts has been open to question.[17]

If we should have a correct idea of the real productive capacity of an industry, it is necessary to find out the appropriate number of shifts and the number of workable days in a year for this industry. These may differ from industry to industry. But these are technical issues which should be capable of being worked out by technical experts. If this is done, the installed capacity would be a satisfactory basis on which to obtain a universally acceptable single series of "estimates of installed capacities and unutilized capacities" for all industries in India. From the point of view of planning the future growth pattern of industries on sound lines and also for taking the remedial measures needed to match actual production with real potential productive capacity it would be useful if such estimates are made availabel by employing the statistical expertise that exists in the country.

We may conclude this section with the statement that the Reserve Bank of India's date in the publications referred to earlier can only be helpful in analyzing the variations in industrial production around the peak output and not for examining trends in the under-utilization of industrial capacity. For the latter, it is the available data on installed capacity which is more appropriate though this data also has some limitations as pointed out above.

SECTION II: EXTENT OF UNDERUTILIZATION OF INDUSTRIAL CAPACITY

Underutilization of industrial capacity becomes a problem only if it exceeds what may be regarded as inevitable and permissible normal level and if it

---

[15]"Excess Capacity and Production Potential in Selected Industries in India," *R. B. I. Bulletin*, April 1969.

[16]Paul, Samuel, *op. cit.*

[17]It is learnt that recently the C.S.O. has adopted a more appropriate shift-pattern for assessing "installed capacity" of industries in India. But data based on this is not available.

tends to persist for several years. Again, the gravity of the problem also depends upon the number of industries suffering from this malady. A full understanding of the nature and extent of the problem in all its aspects would require a detailed analysis of the industry-wise and unit-wise position in respect of the growth of installed capacity and its utilization for a period covering many years. No such detailed study is attempted here. The position in respect of capacity utilization *vis-a-vis* the growth of installed capacity by broad categories of industry like consumers' goods industries, intermediate goods industries and capital goods industries, is indicated, the objective being just to assess in broad terms the over-all intensity of the problem in India.

At the outset, in view of the wide use that has been made of the Reserve Bank's data on potential-utilization ratio to indicate the extent of under-utilization of industrial capacity, it might be appropriate to exhibit this data side by side with the data based on installed capacity to show the difference and support the contention made in Section I that the Reserve Bank of India's data is inappropriate for assessing underutilization of real industrial capacity. The relevant figures are given in Table I.

It is evident from the figures in the table that underutilization of capacity is considerably understated if we use the peak output-utilization ratios as the basis. For all industries, the extent of underutilization works out at only 12.1 per cent, 18.9 per cent, and 20.6 per cent for the three periods

TABLE 1

Average Rates of Utilization of Installed Capacity and the Peak Output-Utilization Rates

| Industry group | Period | | | | | |
| | 1961-1965 | | 1966-1968 | | 1969-1971 | |
	I.C. Approach	P.O. Approach	I.C. Approach	P.O. Approach	I.C. Approach	P.O. Approach
Consumer goods	46.3	88.5	48.6	83.4	53.0	84.6
Intermediate goods	64.3	89.2	60.9	83.6	61.2	78.5
Capital goods	57.6	83.0	42.3	65.3	42.8	59.1
All industries	53.6	87.9	52.1	81.1	54.5	79.4

Note: "*I.C. Approach*" figures indicate the average rates of utilization of Installed capacity as given by Samuel Paul, "Industrial Performance and Government Control." in J.C. Sandesara (ed.), *Indian Economy—Performance and Prospects,* Table II on p. 639.

"*P.O. Approach*" figures indicate the peak output-utilization ratio as worked out by the Reserve Bank of India. Averages for the periods are calculated from the yearly figures given in the *Reserve Bank of India Bulletins* of April 1970, March 1972 and October 1973.

1961-65, 1966-68 and 1969-71 *respectively* according to the peak output-utilization ratios, while as per utilization of installed capacity these figures are substantially higher, being 46.4 per cent, 47.9 per cent and 45.5 per cent respectively. Thus compared to the peak output the actual output is fairly high while compared to installed capacity it is significantly low. It is obvious that it is the latter which would give a truer picture of the real gravity of the problem of idle capacity in Indian industry.

Next, it is necessary to examine the belief that the problem of underutilization is only a recent phenomenon dating from 1966-67, when industrial stagnation is said to have set in. A study of the trends in utilization of industrial capacity in the several years prior to this date shows that the problem of underutilization existed from a very much earlier date. We have the figures worked out by C.N. Vakil and P.R. Brahmananda for the period 1946-54, which are presented in Table 2. The table shows the number of industries classified according to the degree of utilization of the available capacity in each of the years during 1946-54.

TABLE 2

Number of Industries Classified According to Utilization of Capacity

Figures in brackets give percentage

Utilization of capacity	Number of Industries								
	1946	1947	1948	1949	1950	1951	1952	1953	1954
Less than 25%	6 (18)	4 (10)	4 (7)	13 (20)	8 (10)	8 (10)	14 (18)	13 (16)	5 (6)
25% to 50%	9 (27)	16 (39)	18 (32)	20 (31)	25 (32)	23 (30)	25 (31)	27 (33)	24 (30)
50% to 75%	9 (27)	9 (22)	19 (34)	18 (28)	27 (34)	18 (23)	22 (27)	21 (26)	25 (31)
75% and above	10 (30)	12 (30)	16 (28)	14 (22)	19 (24)	29 (37)	19 (24)	20 (24)	27 (33)
Total	34 (100)	41 (100)	57 (100)	65 (100)	79 (100)	78 (100)	80 (100)	81 (100)	81 (100)

(Figures are rounded and may not add up)

Source: C.N. Vakil and P.R. Brahmananda, *Planning for an Expanding Economy*, p. 23.

Note: The figures in the table are worked out by Vakil and Brahmananda on the basis of figures contained in the *Monthly Statistics of Production of Selected Industries in India* which lists more than eighty types of industrial activities. They have worked out the percentage of utilization in each year to the available capacity and have classified the different industries according to the degree of utilization of capacity in each year.

From this data emerges the fact that even during the years before the commencement of planning about 50 per cent of the number of industries had an idle capacity of about 50 per cent. This position continued in the years 1952-54 too. This was a period when the rapid expansion of industrialization, in the sense in which it began since the Second Plan, had not yet begun. Industries in the public sector were relatively less compared to the position which developed since the Second Five Year Plan. Nevertheless, in the post-Independence years 1947-51, thanks to certain favourable factors, Indian industries expanded. In these years the pent-up demand within the country, the spurt given by the Korean boom and the scope for exports stimulated the private sector in India to increase the capacity of the existing industries and to establish new industries. Industrial expansion which took place was largely unplanned. Different business units, planning their expansion schemes independently of one another, under the stimulus of favourable factors noted above exceeded in their total sum of effects, the extent of response required by the stimuli. Thus, we see, on the one hand, an expansion in industrial capacity and on the other, underutilization of capacity—a phenomena which has persisted and become more marked in the sixties.

It is well known that the process of India's industrialization was speeded up from the period of the Second Five Year Plan which placed relatively greater emphasis on basic and heavy industries. With this plan began also a process of marked expansion of the public sector. To what extent the Second Five Year Plan and each of the successive five year plans took note of the idle industrial capacity which existed at the beginning of their respective plan periods and made provision for its fuller utilization while creating new industrial capacity is an important question of industrial planning. On this point, one thing is clear, i.e., the planners were aware of the existence of the problem of underutilization of industrial capacity. This is borne out by the statements relating to the objectives of industrial planning.

The First Five Year Plan[18] itself gave topmost priority to "fuller utilization of existing capacity in producer goods industries like jute and plywood and consumers' goods industries like cotton textiles, sugar, soap, vanaspathi, paints and varnishes." In the Second Five Year Plan[19] programmes of industrial development were conceived in terms of, *inter alia*, "fuller utilization of existing installed capacity in industries where there are wide gaps between capacity and production." The Third Five Year Plan[20] professed to take note of the growing gap between capacity and utilization in certain branches of industry in laying down the order of priorities for industrial planning. The Fourth Five Year Plan[21] also professed to "correct imbalances in the industrial structure" and bring about "the maximum utilization of capacity already built up." The Fifth Five Year Plan[22] again stated "maximization of output from existing capacity" as one of the objectives of industrial planning.

[18] GOI, Planning Commission, *First Five Year Plan*, p. 425.
[19] GOI, Planning Commission, *Second Five Year Plan*, p. 393.
[20] GOI, Planning Commission, *Third Five Year Plan*, p. 459.
[21] GOI, Planning Commission, *Fourth Five Year Plan*, p. 304.
[22] GOI, Planning Commission, *Draft Fifth Five Year Plan*, Vol. II, p. 134.

Despite such declared and professed objectives as above, we find that underutilization of the increasing industrial capacity has continued to be one of the greatest weaknesses of India's industrial economy. The unhealthy trend towards this underutilization which began even before the commencement of planning, as shown earlier, has not been checked by the several five year plans as will be shown in what follows. It has to be noted here that we have to view the problem of underutilization of industrial capacity against the background of the increases in the installed capacity which has resulted from industrial investments made from time to time under the plans. Table 3 shows the trends in rates of growth of installed capacity during 1960-70 by major groups of industries.

TABLE 3
Annual Rates of Growth of Installed Capacity

Period	Consumer goods	Intermediate goods	Capital goods	All industries
1960-64	1.9	11.2	9.1	6.1
1964-67	4.2	8.7	6.6	6.4
1967-70	5.3	4.0	3.7	4.5
1960-70	3.6	8.3	6.7	5.7

Source: Samuel Paul, "Industrial Performance and Government Controls" in J.C. Sandesara (ed.), *The Indian Economy—Performance and Prospects*, University of Bombay, 1974, p. 636.

Following are the salient points which emerge from the figures in Table 3:

(*i*) During the period 1960-70 the industrial capacity as a whole increased at an annual average rate of 5.7 per cent.

(*ii*) The annual rate of growth of industrial capacity which showed a slight increase between 1960-64 and 1964-67 declined markedly from 6.4 per cent in 1964-67 to 4.5 per cent in 1965-70.

(*iii*) The decline in the annual rate of growth of industrial capacity after 1967 was not shared by the consumers goods industries which showed a further increase. This rate increased from 1.9 per cent during 1960-64 to 4.2 per cent in 1964-67 and to 5.3 per cent in 1967-70.

(*iv*) Both the intermediate goods and the capital goods sectors show very marked decline in the annual rate of growth of capacity during 1967-70 compared to the earlier periods. In the case of intermediate goods it declined from 11.2 per cent in 1960-64 to 4.0 per cent in 1967-70 and in the case of capital goods during the same periods the decline was from 9.1 per cent to 3.7 per cent.

According to a study by the IDBI[23] the average annual rate of growth of capacity in major Indian industries during the Fourth Five Year Plan

[23]*GOI, Economic Survey*, 1974-75, p. 12.

period, 1969-74 was only 3.8 per cent.

While the above marked decline in the rate of growth of industrial capacity is to be deplored as being an indication of the slowing down of the country's effort at rapid industrial development, even more deplorable is the fact that even the low rate of increase in industrial capacity could not be utilized adequately, if not fully. Table 4 shows how the marked extent of underutilization of industrial capacity which was shown to have existed during about a decade prior to the Second Five Year Plan continued to exist during the 1960s also.

TABLE 4

The Average Annual Rates (per cent) of Utilization of Installed Capacity

| Industry group | Periods | | |
	1961-65	1966-68	1969-71
Consumer goods	46.3	48.6	53.0
Intermediate goods	64.3	60.9	61.2
Capital goods	57.6	42.3	42.8
All industries	53.6	52.1	54.5

Source: Same as for Table 3, p. 639.

The figures in Table 5 show for the years 1974 and 1975 the position of the bulk of manufacturing industries relating to utilization of installed capacity.

TABLE 5

Number of Industries Classified According to Utilization of Installed Capacity

| Utilization of installed capacity | Number of industries | |
	1974	1975
Less than 40%	37 (26.0)	41 (29.0)
40 to 50%	21 (14.8)	22 (15.5)
50 to 60%	20 (14.1)	21 (14.8)
60 to 70%	17 (12.0)	22 (15.5)
70 to 80%	23 (16.2)	12 (8.4)
80% and over	24 (16.7)	24 (16.7)
	142	142

N.B.: Figures in bracket show percentage to total number of industries.

Source: The figures are worked out on the basis of the data relating to industry-wise actual production against the respective installed capacities given in the Annual Report for 1975-76 of the Government of India, Ministry of Industry and Civil Supplies (Appendix I—Table on pp. 131-36).

It can be seen from the figures in the above tables that during the decade 1961-71 the average annual rate of utilization of installed capacity in industry was just about 53 per cent and that in the years 1974 and 1975 in as many as 41 and 45 per cent of the number of industries utilization was less than 50 per cent of the installed capacity. It was shown earlier that even during 1946-54 about 50 per cent of the number of industries had an idle capacity of about 50 per cent of the installed capacity. Thus, by and large, it can be said that the intensity of the over-all problem of under-utilization of industrial capacity has been more or less the same even from 1946. It is also obvious that for nearly three decades substantial potential has continually existed for stepping up output by just fuller utilization of capacity. *The GOI Economic Survey, 1975-76,* also admitted the "fact that in a number of major industries, a sizeable proportion of capacity remains unutilized so that output can be increased without further investment."[24] This certainly is a sad commentary on the country's effort at planned industrial development.

The industry-groupwise trends shown in Table 4 reveals that while the capacity utilization rate declined very markedly in the case of capital goods and relatively slightly in the case of intermediate goods, it showed a somewhat hopeful improvement in consumer goods sector. Between the periods 1961-65 and 1969-71 the average annual rate of utilization of installed capacity declined from 57.6 per cent to 42.8 per cent in the capital goods sector from 64.3 per cent to 61.2 per cent in the intermediate goods sector and increased from 46.3 per cent to 53.0 per cent in the consumer goods sector.

Viewed particularly against the fact that underutilization of capacity during 1946-54 was greatest in the consumer goods industries, and the fact that in this sector installed capacity has shown a markedly increasing trend (Table 3)—the trend towards an increase—though small—in the rate of utilization of installed capacity is a hopeful sign of improvement in the position. But the worsening of the capacity utilization position in the capital goods and the intermediate goods sector must be reckoned as a major factor which must have contributed to the difficulties that the economy has been facing. In retrospect it reveals the weakness of the Mahalanobis model on which industrial planning since the Second Five Year Plan has been based. The model being chiefly supply-based, assumed that supply equals output and output equals capacity. It ignored the *demand* for capital goods. The Fifth Five Year Plan has recognized this fact when it states that, if the pattern of output capacity is changed in favour of investment goods but there is no corresponding change in the structure of gross national expenditure in favour of investment outlays, the economy would experience underutilization of capacity in the industries producing investment goods and strong inflationary pressures in respect of the consumer goods sectors.[25]

The broad three-fold classification of industries given in Tables 3 and 4 do not give a complete picture of the inter-industry variations in respect

[14]*GOI, Economic Survey, 1975-76,* p.10.
[25]GOI, Planning Commission, *Draft Fifth Five Year Plan,* 1974-79, Vol.I, p.11.

of growth of installed capacity and the extent of idle capacity. Figures presented in Tables 2 and 5 give some idea of the differences that exist among the numerous industries, in the utilization of installed capacity. For instance, in 1975, while about 25 per cent of the number of industries utilized over 70 per cent of their respective installed capacities there were 29 per cent of the number of industries utilizing less than 40 per cent of the installed capacities. Again, each industry comprised of differing number of units whose utilization rates also differ.[26] An analysis by Samuel Paul,[27] for 1965, of rates of capacity utilization in Indian industries covering 39 items shows that while for a few industries like cigarettes, petroleum refinery products, cement, basic metals (Ferrous) and tyres and tubes, the utilization ratio was so high that a further increase in output depended very much on expansion of capacity, for many other industries the utilization ratio was quite low, indicating the potential for increasing output with the existing capacity itself. Another analysis made by Yogindra K. Alagh[28] for the year 1968, showed marked industry-wise variations in the utilization of production potential. In that year, while excess capacity higher than one-third existed in transport equipment, metal products, flour-milling and grinding, sugar and vegetable oil sectors, in the case of electrical equipment, cement, non-ferrous alloys, other metals, leather products and footwear, biscuits and confectionery, jute textiles, fertilizers, glass and glass-ware, dyestuffs, paints and varnishes and drugs and pharmaceuticals sectors excess capacity was higher than a fifth of the potential production. It should be noted that these computations are based on the Reserve Bank of India's data on "potential production" and hence as shown in Section I these figures overstate the utilization. So, the actual excess capacity must be taken to be much higher than "one-third" and "one-fifth" stated above.

Section III: Explanation for Underutilization of Industrial Capacity

Having presented in the previous section a brief picture of the trends in underutilization of industrial capacity in India, in this section an attempt is made to set forth the various factors which can explain this underutilization. For the underutilization of capacity during the period 1946-54, the explanation could be in terms of unplanned industrial expansion. The conjunction of favourable factors such as the pent-up demand for several kinds of goods in the early years of the post-war period, existence of accumulated sterlingbalances, the Korean boom and some export possibilities led entrepreneurs to increase the capacity of existing industries and also to establish new units. But, in the absence of planned regulation, the combined

[26]GOI, Ministry of Industry & Civil Supplies, Report 1975-76, Appendix I, Table on pp. 131-36 gives installed capacities and their utilization for 142 industries for the years 1974 and 1975.
[27]J.C. Sandesara (ed.), op.cit., p.642.
[28]Ibid., p.650.

result of the activities of the several individual entrepreneurs was the creation of capacity in excess of what was warranted by the stimuli. However, the persistence of marked underutilization of capacity even after the First Five Year Plan can only be attributed to faulty planning techniques and inefficient plan implementation.

It must be admitted that 100 per cent utilization of capacity cannot be expected as a normal feature of any industrial economy. Entrepreneurs, in making investment decisions take into account not only the immediate demand but also the level of demand likely to emerge in the foreseeable future. This kind of continuing process of "planned excess capacity" means also some degree of underutilization, but this may have to be taken as a concomitant of an expanding industrial sector in a developing economy.

In some industries, the technological features may make it inevitable that the minimum possible expansion may be more than what is warranted by the demand factor. This leads to what may be called surplus capacity arising from "indivisibilities." However, if this surplus is much, the industry is not likely to be taken up as it would lead to loss. So, this factor may also be taken to account for only a small degree of underutilization.

In a newly industrializing economy there are some *teething* troubles which are perhaps inescapable in a new unit during the immediate period after its commissioning. Some time lag, which differs from industry, is required to overcome the initial difficulties and achieve capacity output.

Besides, some underutilization may result from unforeseen breakdowns in plants as well as closedown of production for necessary periodical repairs and check-up.

Only a detailed investigation into the working of industrial units can show how much of underutilization in Indian industries has been due to the factors noted above, viz., "planned excess capacity," technological "indivisibilities," "teething" troubles and breakdowns and repairs of plants. All these factors cannot account for the chronic underutilization in Indian industries on the scale depicted in the previous section.

Any explanation of India's chronic problem of underutilization of industrial capacity will have to take account of shortages in input supplies, deficiency in demand for the industrial products, inter-industry imbalances, some policy variables, peculiarities of industries, industrial relations, faulty investment allocation and weaknesses in plan implementation. All these factors which are in a way interdependent may be taken to have operated in different degrees in the different industries in India and this is a matter for a detailed industry-wise and even unit-wise analysis which is beyond the scope of this paper. We shall briefly elaborate these factors in what follows.

Shortage in supply of inputs like raw materials, components and spare parts, power, transport facilities and labour is an important contributory factor for capacity underutilization in the various industries at different times. For instance, the M.V. Raghavachari study[29] states as important reasons for idle capacity, shortage of sulphur in the case of sulphuric acid industry and those depending on this industry, shortage of imported tallow in the case of soap industry, benzene shortage in the case of polysterene, shortage of agricultural raw materials in the case of several agro-based industries, non-availability of certain components and spare parts in the case of industries like tractors, diesel engines and cycles. Shortage of power has been one of the widely known features of the Indian economy and this must have necessarily acted as an important contributory factor for idle capacity in several industries even where the demand for the products of these industries justified fuller utilization. The same thing could be said about transport facilities especially with the deepening of the oil crisis. As regards labour though there cannot be said to be any over-all shortages some shortage of certain categories of skilled labour seems to have been felt in some industries.

Inadequate supplies of several inputs was due both to relatively low levels of domestic production as well as to difficulties of making good the deficiency by importation. According to a study[30] made in 1965, "The shortage of foreign exchange for the import of components, raw materials and spare parts is undoubtedly the most important single factor limiting output in the industries studied." It may be said that this factor must have continued to be an important cause for underutilization till the foreign exchange position improved during the last two years. The stoppage of some foreign aid following the hostilities with Pakistan was an unforeseen factor which aggravated the foreign exchange difficulties.

Deficiency in the demand for industrial products may be taken to be another major factor contributing to underutilization of industrial capacity. Broadly speaking, the demand for industrial products is the sum of the demand by households, private sectors enterprises, public enterprises and other countries. The demand by private and public sector enterprises is generally for investment goods and intermediate products going into the production of consumption and investment goods. The demand is governed largely by the demand for the end products of industry by the households which in turn, depends chiefly on the rate of growth of per capita income and the pattern of income distribution. If we examine the trends in per capita income (at 1960-61 prices) we see that between 1960-61 and 1963-64, it ranged between Rs 306 and Rs 318 and having risen to Rs 335 in 1964-65 fell again to lower levels to regain the level of Rs 340 only in 1969-70 and since then it has ranged between Rs 337 and 353. Thus it is found that the per capita income level has not only not shown a steadily rising trend from year to year but it has been generally low. This situation was hardly conducive to the growth of demand for industrial products. The low rate of

[29] Reserve Bank of India Bulletin, April 1969 (reprint), p. 11.
[30] V.K. Ramaswamy and D.G. Pfoutz, Utilization of Industrial Capacity, A joint pilot study by the GOI and the USAID, December 1965.

growth of income was due both to lack of adequate expansion of non-agricultural employment as well as to poor agricultural performance. The latter, in particular, needs to be greatly emphasized. For, as is now widely recognized, Indian planning has been stumbling largely because it failed to achieve, in the initial years, a break-through in agriculture. Even now the "Green Revolution" is said to be limited to a few crops like wheat, bajra and maize and to a few regions only. Besides, some years like 1965-67 have been exceptionally bad agricultural years. Only a nation-wide agricultural transformation can create the necessary conditions to stimulate the demand for industrial products on a scale adequate for fuller utilization of capacity and further marked expansion of capacity. As regards export demand for industrial products the difficulties of export promotion have been well known. In pushing ahead with industrialization largely in accordance with the Mahalanobis model the planners seem to have taken for granted the expansion of demand both domestic and foreign. As G.L. Mehta says, "More attention was devoted by those who planned, to targets in terms of capacity and in allocation of necessary rupee and foreign exchange resources as well as physical and technical resources, for building up this capacity rather than to its actual utilization."[31] There seems to be much truth in this view.

Planning has involved adoption of certain economic policies and appropriate changes thereof from time to time. Some of these "policy variables" have influenced industrial capacity utilization. Policies in respect of allocations of raw material, supplies of power, grant of import licences may have operated in practice inequitably as between different industries/firms thereby creating inter-industry/inter-firm disparities in capacity utilization. Import policy may operate in such a way that the extent of competing imports permitted for different product groups may vary and this affects utilization of industrial capacity. Similarly, under export promotion policy the scope afforded for different industries to push their products abroad may vary. The licensing policy may have been so administered as to create excess capacity in some industries. But, in view of the fact that the rate of growth of installed capacity has markedly slowed down from 1967, this factor cannot be considered to be a major cause for *over-all* underutilization of industrial capacity. However, as has been explained by the Planning Commission[32] the working of the system of licensing and control has created imbalance—excess capacities in some industries and shortage of capacities in others.

An important aspect of policy leading to capacity creation without reference to ensuring its utilization is the "project aid." Big industrial projects were launched chiefly because "specific projects loans" were more easily made available than "general purposes loans" by the foreign-aid-giving countries and institutions. Though the feasibility reports which

[31]G.L. Mehta, *Dilemmas in planning*, Vora & Co., 1972, p. 50.
[32]GOI, Planning Commission, *Draft, Fourth Five Year Plan, 1969-74*, p. 235.

generally preceded the sanction of project loans made an assessment of the availability of local resources and facilities and the demand for the products of the industries, in retrospect, it became evident that thanks to project aid the projects could be completed but this did not ensure capacity utilization.

Another policy variable with which the extent of capacity-utilization is associated is the protection offered to certain industries. High levels of effective protection enable inefficient industries to thrive though they are not capable of utilizing their capacity adequately.

The special characteristics of industries relating to their size and the nature of market for their products affect capacity utilization. It may be said that generally monopolistic market structure tends to restrict output and hence reduces capacity utilization. On the other hand, bigger firms are capable of achieving higher levels of utilization as they enjoy greater economies of scale and are better able to procure the necessary inputs. Whether a monopolistic market situation associated with big business has actually restricted output and thereby contributed to idle capacity in India, however, needs to be verified by empirical studies.

Some degree of underutilization of industrial capacity can be explained by labour troubles leading to work stoppages. At one time or the other most of the industries have been affected by prolonged strikes or lock-outs and consequent underutilization of capacity. The number of man-days lost in industry increased from 3.8 million in 1951 to 13.8 million in 1966 and to 20.6 million in 1970.[33] This source of capacity underutilization could be avoided by better industrial relations.

The several explanations for underutilization of industrial capacity stated above, except a few like unexpected foreign exchange difficulties for importing the required inputs for industries and sudden work-stoppages arising from industrial conflicts, may be traced to inadequate investment, faulty allocation of investment and inefficient implementation of planned policies and programmes. Inadequate supplies of inputs and deficiency of demand for output of industries represent a situation of inter-industry imbalance due chiefly to underinvestment and faulty allocation of investment. Shortages of power and transport facilities indicate inadequate investments in these sectors. Creation of capacity in excess of requirements in certain sectors indicate the directions in which investments could have been reduced. What is, therefore, required is a synchronized growth of interrelated branches of industries which depands, among other things, on a coordinated and integrated pattern of investment. Full account should be taken of the implications of a certain rate of growth of installed capacity in the different industries for allocations in the related sectors like mining, agriculture, transport, etc. An important lesson of the experience of the past three decades is that industrialization cannot be speeded up by a process of mere creating more installed capacity to the neglect of the factors on which adequate utilization of this capacity depends.

[33]C.S.O., *Statistical Pocket Book*, 1972, p. 166.

CONCLUSION

The following are the main points which emerge from the discussion made above of the problem of underutilization of industrial capacity in India.

1. The manifold adverse effects of marked underutilization of industrial capacity have been touched upon in the Introductory section. Especially from 1966-67 as the *GOI Economic Survey* puts it, "The effects of slow capacity creation in the last six years on industrial growth have been compounded by a failure to make an optimum use of available capacities."[34] These adverse effects emphasize the great importance to be attached to the prevention of the occurrence of the problem. Indeed, in a planned economy like ours the continued existence for several years, of a marked degree of underutilization of industrial capacity should not have any place. Such a thing can only be taken to reflect the immaturity of the country's planning techniques and inefficiency of plan implementation.

2. It has been shown that the use of the data on "potential production" and "potential-utilization ratio" based on the "peak-output approach" furnished by the Reserve Bank of India grossly underestimates the problem of underutilization in Indian industries. It is pointed out that the "installed capacity" is a more satisfactory basis to derive the figures relating to the extent of underutilization. However, the absence of universally acceptable series of "estimates of installed capacities and unutilized capacities" for different industries in India is a handicap in a precise understanding of the degree of underutilization and this handicap should be removed.

3. The problem of idle capacity in Indian industry is not a very recent phenomenon, but has existed from the years prior to the introduction of planning. The extent of this idle capacity has remained around 50 per cent of the installed capacity even from 1946.

4. In the consumer goods industries sector the rate of growth of installed capacity from 1960 has been marked and there has also been a slight increase in the rate of utilization of this growing capacity. On the other hand, in the case of both the capital goods industries and intermediate goods industries there has been a decline in the rate of growth of installed capacity as well as the rate of utilization of this slowly increasing capacity. Besides the over-all problem of underutilization of industrial capacity, there exist inter-industry and inter-unit variations and arrangements to keep a continuous record of these variations will help better planning of industrial development.

5. Some degree of underutilization of industrial capacity due to such factors like "planned excess capacity," technological "indivisibilities" and "teething" troubles may have to be accepted as a normal feature, but India's case of chronic excess capacity should be regarded as a major aspect of the failure of Indian planning. Except for such unforeseen factors

[34]*GOI, Economic Survey, 1974-75*, p. 12.

like foreign exchange difficulties arising from sudden stoppage of some foreign aid following the declaration of the Indo-Pakistan war and work-stoppages due to industrial disputes several other factors like shortage of inputs, power and transport facilities, deficiency of demand and certain policy variables can be traced to inadequate investment, faulty investment allocation and inefficient plan implementation. The relative importance of the various factors responsible for underutilization of capacity may vary from industry to industry and among different firms within an industry. This aspect requires detailed investigation.

6. Having allowed the problem of underutilization to become almost chronic, the task presently is to reverse the trend and achieve progressively higher rates of utilization. There is a hopeful sign in that the *GOI Economic Survey* for 1976-77 reports that "Capacity utilization in 1976-77 was at a level appreciably higher than in 1975-76."[35] However, to solve the problem, the plan strategy will have to be adopted to ensure steady flow of inputs and demand for products. These would have to cover many things like the level and pattern of investment, rate of growth of mineral products and commercial crops, buffer stock arrangements, allocation of foreign exchange, etc.

7. Continued underutilization of capacity for several years in many industries must have affected costs and hence prices of the products which in turn may have also adversely affected the demand. This needs a detailed study.

8. Preventing the emergence of substantial underutilization of industrial capacity in the future requires correct monitoring arrangements to sense the trouble in time, so that prompt remedial measures could be taken. More systematic studies regarding domestic demand forecasts for industrial products and potential for their exports as well as regarding the needed inputs and other production requirements should be carried out and the relative rates of growth in installed capacities of different industries should be based on such studies.

[35]*GOI, Economic Survey, 1976-77*, p. 14.

T. K. LAKSHMAN

Economic Growth and the Problem of Inequalities of Income—A Comparative Study of the Developed and the Developing Countries with Particular Reference to India

DEVELOPED COUNTRIES AND THE PROBLEM OF INEQUALITIES OF INCOME

Unequal distribution of income in any country, irrespective of what its magnitude might be, leads to relatively low levels of living and consequently poverty at least among some sections of the population. Townsend traced poverty to inequalities in "the distribution of income, capital assets, occupational fringe benefits, current public services and current private services."[1]

In most of the developed countries, these inequalities do exist in varying degrees, inspite of their higher rate of economic growth, depriving the relatively poorer sections of a fair share in total income and assets. Many factors are responsible for this situations—the differing laws of inheritance; practices of nepotism and class favouritism; discrimination on grounds of race, sex and age; restriction on educational opportunities and specialization of occupations; and the pattern of ownership of physical and human capital. Moreover, the original pattern of inequality is rigidified through institutional arrangements, perpetuating inequalities of opportunities.

The General Theory of Causation of Inequality

Most theories conceive the central problem of income distribution as the determination of the levels of employment and remuneration of the factors of production usually grouped into capital and labour. Neo-classical theory assumed competitive equilibrium in all markets and thus derived returns to factors from purely production relationships and demand patterns, given factor supply conditions. At the other extreme, the classical and Marxist wage theory models assume relatively fixed wages with all surplus values appropriated by the owners of capital. But these theories are inadequate since they do not consider the determinants of the functional division of income. What is mainly missing in these theories is the reflection of determinants influencing the distribution of various forms of assets. The income

---

[1]Quoted from Martin Rein, "Problems in the Definition and Measurement of Poverty," in Peter Townsend (ed.), *The Concept of Poverty*, Meinemann Educational Books, 1970, p. 47.

of any household is derived from a variety of assets; land, privately owned capital, access to public capital goods, and human capital embodying varying degrees of skill. A grouping of households according to the type and productivity of their assets provides more insight into the nature of income determination among the low income groups.

With the result, interest in income distribution progressively rose, as attention was shifted from functional shares, through size distribution, to the poverty line or level-of-living distinctions. The alternative general theory[2] that has been evolved attempts to explain this phenomena of inequality of income and poverty based on three possible hypotheses. They are (a) events which are random in their incidence and which select people for poverty status; (b) social barriers of class, caste and custom, which provide a basis for selection of people for this status and work to reinforce the selection by the differential provision of economic opportunities and (c) personal differences of ability and motivation functions to select people for poverty status.

The first one of these focusses attention on the risk of being subject to very low income and hence poverty due to unforeseen calamities in the family. The second, i.e., the social barriers theory urges the idea that the society deliberately selects people to the occupations of low income and poverty by formal or informal policy decisions. For instance, racial discrimination substantiates this theory. Thirdly personal differences theory suggests that some people would remain at low levels of living because of factors such as lack of education and medical care.

However, much evidence in support of disparities of income leading to low levels of living and poverty in spite of economic growth and on the effects of various policies—fiscal, monetary and social, in reducing the inequalities of income has been gathered both for developed and developing countries of the world.

MAIN TRENDS OF INEQUALITIES OF INCOME IN DEVELOPED COUNTRIES

The trends, in socialist countries reveal that the overall equality in the distribution of income is the highest, since income from ownership of capital does not accrue as income to individuals. The inequality in these countries is mainly due to inequality in wages between sectors and skilled classses. Moreover, since the structural factors operating towards equality is the strongest in these countries, the average income share of the lowest 40 per cent amounted to about 25 per cent of the total income.[3] In respect of non-socialist developed countries, the average income share of the bottom 40 per cent is about 16 per cent, which is lower than the average in socialist

[2]Robert J. Lampman, *Ends and Means of Reducing Income Poverty,* Institute for Research on Poverty, Monograph Series, Academic Press, London, 1971, pp. 36-37.

[3]Montek S. Ahluwalia, "Income Inequality: Some Dimensions of the Problem," *Redistribution with Growth,* Holl's Chenery, Montek S. Ahluwalia, C. L. G. Bell, John H. Duloy, Richard Jelly (eds.), p. 7.

countries but better than most of the developing countries.[4] The average income share of the lowest 40 per cent in the developing countries amounts to 12.5 per cent of the total income.[5] The poverty line defined by the U.S.A. is 50 dollars and in these developing countries about 50 per cent of the population secure less than $ 50 per capita.

The poverty line in European countries was fixed at an annual income level ranging between $ 1500 and $ 3000 at 1962 prices.[6] The Council of Economic Advisers in their Annual Report to the President of America estimated the number in poverty on the basis of the above income range to be as large as 32 per cent of the total number of families in America. This percentage declined to 17 in 1967 due to various fiscal and welfare measures.[7] However, the estimate of the inequality dimension in U.S. in recent years pointed out that the top 10 per cent received about 28 per cent of the total money income and the lowest 10 per cent about 2 per cent of the total.[8] The share of the lowest 20 per cent was about 5 per cent of the total money income.[9] In terms of wealth, the top 10 per cent of the families held over 50 per cent of the total wealth and the lowest one-third only one per cent. Further the top one per cent held three-fourths of the corporate stock.[10]

In European countries like Germany, Denmark, United Kingdom, Netherlands, Sweden and Norway, inequality index comprising concentration ratio of Lorenz curve and Gini ratio of Lorenz curve indicate, however, a falling trend. If expressed in terms of average or median incomes, the trend of the lower incomes over the last ten years was upward and for the highest income groups downward. After tax, inequality index derived from the Lorenz curve for Britain fell by 8 percentage points over 21 years (1938-59); and for Denmark by 7 points over 13 years (1939-52).[11] The inequality index for U.S. fell by 7 percentage points in 1967 corresponding with a reduction along the trend of about 14 years.[12]

Based on the continuous observed percentage reduction of inequality per year, it was estimated, that it would take 50 to 85 years in order to reduce the existing inequality to one-half.[13] Taxes reduced the after-tax income share of the highest decile, and raised, after the Second World War, the share of the lowest decile. If the linear trend in inequality indicators were to continue, halving inequality was estimated to take twenty-five years.

[4]*Ibid.*

[5]*Ibid.*

[6]Robert I. Lampman, *op. cit.*, p. 3.

[7]*Ibid.*

[8]*Ibid*, p. 46.

[9]*Ibid.*

[10]*Ibid*, p. 45.

[11]Jan Tinbergen, *Income Distribution Analysis & Policies*, 1975, pp. 19-20. See Tables 2.1A 2.1B. 2.IIA, 2.IIB, 2.IIIA, 2.IIIB. 2.2. IV.

[12]*Ibid.* p. 22.

[13]*Ibid.* p. 27.

Complete re-distribution by public finance was calculated to reduce the ratio of the upper to the lower quintile from 8 to 2.5 in Denmark (1963) and from 14 to 6.5 in the Netherlands.[14]

In fact, egalitarian thought is doubtlessly deep-rooted in Western civilization. But the dominance of such thinking in political, social and economic affairs is a modern phenomenon. Egalitarianism has brought about various income distribution policies, such as fixation of minimum wages, limitation of dividends, promotion of skills through education, fiscal and various social security measures in several developed countries. Taxes, in particular, are being used as the main instruments of redistribution since the beginning of the 20th century. In this context, direct taxes on income, wealth and wealth increases and indirect taxes on luxuries are currently in vogue. On the positive side of assistance to their poor, social expenditure on health and education, price supports to protect some groups of small producers in agriculture, small scale industry and retail trade are widely prevalent. So also for reducing wealth concentration and its distribution, efforts have been made to disperse economic power, expand social security institutions and private insurance companies and increase workers participation in the enterprise capital.

For instance, the basic policies pursued in England[15] towards the removal of poverty were free contract, cautious extension of education and of suffrage, work relief for the able-bodied poor and work-houses for the disabled paupers. In America, the strategies contemplated[16] towards overcoming poverty were: (i) Establish and facilitate the working of a market system aimed at economic growth and maintenance of high employment; (ii) Adapt the system to the needs of the poor; (iii) Change the poor and adapt them to the system; and (iv) Relieve the distress of the poor. The first one was sought to be achieved through aggregative measures of fiscal and monetary policies. The second strategy aimed at: developing the economics of areas that can be identified as pockets of poverty; legislating and bargaining low wage rates above the poverty levels; offering training and re-training to qualify low-income workers for higher-skill jobs; providing jobs for all able-bodied poor by subsidizing private employers and by public work or work relief; prohibiting discriminatory barriers to employment on account of colour, age, sex or education; and expanding and supplementing presently operating transfer payment programmes to block, more completely, retreats into poverty. Besides it sought to provide public education, health and housing benefits. The third measure attempted to improve the abilities of the poor to seize opportunities to earn more incomes and to change the attitudes, values, motivations, and life-style of the poor and to develop their potential productivity. The emphasis was, therefore on provisions of schools, libraries, information services, hospitals,

---

[14]*Ibid.*
[15]Robert J. Lampman *op., cit*, p.8.
[16]*Ibid.*, pp.6-10.

maternal/child clinics, public housing, sanitation and other environmental improvements for the whole community of the poor. The fourth one sought to implement minimum income guarantees and comprehensive social security plans. This measure was emphasized in the early part of the 20th century. The first three strategies were, however, given top priority in the 1950s and 1960s and the last two during 1970s.

In fact, the per capita total social welfare expenditure in constant 1966-67 prices in America rose from $ 211.34 in 1949-50 to $ 497.14 in 1966-67. Similarly, the corporate income tax with a rate of 14 per cent for over $ 10,000 brackets had the most progressive effect.[17]

ECONOMIC GROWTH AND INCOME INEQUALITY PROBLEM IN DEVELOPING ECONOMIES

The ultimate objective of economic growth in all the developing countries is the promotion of welfare—social and economic—of all the people. The promotion of such welfare involves eradication of poverty and unemployment and a marked rise in the levels of living of the masses. In order to achieve these objectives, all developing economies have endeavoured over the last two decades for a sustained and significant rise in real national income and consequently in per capita income under the assumption and hope that economic growth would eliminate poverty and unemployment. There is also an accepted view that at least in the initial stages of development, an adverse or skewed income distribution is necessary to the attainment of a rapid rate of economic growth. This view is based on the assumption that the marginal savings rate is greater in the higher, than in the lower, income groups and that the larger savings realized from an unequal distribution of income will lead to a higher rate of investment and economic growth. This would happen, if Say's Law prevailed and if the economies of these developing countries behaved like a purely competitive general equilibrium system in which at any moment of time the demand for the different goods and services is exactly what is needed to motivate and absorb the desired rates of production. In fact these are properties of neoclassical growth models in which the sustained growth rate is independent of the saving rate. The long-run growth rate is uniquely determined by growth of the labour force. The growth paths derived from such models are, therefore, sustained by purely competitive temporal and inter-temporal general equilibrium relationships and their application to developing economies will be quite unrealistic. Moreover under conditions of imperfect competition there is the failure of equilibrating mechanism of the price system to produce steady growth or desirable distribution of income. Much less, the hypothesis that inequality is a necessary or sufficient condition of economic progress through saving is taken much less

[17]*Ibid.*, p.13.

seriously by the present generation of economists than by their fore-runners. Apart from this the issue of growth and its impact on the poorer strata of the society has of late caught the attention of economists, politicians and even laymen. There is a feeling that the mechanisms which promote growth also promote economic concentration, and a worsening of the relative and perhaps even absolute position of the income groups. This pessimistic view has led to some questioning of growth-oriented development strategies which have assumed that the poverty problem could be solved without much difficulty, if growth could be accelerated. In this context, the issue of economic growth and worsening of income distribution in developing countries attracted the attention of many economists to structural rigidities. The initial set of structural hypotheses, in fact, was formulated in 1950s by writers such as Paul Rosenstein-Rodan,[18] Ragnar Nurkse,[19] W. Arthur Lewis,[20] Paul Prebisch,[21] Hans Singer[22] and Gunnar Myrdal.[23]

They have explained the phenomena of worsening income distribution and unemployment on the basis of the particular properties of demand and production functions and other specifications of economic behaviour. A major theme in most of their work was the emphasis on the failure of equilibrating mechanisms of the price system to produce steady growth or a desirable distribution of income. Stephen A. Resnick[24] strongly emphasized the above view point by referring to the market imperfections caused on account of fiscal and monetary instrument and the consequent failure of the optimal allocation of resources.

In this context, the experiences of a number of developing countries in their worsening of the distribution of income particularly in 1960s in spite of accelerated rate of growth of income highlighted the need for the reconsideration of the structural problems. The structural rigidities were

---

[18]P. Rosenstein Rodan, "Problems of Industrialisation of Eastern and South-Eastern Europe" *Economic Journal*, June-September 1953, pp.205-16.

[19]R. Nurkse, *Problems of Capital Formation in Under-developed Countries*, Oxford, 1953.

[20]W.A. Lewis, *Economic Development with Unlimited Supplies of Labour*, Manchester School, May 1954, pp.132-91

[21]P. Prebisch, "Commercial Policy in the Under-developed Countries," *American Economic Review*, Proceedings, May 1959, pp. 251-73.

[22]H.W. Singer, "The Distribution of Gains between Investing and Borrowing Countries," *American Economic Review*, Proceedings, May 1950, pp.473-85.

[23]G. Myrdal, *Asian Drama: An Inquiry into the Poverty of the Nations*, Vol. I, 1968, pp.539-63.

Myrdal Pointed out that the proportion of income variation accruing to the very lowest and highest income groupings, i e., the lowest and the highest deciles is larger in under-developed countries than in the developed ones. His study was based on the consumption of various items by different income, social or ethnic groups, by urban as opposed to rural areas by and different regions.

[24]Stephen A. Resnick, "State of Development Economics," *American Economic Review*, May 1975, p.318.

mainly related to the limited ability of the economies to absorb the grow-ing labour force and to the recent disruption to world trade caused by increased oil and food prices, which required substantial adjustment in productive structures. Thus the constraint in the development policy was noticed to exist due to a number of structural factors.

The revival of interest in income distribution added, therefore, a new dimension to structural analysis. The traditional approach, which focussed attention on the division between wage and non-wage income, was found to be ill-suited to developing countries, since most of the wage earners in the modern sector belonged to the middle-income groups. Recent studies by M.S. Ahluwalia[25] brought out the fact that the bulk of the poorest groups in developing countries were self-employed and largely rural. Their incomes depended more on the availability of land and capital and access to public facilities than on wages. Since each of the main poverty groups— small farmers, landless labourers, urban self-employed—had a different set of productive possibilities and constraints, the need for a new form of structural analysis based on the identification of these groups was felt necessary for distribution-oriented policies. The measures found to be less disruptive of development in most countries, were therefore, those designed to redistribute increments in income and new assets. Develop-ment strategies based on this approach were elaborated by Ahluwalia and Chenery. The two authors pointed out the need for detailed profiles of poverty highlighting the economic characteristics of poverty groups. The emphasis was, therefore, on the sectoral distribution of the poor, their occupational characteristics and educational levels, their ownership of productive assets and their access to key production units. These charac-teristics were considered important determinants in the process of income generation among poverty groups. The groups of people which were afflicted by poverty on the basis of the above features were agricultural labourers, artisans, marginal farmers, etc. The poorest groups in underdeveloped countries were estimated to constitute 50 per cent of the population.[26] Of this population, about two-thirds earned their livelihood from agriculture and these were mainly small farmers. Further about 70 per cent of the poverty groups[27] were estimated to live in rural areas. Given thus the scale of the problem and limited capacity of other sectors to expand pro-ductive employment, it was considered that a viable strategy for raising the incomes of the lowest 40 per cent of the population must necessarily focus on the agricultural sector. Besides, they also recognized that a mere shift in sectoral emphasis towards promoting agriculture and allo-cating resources to development is not enough. The impact of government

[25]M.S. Ahluwalia, "Income Inequality: Some Dimensions of the Problem" in H. Chenery *et. al.*, *Re-distribution with Growth*, London, 1974, pp. 21-22.
   [26]*Ibid.*, p.19.
   [27]*Ibid.*

policies on the target population should depend on the distributional incidence of these policies within the agricultural sector. Income distribution in agriculture was therefore, to be determined largely by structural factors such as the distribution of land. Coupled with this measure, other tools contemplated to be used in the development strategy were the following:[28]

(*i*) Intervention in factor markets determining factor prices, utilization levels and factor incomes giving the functional distribution of income;

(*ii*) (*a*) Direction of redistribution of assets (including both physical capital and labour skills) among the population translating the functional distribution of income into a size distribution of income (changes in ownership patterns over time are an important element determining changes in the distribution of income). (*b*) In case of absence of access to particular types of assets by the lower income group, redirection of the pattern of investment in the economy by the Government to create new assets.

(*iii*) Taxation of personal income and wealth so that it may operate on the size distribution of income (this is a fiscal corrective on market determined income).

(*iv*) Provision of public consumption goods or direct income transfers by the state, complement post-tax income distribution patterns and jointly with taxation of personal income determining the net fiscal impact on the size distribution of income.

(*v*) Intervention in commodity markets to influence both the pattern of output and relative prices through taxes and subsidies on domestic production and consumption, tariffs and subsidies on imports and exports, and various terms of quantitative restriction on both domestic production and foreign trade.

(*vi*) Influence of technology on both the level and distribution of income.

THE STUDIES OF IRMA ADELMAN AND TAFT MORRIS

A detailed study on the pattern of distribution of income among different sections of the population in the developing countries consequent on economic growth and changes in their aggregate income level allowing sufficient weightage in the price level was made by Irma Adelman and Taft Morris.[29] These two economists, using 1950-63 cross section data for forty-three developing countries studied the relationship between the shares of income accruing to the poorest households on the one hand and various broad aspects of the nation's economic, social and political performance on the other. According to this study, the primary impact of economic

[28]M. S. Ahluwalia, "The Scope for Policy Intervention" in H. Chenery, *op. cit*, pp. 73-74.

[29]Irma Adelman and Taft Morris, "Development Economics—A Reassessment of Goals," *American Economic Review*, Papers and Proceedings, American Economic Association, May 1975, pp. 302-5.

development on income distribution in many of the underdeveloped countries including Latin American countries was, on the average, to decrease both the absolute and relative incomes of the poor. Their main findings further indicated that the development process in these countries led typically to a trickle up in favour of the middle classes and the rich and did not trickle down to the poor. It was also noticed by them, that the absolute incomes of the poor rose only when the development moved into intermediate levels of development and the poorest segment of the population benefited from economic growth only when the government played an important economic role and when widespread efforts were made to improve the human resource base. Thus the finding of Irma Adelman and Taft Morris clearly demonstrated a conflict in the process of economic development between the growth of overall national income and an increase in the welfare of the poor or their levels of living. Moreover, even the policy programmes considered important from the point of view of economic growth were found to be most ineffective in improving income distribution. In the light of this analysis, they felt the need to decide in advance, while formulating development planning models and development policy, the extent to which increases in the welfare of the poor were to be weighed against simple growth of gross national product. This approach was found necessary, since their analysis clearly highlighted the ineffectiveness of the traditional economic instruments in improving the relative shares of income to the poor. In fact, the two economists attempted to investigate the impact of a variety of traditional economic instruments such as relative product and factor prices (influenced directly through price fixing, taxes, subsidies, and or world prices, and degree of monopoly), rationing of products and services, rationing of credit, Government taxes and transfers, trade policy, labour market policy, technology and inflation, or income distribution. It was found that in spite of these policy measures, the growth of income did not trickle down to the poor. The commonly accepted definition of development focussing attention on the creation of conditions for self-sustained growth in per capita gross national product and development strategies and planning methodologies was found to be unrealistic in the context of raising the levels of living of the poorer sections of the society. Their suggestions were, therefore, for a change in the economic structure, as against the stress mainly on the rate of economic growth, in order to improve the pattern of income distribution which gave a slant towards the poor. The change in the structure implied not only contemplated promotion of equity but also the creation of conditions conducive to continuing improvements in equity by ensuring a progression of mutually balanced strategy mixes. Further an overall view of the development process in some of the non-communist countries like Israel, South Korea, Singapore and Taiwan, with dynamic sequences of strategies, reflected improvements in the incomes of the poor with accelerated growth. The dynamic sequences of processes which contemplated redistribution now and growth later in these countries as against growth now and redistribution later in countries like the USA and Japan were: (*a*) radical asset distribution, focussing attention not only on land, but also on imposing curbs on the use and further accumulation of financial capital; (*b*) extension of human resource base by promotion of skills; and (*c*) adoption of labour-intensive growth policies with appropriately paced agricultural development.

The first one was supposed to set the economic and political conditions in order to ensure that subsequent economic growth did not become highly unequating in its approach. The second one aimed at the redistribution of ownership of human capital on an extensive basis. The third one contemplated a mass consumption market and enlarged domestic demand as a result of larger employment and equitable growth pattern.

Adelman is very emphatic about the above approach of restructuring the assets, which is expected to sustain both equity and growth. A similar conclusion is derived by Richard Jolly,[30] while projecting the case studies of India, Tanzania, Sri Lanka, Korea and Taiwan in respect of their income growth along with inequality proportions. He has highlighted that success in redistribution has been accompanied by the changes in assets, ownership, changes in the structure of economic production, and improved infrastructural facilities.

ECONOMIC GROWTH AND THE PROBLEM OF INCOME INEQUALITY IN INDIA

A study of Indian case in respect of its growth of income and the pattern of distribution of such income, wealth and ecomomic power is of great significance, since it constitutes nearly half of the total population of 550 million representing almost one-sixth of the world's total under abject poverty. The Indian experience, therefore, serves as a good example of the general problems of implementing antipoverty or redistributive policies

The Trends of Economic Growth in India

Sustained efforts have been made over the last more than two and half decades through a series of five year plans to raise the levels of living of the masses by accelerating the rate of growth of real income and per capita income. With the result, substantial proportion of inputs have been ploughed into the various sectors of the economy in order to raise the levels of output. Considering some of the indicators of development, the public sectoral plan outlay has risen from 1960 crores in the first plan to Rs 39,303 crores in the fifth plan.[31] The increase in the gross capital formation as a percentage of gross domestic product is from 9.2 in 1950-51 to 17.2 in 1973-74, (i.e. from Rs 952 crores to Rs 9851 crores both private and public sectors together).

---

[30]Richard Jolly, *An Overview*; H. Chenery, *op. cit*, pp. 245-55.
[31]R.N. Lal, *Capital Formation in India: 1950-51 to 1965-66*, 1970; Central Statistical Organisation, *National Accounts Statistics, 1960-61*, 1973-74, February 1976.

Similarly the gross domestic savings have registered a rise from Rs 973 crores (19.4 per cent) in 1950-51 to 9414 crores (16.4 per cent) in 1973-74.[32] It has further risen to Rs 13,000 crores in 1976-77. The foreign assistance during 1957-58 amounted to about 4 per cent of the gross domestic product and provided as much as 29 per cent of the total finance for capital formation. It has, however, declined in recent years to 5 per cent of India's gross capital formation. There is also a phenomenal increase in irrigation, power, agricultural and industrial output, foreign exchange, the number of literates comprising both technical and scientific personnel and other various allied services. All this increase is to be viewed in the context of a population growth of 2.23 per cent per annum between 1961 and 1971. However, considering the impact of all these factors on the growth of income, the estimation is that the gross national product has risen from Rs 9503 crores in 1950-51 to Rs 70,700 crores in 1975-76 at current prices and the per capita income during the same period from Rs 266 to 1,178. But the relative rates of growth over a series of years has been uneven and fluctuating.[33]

However, although the relative rates of growth is uneven, the absolute increase in the aggregate and per capita income cannot be underscored. But the main issue is the pattern of distribution of income among the different sections of the population of the country since the per capita income does not reflect the real position of accrual of income to each individual or household belonging to different occupational categories. Further, this issue has become all the more important in the light of awareness of accentuation of inequalities of income despite the vast proliferation of socialist and social welfare legislations. The failure to remove social and economic injustice and to secure minimum levels of living embodied as directive principles in the Indian constitution remains glaring. The inequality proportion is in fact highlighted by the evidences of several studies made in the recent years in the country.

Several statistical measures of the extent of poverty[34] have been developed in India by using the data of National Sample Surveys, NCAER, CSO and Reserve Bank of India. Although the data is not quite comprehensive and accurate, a large amount of reasonably good data has helped many studies. Some of the studies considered for this purpose are those of Burdhan, 1970; Dandekar and Rath, 1971; Minhas, 1970; Vaidyanathan, 1971; Ojha-Bhat, 1974; Randive, 1971; Ahmed and Bhattacharya,[35] and the Indian Institute of Public opinion, New Delhi, 1976. These various studies have been reviewed by P.K. Burdhan[36] and they indicate glaring

[32]*Ibid*.

[33]Refer *Basic Statistics Relating to the Indian Economy* ,Vol I, Table 6.2.

[34]Relative or absolute poverty is only a reflection of an unequal distribution of income irrespective of what the income level might be.

[35]P. K. Burdhan, "The Pattern of Income Distribution in India—Review" in *Poverty and Income Distribution in India* (ed) by T.N. Srinivasan and P.K. Burdhan, Statistical Publishing Society, Calcutta, 1974, pp.103-7.

[36]*Ibid*., pp. 103-7.

inequalities in the levels of income and in the consumption expenditure
between the top 20 per cent and the bottom 20 per cent of the population.
According to the NCAER (1964-65), the bottom 20 per cent of the population shared only 7.5 per cent of the total disposable income whereas the
top 20 per cent enjoyed as large a share as 47.5 per cent of the total.
Assessing the rural and uaban households separately the same study (1964-
65), pointed out that the bottom 20 per cent of the rural population shared
only 7.39 per cent of the total income from the rural sector. On the other
hand, the share of the top 20 per cent in the total rural income was as
large as 44.65 per cent. Similarly in the case of the urban bottom 20 per
cent, the share was only 5.52 per cent of the total urban income, and that of
the top 20 per cent 5.4 per cent of the total. The estimate of Ojha-Bhatt[37]
based on the national income data of the Central Statistical Organization
(1974) revealed the share of the bottom 20 per cent of the population as
7 per cent of the disposable personal income and that of the top 20 per
cent as 48 per cent. Ranadive's estimates for 1961-62 were 7.6 to 7.8 per
cent of the total disposable income for the bottom 20 per cent and 45.5 to
46.7 per cent for the top 20 per cent. The estimates of Ahmed and Bhattacharya range round 7.6 per cent of the total personal income for the bottom
20 per cent and 45.6 per cent for the top 20 per cent. Taking the five estimates together, the bottom 20 per cent of the population has a share
between 7 and 8 per cent of the total personal income; and the top 20 per
cent between 45 per cent and 48 per cent. The Lorenz ratio is between 0.35
and 0.39. Burdhan's review of these various studies on the distribution of
income by decile groups further revealed a very large jump in the income
share of the top decile i.e. by nearly 2 to 3 times higher than the preceding
decile and it was actually 13 times of that of the lowest decile[37] indicating
the extreme concentration at the top.

A consideration even from the point of view of consumption expenditure,
which is supposed to give a fairly reliable idea of the distribution in terms
of the levels of living, revealed a share of 8 per cent in the total consumption expenditure for the bottom 20 per cent of the rural population and 39
per cent for the top 20 per cent. In the case of urban population, the share
for the bottom 20 per cent was only 7 per cent. But for the top 20 per cent,
it was as big as 42 per cent..[38] Actually even in terms of per capita consumption expenditure considered necessary to maintain at least the minimum levels of living, which of course, varies from Rs 15 to Rs 20 per
capita per month at 1960-61 prices,[39] the proportion falling below the

[37]*Ibid.*, p. 112.

[38]*Ibid.*, p. 114.

[39]The recommendations of per capita consumption expenditure at 1960-61 prices for
minimum levels of living by the different groups and individuals are as below:
   (*a*) Distinguished study group of the Planning Commission—Rs 20 per capita per
       month.
   (*b*) Minhas (1970) and Vaidyanathan (1974) Rs 20 per capita per month.

poverty line is estimated to be sizeable. Therefore, glaring inequalities in the levels of living can also be reflected through the consumption expenditure. Burdhan[40] using the official agricultural labour consumer price index for deflating the consumption of the rural poor and the official working class consumer price index for deflating that of the urban poor estimated that 54 per cent of the rural and 41 per cent of the urban population (1968-69) were below the poverty line. Again comparing the trends between two periods, i.e. 1960-61 and 1967-68, the estimate by the same economist (Burdhan) showed a marked increase of the rural people below the poverty line from 38 per cent in 1960-61 to 54 per cent in 1968-69. Similarly among the urban population, the percentage below the poverty line increased from 32 in 1960-61 to 41 in 1968-69. Dandekar and Rath's estimation of the proportion of the population below the poverty line which was based on consumer's expenditure showed 40 per cent for the rural and 50 per cent for the urban population.[41] Minhas, assessment (based on NSS data) for different years between 1956-57 and 1967-68, reflecting the percentage shares in total consumption expenditure of different fractile groups of rural population at the current prices of different years, indicates little change in the concentration index over a period of 11 years.[42] Further, the Indian Institute of Public Opinion, New Delhi, taking the Draft Fifth Five Year Plan definition of the poverty line, i.e. "a minimum desirable consumption standard" of Rs 46.60 per capita per month at 1972-73 prices pointed out that Indians below the poverty line rose from 30 per cent in 1960-61 to 45 per cent in 1970-71.[43]

On the basis of all these studies, the possible inference is that in spite of economic growth, the poverty proportions have not been reduced and the inequalities of income, on the other hand, have considerably increased. Added to this, there cannot be any denial of the fact that inflation has further accentuated the income contrasts between the masses and the privileged minority through erosion of wages and salaries and windfall, profits brought by the rising prices for the benefit of employers, traders and industrialists.

The glaring inequalities in income and the consequent differences in the levels of living and welfare can be attributed to the continuance of concentration of asset holding in spite of several taxes on income and wealth.

(c) Dandekar and Rath (1971)—Rs 15 per capita per month for the rural poverty line and Rs 22.5 for the urban poverty line.

(d) P.K. Burdhan, (1970s (a)), 1970 b), (1973)—Rs 15 per capita per month for the rural poverty line and Rs 18 for the urban poverty line

(e) Ashoka Rudra (1974)—Rs 22.73 per capita per month (based on retail prices) for rural India in 1960-61.

[40] Burdhan, *op.cit*, p. 130.

[41] V.M. Dandekar, and N. Rath., *Poverty in India*, Indian School of Political Economy, 1971.

[42] B.S. Minhas, *Planning and the Poor*, 1974, pp. 64-68.

[43] R. Shenoy, "Little Growth and Less Social Justice," *Indian Express*, 16 February 1977.

The income tax laws allowed numerous exemptions and deductions in order to promote various non-tax objectives. This narrowed down the base and extended unrealized capital gains. The tax on capital was estimated to have touched not more than 1 per cent of the total gains,[44] which the top wealth owners derived annually in the form of appreciation of asset values. The average yield in the ten years 1960-61 to 1969-70 was found to be only Rs 4 crores as contrasted with the Kaldor's calculation of 25 crores[45] over a number of years. The capital gains tax did not thus affect the inequalities accruing through the appreciation of the value of wealth. The same study by Bagchi highlighted that the estate duty, gift tax and wealth tax did not contain the accentuation of the inequalities resulting from the concentration of wealth. Moreover, monetary incentives in the form of low rates of interest and various other incentive schemes such as tax rebates, subsidized seed, fertilizers, capital equipment and irrigational facilities did not touch the poorer rural households, and also the mounting educated and illiterate unemployed, since they did not have the productive means to use all the above facilities extended by the Government. The social investment undertaken over the last more than two and half decades in the form of education, medical and other public facilities, credit planning, creation of infrastructural facilities and so on mainly benefited the relatively larger asset holders and hardly the poor.

With the result, the estimates of concentration ratio for assets owned by rural households, according to the study of V.V. Divatia and U.D. Choudhury[46] indicated an increase from 0.65 in 1961-62 to 0.68 in 1971-72. The poorest 20 per cent of the rural households were estimated to own no assets or not even 1 per cent of the total assets. But the top 10 per cent had more than 50 per cent of the assets in 1961 and as well as in 1971-72. In terms of money value, more than one-third of the households had assets of less than Rs 2,500 each and over 50 per cent less than Rs 5,000 each. The value of assets of the former just amounted to 3 per cent of the total. Actually the combined share of the top 50 per cent of the households was 92 per cent of the total assets. Any growth in wealth would essentially, therefore, measure the increase in the assets of the richer households but not of those owning only 8 per cent of the total.[47]

Again, according to another estimation of Sree Lekha Basu, the proportion of total assets (which are nothing but broad dimensions) shared by the top 25 per cent of the households amounted to 74.70 per cent and those

[44]Amaresh Bagchi, "Re-distributive Role of Taxation in India," T.P. Srinivasan and P.K. Bardhan (ed), *op. cit*, p. 441.

[45]*Ibid.*, p. 457.

[46]V.V. Divatia's document "Inequalities of Asset Distribution of Rural House-holds" bases its estimates on the 1971-72 survey result of the RBI. These estimates consider Kuznets', index Gini Co-efficient, V. Value etc., for the different States.

[47]Sreelekha, Basu, "Pattern of Asset-Holding in Rural India: A Study of Top Asset-Holders," *Economic and Political Weekly*, Vol, 11, No.28, 10 July 1976, p. 1037.

of the top 50 per cent, to 91.89 per cent. The remaining 50 per cent shared as small a chunk as 8.11 per cent of the total rural assets.[48] The concentration ratio of asset distribution was found to be as high as 0.66111 and the highest one per cent of the house-holds held 14 per cent of the total assets. The disparity becomes very glaring when the average asset value per household is taken between those of the top 50 per cent and the bottom 50 per cent. In case of the former, it was Rs 20,900 and in the latter, it amounted only to Rs 1836 per household.[49]

All these figures clearly indicate the glaring inequalities in the pattern of holding assets, in spite of various fiscal, monetary and social welfare measures. This feature is conspicuous when inter-state and intra-state proportion of total assets shared by different groups are also compared (See Tables 1 and 2). A look at Table 1 indicates that inequalities have increased in Assam, Gujarat, Karnataka, Orissa, Punjab, Rajasthan and Tamil Nadu. There is a slight fall in the asset concentration in Andhra, Jammu and Kashmir and Kerala due to somewhat effective asset distribution. In states like Bihar, Maharashtra, United Province and West Bengal inequalities remain the same. Considering the all-India situation, the share of the rich "privileged group" in the total assets has improved slightly from 91.3 per cent in 1962 to 91.9 per cent in 1971. The overall picture is that there is no reduction either in the share of the top 50 per cent in the total assets or in the inequality distribution among them. Shares of most of the sub-groups have remained the same except those of the top 5 per cent where ownership of total assets recorded a fall from 37.0 per cent in 1962 to 35.3 per cent in 1971.

The variations in group shares were not very marked in Orissa, Punjab, and Rajasthan. Actually in Andhra Pradesh, Bihar, Kerala, Madhya Pradesh and United Provinces the share of asset holdings for the top 10 per cent has declined, whereas in Gujarat, Maharashtra, and Orissa the share of the top 10 per cent has appreciated.

Among the different types of assets owned, land is the most important for the rural households. The aggregate value of the assets in the form of land was 66.2 per cent (AIDSS 1971). Bihar, Maharashtra, Punjab, Haryana and Tripura have more than 70 per cent of their assets in land. In fact, the top 50 per cent owned 93 per cent of the total land and the lowest 25 per cent possessed hardly any land. On an average, the top 50 per cent households owned land worth about Rs 14,000 per household, compared to only Rs 1050 worth of land by the bottom half.[50] The pattern of actual distribution of economic resources among rural households as shown in Table 3 will spotlight the glaring inequalities.

---

[48] *Ibid.*, p. 1038.
[49] *Ibid.*, p. 1037. The assets compared mostly durables such as ornaments, household utensils, furniture, small huts and livestock.
[50] *Ibid.*, p. 1040.

TABLE 1

Proportion of Total Assets Shared by Various Groups of Rural Households, Period June 30, 1962 and June 30, 1971

(in percentages)

States	Top 5%		Top 10%		Top 25%		Top 40%		Top 50%	
	1962	1971	1962	1971	1962	1971	1962	1971	1962	1971
1. Andhra Pradesh	41.5	40.70	59.3	56.59	81.8	78.33	91.1	89 61	94.3	94.11
2. Assam	27.9	26.50	39.3	40.31	63.0	65.64	79.2	79.83	85.0	83.03
3. Bihar	36.8	37.01	54.5	52.25	78.1	76.29	85.0	87.50	92.6	92.72
4. Gujarat	27.5	30.95	44.4	47.25	70.7	72.80	85.1	85.63	90.4	91.10
5. Jammu and Kashmir	23.7	21.33	34.6	33.50	58.4	55.94	74.2	71.35	81.4	79.42
6. Kerala	43.7	36.44	57.5	51.60	81.4	75.40	91.2	84.82	94.5	91.25
7. Madhya Pradesh	30.6	20.11	44.9	43.16	69.0	68.45	82.0	81.43	88.0	88.41
8. Madras	41.5	39.90	56.3	56.16	80.0	79.33	90.8	90.72	94.0	94.69
9. Maharashtra	33.7	32.42	47.0	48.60	74.2	74.00	87.2	86.25	92.3	92.87
10. Karnataka	37.5	38.40	52.4	52.83	73.4	76.03	86.0	87.60	91.3	92.73
11. Orissa	29.3	31.52	41.5	45.06	65.7	68.01	80.6	82.50	86.5	88.56
12. Punjab	21.2	30.50	40.0	50.30	72.5	79.05	85.8	92.23	92.0	95.21
13. Rajasthan	25.2	29.05	37.8	42.46	61.6	66.35	76.7	80.15	84.1	85.47
14. Uttar Pradesh	33.5	31.35	45.8	43.98	69.5	69.03	81.4	82.33	88.2	88.31
15. West Bengal	33.4	34.00	49.4	49.58	74.1	74.85	86.9	87.31	92.0	92.37
All India inclusive of Goa & Pondicherry	37.0	35.27	50.3	50.56	74.0	74.70	86.2	86.61	91.3	91.89

Source: A.I.R.D.I.S 1961-68 and A.I.D.I.S.—1971.

TABLE 2
Estimates of Gini Coefficients for Asset Concentration

States	Top 50 per cent 1962	Top 50 per cent 1971
1. Andhra Pradesh	0.5436	0.5104
2. Assam	0.3610	0.4178
3. Bihar	0.4791	0.4783
4. Gujarat	0.3969	0.4389
5. Jammu and Kashmir	0.3144	0.2985
6. Madhya Pradesh	0.4340	0.3721
7. Kerala	0.5347	0.5045
8. Madras	0.4692	0.5110
9. Maharashtra	0.4315	0.4262
10. Karnataka	0.4652	0.4973
11. Orissa	0.3818	0.4770
12. Punjab	0.3593	0.4588
13. Rajastban	0.3363	0.4062
14. Uttar Pradesh	0.4155	0.4118
15. West Bengal	0.4407	0.4527
16. All India	0·4566	0.4657

TABLE 3
Distribution of Economic Resources Among the Rural Households (1971-72)

percentage

Items	Poor (a) tenants	Small (b) farmers	Well-to-do (c) farmers
	(a)	(b)	(c)
1. Households	60.28	29.28	10.34
2. Area operated	9.25	37.52	53.23
3. Irrigation (all types)	15.09	38.98	45.93
4. Term loans (outstanding amount in 1973-74)			
(a) Public sector	5.10	32.62	62.29
(b) Private sector	3.96	18.75	77.29
5. Agricultural machinery (value)	4.45	33.30	62.25
6. Total gross value of output (Rs crors)	683.36	2,716.8	3,705.3
7. Marketable surplus as % of total output.	20.1	25.8	45.5

Source: NSS 26th Round.No.215, Agricultural Census of India, Government of India 1975.

Reserve Bank of India, *Monthly Bulletin*, April 1974 and August 1974.

(a) Poor persons—all those who own small plots of land i.e.2.50 acres

(b) Small farmers—all those who own small plots of land i.e.2.50 to 10 acres

(c) Well-to-do farmers all those who own small plots above 10 acres.

Table 3 indicates that at one end are the large or the well-to-do farmers constituting just one-tenth of the total rural households. These households account for more than half (53 per cent) of the total operated agricultural area. At the other end are the poor tenants (landless labourers and farmers cultivating up to 2.50 acres) constituting about 60 per cent of the households and cultivating only 9 per cent of the agricultural land. In between the two are the small farmers comprising about 30 per cent of the rural households and account for 37 per cent of the operated area.

No doubt, the unequal land distribution is only a partial, though fundamental, index of inequality. Considering other items, animals, tools and implements, electric pumps and agricultural machinery and access to irrigation are highly favourable to the large farmers. Similarly with regard to the distribution of term loans by the public as well as private sector banks, the large farmers have received 62 per cent of the total loans, while the small farmers and the poor tenants account for only 33 per cent and 5 per cent of these loans respectively. With the result, the share of the large farmers in the gross value of agricultural output and in the marketable surplus is big.

The glaring inequalities in the asset holding of the rural households can be ascribed partly to the failure in the policies aimed at direct distribution of existing assets and partly to the absence of effective impact of certain policies related to public investment in the provision of various types of facilities and to infrastructure aimed at helping to raise productivity and asset formation on the part of the poor themselves. Regarding the former, the implementation has been hampered on account of various factors such as fictitious transfer of land to close and distant relatives to keep the size of permissible retention high, indifferent local bureaucracy favouring mainly rural oligarchy and slow judicial process. With the result, only a small portion of the land has been redistributed. The following figures borne out by the data of the Bombay weekly for the period ending 9 July 1976 and highlighted in an article, on Trends in Distribution of Property, by Rajkrishna substantiate the negligible redistribution of land.[51]

LAND SURPLUS IN INDIA
(Area in Million acres)

1. Estimated surplus	4.04 (1.5 per cent of the total area owned by rural households)
2. Declared surplus	2.03
3. Acquired surplus	2.02
4. Distributed surplus	0.63

With regard to the latter policies aiming at the building up of infrastructure and asset formation on the part of the poor, the Programme

[51]Rajkrishna, "On Trends in Redistribution of Property," *Indian Express*, 3 March 1977.

Evalution Organization of the Planning Commission has made out that subsidized co-operative credit, extension services from the community development programmes and irrigational benefits have been appropriated only by rich farmers by virtue of their social and economic dominance in the country side and their political and administrative control over these new institutions. This has been by far the trend all over the country and moreover the small farmers lack the finance to invest in tube-wells, pumps and other mechanical devices for supplementary water supplies.

Even Small Farmers Development Agencies and the Agency for Marginal Farmers and Agricultural Labour (MFAL) developed in recent years have not yet made much impact, since the number to be covered is very large and needs identification of the economically viable activities such as farm level infrastructure and required inputs, services and credit suited for the individual small farmers. However, strengthening the general area-level infrastructure (like development of marketing, processing, storage, transport, etc.) has generally benefited those who have relatively larger land and hence enabled them to produce more than the small or the marginal farmer. Further, the credit policies of co-operatives, land development banks and the commercial banks in extending credit are largely governed by the size of the land assets. Therefore, the benefit of inputs has largely accrued to the rich farmers. The tenants and the share croppers do not have any access even to a short-term co-operative bank credit and largely depend on the exploitative moneylenders.

Public investment in human capital formation by spreading educatian is also an important means of bringing about a better distribution of income in the long run. Considering the trends in the participation of higher education, both general and technical, the higher income groups in India are relatively in an advantageous position as compared with those of the poor or low income groups. With the result, the benefits of public investment in education have accrued more to the relatively richer urban groups than to the low income holders or the poor in rural areas.

Another redistributive tool, which is of significance, is that of public investment in rural works programmes. This type of investment is expected to create alternative employment for rural skilled and underemployed labour and produce at the same time durable assets in the form of roads, soil conservation, minor irrigation and afforestation without using scarce inputs like steel and cement. In this context the Crash Scheme for Rural Employment in India which was initiated in every district is worth consideration. This scheme, in spite of its good intentions, failed to provide continuity of employment partly due to the inefficiency of the administrative machinery to prepare technically sound projects suited to specific problems of training, skills and location and partly to the failure to mobilize responsible local participation in terms of financial and organizational efforts. Besides political pulls and regional pressures hindered mobility of labour.

Finally, the government-evolved price, income, and tax-subsidy policies to help the poor are also important. Considering the support prices to food grains and the distribution of procured grains at fair prices, it is very much apparent, that much of the benefit has reached only the big farmers. This is due to the fact that a major part of the marketable surplus comes from the big farmers. In respect of income policy again, it is evident that the statutory stipulation of minimum wages in unorganized industry or agriculture where the overwhelming majority of the poor work is inoperative. So far as the direct provision of public consumption and welfare measure for the poor in the form of health and sanitation, nutrition, drinking water, housing, education, electricity, transport and communication are concerned there is some progress over the last two decades but the minimum needs of many are inadequately met with.

Income Inequality in the Urban Areas

Similarly, an examination of the asset inequalities in the urban areas highlights the failure of the asset redistribution policies. The estimated assets of the top 20 houses for 1966-67 by the Licensing Policy Inquiry Committee was Rs 2089 crores.[52] These assets, according to the findings of the Research Bureau of *Economic Times*, increased to Rs 5110 crores, nearly more than double by 1975-76.[53] Moreover, these assets, which constituted 61 per cent of the paid-up capital in 1965-67 increased to 68 per cent in 1972-73.[54] Actually, the heaviest concentration was only in two top companies, Tatas and Birlas and the assets increased from 968 crores in 1966-67 to Rs 2039 crores in 1975-76.[55]

The overall effect of the concentration of the assets was the increase in the monopoly power and the transfer of income from the masses of consumers to a handful of large-scale producers through the monopolist price mechanism. In fact even the share of the small industries, which was about 42 per cent of the national income in 1960-61 declined to 34 per cent in 1974-75.

In terms of the total sales, according to the study of G.B. Singh,[56] four firms controlled more than half of the total sales in steel, aluminium, transport equipment, petroleum, cement, synthetic fibres, paper, food products, cigarettes and rubber products in 1960, 1965 and 1970. The last six are consumer goods industries where concentration is likely to be associated with direct consumer exploitation.

All these prove, that in spite of various policy declarations and attempts to bring down income inequalities, the results are far below the expected

[52]R.Shenoy, "Little Growth and Less Social Justice," *Indian Express*, 16 February 1977.
[53]*Ibid.*
[54]*Ibid.*
[56]*Ibid.*
[56]*Ibid.*

targets. The general trend has been one of appropriation by the rich a disproportionate share of the benefits of public investment. Moreover with low or negative rates of profits in public enterprises and huge subsidies paid in support of prices to big farmers, there is little surplus left to help the poor. The magnitude of the number steeped in poverty and unemployment continues to be phenomenal. The various policy measures pursued so far to promote distributive justice along with growth have been ineffective.

Major Policy Approaches to Overcome Inequalities

Under these circumstances of persistently continuing and glaring inequalities of income and wealth, there is a need for a reformulation of the developmental as well as other policies designed to promote larger social justice. Although distributional objectives cannot be thought of independently of growth objectives, the basic approach will have to lay relatively greater emphasis on the redirection of investment sector-wise and socio-economic group-wise to raise the level and growth of income of lower income groups. Redistribution of consumption by identifying properly several poverty groups such as small farmers, landless labourers, urban unemployed and others is equally essential. Such an emphasis will monitor development performance not simply in terms of growth of GNP but in terms of the distributional pattern of income growth. In bringing about such a change in the strategy, the Government has to play a vital role by reallocation of investment in various planned programmes so as to maximize welfare, and also endeavour for effective redistribution of the assets such as land, privately owned capital, access to public capital goods and human capital. Land is the major means of production on which the overwhelming majority in India depend for their living. An attempt, therefore, to solve the problems of the small farmers without first correcting the maldistribution of land and other resources will end in a fiasco. Further, the variation in income at the lower levels is due to the lack of skills as well as lack of ownership of physical capital and access to complementary assets and other inputs. Inequality of income can, therefore, be minimized by increasing the ownership of private capital and access to public facilities. This needs a pursuance of a policy, in favour of those factors of production that are owned by the lower income groups; alteration in the pattern of concentration of productive assets over time; and elimination of barriers in order to enable entry into more profitable types of production. With nearly 40 per cent to 50 per cent of the population below the poverty line public investment has to pay particular attention to 473.4 lakhs agricultural labourers deriving their income mainly from unskilled labour and 36.0 lakhs small and marginal farmers relying on a combination of family labour and small amounts of land. These also include self-employed craftsmen, artisans and those engaged in various services in villages. In the urban areas, they comprise both skilled and unskilled workers and a large number of the underemployed engaged in low productivity self-employment. The scope for the productive use of the unskilled labour force depends on the development of skills or human capital through education and this helps for a greater absorption of labour in the modern sector.

While thus stressing on raising the income of poorer groups, the policy evolved should build up linkages among different groups. In fact the policy objectives will have to be one of providing an appropriate mix of education, public facilities, increased access to credit, land reforms and promotion of physical and human capital in order to increase productivity and income of the poor.

Equally important are the policies in the direction of price and income controls. This needs measures to curb concentration of wealth and income. Considering the concentration of assets in the big houses, it is necessary to review the Monopolies and Restrictive Trade Practices Act in order to effectively bring about greater diffusion of economic power and greater equality in the distribution of wealth and income.

With social justice as the ultimate goal of the country a wide range of policies giving maximum manoeuvrability in plan implementation to raise the levels and growth of income in different socio-economic groups are necessary. In a country like India with a mixed economy structure, the strategy of socialization has been pursued. This strategy has, of course, accelerated public sector investment and phenomenally increased the share of the public sector as against the private sector. The main difficulty is that it is by no means certain that the pursuit of this strategy leads to a continuous improvement in the distribution of income. Moreover, the efficiency of public sector enterprises which have led to socialization of assets has become an issue of much concern and attention and the distributional impact of income of these undertakings is mainly limited to the workers employed.

However, apart from this trend of socialization of assets, a policy of direct investment support to raise the income of the lowest income groups coupled with the effective implementation of measures designed to alter the asset concentratiou patterns will accentuate the promotion of distributional objective. Since low income results from the lack of physical capital, access to infrastructure and a wide range of complementary inputs along with asset distribution and direct investment in the poverty sector leading to the creation of capital and employment are necessary. The policy orientation of the present government to the integrated development of the rural areas and increased employment generation is a welcome change, which needs to be expeditiously carried throughout the country in order to successfully eradicate poverty or eliminate inequalities of income. Rural development programmes should accentuate promotion of the rural infrastructure helping land improvement, drainage, small irrigation, feeder roads, credit and marketing institutions.

Equally important is the promotion of skills through education. There is a growing evidence, that the educational expansion involving particularly higher education has tended to be directed disproportionately towards higher income groups than that of the poor in India. Hence the educational programmes will have to aim at the diffusion of human skill in different regions. The main issue here is to adopt broadening programmes of education so as to benefit the poor. The emphasis will have to be, therefore, on vocational training rather than high academic orientation. Education is the best means of promoting growth and equality.

It is also of paramount importance for the government to increase public expenditure on public health and nutritional programmes, family planning and on extension of water supply and rural electrification to ensure basic necessities to the poor. Besides, price subsidies on essential and critical items of consumption need continuation for the benefit of the lower income groups. If policy of the Government is rigidly directed towards maintaining the price of wage goods at a low level, it is as good as the transfer of real income to the poor. This policy is particularly important in view of its impact on the urban poor who receive money incomes and whose real incomes are highly sensitive to wage goods prices.

The subsidies, no doubt, amount to heavy drain on budgetary resources. But the cost of these resources will have to be measured in terms of alternative investment possibilities which could provide the basis for self-sustaining growth of incomes among the poor groups in future.

Finally progressive fiscal and monetary policy measures coupled with labour-intensive industrialization in the poverty stricken pockets will considerably influence both the level and the distribution of income.

In a nutshell, both negative and positive approaches to overcome the inequalities of income are necessary. Radical redistribution of assets, limitation of dividends, direct taxes on income, wealth and wealth increases, indirect taxes on luxuries and curbs on further accumulation of capital are negative in character. Promotion of skills through education, direct investments in poverty pockets and the consequent capital formation and the employment generation, expenditure on social and economic infrastructure are positive approaches.

N. SREENIVASA IYENGAR AND LILA RAM JAIN

On Inflation and its Differential Effects

INTRODUCTION

Price inflation reduces the purchasing power of money incomes in general and its impact on the living standards of households is not uniform. In this paper we propose a method of measuring the intensity of inflation by computing a set of differential price deflators.

The need for differential price deflators arises when one wants to compare two or more distributions of household incomes or expenditures over time or space (Iyengar and Bhattacharya, 1965). Since the pioneering study of Mahalanobis (1962) on the distribution of cereals in India, a number of attempts have been made to measure differential price effects (Iyengar, 1967; Vaidyanathan, 1974; Chatterjee and Bhattacharya, 1974). A brief review of these studies is available in Bardhan (1974).

More recently, Radhakrishna and Sarma (1974) have approached the same problem in a somewhat different manner. Their method relies on the use of linear Engel curves for the computation of index weights. It also makes use of a two parameter lognormal distribution for graduating the observed distribution of levels of living in the reference period. The present study is, however, based on slightly more general specifications, both in respect of the form of the Engel relationships and the parametric form of the expenditure distribution, but the prices used in the two studies are the same. Our empirical results indicate that the intensity of inflation was generally more severe for the poorer sections of the population in recent years.

A rigorous formulation of the problem is given in Section 2. The data and method of estimation are explained in Section 3. Our main results are reported in Section 4 and the major limitations of the study are discussed in the concluding section.

FORMULATION OF THE PROBLEM

Let $P_t = P_{t1}, P_{t2} \ldots P_{tn}$ be a column vector of prices of n items of household expenditure in the period t $(t = O, 1 \ldots T)$ and let $q_t = q_{t1}, q_{t2}, \ldots q_{tn}$ be the corresponding quantities purchased by a household in the same period. The total outlay on q_t at "current" prices is given by

$$E_t = E_{t1} + E_{t2} + \ldots + E_{tn} \tag{2.1}$$

where

$$E_{tj} = P_{tj}\, q_{tj} \tag{2.2}$$

The proportion of total outlay spent on the jth specific item is denoted by w_{tj}. That is

$$w_{tj} = E_{tj}/E_t \tag{2.3}$$

so that $0 < w_{tj} < 1$ and $\Sigma_j w_{tj} = 1$ for every t. The ratios (w_{tj}) are also called Engel ratios, and the mathematical relationships between E_{tj} and E_t are known as Engel curves. The well-known Engel's Law postulates that w_{tj} is a diminishing (increasing) function of E_t if the specific item j is income inelastic (elastic). The inelastic items are usually identified with essential items of mass consumption while the elastic items are treated as luxury. The pattern of household expenditure is, thus, represented by the column vector of budget weights (w_t). The budget pattern is an essential ingredient of a consumer price index, the other ingredient being the price ratios or relatives:

$$r_{tj} = p_{tj}/p_{oj} \text{ for all } j = 1, 2. \ldots n_n \tag{2.4}$$

where p_{oj} is the price of the jth item of consumption in the reference period O. The index of price change between the periods O and t can be written in Laspeyre's form:

$$L_{t,\,o} = 100\, \Sigma_j\, w_{tj}\, r_{tj} \text{ for all } t = 1, 2, \ldots T \tag{2.5}$$

where $(w_o) = (w_{o1}, w_{o2}, \ldots w_{on})$ are the budget weights in the initial or reference year. These weights are, of course, related to the level of outlay E_o in the period.

Let $f(E_o)$ be the frequency function of E_o. This is referred to as the size distribution of expenditure in the initial period. At any point, say E^*_o, on the distribution it is possible in principle to define a set of budget weights w^*_{oj} and compute a specific price index by replacing w_o in (2.5) by w^*_o.

However, it is usually at the mean $\bar{E}_o$ or the median $\tilde{E}_o$ that one would like to compute a price index. Also, it may be of interest to compute price indices for the different frequency intervals in a given distribution of household expenditures and study the inter-class variations in price effects.

If the Engel curves are linear, as in Radhakrishna's case, we may write:

$$E_{oj} = A_j + B_j\, E_o \quad \text{for all } j = 1, 2. \ldots n \tag{2.6}$$

so that

$$w_{oj} = B_j + A_j/E_o \tag{2.7}$$

is a decreasing function of E_o if A_j is positive; it is increasing when A_j is negative. The linear system (2.6) is viable only when the following conditions hold:

$$\text{(i) } E_o > -A_j/B_j \text{ for all } j \tag{2.8}$$
$$\text{(ii) } \Sigma_j \ A_j = O, \ \Sigma_j \ B_j = 1$$

For household living on a total budget of E_o in the initial year the overall rise in prices in a terminal year t is given by (2.5):

$$L_{t,o} = B + A/E_o \tag{2.9}$$

where $B = \Sigma_j B_j \ r_{tj}$ and $A = \Sigma_j \ A_j \ r_{tj}$ are linear homogeneous functions of the price relative and independent of E_o. Obviously, if $A > 0$, then $\overline{L}_{t,o}$ is higher for households with lower value of E_o and vice versa. If $A = O$, there is no such price discrimination and the impact of prices on households is uniform. The case $A > O$ corresponds to the case visualized by Mahalanobis (1961).

In the linear expenditure system of Stone (1954) the Engel curves take the form:

$$E_{oj} = \bar{\bar{E}}_{oj} + b_j \ (E_o - \bar{\bar{E}}_o) \tag{2.10}$$

Here, $\bar{\bar{E}}_{oj}$ represents the "committed" or "irreducible" expenditure on item j and $\bar{\bar{E}}_o$ is the minimum committed (or subsistence) total needs of a household to live in a community. In this model, planning of budgets has no meaning if the household cannot spend more than $\bar{\bar{E}}_o$. Any outlay over and above $\bar{\bar{E}}_o$ is proportionately allocated to the individual items according to the value of b_j. For the system to be additive, $\Sigma_j \ b_j = 1$. In this system, the budget weights are given by:

$$w_{oj} = b_j + c_j/E_o \tag{2.11}$$

where $c_j = E_{oj} - b_j \ E_o$ is positive for all j. Using the above weights in (2.5) we arrive at the following index for price change:

$$I_{t,o} = b + c/E_o \tag{2.12}$$

where $b = \Sigma_j b_j \ r_{tj}$ and $c = \Sigma_j c_j \ r_{tj}$ are linear combinations of the item price relatives. Since c_j and r_{tj} are positive, c is zero when every c_j is zero, that is, when $b_j = E_{oj}/E_o$. This may be interpreted as the pattern of expenditure incurred by the poorest household in a community or society. Equation (2.12) shows that a given price rise always affects the poor more adversely than the rich. Thus, Stone's model provides a strong case for the Mahalanobis's hypothesis. This aspect of the model will be further examined in a subsequent study.

Another interesting model of household expenditure behaviour is the well-known addi-log expenditure system derived from an indirect utility function (Houthakker, 1960).[1] The empirical relevance of this model for

---

[1]The indirect addi-log system was developed originally by Leser (1941). It was further developed and applied to Dutch data by Sommermeyer et al. (1962), and Parks (1969). The

Indian situation was first examined in a paper by Iyengar and Rao (1968), and later adopted by Iyengar and Jain (1973) for projecting consumer expenditures in India. The addi-log model consists of a family of non-linear additive Engel curves represented by the following equations:

$$E_{oj} = \delta_j \, E_o^{1+\Sigma_j} \Big/ \sum_r \delta_r \, E_o^{\Sigma_r} \qquad \text{for all } j = 1, 2, \ldots, n \quad (2.13)$$

where $(\delta_j \, \Sigma_j)$ are constant parameters. The budget weight of the jth item in this model can be written as:

$$w_{oj} = 1 \Big/ \sum_{r=1}^{n} \left(\frac{\delta_r}{\delta_j} \right) E_o^{\Sigma_r - \Sigma_j} \qquad (2.14)$$

The price index for this system can be readily computed if one knows the parameters. These parameters can easily be estimated from grouped expenditure data (see Jain, 1976). In this model one can show that the price index need not always decline with the rising level of E_o. A rigorous proof of this is perhaps difficult because of the intricate nature of the system. One may, instead, resort to empirical methods, taking full advantage of a computer. This is what we propose to do in the following section.

DATA AND METHOD OF ESTIMATION

In this study use has been made of the all-India average wholesale price indices published by the Office of the Economic Adviser to the Government of India. The data actually used cover a period of 21 years beginning from 1953-54. From these data, Radhakrishna and Sarma (1974) have obtained suitable price indices for the following ten composite items of household expenditure, following the National Sample Survey classification: (1) cereals, (2) pulses, (3) milk and milk products, (4) edible oils, (5) meat, fish and eggs, (6) sugar and gur, (7) other foods, (8) clothing, (9) fuel and light, and (10) non-food.

These data, which form a major input in our study, are shown in Appendix Table A-1. The composite price relatives were recalculated after

---

utility function underlying the system is:

$$U \left(\frac{E_o, E_o}{p_1 \, p_2}, \ldots \frac{E_o}{p_n} \right) = \sum_i \lambda_i \left(\frac{E_o}{P_i} \right)^{\sigma_j}$$

The derived demand relationships are:

$$q_i = \frac{\lambda_i \, \sigma_i \, E_o^{\sigma_i} \, p_i^{-\sigma_i^{-1}}}{\sum_j \lambda_j \, \sigma_j \, E_o^{\sigma_j - 1} \, p_j^{-\sigma_j}}$$

$$i = 1, 2, \ldots n$$

Here, λ_j, σ_i are parameters. In cross-sections, the prices p_i are treated as fixed parameters and hence absorbed into λ_i.

shifting the base to 1964-65, since the year 1953-54 was considered unsuitable for our present purpose.

Estimates of budget weights for the base year (1964-65) were taken from the National Sample Survey, 19th round, separately for rural and urban households. The National Sample Survey of India classifies sample households into classes according to their standard of living which is measured by the household's monthly per capita total expenditure. The 13 classes are: Rs 0-8, 8-11, 11-13, 13-15, 15-18, 18-21, 21-24, 24-28, 28-34, 34-43, 43-55, 55-75, 75 and above; and, for each class, estimates of mean expenditures on various items of consumption and their totals are available in the National Sample Survey reports.

However, for certain purposes, it may be preferable to employ size distributions where the relative frequencies in various classes are equalized. The practical advantages of such fractile tabulations are brought out in a fundamental paper by Mahalanobis (1960). Where the data have already been tabulated according to fixed class intervals, it is possible to use some simple interpolations to convert the group means into fractile means. It is also possible to fit a suitable mathematical curve for the observed size distributions and derive the fractile means from the "graduated" distribution. In the present exercise, we have used a three parameter Lognormal curve for graduating the National Sample Survey expenditure distributions of rural and urban households of 1964-65. For a detailed discussion of the properties and estimation of the three parameter lognormal distribution from National Sample Survey data, the reader may see Iyengar and Jain (1974) and Jain (1975).

The expenditure variable E_o is said to be distributed lognormally with parameters $(K_o, \theta_o, \lambda_o)$ if the natural logarithm of the deviation $(E_o - K_o)$ is normally distributed with mean θ_o and standard deviation λ_o. The parameters $(K_o, \theta_o, \lambda_o)$ could be estimated from the same data in more than one way. We have, however, applied the standard method of maximum likelihood and the related "scoring" procedures of Rao (1965) for estimating the lognormal parameters. For the 1964-65 distributions the following estimates were obtained:

TABLE 1

Maximum Likelihood Estimates of Lognormal Parameters, Rural and Urban India, 1964-65

Sector	Parameter		
	K_o (Rs)	θ_o	λ_o
Rural	1.48704	2.97142	0.30469
Urban	4.39656	3.15355	0.51098

The mean expenditures[2] for various fractile classes, as derived from the

[2]For methodology see Jain (1976 b).

estimated lognormal distributions, are shown in Table 2.

TABLE 2

Estimated Fractile Means of Monthly Total Expenditure Per Head, Rural and Urban India, 1964-65

Fractile class (per cent)	Mean total expenditure (Rs)	
	Rural	Urban
00-01	0.06	0.08
00-05	17.86	9.93
05-10	10.28	12.74
00-10	9.06	11.33
10-20	12.48	15.54
20-30	14.93	18.86
30-40	17.27	22.19
40-50	19.71	25.82
50-60	22.43	30.05
60-70	25.67	35.32
70-80	29.89	42.48
80-90	36.32	54.02
90-100	54.41	90.70
90-95	44.95	70.47
95-100	63.87	110.93
99-100	87.88	166.28

The budget weights w_{oj} were obtained for each of the above fractile classes at the corresponding fractile means, using the addi-log formulation (2.13), for which the estimation of parameters was readily available (see, Jain, 1976a). The addi-log parameters were estimated from ordinary doublelog parameters as follows:

Expression (2.13) can also be written as:

$$E_{oj} = E_o / \sum_r \exp\left(\log \delta_{rj} + \Sigma_{rj} \log E_o\right) \tag{3.1}$$

where

$$\delta_{rj} = \delta_r / \delta_j \text{ and } \delta_{rj} = \underset{r}{\Sigma} - \underset{j}{\Sigma}$$

It is easy to show that

$$\text{est. } (\log \delta_{rj}) = \text{est. } (\log \overset{1}{\delta_r}) - \text{est. } (\log \overset{1}{\delta_j}) \tag{3.2}$$

$$\text{est. } \Sigma_{rj} = \text{est. } \overset{1}{\underset{r}{\Sigma}} - \text{est. } \overset{1}{\underset{j}{\Sigma}} \tag{3.3}$$

where $\overset{1}{\underset{j}{\Sigma}}$ and $\log \overset{1}{\underset{j}{\delta}}$ are parameters appearing in the ordinary doublelog relationship

$$\log E_{oj} = \log \overset{1}{\underset{j}{\delta}} + \overset{1}{\underset{j}{\Sigma}} \log E_o \tag{3.4}$$

Parameters $\log \delta^1{}_j$, $\Sigma^1{}_j$ were estimated by the method of least squares using the 1964-65 National Sample Survey data. The estimates of the doublelog parameters $\log \delta^1{}_j$ and $\Sigma^1{}_j$ for selected item of expenditure are given in Table 3.

TABLE 3

Least Squares Estimates of $\left(Log\ \delta_j^1,\ \Sigma_j^1 \right)$ for Selected Items of Expenditures
Rural and Urban India, 1964-65

Sl No.	Items of expenditure	Rural		Urban	
		est. log δ_j^1	est. Σ_j^1	est. log δ_j^1	est. Σ_j^1
1.	Cereals	0.53816	0.59748	1.33079	0.23541
2.	Pulses	−3.08435	1.00343	−1.78600	0.57178
3.	Milk, and milk products	−5.87594	1.89454	−3.71609	1.32173
4.	Edible oils	−3.79585	0.99652	−3.52015	1.01665
5.	Meat, fish & eggs	−3.31571	0.95259	−2.45177	0.77581
6.	Sugar and gur	−4.63675	1.33650	−1.04588	0.60341
7.	Other foods	−2.02071	0.96131	−2.38732	1.19548
8.	Fuel and light	−1.90503	0.66276	−1.73031	0.66745
9.	Clothing	−6.09855	2.03280	−6.48643	1.96500
10.	Other non-foods	−4.09110	1.66830	−5.46730	1.90507

Main Results and Their Discussion

Combining the estimated fractilewise budget weights of the base year with the item price index relatives, we obtain for each fractile class a series of price indices for every year from 1953-54 through 1973-74. Separate sets of index numbers were obtained for the rural and urban sectors, and these are given in Table 4 (R) and 4 (U). From these tables it would appear that the poorer sections of the population were affected by inflation more severely than the rich during the last ten years, though the extent of price differentials itself varied. However, during the period from 1953-54 to 1963-64 the opposite tendency is revealed, when the general prices were lower than the 1964-65 prices. Paradoxically, the same tendency is also revealed, though in a mild form, during the year 1970-72 when the price level was higher than the overall price level of 1964-65. A possible explanation for this paradox could be that the prices of two major food items—cereals, and sugar recorded a temporary fall while the prices of all other household items maintained a steady rise throughout the period from 1953-54 to 1973-74. The weights of these two items in the budgets of poorer households being larger, a fall in their prices could deflate the overall price index. Incidentally, the prices seemed to have reached an unprecedented high level in the year 1973-74 (see Table A-1).

Conclusions and Limitations

A broad conclusion of this study is that there is no general validity for the Mahalanobis hypothesis that inflation always affects the poor more adversely than the rich. No conclusions can, in fact, be regarded as independent of the models from which they are derived. The system of linear Engel

TABLE 4 (R)

Price Indices (with 1964-65 = 100) for 16 Fractile Classes for 1953-54 to 1973-74, Rural India

Sl No.	Fractile class	1953-54	1954-55	1955-56	1956-57	1957-58	1958-59	1959-60	1960-61	1961-62	1962-63
1.	00-01	65.68	59.36	58.52	66.91	69.95	71.98	72.22	74.04	74.33	76.12
2.	00-05	66.10	60.45	59.33	66.72	69.13	72.04	73.54	74.67	75.94	78.71
3.	05-10	66.30	60.79	59.64	66.86	69.22	72.18	73.81	74.92	76.28	79.15
4.	00-10	66.20	60.62	59.48	66.79	69.17	72.10	73.68	74.79	76.11	78.93
5.	10-20	66.48	61.10	59.91	66.99	69.33	73.31	74.05	75.14	76.57	79.51
6.	20-30	66.67	61.43	60.21	67.15	69.46	72.45	74.29	75.39	74.88	79.88
7.	30-40	66.85	61.73	60.48	67.31	69.60	72.59	74.51	75.62	77.16	80.21
8.	40-50	67.03	62.03	60.76	67.47	69.75	72.73	74.72	75.85	77.43	80.53
9.	50-60	67.22	62.35	61.06	67.64	69.91	72.89	74.94	76.10	77.72	80.86
10.	60-70	67.44	62.72	61.40	67.85	70.11	73.06	75.19	76.39	78.05	81.22
11.	70-80	67.70	63.15	61.81	68.12	70.37	73.28	75.49	76.75	78.44	81.65
12.	80-90	68.06	63.76	62.39	68.50	70.75	73.59	75.90	77.25	78.98	82.23
13.	90-100	68.89	65.15	63.71	69.42	71.68	74.32	76.80	78.42	80.22	83.50
14.	90-95	69.49	64.47	63.07	68.96	71.22	73.96	77.37	77.85	79.62	82.89
15.	95-100	69.23	65.72	64.28	69.82	72.10	74.63	77.17	78.93	80.74	84.01
16.	99-100	68.92	66.88	65.41	70.68	72.99	75.26	77.91	79.91	81.78	85.00
17.	bottom 10% minus top 10%	−2.68	−4.52	−4.23	−2.63	−2.51	−2.21	−3.12	−3.63	−4.10	−4.56
18.	bottom 5% minus top 5%	−3.13	−5.28	−4.94	−3.10	−2.97	−2.59	−3.63	−4.26	−4.79	−3.30
19.	bottom 1% minus top 1%	−4.24	−7.53	−6.89	−3.77	−3.04	−3.28	−5.69	−5.93	−7.45	−8.89

TABLE 4 (R) Contd.

Sl No.	Fractile Class	1963-64	1964-65	1965-66	1966-67	1967-68	1968-69	1969-70	1970-71	1971-72	1972-73	1973-74
1.	00-01	83.76	100.00	108.15	127.36	147.74	141.73	146.00	145.54	145.40	171.20	197.96
2.	00-05	85.61	100.00	106.99	126.76	146.38	138.83	145.10	149.66	149.68	171.92	203.92
3.	05-10	85.99	100.00	106.72	126.30	145.57	138.27	144.59	149.75	150.13	171.79	202.91
4.	00-10	85.81	100.00	106.85	126.53	145.97	138.55	144.85	149.72	149.91	171.86	202.93
5.	10-20	86.32	100.00	106.48	125.87	144.86	137.79	144.13	149.75	150.47	171.65	202.81
6.	20-30	86.65	100.00	106.23	125.41	144.10	137.29	143.63	149.79	150.79	171.48	202.63
7.	30-40	86.95	100.00	106.00	124.97	143.41	136.84	143.17	149.61	151.06	171.31	202.41
8.	40-50	87.24	100.00	105.78	124.53	142.72	136.39	142.70	149.50	151.30	171.13	202.15
9.	50-60	87.55	100.00	105.55	124.05	141.99	135.92	142.11	149.36	151.53	170.92	201.85
10.	60-70	87.88	100.00	105.29	123.51	141.16	135.39	141.62	149.18	151.74	170.68	201.47
11.	70-80	88.28	100.00	104.98	122.84	140.15	134.75	140.92	148.92	152.05	170.37	200.97
12.	80-90	88.83	100.00	104.56	121.91	138.76	133.86	139.85	148.53	152.39	169.93	200.22
13.	90-100	90.02	100.00	103.62	119.75	135.56	131.86	137.70	147.49	153.04	168.86	198.33
14.	90-95	89.45	100.00	104.07	120.80	137.11	132.83	138.79	148.02	152.75	169.39	199.28
15.	95-100	90.50	100.00	103.24	118.84	134.21	131.02	136.75	147.02	153.27	168.39	197.49
16.	99-100	91.44	100.00	102.49	117.00	131.51	129.34	139.85	146.02	153.68	167.62	195.74
17.	bottom 10% minus top 10%	−4.21	0.00	3.23	6.77	10.41	6.69	7.14	2.22	−3.22	3.00	4.59
18.	bottom 5% minus top 5%	−4.88	0.00	3.75	7.91	12.17	7.81	8.34	2.64	−3.59	3.53	5.42
19.	bottom 1% minus top 1%	−7.68	0.00	5.66	10.36	18.23	12.39	11.15	10.48	−8.28	3.78	2.22

TALLE 4 (u)

Price Indices (with 1964-65 = 100) For 16 Fractile Classes for 1953-54 to 1973-74, Urban India

Sl No.	Fractile class	1953-54	1954-55	1955-56	1956-57	1957-58	1958-59	1959-60	1960-61	1961-62	1962-63
1.	00-01	65.67	58.77	57.83	66.41	69.47	71.58	71.50	73.32	73.28	75.04
2.	00-05	65.57	59.95	58.46	65.59	68.08	71.51	73.42	74.25	75.60	78.80
3.	05-10	65.80	60.39	58.86	65.76	68.14	71.64	73.87	74.60	76.15	79.50
4.	00-10	65.68	60.17	58.65	65.67	68.11	71.58	73.65	74.43	75.88	79.16
5.	10-20	66.03	60.82	59.25	65.95	68.24	71.78	74.27	74.92	76.66	80.13
6.	20-30	66.30	61.30	59.70	66.20	68.39	71.95	74.71	75.30	77.21	80.78
7.	30-40	66.56	61.76	60.14	66.45	65.56	72.12	75.11	75.65	77.72	81.37
8.	40-50	66.83	62.23	60.59	66.72	68.76	72.31	75.50	76.01	78.21	81.94
9.	50-60	67.14	62.74	61.09	67.04	69.00	72.52	75.91	76.40	78.74	82.53
10.	60-70	67.49	63.32	61.66	67.41	69.30	72.78	76.36	76.84	79.32	83.18
11.	70-80	67.93	64.03	62.36	67.89	69.69	73.10	76.90	77.39	80.01	83.92
12.	80-90	68.54	65.00	63.34	68.59	70.28	73.58	77.59	78.14	80.93	84.88
13.	90-100	69.93	67.18	65.58	70.27	71.80	74.74	79.04	79.81	12.85	56.81
14.	90-95	69.25	66.12	64.48	69.43	71.03	74.16	78.35	78.99	81.93	85.91
15.	95-100	70.46	68.00	66.44	70.94	72.43	75.21	79.54	80.46	83.55	87.48
16.	99-100	71.47	69.57	68.09	72.29	73.72	76.14	80.44	81.63	84.81	88.64
17.	bottom 10% minus top 10%	−4.24	−7.01	−6.92	−4.59	−3.68	−3.16	−5.38	−5.38	−6.97	−7.65
18.	bottom 5% minus top 5%	−4.88	−8.06	−7.98	−5.35	−4.34	−3.69	−6.12	−6.20	−7.94	−8.67
19.	bottom 1% minus top 1%	−5.90	−10.80	−10.25	−5.87	−4.25	−4.57	−8.94	−8.36	−11.54	−13.60

Table 4 (u) Contd.

Sl No.	Fractile Class	1963-64	1964-65	1965-66	1966-67	1967-68	1968-69	1969-70	1970-71	1971-72	1972-73	1973-74
1.	00-01	82.85	100.00	107.97	127.44	152.15	142.83	145.54	144.46	145.08	172.75	199.20
2.	00-05	85.77	100.00	105.85	125.98	146.72	138.97	144.00	151.00	151.75	174.00	207.18
3.	05-10	86.27	100.00	105.60	125.82	145.49	138.27	144.03	152.29	152.77	174.02	208.10
4.	00-10	86.02	100.00	105.72	125.90	146.10	138.61	144.01	151.67	152.28	174.01	207.68
5.	10-20	86.71	100.00	105.39	125.64	144.37	137.64	144.03	153.55	153.61	173.99	208.75
6.	20-30	87.19	100.00	105.18	125.43	143.16	136.96	144.00	154.36	154.43	173.89	209.26
7.	30-40	87.63	100.00	105.00	125.21	142.05	136.34	143.94	155.17	155.11	173.74	209.55
8.	40-50	88.06	100.00	104.82	124.96	140.15	135.73	143.84	155.85	155.70	173.54	209.70
9.	50-60	88.51	100.00	104.64	124.67	139.79	135.08	143.70	156.44	156.26	173.28	209.69
10.	60-70	89.02	100.00	104.46	124.32	138.51	134.36	143.50	156.95	156.79	172.93	209.49
11.	70-80	89.61	100.00	104.25	123.85	137.00	133.50	143.18	157.35	157.30	172.42	209.01
12.	80-90	90.41	100.00	103.99	123.15	135.00	132.36	142.64	157.52	157.78	171.60	207.93
13.	90-100	92.12	100.00	103.51	121.34	130.81	129.00	140.94	156.46	158.02	169.28	203.99
13.	90-95	91.30	100.00	103.73	122.26	132.81	131.08	141.85	157.22	155.04	170.50	206.17
15.	95-100	92.75	100.00	103.37	120.56	129.32	129.00	140.13	155.55	157.83	168.23	201.97
56.	99-100	93.92	100.00	103.16	118.97	126.65	127.34	138.32	153.07	157.05	165.98	197.38
17.	bottom 10% minus top 10%	-6.09	0.00	2.20	4.56	15.28	8.70	3.07	-4.78	-5.73	4.73	3.68
18.	bottom 5% minus top 5%	-6.98	0.00	2.47	5.41	17.40	9.96	3.87	-4.55	-6.07	5.76	5.20
19.	bottom 1% minus top 1%	-10.97	0.00	4.82	8.47	25.50	15.49	7.22	-8.62	-11.97	6.77	1.82

Appendix Table A-I

All-India Weighted Wholesale Price Indices for Ten Commodity Groups—Weights Based on NSS 17th Round Data (1952-53 = 100)

Period	Cereals	Pulses	Milk & milk products	Edible oils	Meat, fish & eggs	Sugar & gur	Other foods	Clothing	Fuel & lights	Other non-foods
1953-54	97.7	91.0	101.6	122.8	93.7	118.7	120.9	103.2	99.7	95.9
1954-55	87.6	59.0	92.0	99.3	94.5	118.6	117.5	108.0	99.2	94.4
1955-56	86.4	62.0	90.5	90.5	101.5	90.4	112.3	105.7	97.9	93.7
1956-57	99.3	81.0	95.0	135.0	96.9	97.0	117.8	116.0	107.7	95.6
1957-58	103.8	82.0	105.8	133.6	97.3	109.1	113.3	116.6	117.0	98.1
1958-59	106.4	104.0	108.9	129.8	111.2	125.4	123.3	112.2	121.2	101.4
1959-60	106.2	94.0	111.3	130.8	115.0	140.9	145.3	117.0	122.6	104.3
1960-61	109.1	93.0	116.5	150.4	116.0	131.3	135.0	128.6	127.3	105.3
1961-62	109.0	92.0	116.4	161.2	135.8	121.1	146.4	129.0	129.5	110.5
1962-63	111.2	105.0	120.8	157.0	140.7	141.4	159.2	128.7	134.3	115.9
1963-64	122.8	115.0	129.5	157.9	150.0	176.2	159.9	135.6	147.9	124.9
1964-65	148.4	165.0	147.6	214.8	171.3	178.8	171.5	139.1	154.5	126.2
1965-66	161.0	162.0	124.6	266.8	191.5	154.4	184.9	144.4	160.1	130.5
1966-67	190.1	196.3	139.2	303.4	226.4	190.0	251.5	154.0	169.5	140.6
1967-68	225.6	278.0	161.8	314.3	253.4	323.8	236.0	161.2	186.9	151.2
1968-69	212.5	190.0	171.1	275.0	234.2	319.7	240.0	164.6	195.4	155.2
1969-70	217.6	203.0	179.2	327.8	221.5	207.9	301.8	171.3	201.3	163.0
1970-71	215.4	219.5	246.6	375.0	242.4	210.9	361.3	184.0	195.4	165.0
1971-72	214.8	250.0	260.5	336.8	276.6	275.8	306.3	206.4	213.9	185.3
1972-73	256.1	303.5	275.5	386.0	306.7	353.3	316.2	214.3	222.7	191.6
1973-74	295.1	378.2	341.6	568.2	412.5	362.5	425.3	246.3	238.5	204.3

curves and the linear expenditure system lead to one type of conclusion, and the non-linear addi-log model leads to another. It is crucial, therefore to first select a proper household expenditure model that is theoretically and empirically more satisfactory. A similar comment holds as regards the assumption about the size distribution of household expenditures. Eventually, it appears that all our conclusions are arbitrary. To argue that they are not requires a good deal of testing.

A second question is: Could you not do away with all your parametric assumptions about the Engel curves and the size distribution of expenditures and just use the given ungraduated or unsmoothed data? The answer could be both "yes" and "no." It is possible to graduate a given set of data using linear interpolations or other crude methods of numerical analysis. On the other hand, testable parametric descriptions of the same data have a wider scope and permit varied extrapolation outside the range of actual observation.

There can be serious questions about the way we have combined all-India wholesale prices with the household budgets. It would have been more appropriate if we could use the consumer prices. But the available consumer price indices of the working class households would not be adequate for our purpose.

The accuracy of data is not known and it is not easy to defend our methods of analysis on strictly theoretical grounds. But exercises of the type we have undertaken are likely to generate further interest in the subject of inflation and its differential effects on the living standards of different classes of population. An interesting exercise would be to investigate the effects of changes in the parameters of growth and inequality in an assumed income distribution on the pattern of price discrimination. This could also involve suitable parametric assumptions about the expenditure-income relationships. A detailed study of the changes in the size distributions of expenditure at constant prices is being undertaken, using the differential price deflators presented in this note.

REFERENCES

Bardhan, P.K., "The Pattern of Income Distribution in India: A Review," *Sankhya, Series C*, pp. 103-38, 1974.

Chatterjee, G.S. and Bhattacharya, N., "On Disparities in Per Capita Household Consumption in India," *Sankhya, Series C*, pp. 183-214, 1974.

Houthakker, H.S., "Additive preferences," *Econometrica*, 28, pp. 248-57, 1960.

Iyengar, N.S., "A Study of Differential Price Movements and Consumer Behaviour: An Application of Fractile Graphical Analysis," *Indian Economic Review, New Series*, 2 pp.177-98, 1967.

Iyengar, N.S. and Bhattacharya, N., "The Effect of Differentials in Consumer Price Index on Measures of Income Inequality," *Sankhya, Series B*, 27, pp. 47-56, 1965.

Iyengar, N.S. and Jain L.R., "Projections of Household Expenditures in India, 1971-75," *Indian Journal of Agricultural Economics*, 28, pp. 56-70, 1973.

————— "A Method of Estimating Income Distributions," *Economic and Political Weekly*, 9, pp. 2103-09, 1974.

Iyengar, N.S. and Rao H.V., "Theory of Additive Preferences: Statistical Implications for Consumption Projections," *Economic and Political Weekly*, 3, pp. 1003-12, 1968.

Jain, L.R., "On Estimating Three-Parameter Lognormal Distribution Using Grouped Data," Discussion Paper No. 122 (mimeo), *Indian Statistical Institute*, New Delhi, 1975.

—————"An Empirical Evaluation of the System of Indirect Addi-log Engel curves," 1976. Discussion Paper No. 80 (Mimeo, revised version), *Indian Statistical Institute*, New Delhi.

—————"On Methods of Demand Projections," Discussion Paper No. 124, *Indian Statistical Institute*, New Delhi, 1976.

Leser, C.E.V., "Family Budget Data and Price Elasticities of Demand," *Review of Economic Studies*, 9, pp. 40-57, 1941.

Mahalanobis, P.C., "Fractile Graphical Analysis," *Econometrica*, 28, pp. 325-51, 1960.

—————"A Preliminary Note on the Consumption of Cereals in India," *Bull. Int. Stat. Inst.Part* 4, 1962.

Parks, R.W., "System of demand equations: An Empirical Comparison of Alternative Functional Forms," *Econometrica*, 37, pp. 629-50, 1969.

Radhakrishna, R. and Sarma, A., "Distributional Effects of the Current Inflation," Discussion Paper, *Sardar Patel Institute of Economic and Social Research*, Ahmedabad, 1974.

Rao, C.R., *Linear Statistical Inference and its Applications*, John Wiley & Sons, Inc. New York, 1965.

Somermeyer, W.H., *et al.*, *A Method of Estimating Price and Income Elasticities from Time Series and its Application to Consumers Expenditures in the Netherlands, 1949-59*, Netherlands Central Bureau of Statistics, Statistical Studies, No. 13 (mimeo) 1962.

Stone, R., "Linear Expenditure Systems and Demand Analysis," *The Economic Journal*, 66, pp. 511-27, 1954.

Vaidyanathan, A., "Some Aspects of Inequalities in Living Standards in Rural India," *Sankhya, Series C*, pp. 215-41,1974.

D. L. NARAYANA

Incomes Policy

Economists cannot afford to define their science too narrowly, if they are to play a part in the art of creating wealth and its better distribution. Their science has got to be nearer to the original concept of political economy. For, without favourable political climate, no economy can grow, no economic stability can be sustained. Without the direction of State policy, no equitable distribution of wealth can be achieved. Economic welfare is not mere accumulation of wealth. It necessitates proper production and equitable distribution of wealth.

KEYNESIAN POLICIES AND ECONOMIC STABILITY

J.M. Keynes is the father of incomes policy. He originated the idea of deferred payment during the Second World War. In his book, *How to Play for War*, he advocated that payment of part of the income earned by individuals during war-time involving greater effort must be postponed for disbursement during the post-war period, so that the excess of income earned in making war effort does not compete for the limited supply of goods and services in the civilian sector. Deferred payment was devised as an instrument of restraining income flow and demand for consumer goods and thereby facilitate price stability. In the post-war period, the disbursement of the accumulated savings under the deferred payment scheme was expected to act as a substitute for the expected steep fall in demand in economy due to the cessation of war effort. Hence the deferred payment scheme was also devised to facilitate stability in the post-war period. With the increasing pressure of inflation in industrial countries in the post-war period, the principle of deferred payment has been enlarged into an incomes policy as an anti-inflationary device.

J.M. Keynes is the father of not only incomes policy, but also mixed economy and macroeconomics. His economic policies facilitated the survival of capitalism with the Hicksian "fixprice" and "flexprice" market sectors corresponding to the "cost-push" or "wage-push" and "demand-pull" pressures on prices.

Keynesianism evolved basic rules for stabilization of an economy. If the national problem is only one of unemployment in industrial countries, the rules of the game are: increase the aggregate demand by government spending, cut the taxes, cut the government surpluses, increase the deficit and make money cheap and abundant. If the economy is suffering only from inflation and nothing else, the rules of the game are: reduce aggregate demand by cutting government spending, raise taxes, increase the size of budget surplus and make money scarce and dear for individuals and business to borrow. The same rules of the game are often applied even in the case of poor countries under planned economic development. Indeed, Keynesian technique, as economic history reveals, worked successfully in the Depression; but it did not seem to work in the reverse direction in effectively curbing inflation and repressing the excesses of a blooming boom.

Although the rules of Keynesianism are quite clear in the case of either unemployment or inflation, a situation of simultaneous unemployment and inflation calls for greater economic artistry, evaluation, forecasting, improvization, and sorting out of values and priorities. If specific advice is needed, it is necessary to decide which is the more serious problem, whether the economy is moving towards more unemployment or worse inflation. If inflation is going to be the greater menace, fiscal and monetary policy should be harnessed towards restraint, if unemployment is going to be a greater social evil, utilize fiscal and monetary stimulus. If increasing unemployment and increasing inflation persist, balancing the aggregate demand and aggregate supply becomes more intricate in terms of policy measures to be applied. If incomes are rising faster than output wages, profits and money incomes are to be curbed. Prices may have to be controlled directly which may emerge as a leading problem. Productivity and supply are to be increased. Even these policy measures may be further complicated if the international impact is not favourable to domestic policies, involving importation of inflation. The economic crisis may be further aggravated and become intractable, if increasing inflation and unemployment are followed by stagnation and deterioration in national output.

The hey-day of Keynesianism for nearly two decades since 1950 landed several countries in rampant stagflation and promoted global inflation betraying the weakness of the Keynesian remedies to check the problems effectively. Indeed chronic inflation has become the malady of the Keynesian mixed economy without known cure better than the disease. The medicines from the Keynesian tool box including incomes policy failed to check the disease successfully. Hence the theoretical validity of Keynesianism is questioned even in advanced countries not to speak of its lack of direct relevance to underdeveloped countries from the very beginning, its policies are being seriously doubted, its theoretical flaws are being projected over the last six or seven years. Probably Keynesianism has created its own Frankenstein in stagflation and global inflation.

The need is felt actually for evolving a new economic theory to comprehend the contemporary economic problems and their solutions in the context of a more progressively emerging world economy, treating national economies as integral parts of global economy, involving supply management and efficient management of resources without depending much on consumption and effective demand, projecting the central role of capital formation and human resources as engines of economic growth.

Keynesian bias will continue till the emergence of a new theoretical framework to guide policy. The need for equality of aggregate demand and aggregate supply to facilitate economic stability may continue further, because of its broader framework and the existing controversy on the matrix of price formation governing the inflationary pressure in terms of monetary, structural, national and international approaches. Indeed, inflation is a complex phenomenon.

LESSONS OF INCOMES POLICY IN INDUSTRIAL COUNTRIES

Incomes policy, as is working in advanced countries, over the last three decades after the Second World War, means the deliberate intervention of Government to determine and regulate the growth of money income so as not to outstrip the growth of output in order to restrain the interaction of cost-push and demand-pull pressure on price level and curb the exploitation of market power by labour, business and such other pressure groups. It also covers the deliberate efforts made in the private sector, often on a nation-wide basis towards the same goal. By controlling incomes and thereby expenditure particularly on consumption, incomes policy tries to maintain balance between aggregate demand and aggregate supply and correct the emergence of a situation of too much money chasing less flow of goods. Thus, it is essentially an anti-inflationary device. Indeed, it constitutes a close adjunct of fiscal and monetary policies and a cure for chronic inflation.

Incomes policy in advanced countries does not cover the whole range of policy with respect to incomes. It is not concerned with income distribution per se, such as the measures for reduction of inequality of incomes, elimination of low wages, removal of poverty and improvement of worker's welfare. However, in practice, some measures are often adopted along with incomes policy, because the trade unions regard measures to improve the position of low paid workers as a pre-requisite for their cooperation in an incomes policy. Thus, incomes policy in advanced countries is essentially a device for price stability with marginal significance to income distribution.

After the Second World War most of the industrialized countries adopted incomes policy at different times under diverse circumstances. The specific objectives and methods of incomes policy differed greatly among the different countries varying with the institutional and political characteristics, a review of which throws light on the practical problems of implementing the policy. Historical analysis of the incomes policy reveals that there are three periods of strong interest in incomes policy: (i) the immediate post-war years, (ii) the early 1960s and (iii) since 1965. Incomes policy in industrial countries stimulated a large number of evaluation studies among the different countries over the three periods. Research literature is too prolific on the subject for any meaningful review here.

Nevertheless it is necessary to note the degree of success of incomes policy in industrial countries and the lessons will be a source of guidance for consideration in the context of developing countries. In Anne Romanis Braun's comprehensive study, *Incomes Policy in Industrial Countries*, she arrives at broad conclusions which are noteworthy.

Despite breakdowns, failures, and even at times perverse effects in worsening the inflationary climate and enhancing the rate of increase in prices and wages, incomes policy in its various manifestations was a valuable instrument for the economic authorities. In a number of European countries, incomes policy contributed to the attainment of full employment and to the maintenance of relative price stability for lengthy periods, facilitating the achievement of a high rate of investment and consequent rapid rise in productivity and real income, and aiding in the maintenance of political stability. In many other instances, incomes policy provided a temporary measure of restraint through price and wage freezes, controls, provisions for justification of particular increases, or even merely by a well-timed effort to influence public opinion. There were occasions, however, when the temporary success in holding down prices resulted in a buildup of pressures, producing an upsurge of inflation when the policy was lifted (or collapsed).

The impressive performance of the democratic planning of the Dutch economy in terms of rapid growth, reasonable price stability, low level of unemployment and considerable narrowing of incomes differentials despite limited natural resources is not a little due to the successful implementation of wage and price policies up to 1963. Even in recent years management of the economy has become easier even in times of crisis because of the possibility of utilizing the institutions and legal framework to control prices and wages by the Government. Sweden, Norway and Denmark also achieved similar good success.

The successful operation of incomes policy restraining demand in Japan stands in significant contrast to its failure in U.K. for want of proper response of trade unions. Apart from checking the rise of price level, it has helped to reduce unemployment, because of the fact that Japanese tried to reduce the overtime, bringing down managerial salaries and discouraging of new wage claims. The result is that the unemployed in 1973 were only 8,30,000 out of a population of 108.35 million as against a similar number of unemployed in U.K. with a population of 55.93 million in 1973.

While some countries achieved impressive success, in general the incomes policy in the industrial countries attained a limited success postulating the need for a more effective and skilful managemant, probably greater control of the economies. On the whole, incomes policy acquitted as "a valuable instrument" of public policy.

The labour organization plays a crucial role in determining the feasibility and effectiveness of incomes policy as a continuing instrument and it cannot be overemphasized. In the case of Scandinavian countries and Netherlands the existence of strong central trade union organizations facilitated the consistent implementation of wage and price policy over lengthy periods. In the case of Australia and New Zealand, the compulsory arbitration provided similar scope for continuity. In U.K. due to the absence of strong central unions pursuit of consistent price-wage stability has been adversely affected and the results were disappointing.

The success of incomes policy in any country depends on sustained public support and understanding of the adversity of the alternative situations of inflation and economic instability by the groups involved. Experience reveals that incomes policy cannot be regarded simply as an instrument of economic management, short-term or long-term, on the same plane as monetary policy. "It is political in widest sense." The adverse alternative to an incomes policy must bring together the rival groups to utilize the institutions for working out a compromise between the competing claims of the various income groups. Negotiation and settlement of increases in wages, salaries and other incomes over a given period, or continuation of the agreement over a longer period depends not a little on the understanding of the problems of the economy by the parties concerned. The practice of central bargaining facilitates the understanding of economic and social considerations as against industry-wise or enterprise-wise negotiations which fail to take cognizance of the national problems. Indeed, the parties negotiating for wage, salary and other income increases must understand the repercussions of the international economic situation on the country's position to come to enlightened conclusions. Public opinion on the correct appreciation of the nation's economic problems matters not a little in moulding the morale of the negotiating parties. "There is no doubt that incomes policy is an instrument that demands extremely skilful management— an essentially political art—as well as correct appreciation of the economic circumstances in which the policy is being applied and of the limits that these circumstances for the policies to be pursued."

OBJECTIVES OF INCOMES POLICY IN INDIA

Whereas incomes policy is three decades old in industrial countries, the idea is under discussion for over a decade in India since the issue was raised by Late T.T. Krishnamachari in February 1963. The concept came into limelight with the publication of Reserve Bank's *Report on a Framework for Incomes and Prices Policy* in 1965 which has drawn attention to the objectives of Incomes Policy.

The three possible objectives of incomes policy in an underdeveloped country are: (*i*) Economic growth as per the policy of planned economic development (*ii*) Income distribution in conformity with the goals of State Policy of achieving an egalitarian society (*iii*) Control of inflation to maintain economic stability.

In underdeveloped countries where the per capita income is still below the level to facilitate the minimum standard of living for population, even an equal distribution of the national income cannot eliminate poverty and it may mean only redistribution of poverty instead of prosperity, especially in a country like India, where forty per cent of the population is still below poverty line with a greater inequality of income. Unless rapid economic growth is maintained outstripping the growth rate of population to reach a level of per capita real income that is at least to the level of desired minimum standard of living in conformity with the goal of welfare state, economic development will be the supreme goal. Incomes policy is to be viewed in the context of augmenting national income through planned economic development which is an inherent condition.

In underdeveloped countries where the incidence of inequality is greater with a larger proportion of the population below poverty line and where income distribution is not according to any principle of equity such as productivity and equal pay for equal work resulting in irrational and chaotic income and wage differentials, equity in income distribution has to be considered as an important objective of incomes policy. As inequality of incomes grows in the initial stages of economic development, it is necessary that appropriate steps are taken to facilitate the evolution of an equitable distribution of income. Growth with justice occurs only when planning is coupled with an appropriate incomes policy and fiscal policy.

As inflation has become an endemic malady of mixed economy even in underdeveloped countries, as it aggravates inequalities of income, incomes policy has to be operated as an anti-inflationary device which has been the prime objective in industrial or advanced countries. Anti-inflationary objective will be complementary to the income distribution objective, as it avoids the potential aggravation in inequalities of income, but the goal of economic development may come into friction with the goal of distribution in the formulation and implementation of state policy involving the need for a suitable reconciliation in shaping the state policies by formulating priorities. For, the level of income equity desired can be of considerable variation.

The report of the Reserve Bank stressed the importance of the growth and equity objectives. "The specific role of income policy is precisely to ensure that the broad pattern of generation of money incomes is consistent with the social objectives of the plan and that the disparity in income distribution and consumption is reduced." Here the egalitarian objective is emphasized, but the report states elsewhere:

One of the major changes implicit in the programmes of development adopted by India is that of augmenting the total supply of capital in the economy, principally through domestic effort. Having regard to this objective in the context of economic transformation it would be desirable not to apply the equity criterion to changes in the proportion of aggregate wages or aggregate non-wage incomes to national income.

Thus the report laid greater emphasis on economic development convey-
ing some contradiction in the statement of objectives.

Elsewhere the Reserve Bank Report did not underestimate the importance of income distribution.

If incentives to work and save are not to be adversely affected, this objective of incomes policy cannot be attained unless its first objective of
maintaining a stable environment, relating to the process of income formation is realized. And a fortiori both these objectives cannot be realized
if the plan itself is not internally consistent. These two functions of incomes policy are thus interrelated and are best attained if overall fiscal,
monetary and other economic policies and the plan strategy are effectively devised.

As regards the anti-inflation objective, the report laid down the negative
principle that the process of inflationary spiral "can be avoided if instead
of each group trying to exert pressure for maintaining and increasing its
share of national income, the groups agree on the criteria for determination
of income rises. It is the function of incomes policy to formulate such
acceptable guidelines and criteria and enforce through appropriate machinery and policy instruments.

The report maintained the view that the incomes policy can be made to
serve multiple purposes. This may be done by evolving the degree of importance of each of the objectives in terms of priorities. But, those who
like to stress only one objective, assert that the achievement of multiple
objectives will be impossible. In this context, Barbara Wootton's statement
(*Social Foundation of Wage policy*) that "it would indeed be an extraordinary stroke of luck of our chosen social ideals proved to be one hundred
per cent economically viable," may be pertinent. Even if incomes policy is
framed to achieve one objective there is no guarantee of automatic success
which depends on the political climate, public support, cooperation of
trade union organizations, administrative system and the commitment of
the Government to the implementation of policies. Even in the case of
advanced industrial countries, where the anti-inflationary device is the main
objective, the success varied tremendously from unique achievement in the
case of Dutch economy and its failure in the U.K., the number of industrial revolution. Indeed the Dutch experiment revealed that the growth and
income distribution objectives are happily blended and reconciled.

There is also evidence to prove that incomes policy cannot control inflation without the integrated approach with the fiscal and monetary policies.
Turner and Loetweij in their I.L.O. Report, *Prices, Wage and Incomes
Policies in Industrialized Market Economies, 1966*, came to the conclusion
that an attempt to control inflation by wages and incomes policy "seems to
be ineffective."

Although the Reserve Bank Report has drawn attention to the need of Incomes Policy towards the end of the Third Five Year Plan, no action was initiated. The Report of the National Commission on Labour, 1969, considered the need for incomes policy. Its views are instructive:

It is the need for ensuring stability of the economy which has led countries like Netherlands, Norway, Sweden, France and the United Kingdom to adopt wage policies which are closely linked with policies relating to incomes and prices. The main aim has been to ensure that wage increases and increases in other incomes do not outstrip the growth in real national product. Wage increases inconsistent with the rate of growth of real output and productivity have been worked upon as a cause of wage price spiral.

The emphasis on practical measures adopted for achieving this stability by the countries referred to above has indeed varied according to the social and political environment in which they operate. Although conditions are different in our country in many respects, the experience does indicate that the wage policy has to be framed taking into account such factors as the price level which can be sustained, the employment level to be aimed at, requirements of social justice, and capital formation needed for future growth.

The Commission then appealed for the recognition of limitations of pursuing an integrated incomes and prices policy in India.

In contrast with advanced countries, which have a predominance of wage employment, self-employment is dominant in our economy. The incomes policy that may be formulated has to take into account this structural feature of the economy and has to be in accord with the pattern of income generation and distribution as envisaged in our development plans. Even so, the social basis of wage policy. . . may require consideration of wage policy as a distinct element of the incomes policy. We have to accept it as a distinct entity in the overall framework of policies for economic growth.

Although the self-employed sector is predominant in Indian rural economy, wage employment is predominant in the industrial and urban sector which is bigger than the corresponding sector in several European countries that have adopted incomes policy.

While the Labour Commission did not formulate any guidelines for an incomes policy for India, the Planning Commission in its *Approach to Fifth Plan* and also in the *Draft Fifth Five Year Plan, 1974-79*, formulated incomes policy covering a ground much wider than any attempted so far and it will be considered in the following section in some detail.

Incomes policy worthy of its name, if not fully at least partially, came into operation with the introduction of anti-inflationary policy covering a series of monetary, fiscal and administrative measures during July 1974, when the country was experiencing the runaway inflation of about 30 per cent per year threatening social and political stability of the country. The anti-inflationary policies comprise essentially of demand management measures in order to restrain the demand pressure on the prices in the economy. There are four measures comprising incomes policy:

(*i*) Restriction of dividends of companies to 12 per cent or one-third of net after tax to promote plough back into capital resources of companies.

(*ii*) Additional emoluments ordinance providing for the compulsory deposit of additional wages and salaries for one year and 50 per cent of additional dearness allowance for two years returnable after one and two years respectively with an interest rate of 10 per cent in five annual instalments.

(*iii*) Restriction of the frequency of the issue of bonus shares by increasing the time lag of issues from 18 to 40 months.

(*iv*) The compulsory deposit scheme requiring those with annual income of Rs 15,000 to Rs 25,000 to deposit 4 per cent, those with Rs 25,000 to Rs 70,000 to deposit 8 per cent in a special account, all repayable after 2 years in five instalments at 5 per cent interest.

These income restrictions along with fiscal measures to raise revenues, monetary policy of enhanced rates of interest and administrative measures covering tax evaders and operators in blackmoney have gone a long way to arrest the runaway inflation and reverse it now in the current year reaching a negative rate of inflation. The demand management oriented anti-inflationary policy of the Government of India has been a tremendous success without any parallel in Indian history or histories of several countries in the world stricken with this malady. Probably the steep rise in interest rate structure and the suppression of speculation-induced inflation have played a crucial role in reversing the galloping inflation while national emergency reinforced its success giving great relief for the country in spite of some current symptoms of recession. Price stability provides a better climate and opportunity for the implementation of an incomes policy oriented towards equitable distribution in the framework of planned economic development.

The Planning Commission in its *Approach to the Fifth Plan* pointed clearly that inflation

tends to accentuate inequality, discourage exports, induce avoidable imports and pushes resources into socially wasteful uses such as real estate, luxury housing, speculative inventories, bullion and jewellery and clandestine foreign exchange balances. Inflation enlivens speculation, stimulates inessential and conspicuous consumption and generates a climate of industrial strike and instability. A falling value of the rupee makes rational accounting difficult. Proper formulation and implementation of plan requires that effective safeguards are provided against inflation.

The public would support these sentiments and welcome the assertion of the Approach document that "inflation is inconsistent with the objectives and strategy of Fifth Plan." Unfortunately the Fifth Plan could not be put into operation due to the unfavourable political climate and inflationary trends. But the current economic and political climate is quite favourable for the implementation of development policies.

If there is threatening inflation, growth with stability becomes the primary objective of planned development. If there is economic stability, growth with social justice based on an integrated incomes policy can be the primary objective of planned economic development. For, organized labour in India has not yet developed traditions to cooperate with policies of wage freeze and salary freeze when prices are rising in order to counteract inflation. Indulgence in violence, gheraos, disturbance and destruction of property have been the normal features of Indian labour scene although they may exist in some measure even in industrial countries. Trade unionism has to develop methods appropriate for collective bargaining for achieving their just demands. Intelligent cooperation of organized labour is a prerequisite for incomes policy to function as an anti-inflationary device. Growth with stability promotes better distribution if an incomes policy is integrated with planned economic development. Economic planning with an integrated incomes policy and without inflation can achieve economic growth with social justice.

INTEGRATION OF INCOMES POLICY WITH DEVELOPMENT PLANNING

A study of the *Approach to Fifth Plan* and the *Draft Fifth Five Year Plan* reveals that the Planning Commission, Government of India has attempted the formulation of a comprehensive incomes policy for the first time as an integral part of development planning with the two strategic goals of "removal of poverty and attainment of economic self-reliance" on the principle that "the process of redistribution must be woven into the process of production itself." The comprehensive incomes policy comprises the measures relating to the mobilization of resources as in the earlier plans and all the other measures brought together in the recent plan documents as policies relating to income distribution. According to the Planning Commission, Government would have to aim at removing several sore spots afflicting the Indian economy. About eighteen measures were suggested to realize the purpose of incomes policy.

(*i*) curb inflation by keeping down deficit financing;

(*ii*) raise the living standards of the poor by ensuring that "essential goods such as cereals, pulses, edible oils, standard cloth and cooking fuels are made available at reasonably stable prices;"

(*iii*) prevent exploitation of consumers by the trade on account of short-term scarcities of essential commodities through safeguards;

(*iv*) stabilize the prices of industrial inputs provided by agriculture such as raw cotton and raw jute;

(v) expand the role of public sector in trade and distribution in order to achieve goals 3 and 4;

(vi) measures to reduce costs of different commodities subjected to high indirect taxes;

(vii) deliberate adjustment of relative prices "as an important policy instrument for the regulation of that economy;"

(viii) to raise labour productivity "the Fifth Plan envisages better food, nutrition and health standards, higher standards of education and training, improvement in discipline and morals and more productive technology and management practices." Rise in wages in relation to productivity is envisaged, while those unrelated to productivity are to be avoided with the exception of the cases of low wages;

(ix) resist the formation of high wage islands "in a determined way";

(x) "it should be explored whether an equitable national wage structure can be evolved which may permit the demands for wage increase to be dealt with in a rational way;

(xi) maximum restraint on the unjustifiable incomes that arise due to numerous malpractices;

(xii) political pressures "for fixing procurement prices at a level higher than what would be reasonably remunerative for farmers" must be resisted;

(xiii) in conditions of scarcity the government should restore market equilibrium by levying excise duty on the producers in order to eliminate corruption arising out of ineffective controls;

(xiv) curb usurious incomes by expanding and diversifying institutional finance including cooperative credit;

(xv) imposition of land ceiling and distribution of the surplus land among agricultural labourers;

(xvi) urban land policy to prevent unearned accretion of wealth by the few and to enlarge housing services at reasonable prices to the people is envisaged. Taxation of windfall gains from urban property is suggested;

(xvii) public investment in low-cost housing should be stepped up; and

(xviii) effective measures against corruption, black-marketing, tax evasion and other anti-social activities in order to reduce the unaccounted incomes;

Indeed some more items can be added to the above list. Its main significance consists in giving a vision of the range of incomes policy apart from fiscal policy as an instrument of income redistribution. It is rather difficult to distinguish the plan goals and the long-term objectives in terms of policy. If all the measures are successfully implemented, a clean egalitarian society can be achieved. Probably the list represents ideological foundations of the economic policies for income distribution. The crux of the problem lies in implementation and practical achievement of the measures. All the objectives cannot be given equal importance and weightage as regards timing, speed and the degree of enforcement. Hence the choice of the items as a strategy becomes inevitable.

In order to eliminate poverty and evolve a rational income structure governed by productivity both in industry and agriculture, wage policy becomes a supreme necessity in view of the economic environment in the country. A policy of generating employment opportunities goes a long way to strengthen the evolution of a rational wage and income structure, both in the short run and long run in view of the work force explosion. Controlling the rate of growth of population through wider and more effective adoption of family planning practices can serve as an important instrument for improving the distribution of income in the long run. For raising the standard of living of the lowest 30 or 40 per cent of our population, generation of additional employment must be a principal instrument of economic policy. Policies intended for income redistribution will generate social tensions which are to be handled carefully.

WAGES AND INCOMES POLICY FOR INDIA

Although the self-employed sector is predominant in India, the wage and salary earning sector is quite significant. Out of 180 million working population according to 1971 Census, the wage and salary earners numbered about 72 million constituting 40 per cent of the total. 78 million constitute cultivators and about 48 million were agricultural labourers. In the organized sector, the public sector accounted for 10.7 million wage and salary earners and the private sector for about 6.8 million. Although the agricultural workers are the most numerous, in terms of economic importance the wage and salary earnings in the organized sector far outweigh others.

A review of the wage and income trends even in the organized sector reveals the evolution of a chaotic wage structure. For instance a fourth grade worker with a less load of work in a public sector institution gets an income which becomes liable to income tax as compared to a similar worker with a heavier load of work in an institution like university fails to get even a minimum wage revealing four to five times wage differentials for a similar type of work.

According to the National Labour Commission real wages in Indian Industry since Independence are showing a declining tendency, wage cost as a ratio of total cost of manufacturing is also declining, wages are not keeping pace with increasing productivity, not to speak of profits. The Commission also noted that wages in industries where labour is well-organized are high. It also commented that the underlying strategy of government wage policy has been one of taking care of immediate pressing problems through legislation.

The experience of wage policy reveals that the Government has evolved a politically viable wage policy which has ensured some restraint on the wage level and some equity in the movement of industrial wages on the

other. The best wage policy would be a proper integration of the existing
wage structure with incomes policy.

The Chakravarthi Committee on Wage Policy has formulated the following objectives in conformity with the two major tasks of the Fifth Plan,
elimination of poverty and achievement of self-reliance.

(*i*) to ensure minimum wages not less than the poverty line in the interest of health and efficiency of workers;

(*ii*) to ensure the workers and employees a due share in the fruits of
growth;

(*iii*) to rationalize inter-occupational, inter-industrial and inter-regional
wage differentials and reduce disparities in a phased manner;

(*iv*) to eliminate, progressively, unjustified wage differentials between
the organized and the unorganized sectors;

(*v*) to compensate workers and employees for exceptional hazards to
health and life involved in certain occupations or for other exceptional
disadvantages (like temporary / short-term tenure; and remote or backward location);

(*vi*) to compensate workers and employees to an appropriate degree for
the rise in the cost of living;

(*vii*) to avoid pushing up wages to a level as would encourage substitution of capital for labour or reduce the overall demand for labour;

(*viii*) to provide incentives for higher productivity and acquisition of
skills;

(*ix*) to promote vertical and spatial mobility of labour;

(*x*) to reduce wage disputes to the minimum and thus contribute to
healthier industrial relations; and

(*xi*) to eliminate malpractices in payment of wages.

The Committee also laid down the principles for evolving a national
wage structure on the basis of (*i*) minimum wage, (*ii*) skill differential,
depending on the grade, (*iii*) compensation for exceptional hazards, (*iv*)
growth dividend, (*v*) dearness allowance, and (*vi*) share-in profits.

The Document, *Approach to Fifth Plan*, rightly observes "that there is
little chance of carrying conviction with the workers and employees about
the need to exercise due restraint in putting forth wage claims if a similar
discipline cannot be imposed on those who draw their income from property and enterprise." As wages and profits come from a common source,
the net value added in the organized sector, they constitute competing
claims at a point of time. Hence wage policy necessitates a correlative
profits policy. The main components of such a profits policy should be
the following according to Chakravarthi Committee:

(*i*) to eliminate and, if that is not fully practicable, take over through
fiscal devices, price and distribution controls, and other methods, the
excessive profits resulting from the exercise of monopolistic and oligo-

polistic power;

(*ii*) to reduce excessive profits in sweated industries to reasonable levels by eliminating the exploitative features of the industries;

(*iii*) to bring unaccounted profits to the surface;

(*iv*) to provide for an appropriate share of profits to the workers;

(*v*) to create conditions for an adequate return on the capital employed, taking into account the specific features of the industry concerned;

(*vi*) to appropriate a reasonable proportion of profits into the national fisc through direct taxation; and

(*vii*) to promote adequate plough back of profits.

To work out a rational wage and incomes policy, the Wages and Income Commission has gone into the question of laying down the policy in detail for introduction and implementation.

As the evolution of wage and incomes policy takes long time, policy for income distribution must lay more emphasis on those specific policies which can be implemented immediately like the control of anti-social activities involving blackmoney.

M. SEBASTIAN

External Assistance to India: The Real Aid Element in it

The world economy has been undergoing a process of international economic integration for more than four centuries; but it is in the last quarter of a century that the international community has recognized the special problems of the poor countries. One distinguishing feature of this period is the emergence of a number of *genuinely international* economic institutions like the I.M.F., I.B.R.D., G.A.T.T., F.A.O., U.N.C.T.A.D.,[1] to mention but a few of them among others. Another feature of this period is that all countries, irrespective of their ideologies, have come forward to help developing nations to free themselves from the vicious circle of poverty and want, so that the poorer countries can hopefully look forward to a golden age of prosperity and plenty. It is indeed "a Partnership in Development."[2] The motives behind this aid are certainly coloured by the ideologies of donors, though humanitarian considerations seem to be the common ground for all of them.

PURPOSE OF AID

Ideologies have influenced the nature and character of assistance given to developing countries. The dominant ideologies are the East European Socialism and the Western Capitalism. The characteristic features of the assistance given by these two groups are definitely different and each group has claimed success for its approach to the solution of the problem of developing underdeveloped countries, decrying the harmful or the exploitative character of the opposite group. It would be an interesting study to make a comprehensive evaluation of East-West "Partnership in Development" of developing countries. It would be an immense task. Our purpose in this paper is to find out the real aid element in the assistance that has flowed into India both from the West and from the East. Before we take up the

---

[1]I.M.F.=International Monetary Fund; I.B.R.D=International Bank of Reconstruction and Development (or World Bank); G.A.T.T. = General Agreement on Tariffs and Trade; F.A.O.= Food and Agricultural Organization; U.N.C.T.A.D. = United Nations Conference on Trade and Development.

[2]Lester, Pearson, *Partners in Development*, Pall Mall, London, 1969.

main issue, it would be worthwhile to review briefly the special features of aid from the East and from the West.

THE WESTERN APPROACH TO AID

The Western approach to international aid is based on the consideration that there is widespread poverty and misery in large parts of the world. "Poverty anywhere in the world is a danger to everywhere." Poverty needs to be overcome by appropriate help from rich countries. Development, first and foremost, consists in providing the basic necessities of life. Therefore, agricultural development should be given pride of place. Industrialization should be on the basis of comparative cost and specialization principles which means that infrastructure and basic industries should be developed. The state should play only a minor role, leaving the private enterprise responsible for shouldering the burden of development; or just help the private enterprise to play its part. For, competition will ensure the viability of an industry. The Government entering the field of production or putting up heavy industries is a wasteful expenditure. Such projects would be just "white elephants" or "modern pyramids."[3] Hence assistance of this type should not be given.[4]

SOCIALIST OBJECTIVES

The Socialist approach to assistance is that the developing countries have long been colonies and suppliers of raw materials for the industries of the West. Poverty of these countries is primarily due to the exploitation by the West. Hence, socialist countries would like to help developing nations to free themselves from dependence on the West, the ultimate aim being self-sufficiency in major sectors of the economy. Hence aid would be given to those sectors of the economy where dependence is greatest, that is, to the heavy industrial sector; socialist countries would certainly come forward to help develop basic and heavy industries in these countries. The assistance would be made attractive by repayment being effected through exports of locally produced goods to the donor countries. There will be no burden of repayment in convertible currency. Aid and trade would be integrated. The spirit behind this approach should be not profitability, but equality and mutual benefit.[5]

Whatever be the ideologies of these two opposing groups, the developing countries including India welcome assistance from both sides, provided it

[3]M. Friedman, "Foreign economic Aid: Means and Objectives," June 1958.
[4]M. Sebastian, *Soviet Economic Aid to India*, N.V. Publications, New Delhi, 1974, Chs. 4 and 7; P.J. Eldridge, *The Politics of Foreign Aid to India*, Vikas, New Delhi, Ch. 3.
[5]M. Sebastian, *op. cit.*, Chs. 2,4,6 and 7; P.J. Eldridge, *op. cit.*, Ch. 4. V; Koptevsky, *Economic Cooperation between CMEA countries and India*, Allied Publishers, Delhi, 1976, Ch. 2, pp. 22-37.

is useful. These countries' ambition is fast economic growth so that they are able to narrow the gap of poverty with the developed world in as short a period as possible. They are ready to accept whatever assistance is available from the West and from the East. In the given context, this seems to be the most sensible and pragmatic approach for most developing countries of the world.[6]

ACTUAL AID

India started to receive assistance from other countries about the year 1950. Since then, twenty-six years have passed. External assistance authorized by all countries up to March 1976 was Rs 16,306.62 crores, of which India utilized Rs 13,871 crores up to March 1976, which is 85 per cent of the aid authorized by various countries to India. Of this amount, grants authorized up to the above date is Rs 1260.64 crores of which Rs 1058.96 crores were actually utilized. This is about 84 per cent of the total grants authorized. Total amount of loans sanctioned by various countries up to March 1976 was Rs 12,730.18 crores of which Rs 10,535.95 crores were actually utilized. This is about 84 per cent of the total grants authorized. Total grants utilized against total assistance utilized up to the above date is less than 8 per cent. The assistance which was utilized very fast was the one given under P.L. 483 and 665 titles. Authorized amount was Rs 2315.80 crores and utilized amount was Rs 2276.48 crores which was more than 98 per cent of the former (see Table 1).

Bloc-wise analysis of aid is of interest to us presently. Assistance authorized from socialist countries up to March 1976 was Rs 1235.67 crores, of which India utilized Rs 979.05 crores, and this is a little over 76 per cent of the authorized amount. Under Western aid we include Japan and the international agencies, namely, I.D.A. and I.B.R.D. The total amount sanctioned by them up to March 1976 was Rs 16,306.62 crores of which India utilized Rs 13,871.38 crores. This is a little more than 83 per cent of the authorized amount. About 91 per cent of the utilized aid comes from the West and only about 6.5 per cent of the utilized aid come from the socialist sources. The 6.5 per cent is shared by six countries of which about 5 per cent is accounted for by the Soviet Union. The Western aid is shared by 16 different countries and international organizations. The largest donor among them, the U.S.A, accounts for 40 per cent of 91 per cent utilized aid, followed by international organizations accounting for 18.5 per cent, West Germany 9.4 per cent and U.K. 3.3 per cent. The other 20 per cent is shared by 11 other countries. Thus percentage-wise analysis makes the Soviet Union take the seventh rank among donors of India (see Tables 2 and 3). Taking the face value of the absolute quantity of aid given to India, the West has shown greater generosity than the East.

[6]M. Sebastian, *op. cit.*, pp. 107 ff and 163 ff.

AID CONTENT

The next question concerns the real aid content of external assistance. Economic aid is defined as "the transfer of capital and know-how from one country to another which is made on concessional terms, that is, on terms more favourable than those obtaining currently in world capital and labour markets."[7] The criterion of real aid should be based on the real aid element in the total amount of goods and services transferred from one country to another. If a large amount of aid is disbursed by a country, but under stringent conditions, with hardly any aid element in it, such resources transfer cannot be called aid at all. Secondly, resources transfer may be of little use to the recipient of aid. Thirdly, even if assistance were small, it may be of such a nature, that it plays a vital role in the development of the country; the aid may be in the key sector of the economy and thus have a permanent favourable effect on the country. These are the features which we need to study in order to evaluate the real value of aid given by various countries.

THE GRANT ELEMENT

The first and most important study in this section is to find out the grant element in the aid given by various countries. The factors that go to make the grant element are: low interest rates, easy instalment repayment arrangements, repayment spread over many years with a long grace period of no interest and no repayment commitment. These will surely he helpful to the recipient of aid to long-range planning for development without the constraint of the heavy annual repayment burden. This would, of course, mean a sacrifice and a loss to the donors. In order to calculate this grant element in the external assistance received by India, we shall use the following formula:

$$S = \left(1 - \frac{i}{q}\right) \left(1 - \frac{e^{-qG} - e^{-qT}}{q(T - G)}\right).[8]$$

where S = grant element as a percentage of the face value of aid.

---

[7] M. Sebastian, *op. cit.*, p. 2; I.G. Patel, "Retrospect and Prospect of Foreign Aid," in Research Committee on Foreign Aid, *Foreign Aid: A Symposium and an Appraisal*, Indian Council of Foreign Affairs, Calcutta, 1968, p. 414; Gerald Meier, Problems of Cooperation and Development, Oxford University Press, New York, 1974, p. 18.

[8] R.K. Sharma, "Grant Element in External Assistance to India," *The Indian Economic Journal*, Oct.-Dec. 1973, pp. 124-31. We have borrowed the formula from the above author. We find this formula quite comprehensive and also well suited for our purpose.

i = interest rate charged by the donor.

q = discount rate.

G = grace period.

T = maturity period

e = constant factor equal to 2.7182818

Discount Rates

All the variables in the above formula are self-explanatory except perhaps q which is the discount rate. This needs to be explained at some length. If the U.S.A gave an assistance of $100 million at 4 per cent rate of interest in 1960 and if at the end of ten years when repayment is due, the value of the repayment should be $148 million. The question is whether the U.S.A has really gained $48 million during the ten year period. We know that the value of money changes from year to year. The value of the dollar in 1960 is not the same as the value of the dollar in 1970. And so, for this purpose we use discount rates to find the present value of future payments. As the guide line for assessing the appropriate discount rate, we may have to find out the long-term lending rate or the marginal domestic long-term return on capital investment. It is the domestic opportunity cost.[9] Or we can choose the international lending rate "which in the virtual absence of a private long-term market for lending to underdeveloped countries, is presumably represented by the I.B.R.D lending rate.[10] It is claimed by some like I.M.D. Little, and J.M. Clifford,[11] John Pincus[12] and E.K. Hawkins[13] that the discount rate should reflect the social rate of return on capital investment. Social rate of return on capital investment is obtained by taking into account the domestic borrowing rate, the expected rate of return by investors and also a risk premium.

Keeping these points in mind, we will use two methods[14] to find out the grant element in external assistance to India. For the first, we would base ourselves in the U.N.O., Statistical Year Book of 1975.[15] We would take the average of official discount and money market rates for about 5 to 10 years for various countries and use that as our discount rate (see Table 3). In the second method, we would introduce the social rate of return

[9]John Pincus, *Economic Aid and International Cost Sharing*, John Hopkins, Baltimore, Maryland, 1965, p.124; and "The Cost of Foreign Aid," Article No.6, in *Foreign Aid*, Jagdish Bhagwati and Richard S. Eckaus(ed), *Penguin Modern Economic Readings*, England, 1970.

Stephen A.Marglin, "The Opportunity Cost of Public Investment," *The Quarterly Journal of Economics*, May 1963, pp. 274 ff.

[10]John Pincus, *Economic Aid and International Cost Sharing*, p. 124.

[11]*International Aid*, George Allen and Unwin, London, 1968, p.63.

[12]"The Cost of Foreign Aid," *Review of Economics and Statistics, November 1963*, pp. 360-67.

[13]*The Principles of Development* Aid, Penguin Modern Economics, 1970, Ch.2.

[14]M. Sebastian, *op.cit.*, pp. 31-32; S.A. Marglin, *op.cit.*, pp.95 ff.

[15]United Nations, *Statistical Year Book, 1975*, Tables 197 and 198

on capital investment as defined by us earlier. Relying on other studies made earlier by Little and Clifford,[16] John Pincus,[17] and Alstair McAuley and Dubravko Matko,[18] and Judith Thornton[19] we would take 15 per cent as the social rate of return on capital investment both for the developed and East European countries.[20]

RESULTS OF CALCULATIONS

The results of our calculations are found in Table 3 (A & B).[21] A close study of Table 3 A shows that the highest percentage of grant element in loans, namely, 74 per cent is found in I.D.A. assistance while the I.B.R.D. loans carry a small grant element of 5 per cent only. Three big donors of India are U.K., West Germany, and the U.S.A. Assistance from the U.S.A. has flowed from various sources; of these, assistance from AID has the highest, i.e. 66 per cent, grant element. P.L. loans carry a modest 12 per cent grant element. Taking the total loan assistance for the U.S.A. up to 1976 March, the grant element is about 30 per cent. If the actual grant of Rs 184.14 crores were added on to the grant element, then the grant element in the total assistance would rise to 32.5 per cent. For West Germany, the grant element in loans is only 4 per cent. If grants also were included, then the grant element rises to 7.9 per cent. Grant element in U.K. loans to India is 21 per cent and if grants also are included, then total grant element in total assistance would be nearly 26 per cent. Japanese aid to India has been somewhat low and the grant element in their assistance is around 11 per cent only.

For the socialist countries, since little authentic information is available regarding official lending rates, we employed the I.B.R.D. lending rates as the discount rate for them. Interest rates charged by various socialist countries are around 2.5 per cent. There is a slight variation only in the case of Yugoslavia. The grant element in loans given by the socialist countries is uniformly 22 per cent; for Yugoslavia it is 20 per cent. If the actual grants also are to be taken into account, there may not be much of a change in

[16]*Op.cit.*, p. 63.

[17]*Op.cit.*, pp. 360-67. These authors estimate that the social rate of return on capital investment in developed countries would be around 15 per cent, i.e., 10 per cent as opportunity cost and 5 per cent as risk premium.

[18]"Soviet Foreign Aid," *Bulletin of the Oxford Univ. Institute of Economics and Statistics, Nov. 1966*, pp. 261-71.

[19]"Estimation of Value Added and Average Returns to Capital in Soviet Industry from Cross Section Data," *Journal of Political Economy, Dec., 1965*, p. 634, Thornton, estimated that the average return to capital in Soviet industry was 12.9 per cent in 1960. A Russian economist, V. Bacharov estimated that the normative coefficient of effectiveness of production in Soviet Union was equal to approximately 15 per cent in early 1960s.

[20]M.Sebastian, *op.cit.*, pp. 31ff.

[21]The interest rates charged for different loans of each country vary. We have taken the average or the most common rate charged by particular countries.

the percentage above calculated, since grants do not play any significant role in socialist aid (Table 3A).

The overall picture we get from this method is that the grant element in Eastern and Western assistance or the cost of aid to the East and to the West is quite substantial. Among Western countries the U.S. assistance has more than one-third as the grant element in its aid. Taking all the Western countries together, leaving out the large donors, the grant element is only around 6 per cent. Some of them have very low grant element in their assistance. Austria, Belgium, Netherlands, France, Italy, Norway and Switzerland have only 4 per cent grant element in their loans. When grants are taken into account, then the grant element in their loans for these countries rises to about 38 per cent. The reason for this is that countries like Canada, Sweden, Norway and Australia gave large amounts of grant or gave only grants. I.D.A. assistance naturally has a very high percentage of grant element, namely, 74 per cent and practically all the contributors of this money are Western countries. Therefore, we may conclude that Western assistance has more grant element than Socialist assistance from an overall point of view, though the difference between the two may not be very significant. Thus the Cost of assisting Indian economic development for both the groups is quite high (Table 3A).

Table 3B uses the social rate of return on capital investment for every country as the discount rate. According to our calculations, the grant element in the whole assistance for all countries is over 30 per cent. Among Western countries, U.S.A. assistance carries the highest grant element of nearly 70 per cent. Assistance given from AID funds had a substantial grant element. For U.K. and West Germany, the grant element in or the cost of 90 per cent aid to India is 52.5 per cent and 53.1 per cent respectively. The overall picture is that nearly half the assistance from the West is grant if social rate of capital investment is used for discounting. For Socialist countries, this calculation gives the result of 48 per cent. And so comparing the two groups of countries, the cost of assistance to India for both groups is very high; but more or less the same. The cost to the West is slightly higher.

OTHER AID ELEMENTS

Another important feature of this assistance is the problem of repayment. The socialist aid was integrated with trade and repayment was effected by exporting goods from India. On the other hand, in Western aid of Rs 11, 782.19 crores, nearly 80 per cent had to be repaid in convertible currency and that has been a heavy burden for a developing country like India. But then, some of the leading donors came forward to reschedule India's debt. The total amount of debt relief granted to India till March 1976 was Rs 529.59 crores; this covers about 5 per cent of all the loans from the West, and used by India. For individual countries, West Germany generously gave debt relief for about one-fifth of her loans and U.K. for one-tenth of her loans. The U.S.A., however, has not been that generous in granting debt relief. Total debt relief from that country was about 1.6 per cent loans utilized by India. Smaller donors like Austria, Belgium and France were more generous in debt relief services (Table 4).

A few other elements which can be considered are the nature of aid, whether tied or untied, project or general purpose, developmental or consumer aid and so on. Socialist aid has generally been project tied and for setting up heavy and basic industries, including their maintenance. Over 80 per cent of aid from this source has been for such purposes. On the other hand, in Western aid, there is a very good mixture of multi-purposes, and so industrial project aid would be less than half of the assistance given to India. Food and consumer goods in general claimed a very large slice of aid, for example, in the U.S.A. assistance, about 56 per cent was for food and commodity imports. Industrial development, power and irrigation got about 36 per cent only. In U.K. aid, about 36 per cent of the total was for industrial development, but then, nearly 50 per cent was in the nature of maintenance imports. A similar proportion of West German aid also went to industrial development of which again maintenance imports claimed a lion's share.

In the overall study, we find that socialist countries' emphasis has been for industrial projects, while barring a few cases like U.K. and W. Germany, more than half of Western aid went to food and commodity imports. Another element that can be studied is trade contribution to aid and the grant element contained in it. But that will take us too far and so we do not include that factor in this study.

CONCLUSION

The conclusion that we derive from the above analysis is that neither the East nor the West has exploited India in giving assistance. The study of the grant element in the assistance given by both the groups shows us that it has cost all the countries much to extend assistance to us. In the case of individual countries, grant element has been very high in U.S.A aid; I.D.A assistance also carried a very high grant element. Comparing East European or socialist assistance and Western assistance, barring cases like West Germany, France and Japan, Western aid carried a very high grant element with it. Socialist aid also had a high grant element in it, but it was slightly less than the Western aid. Considering other grant elements like non-convertible currency assistance, debt relief, developmental assistance and so on, on the balance, aid from the East and from the West have been welcome and helpful to India. As far as India is concerned, they have been complementary. In the overall evaluation of external assistance, Western aid has a slight edge over socialist aid.

TABLE 1

Aggregrate External Assistance to India

Period	Authorized				Utilized			
	Loans	Grants	PL 480 665	Total	Loans	Grants	PL 480 665	Total
Up to III Plan	3784.54	391.89	1598.28	5774.71	2759.80	336.95	1403.10	4499.8
1966-69	2279.60	166.14	621.37	3007.11	2200.48	225.79	719.43	3145.7
1969-74	3812.57	197.44	96.15	4106.16	3523.82	159.62	153.95	3837.3
1974-75	1153.38	132.11	—	1285.49	859.18	71.65	—	930.8
1975-76	1760.09	373.06	—	2133.15	1192.67	266.95	—	1457.6
Grand Total	12,730.18	1260.64	2315.80	16306.62	10535.95	1058.96	2276.48	13871.3

Source : Report on Currency and Finance, Volume II, Statistical Statements, 1975-76, Reserve Bank of India.

Table 2

External Assistance Source-Wise
(Up to March 1976)

Source	Loans		Grants		PL 480/665		Total	
	Authorized	Utilized	Authorized	Utilized	Authorized	Utilized	Authorized	Utilized
Western countries, Japan and international organizations	9882.32	9505.71	1251.36	895.64	2315.80	2276.48	16306.62	13871.38
East European countries	1225.39	971.29	9.28	7.76	—	—	1235.67	979.05
Bulgaria	8.25	—	—	—			—	—
Czechoslovakia	141.08	84.36	0.4	0.4	—	—	141.08	84.76
Hungary	30.00	3.82	—	—	—	—	30.00	3.82
Poland	31.56	29.84	—	—	—	—	31.56	3.82
USSR	945.77	784.79	8.88	8.36	—	—	954.65	793.15
Yugoslavia	69.73	68.33	—	—	—	—	69.73	68.33
Others	895.64	68.89	—	—	—	—	895.64	68.89
Grand Total	22004.64	10834.89	1260.64	903.40	2315.80	2276.48	18437.93	15208.32

Source : *Report on Currency and Finance*, Vol. II., Statistical Statements, 1975-76, Statement No. 95.

TABLE 3 A

Grant Element in Assistance Received by India
up to March-1976

(Discounted at the long-term lending rates in various countries)

Serial Number	Country	Loan amount L (in Rs crores)	Interest rate I %	Discount rate Q %	Grace period G	Maturity period T	Grant element as % S	Grant element in loan amount E in Rs crores	Actual Grant A	Total Assistance $(L+A)$	Grant element in total assistance in Rs crores $E(t)$	Grant element in total assistance in %
1	2	3	4	5	6	7	8	9	10	11	12	13
1.	U.S.A.											
	AID	1765.63	0.75	6	10	40	66	1165.32	—	—	—	—
	Exim Bank	302.94	5.75	6	4	16	2	6.06	—	—	—	—
	PL-Loans	2273.70	5.00	6	4	40	12	272.84	—	—	—	—
	Others	589.29	5.00	6	1.5	15	6	35.36	—	—	—	—
A	U.S.A. Total	4931.56	—	—	—	—	30.00	1479.58	184.14	5115.70	1663.72	32.5
2.	West Germany	1170.00	5.5	6	5	20	4	46.80	37.00	1207.00	83.80	7.9
3.	United Kingdom	1352.00	6.5	9	7	25	21	283.92	88.89	1440.89	372.81	25.9
4.	Japan	508.00	6.0	8	—	15	11	55.88	0.59	508.89	56.47	11.1
B	Total (2—4)	3030.00	—	—	—	—	12.8	386.60	126.48	3156.78	513.08	16.2
	Others (Western)											
5.	Australia	—	—	—	—	—	—	—	122.12	122.12	122.12	100
6.	Austria	25.24	6	7	—	10	4	1.01	1.40	26.64	2.41	9.0
7.	Belgium	55.00	6	7	—	10	4	2.20	0.62	55.62	2.82	5.0
8.	Canada	369.19	6	7	5	20	8	29.54	462.92	832.11	492.46	59.2
9.	Denmark	16.84	4	7	5.5	20	25	4.21	1.71	18.55	5.92	31.9
10.	France	315.87	6	7	—	10	4	12.63	—	—	—	4.0
11.	Italy	166.42	6	7	—	10	4	6.66	—	—	6.16	4.0

1	2	3	4	5	6	7	8	9	10	11	12	13
12.	Netherlands	127.76	6	7	—	10	4	5.11	17.73	145.49	22.84	15.9
13.	Norway	0.17	6	7	—	10	4	0.01	9.87	10.04	9.88	98.0
14.	Sweden	72.06	2	7	5	20	40	28.82	42.31	114.37	71.13	62.2
15.	Switzerland	32.08	8	7	—	10	4	1.28	—	32.08	1.28	4.0
C	Total (Western) (5—15)	1180.63					6.9	91.47	658.68	1839.31	750.15	40.8
	(A+B+C) Grand Total	8142.19					21.4	1957.65	969.30	10,111.79	2926.95	28.9
16.	Other countries	357.89	6	7	—	—	4	14.32	—	357.89	14.32	4.0
17.	IBRD	669.00	6	7	—	15	5	33.45	—	1630.00	33.45	5.0
18.	IDA	1804.00	0.75	7	10	50	74	1334.46	—	1804.00	1334.96	74.0
	East European											
19.	USSR	784.79	2.5	7	1	12	22	172.65	8.36	793.15	181.01	22.8
20.	Bulgaria	0.40	2.5	7	1	12	22	0.09	—	0.40	0.09	22.3
21.	Czecoslovakia	84.75	2.5	7	1	12	22	19.05	0.40	85.15	19.05	22.0
22.	Hungary	4.84	2.5	7	1	12	22	1.06	—	4.84	1.06	22.0
23.	Poland	30.09	2.5	7	1	12	22	6.62	—	30.09	6.62	22.0
24.	Yugoslavia	54.70	3.0	7	1	12	20	10.94	—	54.70	10.94	20.0
	Total East European	959.57					21.9	210.01	8.76	968.33	218.77	22.8

Source : *Report on Currency and Finance*, Vol. II, 1975-76.

Note (1) Columns 8 & 9. Result is obtained by using the formula $S = \left(1 - \dfrac{i}{q}\right) \left(1 - \dfrac{e^{-qT} - e qG}{q(T - G)}\right)$

(2) Columns 12 and 13, we add the total grant to the grant element.

TABLE 3 B

Grant Element in External Assistance to India
up to March 1976

(Discounted at 15 per cent)

Serial Number	Country	Loan amount in Rs Crores L	Interest rate % I	Discount rate % Q	Grace period G	Maturity period T	Grant element in % S	Grant element in loan amount in Rs crores E	Actual Grant A	Total assistance (L+A)	Grant element in total assistance in Rs Crores E(t)	Grant element in total assistance %
1	2	3	4	5	6	7	8	9	10	11	12	13
1.	U.S.A.											
	AID	1765.63	0.75	15	10	40	90	1589.06	—	—	—	—
	Exim Bank	302.94	5.75	15	4	16	47	142.38	—	—	—	—
	PL 480/665	2273.70	5.00	15	4	40	60	1304.22	—	—	—	—
	Others	589.29	5.00	15	1.5	15	44	259.29	—	—	—	—
A.	Total U.S.A.	4931.56	—	—	—	—	68.03	3354.95	184.14	5115.70	3539.09	69.20
2.	W. Germany	1170.00	5.5	15	5	20	51	596.70	37.00	1207.00	633.70	52.50
3.	United Kingdom	1352.00	6.5	15	7	25	50	676.00	88.89	1440.89	764.89	53.10
4.	Japan	508.00	6.0	15	—	15	36	182.88	0.59	508.50	183.47	30.20
B.	Total (2—4)	3030.00	—	—	—	—	48.04	1455.58	126.48	3156.48	1582.06	50.15
	Others (Wertern)											
5.	Australia								122.12	122.12	122.12	100.00
6.	Austria	25.24	6.0	15	—	10	29	7.32	1.40	26.64	8.72	32.90
7.	Belgium	55.00	6.0	15	—	10	29	15.95	0.62	55.62	16.57	29.80
8.	Canada	369.19	6.0	15	5	20	49	180.90	462.92	832.11	643.82	79.70
9.	Denmark	16.84	6.0	15	5.5	20	60	10.10	1.71	18.55	11.81	63.60
10.	France	315.87	6.0	15	—	10	29	91.60	—	315.87	91.60	29.00
11.	Italy	166.42	6.0	15	—	10	29	48.26	—	166.42	48.26	29.00

1	2	3	4	5	6	7	8	9	10	11	12	13
12.	Netherlands	127.76	6.0	15	—	10	29	37.05	17.73	145.49	54.78	37.60
13.	Norway	0.17	6.0	15	—	10	29	0.05	9.87	10.04	9.92	98.80
14.	Sweden	72.06	2.0	15	5	20	70	50.44	42.31	114.37	92.75	81.00
15.	Switzerland	32.08	6.0	15	—	10	29	9.30		32.08	9.30	29.00
C	Total others (Western) (A+B+C)	1180.63					38.2	450.97	658.68	1839.31	1109.65	60.40
	Total Western	9142.19					—	5261.50	969.30	10,111.79	6230.80	61.60
16.	Other countries	357.89	6.0	15	—	10	29	103.79	—	357.89	103.79	29.00
17.	I B R D	669.00	6.0	15	—	15	36	240.48	—	669.00	240.84	36.00
18.	I.D.A.	1804.00	0.75	15	10	50	91	1641.48	—	1804.00	1641.64	91.00
	East European											
19.	U.S.S.R.	784.79	2.5	15	1	12	48	376.70	8.36	793.15	385.66	48.5
20.	Bulgaria	0.40	2.5	15	1	12	48	0.19	—	0.40	0.19	48.0
21.	Czechoslovakia	84.75	2.5	15	1	12	48	40.68	0.40	85.15	41.08	48.2
22.	Hungary	4.84	2.5	15	1	12	48	2.32	—	4.84	2.32	48.0
23.	Poland	30.09	2.5	15	1	12	48	14.44	—	30.09	14.44	48.0
24.	Yugoslavia	54.70	3.0	15	1	12	46	25.16	—	54.70	25.16	46.0
	Total East European	959.57					48.8	459.49	8.76	968.33	468.25	48.2

Source : Report on Currency and Finance, Vol. II, 1975-76, Reserve Bank of India.

Note: 15% discount rate is the social rate of Return to capital Investment for Western and Socialist countries, as explained in the text.

TABLE 4

Debt Relief Granted
up to March 1976

(*in Rs Crores*)

Country	Debt relief	Loan amount	Total relief as % of loan amount
Austria	9.94	29.24	39.4
Belgium	9.60	55.00	17.5
W. Germany	232.11	1170.00	19.8
France	43.48	127.76	24.0
United Kingdom	141.72	1352.00	10.5
Italy	15.13	166.42	9.1
U.S.A.	77.61	4931.56	1.6
Total	529.59	7827.98	6.8

Source: Report on Currency and Finance, Vol. III, 1975-76, Reserve Bank of India.

M.H. GOPAL

Slums in India—An Approach

Slum improvement in India, as contrasted with that in advanced countries, requires more a socio-psychological approach than an economic one. Slums, known for their squalid housing, insanitation and disease, not to speak of congestion and poverty, are not the monopoly of any single nation, or even of backward and developing countries. They are found in developed nations too. For instance, in the U.S.A., the richest and most advanced country, their presence is conspicuous in Harlem in New York, in the ghettos of Boston, and in Chicago, Detroit, Pittsburgh and Philadelphia. The major cause of these social blots in rich countries is economic, i.e., maldistribution of income. For, there is an adequate GNP to go round, but it has not equitably percolated, largely because of the highly competitive nature of that society.

In countries like India, however, the root cause appears to be different. Compared to the U.S.A, for instance, slums here are more numerous, more widespread and more depressing. The *cheris* of Madras, the *bustis* of Calcutta, the displaced persons' colonies in old Delhi, the slums in Chinchpokli, Charni Road, Parel, Bandra and Kamatipur in Bombay, and, nearer home, in Bangalore and Mysore are distressing examples of this evil.

Slums are often, but not necessarily, a concomitant of urbanization and industrialization, especially where this growth is unplanned and forced. It is also true that, with these structural changes, the deplorable conditions get accentuated. Such a situation raises two types of broad policy issues: basic and partly operational ones. The former, so tellingly but ineffectively spotlighted by Gandhiji, asks: Is high industrialization and rapid urbanization necessary and desirable for India? Are their social costs, as in the growth of slums, worth incurring in the larger and long-term interests of the community? The core of the second issue is: *If* this growth is inevitable, could there not be a wider locational distribution of industry and of population?

While these policy issues also are there for consideration, I shall revert to the one mentioned earlier—the operational part: How the root cause for the continuance of slums in India appears to be different from that of the richer nations and therefore, in the short and intermediate terms, the, remedial approach both of the academic analyst and of the practical worker will have to be different from that in vogue today. My analysis below is only a hypothesis for consideration and verification.

In a city like Mysore or Bangalore there is, at present, not the same degree of urbanization as in Bombay, Calcutta or Kanpur. Still, slums not only exist but have persisted for decades. Sixty years ago slums were found in Bangalore when its population was hardly $1\frac{1}{2}$ lakhs, and they exist even today when nearly 20 lakhs inhabit the city. Why is there such persistence of this social evil?

There are two major economic reasons for this. One is the maldistribution of income. As suggested above this is the primary cause of slums in rich countries. It is, however, a secondary cause in India because our national product is so low that even with a more equitable spread-out and with extended welfare measures, there would not be enough resources to abolish the slums. A recent report on Calcutta stated that, in 1970-76, 1400 *bustis* were cleared but that many more remained and perhaps new ones were appearing. The second reason, comparatively minor but more important than the first, relates to production. The total value of GNP in India is small relative to her potential, to the population and to her needs, and also compared to other countries. These economic causes suggest two economic remedies: more outlay on welfare measures, and increased production.

But, the most important cause for the persistence of slums in India is socio-psychological or cultural. This aspect has three dimensions: *First,* the slum dweller does *not fully realize* the repercussions of the subhuman conditions he lives in on his health, efficiency, productivity, and mortality. This may be termed as the factor of ignorance, fortified by superstition and resulting in a resignation to "Fate." The *second* is his *reluctance* to change the prevailing conditions, and, even where State or external action improves his material environment, his unwillingness to pick up the lead and forge ahead. This may be termed as the factor of personal indifference and habit of public dependence. *Thirdly* is the residents' *inability or unwillingness to cooperate* among themselves in facing the evils, and to keep on collectively trying to improve. This is the factor of mutual distrust and misplaced self-interest.

Some time ago I casually verified this hypothesis with an experienced social worker. He was a *sanyasin* and had been living among slum dwellers for some years. His experience, supporting my hunch, was that for the weekly functions at the Rama Mandir or to listen to his discourses, his "flock" readily assembled, but when it came to clearing the drains, cleaning the roads, or anything worthwhile to improve their lot physically, there was little interest, less cooperation among themselves, and more resignation to the "inevitable."

No community of slum inhabitants can look for bettering their conditions over a long period, if they themselves do not desire or work for it. Even in a Communist society, where slums are almost non-existent, the initiative and resources apparently flow from the State. But actually, the State efforts are indirectly those of the beneficiaries themselves. In non-Communist countries, only a part of the resources comes from the State and the balance has to come from the individual.

If this thesis is valid, even partially, the slum problem in India will need a three-pronged approach:

(*i*) *Resources*: This concerns the State. Any help to overall planning, in financial outlay and in administration can come from the State; and the State in India is already doing this. I, however, wonder if a more realistic, though less spectacular, utilization of public resources cannot be effected, for example—partly, on human build-up. At the moment, greater attention is being paid to the material rather than the human side.

(*ii*) *The direction of slum research*: This concerns the academic enthusiast: (*a*) He himself has to learn more about his area of interest. So far, the investigator has used, for example, participant observation as a mere supporting tool of information by casual visits and personal interviews. To be effective, he has to *live with* the slum dweller for some time and build up *rapport*, as for instance Verrier Elwin did among the tribals. This is hard and not pleasant, but that is the only way to understand the slum dweller's difficulties. (*b*) The researcher has to learn more about the *psychology* of his population, their prejudices and preferences and the limitations to change, effort and concerted action. (*c*) The direction of his research, therefore, needs a shift from data collection to their collation and from mere facts to meaningful interpretation. So far, field surveys of slums have been merely gathering obvious repetitive data. There are in India today enough of such field reports, and further effort in this direction may not significantly add to or alter such data. *If at all* necessary, *a resurvey* in outline may be made to follow the changes in the situation, as, for instance, the L.S.E. Resurvey of London did *vis-a-vis* the earlier Charles Booth's Survey. What is now required of the academic researcher is, therefore, to look at the available information from a different angle; to put them together so as to compare different areas, and changes between two periods and in different social groups. In other words, shift the emphasis in research from collection of facts to inferential analysis. (*d*) He has also to view these facts and inference against the wider socio-economic and cultural background to arrive at realistic remedies such as the third step mentioned below.

(*iii*) *Self-help*: As already indicated, State effort can look to only a part of the solution. Since self-help is the crux of slum eradication, any reform should concentrate on the slum dweller. This is the sociological aspect of the solution—partly cultural and partly psychological. Efforts in this direction should make the slum dweller aware convincingly of his own manifold problems and their repercussions and the prime importance of self-reliance and cooperative action; and this effort has to be at the *dweller's* socio-psychological level—(and not to be at a theoretical, academic one)—utilizing maximally the existing local, trusted agencies such as the Rama Mandir and the Elders' Council. For instance, a mistake committed in a different context by the Community Development and Extention Service Organizations was not in their intention but, in the *hiatus* between the external agency trying to help and the local distrust of such an agency.

For the academic and the social worker to succeed in this direction a mature, sympathetic and dedicated approach is essential—the slums are to be viewed not so much as a theme of mere academic discussion but as the field of practical social work.

N. BASKARA RAO

Population in Economic Thought

The number of people living in a society has been engaging the attention of man since ancient times. Early writings on population were, with a few exceptions, generally rudimentary in analysis. However, with the passage of time, population analysis gained greater rigour and depth along with the growth of specialized fields of study, such as, economics, sociology, geography, human ecology etc. Presently, demography or population study is a specialized field of study by itself, with its own data and techniques of analysis. However, research scholars have quite often tried to understand and analyze the population problem within the framework of the theoretical systems developed in other disciplines mentioned earlier. Economics and Population have perhaps the longest association and economists have made substantial contributions to the study of population. Studies on the economic aspects of population are quite varied. During the preceding two centuries or so, economists have tried to understand the interrelationship between population size and growth on the one hand and economic production and distribution on the other. More recently quantitative or statistical models have been used to measure the interrelationship between population growth and economic development. Further, a number of studies have attempted to understand the interrelationship, at the macro and micro-levels, between the components of population growth, that are mortality, fertility and migration on the one hand and economic factors on the other.

The present paper tries to examine the role given to population by the economists who have contributed to the development of economic thought. The contributions to the study of population made by Malthus, Ricardo, J.S. Mill, Marx and several others, the ideological background of these writers and the times during which they lived constitute a fascinating field of study by itself. No attempt is made in this paper to examine in detail the individual contributions of these writers. However, we have tried to present here the major currents in the development of population theory or certain principles governing the relationship between population, and economic production and distribution. The material for this paper is mainly from the *The Population Debate* by E. P. Hutchinson and the essays of J.J. Spengler on Population Economics.

The latter half of the eighteenth century and the nineteenth century, the latter in particular, are important from the point of view of the development of population theory. However, for a better understanding of the developments that took place in the eighteenth and nineteenth centuries it is necessary to go back to the preceding periods. Many of the population concepts and principles discussed during the nineteenth century and later, had their origin in the preceding few centuries.

THE SIXTEENTH CENTURY AND BEFORE

Early Greek and Roman writers considered whether or not a certain size of population was advantageous from the point of view of political stability and military strength. During the 14th century and later, economic effects of a growing population came to be recognized by a few writers. The Khaldun (1332-1406), an Arab scholar, thought that a large population could lead to a greater division of labour and consequently to more effective utilization of resources and higher income. According to him there are cyclical movements in political stability, population growth and prosperity: political order and economic prosperity stimulate population growth and a stage is reached when increasing luxuries, taxes, etc., lead to political decay, economic decline and depopulation.

Another writer who deserves to be mentioned here is the Italian thinker, Giovanni Botero (1547-1617) who is generally considered to be the intellectual predecessor of Malthus. Botero saw the incompatibility between the power of procreation and the means of subsistence. Though human population can theoretically increase indefinitely, in practice it can increase only up to the limit set by the available supply of food. Any further increase beyond this limit is checked by war and strife, emigration and "inability to marry."

In general, early writers during this period tended to regard population as a means for maintaining political order and military strength. Later writers, however, recognized the importance of the economic effects of population growth. A growing population was thought to bring prosperity according to Ibn Khaldun and Jean Bodin, and poverty according to Machiavelli and Botero.

THE SEVENTEENTH CENTURY

During the Seventeenth century, population analysis became relatively more specific. This was the time when John Graunt (1620-74) analyzed the "Bills of Mortality," the earliest version of the modern Life Table. And demography can be considered to have had its origin in the "political arithmetick" of Willam Petty (1623-87).

Compared to the politico-military considerations of the preceding period, during the seventeenth century economic conditions figured prominently in population thought. The Mercantilists, whose emphasis was on the power and wealth of the state, expansion of foreign trade and industry, favoured a large and growing population. It was believed that in sparsely populated societies people could earn their livelihood without much effort and so they would become lazy and inefficient. On the other hand in densely populated societies, a growing population would depress wages which induce the workers to work for long hours. All these would result in greater aggregate national income or the "excess of national income over the wage-cost of production." The mercantilists sought the intervention of the state to stimulate population growth by encouraging marriages, large families and immigration of skilled workers. William Petty, Josiah Child, Devenant, among others were notable mercantilists known for their populationist views. It must be stated here that those who expressed populationist views did not say that population growth would necessarily do good to the society whatever be the other conditions. According to some writers the advantage of a growing population were conditional upon the "good use of land and inhabitants," "industriousness of the people, quality of the people" etc.

However, Mathew Hale and others were sceptical about the desirability of a large and growing population. Mathew Hale (1609-76) argued that the power of population increase was quite strong and that the growth of numbers would be kept in check by wars, famines and diseases. Mathew Hale's concepts of "geometric progression" and "checks" to population growth figured prominently in the Malthusian theory of population during the eighteenth and nineteenth centuries.

Those who favoured population increase were generally optimistic about the future of their societies, and those who saw unchecked population growth as a threat to the living conditions of the people were rather pessimistic about the future. The general living conditions of the people, the incidence of diseases and war, and their impact on the number of people had some influence on the optimistic/pessimistic views of the writers.

The Eighteenth Century

Both the optimistic and pessimistic thoughts of the preceding century spilled over into the eighteenth century with some variations. However, it appeared that the ill effects of population growth were more forcibly stated, and the essential elements of the Malthusian theory were anticipated and discussed during this period. Though estimation of the time required for the doubling of population was not new to the eighteenth century, many such estimates were made during the eighteenth century. Maurice de Saxe, Hume and Robert Wallace made theoretical estimates of the time required for the doubling of population which was generally considered to be "one generation" or about 30 to 33 years under certain assumptions. Adam Smith, on the basis of empirical evidence, stated that the American colonies doubled every 25 years. Another development during this period was that some attention was given to the relationship between population and distribution, i.e., the effects of population growth on wages and rent, though the debate on population was generally in the context of the production theory.

Population and Production

On the production side, population growth and size were related to the resources of the land, the means of subsistence etc., and different conclusions were reached. William Godwin (1765-1836), and others who were optimistic about population growth, spoke of the inexhaustible resources of the earth and thought that production would increase in proportion to population and supply of labour. Other writers expressed qualified optimism. They thought that a mere increase in the number of people would not be beneficial without the operation of other factors, such as, the fertility of the soil, the quality and composition of the population, the employment opportunities, skills and industriousness of the people etc.

The pessimistic side of the population question was also well stated. The essential elements of the arguments about the ill effects of population growth, developed during the preceding centuries, were examined and restated during the eighteenth century. These arguments were mostly centred around the power of population increase, limitations on population growth imposed by the means of subsistence, the tendency of population to reach or exceed subsistence limit, checks on population growth and the consequences of overpopulation. As stated earlier, under certain assumptions, population was thought to double its size every 25-30 years. Following Botero, Bacon, Raleigh and Hobbes of the preceding period, James Stuart, Adam Smith and others thought that food supply would limit the number of people. Francois Quesnay (1694-1774) of the Physiocratic school of thought rejected the mercantilist arguments and stated that population always tended to exceed the means of subsistence and that widespread poverty was not due to the maldistribution of wealth, but to the excess of population over available resources.

Population and Distribution

The possible effects of population on the elements of distribution, wages, rent etc., were vaguely understood during the seventeenth century and these ideas were further examined and developed during the eighteenth century. Generally, it was thought that population growth would have a negative effect on wages and positive effect on rent and prices. Greater attention was given to the effects of population increase on wage levels than on rent or profits.

According to Adam Smith, if wages are higher than that necessary for subsistence, population and labour supply will increase due to lower mortality and higher fertility and soon population and labour will exceed the demand for labour, thereby depressing the wages to the subsistence level. Population increase influences the supply of labour available for production and also the demand for consumption through the increase in the number of consumers. However, these twin effects of population were analyzed separately. For wage determination the supply side of population was considered, while in the case of rent and prices the demand side was considered i.e. increase in the number of consumers would push up rent and prices. However, a few writers understood the interrelationship between population, wages, rent and prices, and argued that the price of commodities are determined by the cost of production rather than by the volume of demand and that if the growth of population leads to reduced wages, lower wages in turn should reduce the prices. But it was generally accepted that population increase would depress wages and raise rent and prices. And these views further strengthened the pessimistic position.

The Nineteenth Century

The Malthusian theory of population and the principle of diminishing returns held sway during the early decades of the nineteenth century. It was thought that population increase would cause the operation of diminishing returns and that population had the power to exceed the means of susbistence, though in actuality population growth would be restrained by the operation of positive and preventive checks. However, as the nineteenth century progressed it was realized that the principle of diminishing returns was more applicable in certain sectors of production than in others, more in agriculture than in manufacturing. With the improvements in levels of living observed during the late nineteenth century in England and a few other European countries, the growing importance of capital and technology which could counteract the tendency to diminishing returns, the Malthusian fears regarding poverty and misery were relegated, if not eliminated, to a distant future and secondly population became, not the key variable, but one of the several variables affecting production.

On the distribution side, the Malthusian theory, the principle of diminishing returns and the Ricardian theory of rent constituted the core of the theory relating population and distribution during the early part of the century. It was recognized that population, wages, rent, prices and profit could interact in complex ways. Here also, as in the case of production theory, there was a tendency, during the latter part of the century, to give less emphasis to population in view of the recognition that capital and technology could significantly influence the levels of living. Further, there was a growing acceptance of the concept of "natural" wages determined not necessarily at the subsistence level but at a level consistent with the "habits and customs" of the people, and that population and labour supply would adjust in such a way that wages would settle at higher than subsistence levels.

With the recognition of the possible effects of the standard of living on population, the emphasis shifted from an analysis of the consequences of population to an investigation of the causes or determinants of the trends and differentials in population growth and fertility.

The debate over the relationship between population growth and the operation of the increasing and diminishing returns led to the concept of optimum productivity and then to the optimum population theory. Though the idea of an optimum population was vaguely understood during the

preceding centuries, a logical exposition of the optimum population within
the economic framework took shape by the end of the nineteenth century.

Population and Production

The first edition of the *Essay on the Principle of Population* by Malthus
appeared in 1798 and he revised and expanded his ideas in the subsequent
five editions. The ideas of Malthus have been variously interpreted. What
is presented here is only the barest outline of his thesis. According
to Malthus (1766-1834), population increases in geometric progression and
the means of subsistence in arithmetic progression; and hence population
has the capacity or power to outstrip the means of subsistence and quite
often population does approach the limits of subsistence leading to some
consequences. The power of the population to exceed the subsistence level
is restrained by the operation of positive checks such as food shortage,
poverty and misery. Alternatives to these positive checks are preventive
checks such as postponement of marriage and moral restraint. To these
positive and preventive checks, Malthus added "vicious customs with
respect to women, great cities, unwholesome manufactures, luxury, pestilence, and war." Citing the example of American colonies Malthus argued
that population doubled its size every 25 years and with some difficulty
subsistence could be doubled in 25 years but it could not be doubled
again during the next 25 years. On observing poverty in a few European
countries Malthus attributed poverty in general to excess population.

The Malthusian ratios regarding population growth and increase in subsistence did not carry much conviction with the scholars of his times till the
principle of diminishing returns was formally stated and accepted during
the early part of the nineteenth century (Hutchinson, 1967: 158). It was
thought that population increase would underline the need for greater
volume of production. As a result lands of poorer fertility, and less
favourably situated land would be brought under cultivation and recourse
would be made for a more intensive cultivation. All these, at a certain
stage, would lead to diminishing returns from the land. The principle of
diminishing returns provided a scientific basis to the Malthusian theory of
population.

However, Malthus did not lack critics. Simon Gray, William Godwin,
Richard Whateley, John McCulloch, Friedrich List and others questioned
the assumptions behind Malthusian theory of population and the principle
of diminishing returns. The vast stretches of unused lands in the U.S.A and
in some parts of Europe and the actual improvements in the levels of
living in spite of population increase in England were cited as evidences
against the Malthusian prognostications. Godwin tried to show, on the
basis of census data from the U.S.A, that population growth in the U.S.A
was exaggerated due to immigration, and the natural increase (the balance
of births and deaths) was not as high as believed by Malthus. McCulloch,
List and others pointed out that inventions and improvements in the
techniques of production would postpone the operation of the law of

diminishing returns. Gray argued that population growth, though high at the subsistence level, would decline along with an increase in the comforts or the standard of living enjoyed by the people.

On the other hand David Ricardo (1772-1823), James Mill (1773-1836) and John Stuart Mill (1806-73) believed, with some minor variations, in the pressure of population on the means of subsistence. According to James Mill the crucial variable was not population growth but the relative rates of increase in population and capital. If population increase was greater than that of capital, diminishing returns, poverty and higher mortality would follow. J.S. Mill was aware of the principle of increasing returns. However, he thought that in countries that had advanced beyond the early stage of agricultural development population pressure would lead to diminishing returns, unless checked by improvements in the methods of production. And he was not very hopeful of continuous advances in the techniques of production along with the increase in population.

After J.S.Mill, due to various reasons the pessimistic notions about population were on the wane and the general tendency was one of cautious optimism. During the time when Marshall lived (1842-1924) there was a general improvement in the living conditions of the people. The death rates and birth rates in England were on the decline, and the rate of natural increase, after a temporary increase during 1870-80, declined consistently. Emigration was high. Import of food stuff and real income per head were generally on the increase. Alfred Marshall, aware of the role of capital, technology and skills in production, and the improving living conditions in England and other industrialized countries, thought that the pressure of population on subsistence could be postponed to a distant future. Further, when the rate of increase in population was less than or equal to that in wealth, and under certain other conditions a growing population would be beneficial from the point of view of the economies of production, of skills and machinery, improved communication etc.

Optimum Population

Starting from Aristotle several writers had some idea of the optimum or ideal number of people that would be useful to a society. However, the logical formulation of the optimum theory of population took shape during the last few decades of the nineteenth century. From the discussion on population and production in the nineteenth century it was clear that some writers recognized the operation of increasing returns as opposed to diminishing returns. Further, in spite of the pessimistic views regarding population growth, it was pointed out that population growth up to a certain stage would be beneficial from the point of view of the economies of large-scale operations, better division of labour etc.

All these observations implied that there must be a point up to which population growth would be beneficial and beyond that point population growth would lead to hardships. J.S. Mill was perhaps aware of this when he said that after a certain degree of population density, further population growth would adversely affect the living conditions of the people. Sidgwick also stated in 1883 that productivity of labour in agriculture and mining would decrease after a certain density of population was reached and that this density varied with the progress in the "industrial arts, and the accumulation of capital." The concept of "productivity/optimum population" was further examined and elaborated by Edwin Cannan (1861-1935), Knut Wicksell (1851-1926) and a few others.

According to Cannan, when "the greatest productiveness of industry" is achieved at a point in time, the population at that point can be considered as optimum. Underpopulation and overpopulation exist when there are too few or too many people respectively to allow the attainment of maximum productivity. In the case of underpopulation, an increase in population through better division of labour will lead to greater productivity. However, in case of overpopulation, a decline in population per se will not guarantee greater productivity. Cannan recognized that the optimum population is subject to changes every now and then, while the actual population can adjust to these changes only slowly. Further, the concept of optimum population is applicable to a closed economy and in practice it will be difficult to prove the existence of under or overpopulation. Whatever be the problems in the practical application of this concept, the theoretical significance of the optimum population theory lies in the fact that population growth per se cannot be considered as favourable or unfavourable, it all depends on the socio-economic conditions in which population changes occur.

Population and Distribution

Inquiries into the relationship between population, rent, prices, profits and wages which started in the nineteenth century continued in the nineteenth century. The Ricardian theory of rent and the subsistence theory of wages with their pessimistic overtones were generally popular during the first half of the nineteenth century. However, during the second half of the century, as in the case of production, there was a shift in the role of population in economic distribution and the observations regarding population were less pessimistic.

Rent. Ricardo formulated his theory of rent on the basis of the differential fertility of the soil, difference in the location of fertile lands, the principle of diminishing returns and the pressure of population on land and the volume of production. According to Ricardo, as a result of population growth, cultivation will be extended to lands of inferior quality and less favourably situated land, and more intensive cultivation of existing lands will also be resorted to. These changes will lead to an increase in transportation costs and capital requirements. The overall profits, that are determined by the least profitable use of capital in agriculture, will decline. Because of the increasing difference in net returns between the better situated/better quality lands, and unfavourably situated/poor quality lands, rents will increase. Though population raises rent, population growth itself is regulated by the "wealth" of a country or by "funds" meant for employing labour. In other words, increasing "wealth" and the consequent growth of population will push up rent.

Malthus, however, had a slightly different explanation for rent. He believed, along with Ricardo, James Mill and others, that a growing population would lead to a rise in rent. J.S. Mill was aware of the interrelationship between rent, prices, profit and wages and tried to analyze the effects, individually and together, of four variables, population, capital technology (techniques of agricultural production) and habits and customs of the people on rent, prices, profits and wages. To be brief, an increase in population alone or in both population and capital could raise the rent. This is because with the need for more production to feed the growing population and the operation of diminishing returns, poorer lands are brought under cultivation and rent increases. The effect of an increase in capital alone is to raise real wages and improve the living conditions of the workers. However, the better living conditions of the people could result in a greater demand for food which in turn, through the causal chain described before, leads to higher rent. The only case where rent declines is when the real wages and habits of people are constant, and capital, population and technology all advance, but technology advances faster than population.

Price and profits. With regard to price, it was generally thought that with population growth, prices would increase due to the greater demand for consumption, and/or due to the higher cost of production necessitated by the need for more production and by the operation of diminishing returns. However, it was recognized that the effect of population growth on prices would be different depending upon the agricultural/manufacturing sectors of production. Ricardo, for example, thought that prices in manufacturing, in spite of the increasing prices of raw materials, would decline along with the "progress of wealth and population" because of the greater scope for division of labour, improvements in skills, machinery, etc.

Regarding profits it was generally accepted that population growth would eventually lead to a decline in profits. Ricardo and Malthus were aware that population growth could raise profits by depressing wages, but continued growth of capital and population would eventually lead to declining profits due to the operation of diminishing returns and due to lowered productivity of the additional units of capital and labour used for production. Malthus, McCulloch and J.S. Mill admitted that improvements in the methods of production could prevent profits from declining, but they were convinced about the eventual decline in profits.

Wages. For wage determination, different explanations were attempted and whatever be the explanation, several writers agreed that the population growth would depress wages. But there was a growing recognition that wages would stabilize, not at the subsistence level as was thought in the nineteenth century, but at a level in keeping with the "habits and customs" of the people or the standard of living.

According to Ricardo, if population grows faster than the supply of capital wages will be depressed. Here the demand for labour is determined by capital, and population growth influences the supply of labour. According to Malthus wages are determined by the demand for and supply of necessities required for the maintenance of workers. In the case of demand and supply of labour, the supply side is governed by the population growth while the demand for labour is determined by the "wages fund" or that portion of capital meant for the employment of labour. In the case of the supply and demand for necessities, the effect of population is, through greater demand for necessities, to push production beyond the stage of diminishing returns with the consequent effects on productivity, rent, profits and wages. In general as a result of the population-wages interaction, wages would stabilize at the subsistence level, however, Malthus admitted that wages could settle at higher than the subsistence level because of changes in "the habits of the people." Similar views were expressed by J.S. Mill also. According to him, wages are determined by the supply of labour, and on the demand side, by the circulating capital or that part of capital used for employing labour. A decline in real wages caused by a rise in the price of food will lead to a reduction in labour supply and in population, either through mortality or fertility, and consequently real wages will be restored to the original level. On the other hand a decline in prices and a rise in real wages can lead to more comforts, if the higher standard of living does not act as an impetus for further growth of population.

In short, during the first half of the nineteenth century, analysis of the role of population in the distribution theory was based mainly on the Malthusian theory of population, the principle of diminishing returns and the Ricardian theory of rent. It was thought that population growth would push up rent and prices, depress wages and profits, and in general would lead to a worsening of the living conditions of the people. However certain factors restraining these pessimistic tendencies were also observed and stated. Increase in capital and improvements in techniques of production could, at least for a short period, forestall the unfavourable effects of population growth. Secondly there was a growing recognition of the influence of the "habits of the people" or the standard of living. The population-wages interaction could lead to a stabilization of wages, not necessarily at the subsistence level, but at a higher level in keeping with the standard of living. Further, stabilization of wages could take place not necessarily through population changes but also through adjustments in the levels of living. Thirdly, several writers appeared to be aware of the actual operation of preventive checks. In other words adjustments in the number of people need not be through the painful process of mortality, but could be through a reduction in fertility.

During the latter half of the nineteenth century, as the case of production, the role of population in economic distribution was to a certain extent relieved of the pessimistic overtones. Further, with the recognition of several factors affecting wages, rent, profits and prices, there was a general tendency to de-emphasize the role of population.

So far the relationship between population, production and distribution, described in the preceding pages, was in terms of the consequences of population growth. However, nineteenth century was a witness to several attempts made to analyze the causes or determinants of population growth and size. As an offshoot of this, the determinants of fertility or the relationship between fertility and socio-economic status became objects of inquiry. In this way population came to be viewed in a wider framework including economic and non-economic factors.

Population in Socialist and Marxist Thought

The treatment of population in the nineteenth century will not be complete without reference to the socialist and Marxist writings.

Early socialist writers did not discuss about the population problem in great detail. They thought that the problem of overpopulation could be solved through greater production and better social organization.

Karl Marx (1818-83) maintained that there could be no law of population historically applicable to different types of societies. Marx's treatment of population is closely related to the "organic composition" of capital. Capital consists of fixed capital i.e., capitalists' outlay on machines, raw materials, buildings, etc., and variable capital i.e., that part of capital spent on the purchase of labour. And it is variable capital that creates demand for labour.

During the period of early capitalism the ratio of variable capital was constant. In these conditions, if population increased faster than capital (or variable capital because of the constant ratio) wages would decline and profits would increase. And wages would rise if capital increased faster than population. Since increasing wages would be unfavourable to the employers, this trend would not be allowed and through state action the problem of underpopulation would be solved. The enclosure movement in England which separated the serfs from their means of production and the slave-hunting in Africa were cited as measures used to alleviate labour shortage.

Late capitalism or industrial capitalism is characterized by a continuous decline in the share of the variable capital which in turn leads to a decline in the demand for labour, low wages and unemployment. A favourable population-variable / capital ratio can lead to an increase in wages, but emloyers will counter this tendency by substituting machinery for variable capital. This substitution of machinery for labour will result in a relative surplus population which was variously categorized by Marx as the floating population i.e., population displaced by machinery and by structural changes in industry, the latent or those on the verge of moving to cities because of the encroachment of capital into agriculture and the stagnant or those workers with irregular employment. The relative surplus population which maintains low wages and high surplus value and profit is essential for the functioning of the capitalist system.

With a few exceptions, later socialist writers branched off into several groups, some supporting population control and some others opposing it. There are various interpretations of the stand taken by Marx and Engels on population control. However, induced abortion was legalized in Russia as early as 1920 and Lenin defended birth control as one of the basic human rights. In course of time most of the socialist and communist countries opted for population control with minor adjustments depending upon the actual trends in birth rates and population growth.

Recent Theoretical Developments

Interest in population, slightly on the decline during the close of the nineteenth century, fluctuated with the actual trends in population growth. The low birth rates during the early 1930s followed by a "baby boom" during the post-war period in many of the industrialized countries, relatively high growth rates caused by a faster decline in mortality in the developing countries and the greater awareness of the tenuous relationship between population and finite resources in the world as a whole have led to a revival in the study of population. At the theoretical level attempts have been made to identify certain stages in the demographic history of the developed countries and to understand the determinants of these changes. Further, the interrelationship between population growth and economic development, especially among the developing countries has been studied.

Early attempt to identify "demographic stages" is traced to Laudry in 1909. However, Thompson and later Blacker are credited with the development of the concept of demographic transition. Thompson, on the basis of the demographic experience of the European countries, grouped these countries into three categories on the basis of the relative rates of change in birth rates and death rates and the trends in growth rates. Blacker in 1947 identified five stages in demographic evolution:

(i) the high stationary stage with high levels of birth and death rates,

(ii) the early expanding stage characterized by constant birth rates and declining death rates,

(iii) the late expanding stage with declining birth, and death rates, but death rates declining faster,

(iv) the low stationary stage with low birth and death rates more or less balancing each other and lastly,

(v) the declining stage with low birth and death rates, but death rates exceeding birth rates.

Later a number of studies have elaborated on these stages and have attempted to relate demographic evolution and the socio-economic development of the countries, with a view to predict the course of events likely to take place in the developing countries.

In general, according to the transition theory societies pass through certain stages in the demographic and socio-economic evolution. In socie ties with very low levels of development, birth rates and death rates are quite high and consequently population grows only slowly. With no control over the demographic events and the environment, population growth rates could be quite often negative due to famines, pestilence, wars, etc. At the next stage, due to economic development, improvements in sanitation, medicine, etc., death rates decline while the birth rates remain constant. This stage is crucial because a declining death rate and a constant birth rate leads to an "explosive" growth rate if there is no large-scale emigration. The lag in the decline of birth rate is attributed to the fact that motivational factors related to reproduction are more difficult to change than those related to death control. In course of time birth rate also declines and a stage is reached when both death and birth rates are quite low and population either stabilizes or grows slowly. Transition theory has been criticized on several grounds. Without going into the details, it can be said that there are instances in the history of nations when death rates and birth rates declined simultaneously. In some countries birth rates declined before industrialization and economic development, in others birth rates declined only when industrialization was well under way. The post-war "baby boom" in the developed countries cannot be explained within the framework of the transition theory. Further, if decline in birth rates depends only on economic development, the implications for both population and economic development in developing countries are not difficult to understand. However, it is too much to expect from the transition theory an explanation of the diverse demographic trends in various countries. The interrelationship between economic, sociological and cultural factors, and the demographic events is quite complex and it will be difficult to predict the course of demographic events in specific countries. The transition theory indicates only the broad pattern of demographic changes that could occur under certain conditions and to that extent it is useful.

The interrelationship between population and economic development has been studied, by Sidney Coontz, Harvey Leibenstein, Hirschman and others. It is difficult to examine in detail their contributions and the selected findings presented here could serve only as illustrations.

Coontz has tried to relate population with the supply and demand for labour. The crucial variable here is the quality of labour. Low quality labour is relatively cheap and needs less preparation, while high quality labour involves time for preparation in terms of education, skills, etc., and hence it has a higher price. Decline in fertility can take place only when the demand for better quality labour is greater than that of the low quality labour. Relative lack of demand for low quality labour will induce fertility to adjust to the declining mortality.

According to Leibenstein, bearing and rearing children involve certain costs as well as utilities, such as, psychological satisfaction to parents, contributions to family income and a source of security during the parents' old age. In underdeveloped countries utilities may out-weigh costs resulting in large family size. With economic development excess of utility over cost declines and this leads to small family size. Early developments in economic conditions will lead only to a decline in mortality and not fertility and the consequent increase in population growth rate will revert the economy back to the subsistence equilibrium. Economic development has to be sufficiently rapid such that the utilities decline and costs increase and then only fertility can decline. In other words, displacement from the quasi-stable equilibrium of the subsistence economy can be achieved only from, what he calls, the "critical minimum effort" which involves technological progress, massive investment of capital, emigration, etc.

Some writers have stressed the critical importance of a "persistent agricultural surplus" and technological progress if the underdeveloped countries are to escape from the "low-level equilibrium trap." Some others argue that population pressure itself could stimulate forces of development. Population pressure would force people to make efforts to maintain the traditional standard of living and these efforts could lead to better organization, and greater control over environment, and consequently to economic development.

To conclude, what we have presented in this paper constitute only the bare outlines of the theoretical aspects of population economics. We have omitted the biological theories of population. Similarly we have not reviewed certain sociological explanations of population growth and fertility, though the demographic transition theory implies the operation of economic and sociological factors. In fact, from Ibn Khaldun to Leibenstein and from the Malthusian theory to the demographic transition theory, the variables considered and explanations offered are so many and so varied that sometimes it appears that whatever that can be said on population has been stated! However, we will agree with Warren C. Robinson (1971) who, while concluding his observations on the transition theory, states that ". . . ultimately it [transition theory] too may be replaced by some presently totally unsuspected view of why population growth occurs."

REFERENCES

Blacker, C.R., "Stages in Population Growth," *The Engenics Review*, No. 39, 1947.

Coontz, Sydney, H., *Population Theories and The Economic Interpretation*, London, Routledge and Kegan Paul Ltd., 1968.

Cowgill, D.O. ,"Transition Theory as General Population Theory," *Social Forces*, V ol.41, No. 3, 1963.

Higgins, Benjamin, Selected Chapters in *Economic Development, Problems, Principles and Policies*, Allahabad, Central Book Depot, 1966.

Hirschman, A.P., *The Strategy of Economic Development*, New Haven, Yale University Press, 1958.

Hutchinson, E.P., *The Population Debate. The Development of Conflicting Theories up to 1900*, Boston, Houghton Mifflin & Co. 1967.

Kuznets, Simon, *Modern Economic Growth, Rate, Structure and Spread*, Ch. 2, New Haven, Yale University Press, 1966.

Leibenstein, H., *A Theory of Economic-Demographic Development*, Princeton, Princeton University Press, 1954.

————*Economic Backwardness and Economic Growth*, New York, John Wiley and Sons Inc., 1957.

Morris, Judy,K., "Professor Malthus and His Essay," *Population Bulletin*, 22, no. 1, 1966.

Nelson, R.R, "A Theory of the Low-Level Equilibrium Trap in Under-developed Countries," *American Economic Review*, Vol. 46, 1956.

Nickerson, Jane Soames, *Homage to Malthus*, Port Washington, NY, Kennikat Press, 1975.

Penrose, E.F., *Population Theories and Their Application*, Stanford, Food Research Institute, 1934.

Peterson, William, "Marx Versus Malthus: The Men and the Symbols," in Kenneth C.W. Kammeyer (ed.), *Population Studies*, 1971.

Population Economics, Selected Essays of Joseph J. Spengler, Compiled by Roberts S. Smith, Frank T. de Vyver and William R., Allen, Durham, Duke University Press, 1972.

Robinson, Warren C., "The Development of Modern Population Theory," in Kenneth C.W. Kammeyer (ed.), *Population Studies*, 1971.

Sauvy, Alfred, *General Theory of Population*, New York, Basic Books Inc., 1969.

Spengler, J.J., "Economics and Demography" in Philip M. Houser and O.D. Duncan (eds), *The Study of Population 1959*, Chicago, University of Chicago Press.

Taeuber, I.B., "The Future of the Transitional Areas" in Paul Hatt (ed), *World Population and Future Resources*, New York, American Book Co., 1952.

United Nations, "The Determinants and Consequences of Population Trends," *New Summary of Findings of Demographic, Economic and Social Factors*, Vol. 1, New York, 1973.

R.P. MISRA

Target Groups and Regional Development

INTRODUCTION

The purpose of this paper is to outline a development policy which divests the current theorties and practices of regional development of their macro-economic bias and considers rapid improvement in the living conditions of weaker sections of the society as its prime task.

All development processes aim at human welfare; regional development is no exception to this. The latter, however, not only aims at increased welfare in aggregate terms but also at more equitable distribution of it among areas and groups of peoples. If development could be seen in rural terms alone, regional development would go a long way in creating an egalitarian society. The nation is however, not merely a territory—it has to be fundamentally viewed as a people. Just as increase in gross national product does not necessarily mean an increase in the real welfare of all the people, increase in gross regional product, need not imply that all the people inhabiting the region benefit from it.

Within any sub-national area or region, no matter what its size, there exist interpersonal and intergroup differences in income, earning capacities and quality of life. These differences may have historical and cultural roots but they invariably emerge from social class relations which determine the economic and social *locus standi* of each individual and group in the production-distribution cycle. The inequities in development whether seen in national, regional or group perspective, emanate from these social relationships.

These inequities in development—regional as well as interpersonal—have thus to be seen as symptoms of something more deep-rooted, more fundamental and basic. Current development policies do not, however, take serious cognizance of these basic and fundamental issues. They are more concerned with the symptom, and are built on the premise that the task of development planning is to stabilize and re-inforce the social system by way of resolving the problems it gets into because of its archaic character. and inner contradictions. This is reflected from the view of even such liberal social scientists like Myrdal. *A man is poor because he is poor.* The real fact, however, is that *a man is poor because he is made to be poor-* The answer lies not alone in attempting to improve the economic conditions of the poor; it lies in a simultaneous attack on the cause of poverty, which is none other than the prevailing class relations.

Regional planning has many a success to its credit. It has boosted the economies of very many sub-national areas which lagged behind their richer counterparts. Economic incentives of various types to attract new capital and entrepreneurship to the backward regions apart, a new sense of direction, initiative and strategic intervention have helped such chronically backward regions like S. Italy and N.E. Brazil, for example, to improve their share in the GNP. But they have failed to solve the problems of those who were unprepared to participate in new ventures and opportunities. Instances where conditions of such people further deteriorating in the wake of development planning are legion.

It is, therefore, the contention of this paper that dichotomous development leading to higher GNP but greater poverty is embedded in the very social structure and the development policies pursued today. Unless development is carried out within a comprehensive social policy frame which attacks the cause of poverty and underdevelopment directly, it would fail to find a lasting solution of persisting poverty among regions and communities.

AIMS OF REGIONAL DEVELOPMENT

Regional development has three major aims—productive, social and biological.[1] It attempts to secure best conditions and possibilities for all-round development for all; minimizes and ultimately eliminates inter-regional and intra-regional differences in quality of life and makes the best possible use of the natural endowments and human values of the region to secure the first two. The above aims bring to focus a few important features to be noted here. In the first place, it is comprehensive in nature and is not restricted to economic aspects alone; secondly, distributive justice is of prime consideration, for, then and then alone, differences in the levels of living can be eliminated; and finally, it aims to create conditions—including social—for all-round development of all the people of a region.

The prevalent theories and practice of regional development, however, are not so all-inclusive, comprehensive and social goal oriented as to meet the above aims adequately. They are adapted from Western Macro-economic theories[2] and are disaggregated versions of economic growth models. When development is conceived and pursued essentially in terms of steady growth of production and income, the social aspects of it are subsumed in the economic policy, and the social class interest and group relations which form the basis of the distribution of the fruits of development are assumed

[1]R.P. Misra, *et. al.*, *Regional Development Planning in India—A New Strategy*, Delhi, Vikas, 1974, Ch. 1. See also Barbara Prandecha, "The Goals of Regional Policy in Relation of Regional Development," *Gospodarka i administracja terenowa*, Warszawa, 1969, p. 26.

[2]Among these is alo included the circular causations theory of Myrdal who considers underdevelopment as a special product of capitalistic production process.

to change as productivity increases. Human beings become factors of production (and not the goal of production) and "as the recipients of particular marginal investment" through public expenditure in the form of social programmes (health, education, housing, social security, and so on). Social policy is essentially limited to the operational allocation of various residual resources deriving from the national system of redistribution, and covering obviously only partially the accumulated deficit in certain social welfare services.[3] In such situations, even when the average and aggregate production and income improve, the decline in the welfare of a large number of marginalized people, is not only possible but also certain.

As against this, where development encompasses not only productivity and income but also structural change in class and interest group relations involving "the individual and the community in the multiple roles of subjects, objects and beneficiaries of development,"[4] larger and larger number of people are able to participate and share in productivity leading to increased welfare in gross as well as "net" terms.[5] Thus a new regional development policy must reject the thesis that poverty can be attacked through growth rates filtering down to the masses. It must be based on the premise that poverty is the end product of the process of monopolization of means of production and consequent marginalization, from productive and distributive processes, of a larger segment of population. It is inherent to the prevailing social relations, and that it should be attacked on two fronts simultaneously curbing the monopolization process and improving the capacities of the poor to participate and share in the development processes.

SOCIAL STRUCTURE AND REGIONAL DEVELOPMENT

The social structure of the developing societies, whether conceived at the national or regional levels, inhibits real development. The benefits of increased investment in economic and social activities in these areas go to those who need them least. It is not infrequently, that it further accentuates poverty. Let us see how it happens.

To explain this, we would make use of an analogue model from earth sciences. There are three types of model structures: porous, permeable and impermeable (Fig. 1).

The porous structures with equal size particles allow liquid to get to the whole stratum through percolatory or capillary action. The structures are

---

[3]J.B.W. Kuitenbrouwer, "On the Concept of Process of Marginalization," *Occasional Paper No. 37*, The Hague, ISS, 1973.

[4]*Ibid.*

[5]Net welfare is the aggregate welfare of individuals minus the welfare of individuals beyond the minimum desirable. If per capita income is considered as an index of welfare, then net welfare=total income of all individuals—the income of individuals exceeding double the per capita income.

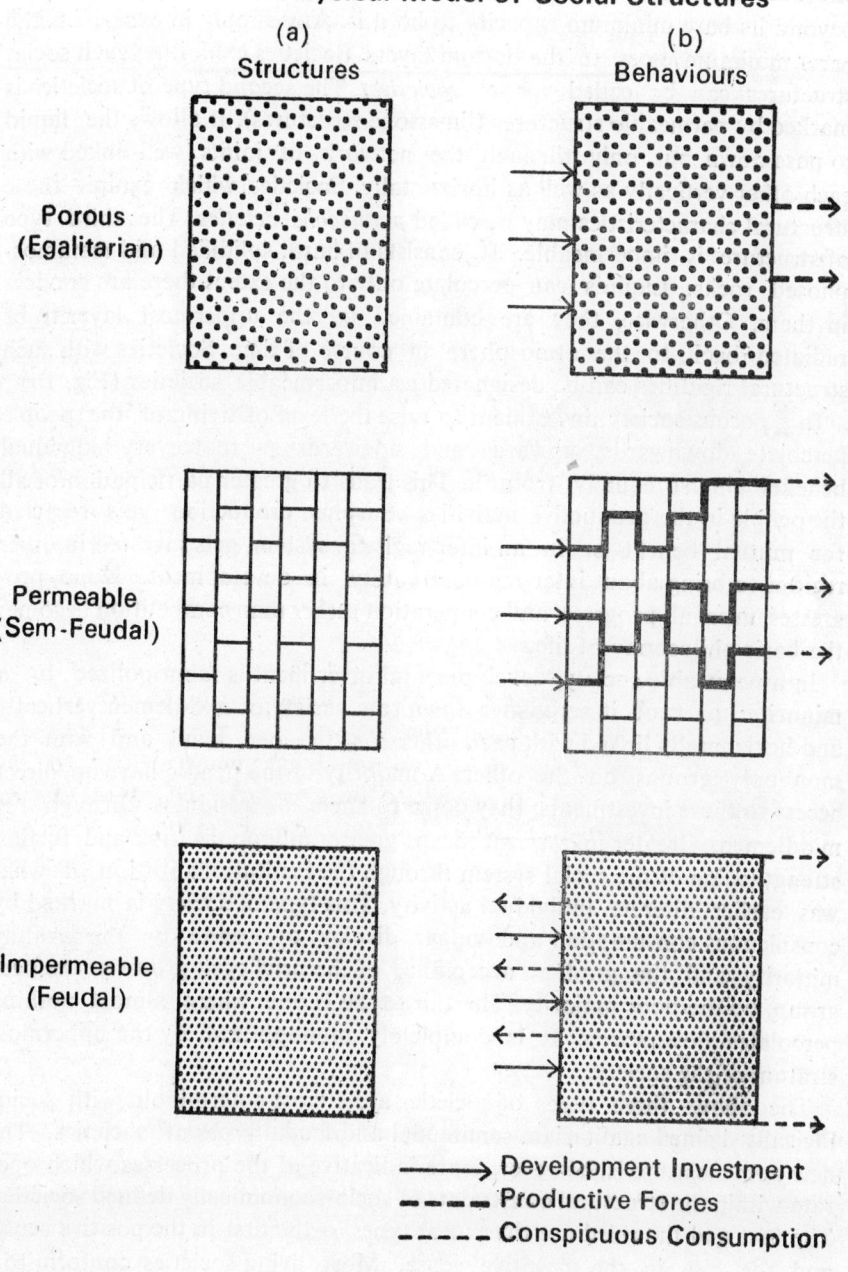

Physical Model of Social Structures

	(a) Structures	(b) Behaviours

Porous (Egalitarian)

Permeable (Sem-Feudal)

Impermeable (Feudal)

→ Development Investment
‑‑→ Productive Forces
‑‑‑→ Conspicuous Consumption

such that the liquid cannot by-pass any particle, whether the process is percolatory or capillary, so long as there is enough liquid to fill the stratum. Nor does it allow retention of the liquid by individual particles beyond its bare minimum capacity to hold it. Any supply in excess of the bare minimum goes to the bottom layers. Societies exhibiting such social structures can be called *porous societies*. The second type of societies is marked by permeable structures (limestone structures). It allows the liquid to pass down but only through the network of joints well-linked with each other vertically as well as horizontally. Societies which exhibit these structural characteristics may be called *permeable societies*. The third type of structure is impermeable. It consists of hard, solidified and metamorphosed rocks. Liquids can percolate only to the extent there are crevices in them. Otherwise, they are contained by the uppermost layer to be radiated back to the atmosphere in course of time. Societies with such structural rigidities can be designated as impermeable societies (Fig. 1b).

In a porous society, investment to raise the level of living of the people percolate downwards, upwards and sidewards so that every individual benefits almost equally from it. This leads to greater participation of all the people in the productive activities. Surplus production gets recycled for mutual benefit or in an inter-regional system, gets invested in other regions to bring about inter-regional equity in development. None progresses unless all progress; and cooperation rather than competition becomes the basic philosophy of life.

In a permeable society, developmental investment is monopolized by a minority; part of it percolates down to a variety of middlemen vertically and horizontally linked with each other on the one hand and with the monopoly groups on the other. A majority of the people have no direct access to these investments; they come to them as residuals through the middlemen. Greater investment means greater monopolization and further strengthening of the social system through the institutionalization of what was earlier discrete individual activity. This type of society is marked by conspicuous consumption and vulgar display of wealth by the wealthy minority and the gradual acceptance of the privileged group as the peer group, by the poor majority. The third type is one where almost nothing percolates downwards. It is completely monopolized by the uppermost stratum of the society.

The above three types of societies are almost coterminous with sociologically defined egalitarian, semifeudal and feudal types of societies. The new nomenclature is, however, more indicative of the processes which operate within the structural constraints of socio-economically defined societies. The first and the third are the "ideal types"—the first in the positive sense, and the last in the negative sense. Most living societies conform to a variant of the second type; and it is this type with which we are concerned in this paper.

When we examine the problem of poverty of a region or a group of people within the framework of the social realities explained above, we cannot but conclude that to think of poverty as the cause of low productivity of the masses, and to approach the problem of poverty in terms of productivity alone is ridiculous:

Many of the traits that characterize developing societies such as the lack of productive and remunerative employment, the inability to distribute the fruits of growth so as to relieve mass poverty or to narrow the gap between minorities enjoying modern consumption pattern and the rest of the population, the inability to accord the masses either the reality or the feeling of participation in decision-making have in different combinations become prominent in advanced countries (too) and have weakened their credibility as models for the development of the rest of humanity.[6]

Yet our models of development persistently ignore the social structural inability to assimilate change and to diffuse the benefits of development to those who have been by-passed by historical economic forces and processes. They rely heavily, if not completely, on truncated thinking on investment and production as the basis for all developments.

The old strategy based on the assumption that poverty can be taken care of through growth which must trickle down to the poverty stricken masses, has not borne fruit for the simple reason that the existing class relations are inimical to it. Wherever it has been pursued without adequate safeguards, it has proved to be counter-productive further strengthening the process of monopolization. We know fully well that:

. . .development is not merely a question of how much is produced, but what is produced and how it is produced. Institutions which create growth are not neutral as to its distribution. Thus, if growth institutions are characterized by disparities in land-holding and concentration of industrial wealth, the process of growth will strengthen them further and they will resist and frustrate all future attempts to take away their powers and privileges through orderly reforms.[7]

It is exactly the situation in which national and regional development efforts are being made in India. Each plan and programme for development has led to more poverty and more unemployment. Economy as a whole has indeed grown; national strength has improved at times beyond expectations. But the institutional reforms to strengthen the "filter down" process and to enable the masses to participate in national endeavours and to benefit from the contributions they make to it, has been frustrating. After going through several cycles of land reforms, we find ourselves where we were to

[6]J.B.W. Kuitenbrouwer, *op. cit.*
[7]*Ibid.*

begin with. These and other reforms have yet to make a major dent in the semi-feudal or permeable social structure we inherited from the British Raj. Twenty-five years of planning has now brought us to that fundamental problem of which we ought to have been adequately aware—mass poverty resulting not so much from lack of production as from the lack of opportunities to produce.

SOCIAL POLICY FRAMEWORK

In the light of the above, development has to be redefined as the process or processes through which a society acquires greater porosity within its own body politic and thus enables its members to gain greater control over themselves and their environment. To achieve this, all societies, but more so the developing ones, whether conceived in the national, regional or local[8] terms must consider structured social change as their major task. It is this change which should form the major component of social development. The provision of health, education, recreation and similar other facilities is only a secondary aspect of social development. What is primary is the transformation of a permeable society into a porous one. That is at least the direction in which we have to move to weaken, if not to eliminate completely, the monopolist minority and to bring them in the mainstream of development.[9]

Following Utria,[10] we could list the following main objectives of a social development policy suited to developing countries like India:

(a) to motivate, prepare and organize individuals and the community to replace the traditional concepts, motivations and attitudes by others which are more favourable to development; and

(b) to transform social structures and institutions, through the individual and the community, particularly as regards (i) re-structuring of production, (ii) changes in social structures; (iii) cultural change; and (iv) changes in political (and legal) structures;

[8]The processes of monopolization and marginalization cut across political and administrative boundaries and operate at international, national and local levels leading to inter-areal and inter-personal disparities in development. While at the internationa levels the national states and multi-national corporations monopolize the resources, atl the national level the regional governments, monopoly houses and their feudal subordinates do the job. The malady is so deep-seated that values of monopolization pervade down to local and individual levels and each person tends to exploit the others.

[9]The concept of mainstream needs some definition. It is often said that one of the objectives of development is to bring the poorer sections of the society into the mainstream of development. If development is conceived in terms proposed in this paper, then it is the upper stratum of the society consisting of large farmers, "intellectuals," businessmen, political bosses, bureaucrats and their allies, who have to be brought in the mainstream.

[10]R.D. Utria, Appendix to "Social Aspects of Regional Development in Latin America," *International Development Review*, No. 4, United Nations, New York, 1972.

(*c*) to accelerate *social mobility* so as to involve the population fully in the benefits of development and facilitate a steady improvement in the social condition of its under-privileged sections through the intro-duction of more dynamic structures for the ownership and use of pro-ductive resources and through an effective system of income distribution and redistribution;

(*d*) to create and fortify an *economy and an economic policy* that will ensure productive employment for the whole population. . . the expan-sion and efficient use of national resources and an adequate supply of goods and services to meet the genuine needs of all sections of the popu-lation;

(*e*) to accelerate and direct the general process of *modernization* by the absorption and assimilation of appropriate technological and scien-tific advances in all walks of life and activity, especially those which sustain the poorest among the poor;

(*f*) to consolidate and raise the level of *social well-being* by improv-ing the organization and aims of social services and other elements of the level of living with special attention to those who are marginalized;

(*g*) to promote and mobilize *popular participation* at all levels and on all fronts, both in decision-making and in the execution of development tasks by focusing on those aspects of development which concern the poor majority;

(*h*) to create a *national image* and a sense of achievement through systematic efforts to speed up development by carrying out a task which was perceived to be too difficult;

(*i*) to concern itself with the various phenomena and circumstances involved in the *self-fulfilment of the individual and the community* and the preservation of human dignity; and

If we accept the above, then social policy becomes the main dynamic factor of development; it brings economic policy in tune with social ob-jectives and proves beyond doubt the

. . .irrelevance and uselessness of social policies and programmes whose scope and objectives are limited to filling selected gaps in particular social services such as housing, medical assistance, education, recreation and so on. It also shows how undesirable it is to formulate economic policy without previously giving due consideration to social problems and to the social implications of economic development model and strategy adopted.[11]

[11]R. D. Utria, *op. cit.*

TARGET GROUPS AND REGIONAL SOCIAL POLICY

It has been emphasized earlier that the poorer sections constitute a large segment of developing societies. This applies equally well to developing sub-national regions and areas. It is these poverty-stricken people who should constitute the target groups in our planning exercises. Our social development policy must aim at full participation by these people in the production and distribution processes.

But who constitute the target group? Attempts have been made by individuals and national and inter-national institutions[12] to evolve indicators of poverty and development. A universally acceptable set of indices has proved to be illusive. In our own country, several seminars and symposia have been organized to evolve methodologies for identifying the poor.[13] We may perhaps continue these exercises for the benefit of researchers. In the mean time, lest our work is hindered, we could use a simplistic procedure to get quick results. Poverty is not an abstract phenomenon. It is here and everywhere. One has only to turn to one's own backyard. We need not, therefore, wait for research reports before formulating policies and the action programmes to implement plans, programmes and projects designed to improve the conditions of the poor. In the case of India, we could use three criteria to identify the poor. These are: (i) Social status as indicated by caste/community, (ii) Educational status, and (iii) Income or property status.

For the purposes of identification of the poorest among the poor, a set of cordinal and/or ordinal indices could be worked out, on the lines suggested below.

Class ordering	Index	Caste ordering	Education ordering	Income ordering
Upper	4	Upper caste touchables	Graduate +	More than 20 times PCI*
Upper middle	3	Intermediate caste touchables +	High school +	10 to 20 times PCI
Lower middle	2	Lowest Caste touchables	Primary school +	5 to 10 times PCI
Lower	1	Untouchables	Literate	Less than 5 times PCI
Lowest	0	Tribals	Illiterate	Less than PCI

*PCI=Per capita income in the country.

[12]Specially, UNRISD, Geneva.
[13]This refers to ICSSR sponsored workshops in different parts of the country.

Supposing that two persons get the following rating

	A	B
Caste	3	1
Education	2	0
Income	1	1
	6	2

It could be said that *B* is thrice as backward as *A*. The maximum score one can get is 12 and the minimum is 0. Now we can link the various classes with scores.

Class	Score range
Upper	11—12
Upper middle	9—10
Lower middle	6— 8
Lower	3— 5 ⎤ Target group
Lowest	0— 2 ⎦

The above classification can be fruitfully used to identify the target groups. The people with lowest status rating should be the immediate concern of the planners. The planned action must aim at improving their social, educational and income status. To improve their bargaining power *vis-a-vis* the kulaks, monopolizers, and other vested interest groups, the concept of social development would have to concern itself primarily with social relations and only secondarily with the provision of social facilities like health, education, recreation, etc.

In the first place, a massive effort will have to be made at the national and regional levels to bring the children of the target groups to the school. The proposition is, however, not so simple to implement, for the obvious reason that a child is the product of the status of the parents. He inherits the poverty in all forms—social, economic and others. He is guided by the aspirations of the parents and the over-all environment in which he is born and brought up. It is, therefore, suggested that at least one standard primary school should be built by the Central Government in all the taluks/tehsils of India, during the Sixth Five Year Plan. These schools would have the same facilities which the best urban schools have, plus the lodging and boarding facilities. Half of the children of these schools should be drawn from the target groups and the other half from the rest of the people. Integrated development of the two groups is essential from the long-term social point of view. The task of these schools should be to see that every child admitted progresses on desired lines and goes to higher schools where he gets full support from the government to move ahead. More such schools can be built gradually to cover all the members of the target group. Space does not permit further elaboration of this scheme here. Suffice it to say that if implemented in right earnest, it would raise the educational level of the poorer sections within a decade.

As regards the economic status, the social development policy should aim at immediate nationalization of all natural resources including land. It should also prohibit acquisition of property for social exploitation. The property may be categorized into three types (*i*) private property, (*ii*) trust property, and (*iii*) state property. No single family should be allowed to own private property worth more than 50 times the per capita income. If the per capita income in 1980 is likely to be Rs 1000 per annum, during the decade 1970-80, a family of six members can have private property worth Rs 3 lakhs. The remaining private property should be declared as trust property and suitable rules could be made for its administration. The benefits accruing from a trust property should go to the welfare of the weaker sections. The above property classification should apply to urban and rural areas alike and similarly to agricultural and industrial sectors alike.

Since a majority of the people belonging to the poorer sections of the society live in the rural areas, the land resources after nationalization have to be so distributed that the poor become the major beneficiaries. In this regard the following proposals could be considered seriously for implementation:

(*i*) the available land should be distributed among agricultural families equitably so that each family would get about 1 to 2 hectares. The compensation for the land acquired from large farmers should be for a maximum of five hectares minus the land assigned for him after redistribution. The compensation should be given in the form of new agricultural enterprises like dairy, poultry etc., so that the maximum desirable level of household income is not reduced. Since better off farmers are more prone to adopt innovations, this policy would not force them out of agriculture;

(*ii*) the farm families should be grouped into a set of twenty or twenty-five and massive assistance in terms of new enterprises services, input, and marketing channels should be given to each group to increase productivity;

(*iii*) to accomplish the above, the local and regional services through decentralization and even at the cost of national and state level services should be strengthened and entrusted with the task of being at the service of the people.

The implications of the above for regional development are indeed far reaching. Regional development then can shed its obscurantist task of drawing regional boundaries, and allocating funds to uncoordinated schemes of development, and tune itself to the task of comprehensive socio-economic planning and development at a variety of areal levels—blocks, talukas, districts, states, etc. There could be three approaches to development then: (*i*) Area approach—development of the physical and human resources; (*ii*) Target group approach—development of the weaker sections; and (*iii*) Economic approach—developments designed to maintain and improve the productivity of the region *vis-a-vis* other regions.

The first approach should lead to the development of natural resources—land, water, flora and fauna and physical and social infrastructure, etc. If the underground water is available only in a given zone, it has to be tapped and used by whosoever has the land near the source. Similarly, a canal can give water to fields on the lower side of its own level. If a major road has to be built, it has to follow a given alignment; there is nothing that can be done about it. But what can be organized is compensatory development projects for those who have not benefited from the area approach projects.

To carry the benefits of development to those who do not benefit from the area approach because of disabilities imposed on them by the society and its laws, target group approach to development would have to be resorted to. Each household of the target group should be given a package of activities which enables it to become economically viable—here viability means earning capacity equivalent to prevailing per capita income. We should be able to evolve models of viable rural families within which households with different economic and socio-cultural status could be fitted.

For the success of a social policy outlined above, development has to be attempted in a multilevel territorial framework. Region should not be construed to be an isolated sub-national territory. It should be considered as a sub-set of a larger set linked vertically as well as horizontally with each other. Each region or sub-region has its own peculiarities with respect to the social situation. While it is true that much of what can be done at the regional level in terms of social development would have to be decided at the national level, it is equally true that a national policy to be of any operational significance must be interpreted in regional and local terms. Here lies the importance of regional sociology and regional social structure.

As an operational strategy, we could consider a two-sector model of rural development—the private sector and the co-operative sector. It is the co-operative sector which needs to be made broad-based and strong. If necessary, each village should have special purpose co-operative, catering to needs of the weaker sections exclusively. To make them viable, their activities should encompass production and agro-services too. Instead of each small farmer owning every piece of agricultural implements, etc., it could very well be owned by co-operatives which can do custom job for the co-operators. This may ultimately lead to co-operative farming.

CONCLUSIONS

In conclusion, we can restate that the existing approaches to regional development lack a comprehensive social policy with the result that the poorer sections of the society do not benefit adequately from the planning and development activities. Social development involves far more than provision of certain social facilities like education, health, housing, etc. It involves a conscious effort to make structural changes in the society and aims at a porous or egalitarian society.

Given a comprehensive social development policy, the approaches to regional development should be two-fold—area approach and household approach. The latter approach is to attack the problem of poverty at its grassroots level. The households of the poorer sections of the society should constitute the target group in regional development. The objective should be to make each household viable through co-operative endeavours.

N. S. P. REBELLO
M. G. CHANDRAKANTH

Crop Insurance in Area Development

INTRODUCTION

Agriculture contributes half of the national income of India and sustains about two-thirds of the population. It is closely interrelated to and interdependent with other sectors of the economy and any turmoil in it affects the economy, as a whole. Agricultural production has a key role to play in area development. Any area development programme has to be built on a base or foundation of agricultural development.

Technological change, specially in crop production, is of prime importance in area development, especially in an agrarian country like India. It involves the use of an enormous quantity of the resources and heavy investment in durable, as well as non-durable factors, as much at the micro-level as at the macro-level. Not only has the State and the economy to provide a strong infrastructure that will encourage and sustain increased production, but farmers have to spend considerable sums of money on land improvement, equipment and purchase of material inputs, such as, seed, fertilizer and chemicals. Considering that most crop production is carried on under rain-fed conditions, the possibilities of loss of the meagre resources at the disposal of the farmers, especially the "small and marginal," assumes great importance.

Crop production is fraught with uncertainties, especially under rain-fed conditions. Most of these arise directly or indirectly from natural hazards, which the farmers generally accept and endure as "acts of nature." However, in recent times, as a result of the improvement in scientific technology and economic institutions, there is an increasing awareness that uncertainties can be actively "coped with." Crop insurance is one such means of counteracting the uncertainties involved in crop production.

Crop insurance can be an important means of relief to farmers from the vagaries of nature, helping them to ward off the fear of crop loss and infusing in them confidence to use modern technology. It is a device through which:

(*i*) the uncertainty faced by the individual farmers is transferred to an agency or the insurer through their participation, in large numbers, in the programme, for which benefit, they pay a risk premium;

(*ii*) the total loss is shared by all the participating farmers, horizontally spread over a wide area and vertically over years;

(*iii*) the risk premium is reflected in the group risk assumed by the insurer; and

(*iv*) an indemnity is paid to the insuring farmer when the loss due to insured causes beyond his control occurs, as long as, he enters into a contract with the insurer and pays the premium.

Uncertainty Risk and Insurance

A distinction has been made by Knight[1] between risk and uncertainty, the latter being a subset of the former. Risk is defined as a situation where the outcomes, as well as their probabilities, are known, and therefore, an expectation of the result can be obtained. A situation, where the outcomes are not clearly known or their probability is unknown, is defined as uncertainty. A situation of uncertainty to an individual is often one of risk to a group of individuals. Even when the individual may not know whether and when rain may fail over time, the probability of rain failure and consequent loss in an area can be estimated. On the basis of this, the total loss over the area in the given period can also be predicted. If this estimated total loss is spread over or shared by all the individuals in the group, the threat of loss becomes relatively small. This is the logic behind a crop insurance programme.

The yield levels and losses in a group of farmers over a period of time, as well as, their probabilities and standard deviation can be estimated. Thus, the situation can be converted to one of risk, using the theory of large numbers and, therefore, becomes insurable.

Friedman and Savage[2] presented a theory explaining insurance and gambling, based on the nature of the utility curve of the individual. An individual is faced with two eventualities: He could obtain normal, reasonably high income of I_1 or incur loss, so that the income would be much lower, say I_2. If the probability of the latter is p, the probability of the former, $q = (l—p)$. The average can be given by $I = p (I_2) + q (I_1)$, which would have an utility to him and say $\bar{U}$. It is possible that the individual could insure an income I^* which has an utility U^* to him. His decision to take up insurance will then depend upon the nature of his utility function with respect to income.

If the utility curve is convex, the utility U^* of the insured income I^*, is higher than the utility $\bar{U}$ of the average income $\bar{I}$. Therefore, he will insure. Thus, an individual tends to insure when the utility of income falls at an

[1] F.H. Knight, *Risk, Uncertainty and Profit*, The University of Chicago Press, Chicago, 1971, pp. 233-34.

[2] M. Friedman and L.J. Savage, "The Utility Analysis of Choices Involving Risk," *The Journal of Political Economy*, Vol. 56, 1948, pp. 279-304.

increasing marginal dis-utility of loss. Here he is willing to exchange an

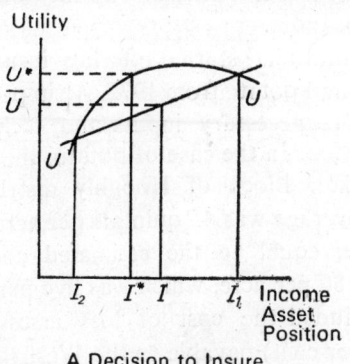

A Decision to Insure

Fig. 1

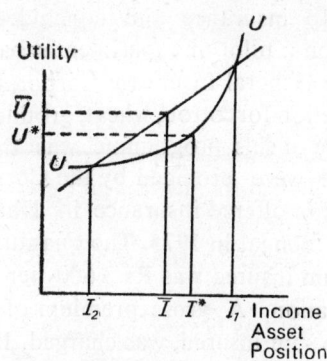

A Decision to Gamble

Fig. 2

uncertain situation for a certain situation, even though it involves a (known) cost.

If the utility curve is concave, the utility $\bar{U}$ of the average income $\bar{I}$ is higher than the utility U^* of the insured income I^*. Hence, he will prefer to take a chance. Thus, an individual tends to gamble when the utility of gains increases at an increasing rate. Here, the individual prefers an uncertain situation to a certain situation, rather than incur a cost to convert the former into the latter.

It is possible that an individual will insure and gamble, if the utility curve is convex up to a certain level of income and concave thereafter.

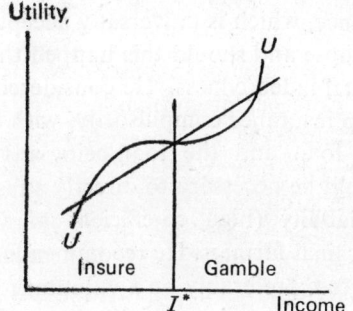

A Decision to Insure or Gamble

Fig. 3

In the first region, he tends to insure and in the second, he gambles.

EARLIER RESEARCH IN INDIA

Borude and Joglekar[3] estimated premium rates for Bajra and Jowar in Maharashtra State. For Rabi Jowar, the pure premium worked out to 4.48 pounds per acre for a quantum coverage of 162 pounds, forming 2.76 per cent of it.

[3]S.G. Borude and N.M. Joglekar, "Crop Insurance to Protect the Farmers Under Dry Farming Conditions in Maharashtra," *Indian Journal of Agricultural Economics*, Vol. 26, 1971, pp. 307-17.

Narain[4] examined the economic, financial and actuarial implications of crop insurance and concluded that it is not advisable to introduce it even on a pilot or experimental basis in India.

The General Insurance Corporation of India[5] started offering insurance protection for cotton, wheat, groundnut and potato from 1972. An important feature of this programme was that the necessary inputs and technical advice were provided by the Corporation. In the case of potato, the Corporation offered insurance in Dhanyakali Block of Hooghly district in West Bengal in 1975. The quantum coverage was 45 quintals per acre and the sum insured was Rs 3,600 per acre, equal to the estimated cost of cultivation. A gross premium of Rs 180 per acre, which was five per cent of the sum insured, was charged. It included the cost of loss assessment and service charges of Rs 36 (one per cent) payable to the West Bengal Agro Industries Corporation. Production finance was also provided to the insured farmers by the nationalized banks.

Dandekar[6] made many important observations and recommendations, regarding crop insurance and its applicability under Indian conditions. According to him, crop insurance should be a part of the infrastructure essential for the development of agriculture, which is basically insecure. Without such protection, the entire structure of agricultural finance, which is universally accepted as important, would be in danger of collapse and should this happen the cultivator will be again back in perpetual indebtedness. He considered that it is necessary to link finance with crop insurance compulsorily, with the premium being treated as a part of the loan and the loan being adjusted from the indemnity. He felt that it would be necessary to directly subsidize premiums in areas with high yield variability (high co-efficient of variation) and in the case of small and marginal farmers. He recommended that area yield insurance should be started, preferably on a voluntary basis, available to all farmers.

Methodology

An illustration of the normal curve technique[7] in rate making applied to the potato crop in Hassan taluk of Karnataka, where the crop is being grown under rain-fed conditions, is presented here.

The yield on an individual farm is invariably different from the average yield for the area, as a whole, on account of the differences in soil fertility, weather conditions and such physical factors, as well as, in inputs used, practices adopted and other managerial factors. In the use of this technique, the frequency distribution of the yields on individual farms over the area

[4]V.M. Dandekar, "Crop Insurance in India," *Economic and Political Weekly*, Vol. II, No. 26, June 1976, p. A-61.

[5]Correspondence with R.V. Madhava Rao, General Manager, GIC, Bombay-400020, dt. 13-8-1975.

[6]V.M. Dandekar, *op. cit.*, pp. A-61 to A-80.

[7]R.R. Botts and J.N. Boles, "Use of Normal Curve Theory in Crop Insurance Rate Making," *Journal of Farm Economics*, Vol. 40, No. 3, 1958, pp. 733-40.

needs to be normally distributed.[8]

This is a crucial assumption, which has to be fulfilled to a reasonable extent before this technique can be used. This procedure of estimating premium is currently adopted by the Federal Crop Insurance Corporation (FCIC) of the United States of America, as well as, the Manitoba Crop Insurance Corporation (MCIC) of Canada.

The symbols used in this study are given below:

Sym-bol	Description
$\overline{Y}$	Average yield over five years of 150 farmers in Hassan taluk express-ed in tonnes per hectare.
P	Price options; in this case, $P_1 =$ Rs 600, $P_2 =$ Rs 650 and $P_3 =$ Rs 700, per tonne of potato.
L	Average annual loss cost or pure premium rate in tonnes per hectare.
C	Coverage levels per hectare, ranging from 45 per cent of the long-term average yield to 100 per cent of the long-term average yield.
y_i	Yield in a given year in tonnes per hectare (for which rate calculation is made).
Y	Mean of per hectare yields (y_i) in a particular year calculated by using the frequency distribution formula for mean.
n	Number of hectares with an yield less than the coverage in a given year.
N	Total number of hectares used in calculating Y in a given year.

[8]Some definitions of terms used here are given as follows:

Area yield insurance: Here, premiums and indemnities are based upon the yield in an area, i.e., homogeneous and of uniform crop conditions. Indemnities are paid to all insured farmers in any area, in which the mean yield in the area is less than the insured yield. *Coverage:* This is the insurance protection offered, it can be distinguished into: (a) the "level of coverage"—when expressed as a percentage of the long-term average yield; (b) the "quantum coverage"—when expressed in terms of physical units, for ex. —tonnes; and (c) the "monetary coverage"—when expressed in monetary terms, taking into account, a specific price. *Gross Premium or Premium or Premium Rate*: This is the final premium charged by the insuring agency. It includes the pure premium based on loss, loss adjustment cost, administrative cost and the reserve fund component. *Indemnity:* It is the compensation payable to the insured farmer for a crop loss arising from the insured cause. It is the quantity by which the yield is less than the coverage. *Insured:* is the party (farmer) who has to be indemnified by the insuring agency (insurer) when a loss is incurred due to the insured cause. *Loss Ratio:* is the ratio of the sum of the indemnities paid by the insurer to the total premiums received, in any crop year. Monetary coverage: is the quantum coverage multiplied by a given price and expressed in rupees. *Pure Premium Rate*: is the definite amount payable to the insurer by the insured for the insurance protection offered to him. It is equal to the average of the indemnities paid to farmers over years for a unit of area.

R Mean yield in tonnes per hectare on indemnified hectares in a given

year$=\sum \dfrac{y_i}{n}$ where y_i is the yield in tonnes per hectare, when it

is less than the coverage.

s Standard deviation of the per hectare yields y_i around the area yield Y in a given year, calculated by using the frequency distribution formula for standard deviation. s varies from year to year.

d Height of the ordinate at C in the frequency distribution of yields.

A Proportion of the total hectares with the per hectare yields y_i less than the coverage in a given year. A is also called the crop loss probability. $A=n/N$.

The total indemnity payable in any given year,

$$I=\Sigma (C-y_i) \qquad\qquad \ldots 1$$

The average annual loss cost which is the total indemnity distributed over N hectares,

$$L= \frac{1}{N} (nC-\Sigma y_i) \qquad\qquad \ldots 2$$

Since $R= \dfrac{1}{n} \Sigma y_i, \quad \Sigma y_i=nR$

Substitutiug R in equation 2, the average annual loss cost or pure premium rate per hectare in any given year,

$$L= \frac{1}{N} (nC-nR)= \frac{n (C-R)}{N} \qquad\qquad \ldots 3$$

and $I= n (C-R)$

Substituting $A = n/N$ in equation 3, the pure premium rate per hectare in any given year,

$$L=A (C-R)=AC-AR \qquad\qquad \ldots 4$$

It can be demonstrated that in a truncated normal distribution on an average[9]

$$R=Y- \frac{ds}{A} \qquad\qquad \ldots 5$$

[9]The mathematical proof of the same is discussed in great detail in the original article. See R.R. Botts and J.N. Boles, *op. cit.*, pp. 739-40.

where d is the height of the ordinate at C in the frequency distribution of yields and s is the standard deviation of the yields. Substituting 5 in 4, the pure premium rate per hectare in any given year,

$$L = AC - A \left[Y - \frac{ds}{A} \right]$$

$$L = AC - AY + ds$$

$$L = A\,(C - Y) + ds \qquad \qquad \ldots 6$$

This formula gives the pure premium rate for any given year in commodity units. If only Y, $\overline{Y}$, C and s are known, the following conversion needs to be made in order to obtain L.

Coverage C can be converted to the standard normal variable Z using the formula,

$$Z = \frac{C - Y}{s}$$

After obtaining Z, the value of A and d can be obtained from the statistical tables.[10] The pure premium rate L is then estimated by substituting the values of A, C, Y, d and s in equation 6.

The computational procedure used to estimate the premium and indemnity by using this approach is as follows:

The range of the yield per hectare during each of the five years (1971-1975) was divided into fifteen classes, the class interval worked out to 1.3 tonnes. The frequency distribution was then obtained. The estimates of the mean yield, the standard deviation, the co-efficient of variation and the pearsonian skewness were calculated, using the formulae involving the frequency distribution[11] for each of the five years. X^2 (Chi-square) test was applied to the frequency distribution each year to test whether the yields were normally distributed.[12] The pure premium rate was then calculated using the formula $L = A\,(C - Y) + d\,s$.

Results and Discussion

Variability in yields. The degree of dispersion of the yield of potato was studied by considering the variability within each year and between the five years. The measure of variability within each year is presented in Table 1. The mean yield was the lowest, 8.57 tonnes per hectare, in 1971 and was the highest, 9.45 tonnes per hectare, in 1975. The co-efficient of

[10]J.S. Fowlie, *Statistical Tables for Students*, Oliver and Boyd, Tweeddale Court, Edinburgh-1, 1969, pp. 4-5.

[11]F.E. Croxton and D.J. Cowden, *Applied General Statistics*, Second ed., Prentice-Hall of India (Pvt) Ltd., New Delhi, 1964, pp. 173-239.

[12]*Ibid.*, pp.681-93.

varition was the highest, 46.75 per cent, in 1971 and lowest, 38.45 per cent, in 1975. Drought was probably the reason for low yield coupled with high variation in 1971. In general, study of the co-efficient of variation indicated that the potato crop was found to be a high risk one, posing a constant threat of loss to farmers, in Hassan.

TABLE 1

Variability in Yields

Years	Mean yield in tonnes per hectare	Median yield in tonnes per hectare	Standa- rd de- viation	Co-efficient of variation (in percentage)	Pearso- nian skewness
Yield variability between farms					
1971	8.57	8.40	4.007	46.75	+0.042
1972	9.06	8.99	4.030	44.50	+0.050
1973	9.28	9.12	3.810	41.07	+0.130
1974	9.35	9.18	3.820	40.84	+0.130
1975	9.45	9.54	3.630	38.45	−0.074

Yield variability between the years

Long term average yield in tonnes per ha.	Long term Median yield in tonnes per ha.	Standard deviation	Co-efficient of variation (in percentage)
9.14	9.04	0.35	3.84

The long-term average yield was 9.14 tonnes per hectare. The variability was comparatively lesser between the years than between farms within the year. Yet, the premium and indemnity payable varied from year to year, based on the annual mean yields and their variability, which are affected by the inputs used, technology adopted, weather conditions and other extraneous factors.

Cost of production: The expenditure—pre-harvest, operating and total[13]

[13]Pre-harvest expenditure included the cost of seed, farm yard manure, fertilisers, plant protection chemicals, labour and incidental charges incurred in the planting and tuber-initiation stages. Operating expenditure included the pre-harvest expenditure and the harvesting expenditure. Total expenditure included the operating expenditure and overheads, such as, interest on operating expenditure, repairs, depreciation and land revenue.

The potato crop comes to harvest in 90 days. The growth period can be divided into three stages, depending upon the risks involved for the purpose of determining the amount of indemnity payable to the farmer:

1. The Planting Stage: which covers forty days from sowing the seed tubers. The crop takes about 20 to 25 days for successful germination, however, depending on the receipt of rainfall at sowing time, availability of disease-free seed tubers, the type of soil, etc.

2. The Tuber Initiation Stage: which extends over 30 days after the planting stage. During this stage, the crop is prone to hazards, such as, late blight and brown ring rot

were estimated for three stages of production, namely, planting, tuber initiation and harvesting, along with overhead expenditure. The cost of production is presented in Table 2.

The cost of seed tubers was the largest component of the expenditure, amounting to Rs 1,112 per hectare on an average and forming about 30 per cent of the cost. Fertilizer was another important component, accounting for Rs 969 per hectare, constituting about 26 per cent of the cost. Of this, Rs 734 was spent on the basal dose and Rs 235 on the top dressing.

The expenditure during the planting stage was Rs 2,847 per hectare or 78 per cent of the total expenditure. Thus, most of the expenditure was incurred in the planting stage itself. The cost incurred up to the harvest was Rs 3,251 per hectare. The operating expenditure was Rs 3,441 being about 95 per cent of the total expenditure. The total expenditure was Rs 3,641 per hectare.

The goodness of fit test and the frequency distribution of expected yields. The data on the goodness of fit test applied to the frequency distribution is presented in Table 3. It can be observed that the normal curve assumption was satisfied, as seen from the chi-square values obtained for the observed and expected yield frequencies. The Pearsonian coefficient of skewness was also not significant.

Fixed coverage level. The level of protection offered against crop loss depends upon the type of cost that is to be covered and the risks affecting the crop. The coverage level offered should not exceed the average expenditure incurred in producing the crop, in other words, it should not cover profit. In Table 4, the coverage level, the quantum coverage and the monetary coverage, to be offered in order to cover cost, when loss occurs at different stages of production, are shown.

In order to cover the operating expenditure of Rs 3,441 per hectare, a quantum coverage of 5.3 tonnes per hectare, which corresponded to a coverage level of 58 per cent was necessary. Taking into account, the average price of Rs 650 per tonne,[14] the monetary coverage at this level worked out to Rs 3,445 per hectare. If a choice of a lower or higher price were to be given to the farmer, the monetary coverage would be lesser or greater than the operating expenditure. The pure premium, as well as, the quantum coverage can be expressed in physical units only, which would not be dependent on the price level.

On the other hand, as is in vogue in the United States of America, only the pre-harvesting expenditure could be covered. The guarantee could be

---

(wilt). Besides these, inadequate rains can also reduce the yields drastically.

3. The Harvesting Stage: which extends over about 20 days after the tuber initiation stage. Some varieties like Holland come to harvest in about 80 days from planting, while many of the Simla varieties take about 90 days. So, 20 days were taken to adjust for differences in duration.

[14]Rs 650 per tonne was the average of the actual prices received by the farmers during the five year period (1971-75).

TABLE 2

Cost of Production

(Per hectare)

Sl. No.	Stage and item	Unit	Quantity	Price (Rs)	Pre-harvest expenditure		Operating expenditure		Total expenditure	
					Rupees	Per cent	Rupees	Per cent	Rupees	Per cent
1. Planting Stage (up to 40 days from planting)										
1.	Ploughing	Plow pairs	25	10	250	7.69	250	7.26	250	6.87
2.	Farm yard manure	Tonnes	20	24	480	14.76	480	13.95	480	13.18
3.	Seed tubers	Kgs	927	1.20	1112	34.20	1112	32.32	1112	30.54
4.	Fertilisers N	Kgs	54		734	22.58	734	21.33	734	20.16
	P 205	Kgs	42 }							
	K 20	Kgs	42 }							
5.	Plant protection chemicals	Rs			38	1.17	38	1.10	38	1.04
6.	Labour	Mandays	49	4.00	196	6.03	196	5.70	196	5.38
7.	Transport and other incidental charges	Rs			37	1.14	37	1.07	37	1.02
	Expenses up to planting stage				2847	87.57	2847	82.74	2847	78.19
2. Tuber initiation Stage (41st to 70th day)										
8.	Interculture	Plow pairs	5	10.0	50	1.54	50	1.45	50	1.37
9.	Fertilisers N	Kgs	49	4.8	235	7.23	235	6.83	235	6.45
10.	Labour	Mandays	22	4.0	88	2.71	88	2.56	88	2.42
11.	Plant protection chemicals	Rs			31	0.95	31	0.90	31	0.85
	Expenses up to tuber initiation stage				3251	100.00	3251	94.48	3251	89.28

Table 2 (Cont.)

3. *Harvesting stage (after 70th day)*								
12. Harvesting	Plow pairs	5	10.00	50	1.45	50	1.37	
13. Labour for picking	Mandays	35	4.00	140	4.07	140	3.84	
Expenses up to harvesting stage				3441	100.00	3441	94.50	
Overhead								
14. Interest on operating capital	Rs					126	3.46	
15. Depreciation and repairs	Rs					66	1.81	
16. Land revenue	Rs					8	0.22	
Total expenditure						3641	100.00	

TABLE 3

Goodness of Fit Test and the Frequency Distribution of Observed and Expected Yields

Class limits tonnes/ha	Mid value	1971 Frequency of observed yields	1971 Frequency of expected yields	1972 Frequency of observed yields	1972 Frequency of expected yields	1973 Frequency of observed yields	1973 Frequency of expected yields	1974 Frequency of observed yields	1974 Frequency of expected yields	1975 Frequency of observed yields	1975 Frequency of expected yields
Under 1.25	0.6	5	5.04	4	4.02	3	2.68	3	2.55	2	1.83
1.25 to 2.55	1.9	6	4.98	5	4.03	4	3.19	3	3.07	2	2.85
2.55 to 3.85	3.2	9	7.83	6	6.72	4	5.79	5	5.61	7	4.86
3.85 to 5.15	4.5	11	11.80	12	10.50	8	9.34	8	9.12	8	8.58
5.15 to 6.45	5.8	12	15.06	13	13.89	13	13.42	14	13.63	12	13.06
6.45 to 7.75	7.1	20	18.39	14	17.01	23	17.25	19	17.14	15	17.50
7.75 to 9.05	8.4	24	19.06	22	18.82	19	19.72	21	19.68	20	20.61
9.05 to 10.35	9.7	14	18.33	18	18.82	19	19.54	20	19.57	24	20.19
10.35 to 11.65	11.0	14	16.41	17	17.01	17	18.90	15	18.46	20	19.63
11.65 to 12.95	12.3	13	12.40	14	13.89	14	14.86	14	15.10	16	15.87
12.95 to 14.25	13.6	9	9.01	10	10.23	11	10.75	13	10.99	10	11.26
14.25 to 15.55	14.9	6	5.53	6	6.99	5	6.94	6	7.15	6	6.88
15.55 to 16.85	16.2	4	3.25	4	4.03	6	3.99	4	4.14	5	3.94
16.85 to 18.15	17.5	2	1.62	3	2.19	3	2.05	4	2.14	2	1.92
Over 18.15	18.8	1	1.26	2	1.83	1	1.53	1	1.60	1	1.26
Total		150	150	150	150	150	150	150	150	150	150

	1971	1972	1973	1974	1975
	$X^2 = 4.199$	2.070	5.28	3.504	3.223
	N.S. at 5%	N.S. at 5%	N.S. at 10%	N.S. at 5%	N.S. at 5%
	D.F.=12	D.F.=12	D.F.=12	D.F.=12	D.F.=12
Mean=Y (Tonnes/ha)=	8.57	9.06	9.28	9.35	9.45
Median (tonnes/ha) =	8.40	8.99	9.12	9.18	9.54
Standard deviation (tonnes/ha) =	4.007	4.03	3.810	3.820	3.633
Co-efficient of var.,(%)=	46.75	44.50	41.07	40.84	38.45
Pearsonian Skewness =	0.042	0.050	0.130	0.130	−0.074

N.S.=Non-significant.   D.F.=Degrees of Freedom.

TABLE 4

Fixed Coverage Level

Stage of crop damage	Type of production expenditure covered		Coverage level (per cent)	Quantum coverage (tonnes per hectare)	Monetary coverage at Rs 650 per tonne (Rs)
	Type	Rs			
Planting	Pre-harvest expenditure	2,847	48	4.39	2,854
Tuber initiation	-do-	3,251	55	5.03	3,270
Planting	Operating expenditure	2,847	48	4.39	2,854
Tuber initiation	- do -	3,251	55	5.03	3,270
Harvesting	- do -	3,441	58	5.30	3,445

increased by a specified amount, if the crop were harvested, in order to cover the cost of harvesting.[15] The quantum coverage sufficient to cover the pre-harvest expenditure, which in this case was Rs 3,251 was 5.03 tonnes per hectare and this worked out to a coverage level of 55 per cent.

Average pure premium rate. The average pure premium rate and the pure premium expressed as a percentage of the quantum coverage, as well as, the long-term average yield are presented in Table 5. At the coverage level of 58 per cent, the average pure premium was 0.33 tonne per hectare. It was 6.24 per cent of the quantum coverage and 3.62 per cent of the long-term average yield. The minimum pure premium rate was 0.18 tonne per hectare, at a coverage level of 45 per cent and constituted about 2 per cent of the long-term average yield.

TABLE 5
Average Pure Premium Rate

Coverage level (per cent)	Quantum coverage (tonnes per hectare)	Average pure premium (tonnes per hectare)	Pure premium as percentage of the quantum coverage (per cent)	Pure premium as percentage of the long-term average yield (per cent)
45	4.11	0.1797	4.37	1.97
50	4.57	0.2289	5.01	2.50
55	5.03	0.2895	5.76	3.17
58	5.30	0.3305	6.24	3.62
60	5.48	0.3603	6.57	3.94
65	5.94	0.4468	7.52	4.89
70	6.40	0.5483	8.57	6.00
75	6.86	0.6668	9.72	7.30
80	7.31	0.8003	10.95	8.76
85	7.77	0.9565	12.31	10.46
90	8.23	1.1322	13.76	12.32
95	8.68	1.3245	15.26	14.49
100	9.14	1.5150	16.58	16.58

Long-term average yield=9.14 tonnes per hectare.

[15]The bushel guarantee per acre in the United States Federal Crop Insurance Policy is the pre-harvest coverage. If the crop is harvested, the bushel guarantee will be increased by the following amounts to cover the harvesting cost:

Crop	Bushel increase
Wheat	1.5
Barley	2.0
Flax	0.7
Oats	3.0
Rye	1.5
Corn	3.0
Soyabeans	1.5

For details see H.W. Delvo and L.D. Loftsgard, "All Risk Crop Insurance in North Dakota," Dept. of Agrl. Econ. Bull No. 468, North Dakota State University, Fargo, North Dakota, March 1967.

The formula adopted by the Federal Crop Insurance Corporation of the United States of America,[16] established $0.01152\,\overline{Y}$ as the proper minimum annual loss cost. In this study, however, it worked out to 0.105 tonne, which is much lower than the pure premiums presented in Table 5. This minimum pure premium rate is to be charged at any coverage level, even those less than 45 per cent of the long-term average yield.[17]

The maximum pure premium rate was 1.51 tonnes, at a coverage level of 100 per cent. It formed 16.58 per cent of the quantum coverage, indicating that the premium payable for every tonne of quantum coverage would be 0.1658 tonne.

Pure premium rate in monetary terms. When the average price of Rs 650 per tonne was taken, the monetary pure premium rate was, as presented, for 12 coverage levels, in Table 6. At a coverage level of 60 per cent, the monetary coverage was Rs 3,562 per hectare and the monetary pure premium was Rs 234 per hectare, i.e., Rs 6.57 for every Rs 100 of monetary coverage. It should be noted that the price does not affect the proportion of the premium to the coverage or indemnity, though it has affected the monetary coverage and the premium.

Schedule of annual pure premium and indemnity: The pure premium payable and the indemnity per hectare, corresponding to 13 coverage levels,

TABLE 6

Pure Premium Rates in Monetary Terms

Coverage level (per cent)	Quantum coverage (tonnes per hectare)	Monetary coverage at Rs 650 per tonne (Rs)	Monetary pure premium at Rs 650 per tonne (Rs)
45	4.11	2,673	117
50	4.57	2,971	149
55	5.03	3,270	188
58	5.30	3,445	215
60	5.48	3,562	234
65	5.94	3,861	290
70	6.40	4,160	356
75	6.86	4,459	433
80	7.31	4,752	520
85	7.77	5,051	622
90	8.23	5,350	736
95	8.68	5,642	861
100	9.14	5,941	985

[16]R.R. Botts and J.N. Boles, *op. cit.*, pp. 735-36.

[17]However, some loss can be expected regardless of the size of the crop. One per cent of the long-term average yield may be sufficient at low coverage levels, but at the higher-coverage levels, two per cent would be more appropriate. The losses will be small in the years with good yields, if the variations in the yields from the mean is low. M.R. Peterson, personal correspondence, dt. 9-10-75. (Mr Peterson is The Manager, Federal Crop Insurance Corporation, USDA, Washington D.C. 20250).

TABLE 7
Schedule of Annual Pure Premium and Indemnity

(Tonnes/Hectare)

Coverage level (per cent)	Quantum coverage (tons/ha)	1971 Pure premium	1971 Indemnity	1972 Pure premium	1972 Indemnity	1973 Pure premium	1973 Indemnity	1974 Pure premium	1974 Indemnity	1975 Pure premium	1975 Indemnity	Average pure premium
45	4.11	0.27	2.01	0.21	1.95	0.15	1.76	0.15	1.71	0.11	1.59	0.1797
50	4.57	0.33	2.11	0.27	2.01	0.20	1.84	0.19	1.79	0.15	1.67	0.2289
55	5.03	0.41	2.19	0.34	2.12	0.25	1.92	0.25	1.87	0.20	1.75	0.2895
58	5.30	0.47	2.27	0.38	2.16	0.29	1.98	0.28	1.92	0.23	1.81	0.3305
60	5.48	0.51	2.30	0.41	2.22	0.32	2.01	0.31	1.98	0.25	1.83	0.3603
65	5.94	0.62	2.42	0.51	2.30	0.40	2.10	0.39	2.08	0.32	1.92	0.4468
70	6.40	0.74	2.52	0.62	2.42	0.49	2.21	0.48	2.18	0.41	2.00	0.5483
75	6.86	0.89	2.66	0.74	2.55	0.60	2.32	0.59	2.29	0.51	2.13	0.6668
80	7.31	1.05	2.77	0.88	2.64	0.73	2.43	0.71	2.40	0.62	2.22	0.8003
85	7.77	1.23	2.92	1.04	2.79	0.88	2.56	0.86	2.53	0.76	2.36	0.9565
90	8.23	1.43	3.06	1.23	2.94	1.05	2.70	1.03	2.66	0.92	2.48	1.1322
95	8.68	1.65	3.38	1.42	3.07	1.24	2.83	1.21	2.80	1.10	2.63	1.3245
100	9.14	1.84	4.13	1.57	3.35	1.45	2.99	1.42	2.98	1.30	2.78	1.5150
Mean yield (Y) T/Ha		8.57		9.06		9.28		9.35		9.45		
Co-efficient of variation (%)		46.75		44.50		41.07		40.84		38.45		

are indicated in Table 7, for each year from 1971 to 1975. In 1971, at a coverage level of 60 per cent, the pure premium payable was 0.51 tonne per hectare and the indemnity was 2.3 tonnes per hectare. The pure premium rate declined to 0.25 tonne per hectare and the indemnity to 1.83 tonnes per hectare in 1975. This was mainly the result of the reduction in the yield variability, from 47 per cent in 1971 to 38 per cent in 1975. No weightage was given for deterioration in crop quality in estimating the indemnity payable, since the procedure involved in determining quality was complicated.

Opinions of farmers. Information on the opinions of the farmers, regarding whether the crop was risky or not, measures used to overcome the risk, their willingness or unwillingness to insure the crop, the reasons for the latter and their preference for voluntary and compulsory crop insurance, have been presented in Table 8. It was observed that 76 per cent of the farmers considered potato as a risky crop. About 28 per cent had already reduced the area under potato to some extent, because of the high risk and expenditure involved. About 45 per cent, however, did not vary the area under the crop, mainly because they felt sure that a good crop would be obtained in the forthcoming years. Only 3 per cent of the farmers planned to give up potato cultivation altogether. The remaining 24 per cent did not consider potato as a risky crop. They stated that, since they were able to obtain good quality seed tubers, they did not face any difficulty in recovering the expenditure.

Of the farmers interviewed, though 76 per cent felt that the crop was risky, only 55 per cent were willing to insure. They, however, wanted to

TABLE 8
Opinions of Farmers

No.	Opinions	Percentage of farmers	Cumulative percentage
1.	Acceptance that potato cultivation is a risky venture	76	
2.	Wish to reduce the area under potato crop	28	28
3.	Did not wish to vary the area under potato crop, since there is surity of getting a good crop in the next year	45	73
4.	Wish to leave potato cultivation in future	3	76
5.	Willing to insure		
	(a) for a premium upto Rs 247 per hectare	37.33	
	(b) for a premium upto Rs 125 per hectare	5.33	42.66
	(c) for a premium upto Rs 85 per hectare	8.66	51.32
	(d) for a premium upto Rs 75 per hectare	4.00	55.32
6.	Unwilling to insure		
	(a) due to high premium rate	5.33	
	(b) due to lack of faith in the insurance organization, with respect to its functions	39.33	44.66
7.	Insist on voluntary insurance	44.66	
8.	Agree that insurance must be compulsory	10.66	55.32

make the supply of good quality seed tubers a precondition to insurance. The other 45 per cent of the farmers rejected insurance altogether. The main reason (in the case of 39 per cent) for this was their lack of faith in the successful working of an insurance programme. Some of them had a bad experience, of one kind or the other, with life or property insurance in the past. They felt very strongly that in the case of loss, the procedure of getting compensation was cumbersome, that even when the insurer was intimated promptly of the loss, the indemnity payment was delayed or not paid at all. Many of them stated that bribes had to be paid. They did not also believe that an insurance organization would take the responsibility of supplying good quality seed tubers. Only five per cent of the farmers rejected crop insurance, because the pure premium rates were too high.[18] Efforts were also made to ascertain the maximum pure premium the farmers were willing to pay for potato insurance in Hassan. It was found that 4 per cent were willing to pay Rs 75 per hectare, 9 per cent were willing to pay up to Rs 85 per hectare, 5 per cent were willing to pay up to Rs 125 per hectare and 37 per cent were willing to pay even Rs 247 per hectare. Thus, it was observed that 55 per cent would pay a pure premium of Rs 75 per hectare, 51 per cent were willing to pay up to Rs 85 per hectare, 43 per cent were willing to pay up to Rs 125 per hectare and 37 per cent were willing to pay up to Rs 247 per hectare. At a coverage level of 58 per cent, at which the operational cost was just covered, the pure premium worked out to Rs 215. Therefore, only 37 per cent of the farmers would be willing to insure at this level. If at least 55 per cent of the farmers should insure,[19] the coverage level should be much below 45 per cent, when even the planting cost can not be covered. Actually, to cover planting cost, the pure premium should be at least 0.21 tonne or Rs 136 per hectare.

It was also observed from Table 8 that about 44.5 per cent of the farmers preferred voluntary crop insurance and only 10.5 per cent were of the opinion that insurance should be compulsory. The main reason for the latter was that farmers would make serious efforts to grow the crops successfully, particularly take up plant protection measures, only in such a case.

Conclusions

The most important causes of yield variability, especially of the low yields obtained, were:

---

[18]Since no insurance premium were computed earlier to data collection, the farmers were asked for their opinion using an ordinary schedule of premiums ranging from Rs 75 to Rs 247 per hectare. They were first asked whether they would purchase crop insurance if the premium were Rs 75 per hectare. If they agreed, the premium was increased progressively until they would no longer purchase insurance. Here, 5 per cent of the farmers rejected crop insurance even at a premium of Rs 75 per hectare.

[19]In the U.S. the FCIC offers crop insurance in a county only if a minimum of 200 or 1/3 of the farmers participate.

(*i*) the failure of rain during the critical periods of planting and tuber initiation; and

(*ii*) the use of poor quality seed tubers, especially those affected by seed borne wilt or bangle disease.

It is necessary to note that, whereas the risk of crop loss due to the first cause is insurable, the risk due to the second is not insurable, since it is an avoidable hazard.

Though, most of the farmers felt that potato cultivation in Hassan is risky, 55 per cent of the farmers were willing to insure when the premium was Rs 75 per hectare and only 37 per cent were willing to insure at a premium of Rs 247 per hectare. At a coverage level of 58 per cent, at which operating expenditure is just covered, the pure premium would be Rs 215 per hectare. When other charges, such as loss adjustment cost (estimated at one per cent of the coverage) which works out to Rs 34 per hectare, are included, the premium would be at least Rs 249 per hectare.

An almost necessary condition for potato insurance to be feasible in Hassan area is the provision of good quality seed to the farmers.

REFERENCES

S.G. Borude, and Joglekar, N.M., "Crop Insurance to Protect the Farmers Under Dry Farming Conditions in Maharashtra," *Indian Journal of Agricultural Economics,* Vol.26, 1971, pp.307-17.

R.R., Botts, and Boles, J.N., "Use of Normal Curve Theory in Crop Insurance Rate Making, *Journal of Farm Economics,* Vol. 40, No. 3, August 1958, pp.733-40.

M.G.Chandrakanth, A feasibility study of crop insurance for potato in Hassan taluk of Karanataka State, unpublished M.Sc. (Agri.), thesis, Dept. of Agri. Econ., University of Agricultural Sciences, Bangalore, 1976.

F.E. Croxton and Cowden, D.J., *Applied General Statistics* (second ed.), Prentice-Hall of India (Pvt) Ltd., New Delhi, 1964, pp. 173-239.

V.M. Dandekar, "Crop Insurance India," *Economic and Political Weekly,* Vol.11, No. 26, 26 June 1976, pp. A-61 to A-80.

H.W. Delvo and Loftsgard, L.D., *All Risk Crop Insurance in North Dakota,* Dept. of Agri. Econ., Bul.No.468, North Dakota State University, Forgo, North Dakota, March 1967.

J.S. Fowlie, *Statistical Tables for Students,* Oliver and Boyd, Tweddale Court, Edinburgh 1, 1969, pp.4-5.

M. Friedman and Savage, L.J., "The Utility Analysis of Choices Involving Risk," *Journal of Political Economy,* Vol.56, 1948, pp. 297-304.

B. K. NARAYAN

Backward Area Development: A Conceptual Framework

Primarily the issue of backward areas impresses itself as it is an universal problem. There is no region or state in our country which could claim that it is not backward. An instance in point is Vidharbha in Maharashtra, Eastern Districts in West Bengal: they all present as difficult a problem as the backward areas of Orissa or Bihar. These problem areas exist in all States, rich or poor. It would be a difficult proposition to think in terms of evolving suitable economy where this problem would be mainly, if not fully, eliminated.

CONCEPT AND DEFINITION

At the outset let us begin with the definition of a backward area. There are a number of definitions, nay descriptions, of backward areas. Even so, most of them agree on the indices, such as ratio of regional unemployment to average national unemployment, per capita regional income to per capita national income, regional infrastructure equipment, the level of economy in terms of capital equipment, etc. If one is not careful and adopts too many indices, he is likely to end up in a paradox. If we take unemployment as a criteria then possibly Maharashtra will qualify for attention. Even so, to be pragmatic, one should identify backwardness as otherwise precious little can be done.

GENESIS

Yet another question that would arise is how did backwardness appear— it may be primarily due to poor agricultural endowment with low productivity per head, gradually engulfing the neighbouring areas. It could be due to inferior land and low return from land. Yet another possibility is low industrial productivity resulting in smaller increase in standard of living. In both situations any improvements in productivity would benefit better endowed regions calling in quick succession development of infrastructure, increasing productivity, development of inter-regional trade (both in primary and industrial products).

[1]Economic Development of Backward Regions: Problems and Prospects (ed) H.M. Patel *et al.*, Rao Pura, Baroda, 1974.

Apart from this, the movement of population from marginal agriculture into industry and technical progress has the built-in effect of developing one area at the expense of the other and further the movement of population has had effects on all other sectors of the economy. The other facet is that of backwardness of the area which was once in the forefront of growth and subsequently declined—the coal fields of Raniganj is an example. Such a phenomenon calls for vigilant care of even developed regions which are in the periphery. It may be observed in passing that the chances for development of a particular area depends not only on historical reasons, but also on factor endowment perspective.

A FEW QUESTIONS

A number of questions arise in this connection. How do we tackle the problem of initial development as against revitalization of a region? Who should do the job—the Government or the private entrepreneur? What is the type of action that is necessary? If the Government has to do it, to what length should it go? Should it only create general endowment activity or straightway plunge into development process on a national scale? The answer in the context of Indian Economic environment is clear. We may have to support a more active policy both on socio-political and economic grounds. This is so because the private entrepreneur in making his decision about the location of the new activity will consider his own interest (profit) more important than the point relevant to national interests. The issues pervading national interest are of no immediate consequence to him and even he may attempt to minimize the investment in social capital, while making best use of the existing and potential social capital.

RATIONALE

If one trusts the autonomous force of growth, it may lead to excessive concentration of growth in a few areas: may be development would move into areas which are already overconcentrated and overurbanized. Further, even the concentration of activity in a small number of centres may lead to excessive size growth. To avoid this, it should be necessary to select a number of centres providing for diffusion of development. Finally, the diffused location of growth centres[2] will call for greater mobility of resources leading to better resource utilization and higher income per head, i.e., it would provide for a sort of socialism in spatial terms. If the mobility is not provided for, it has dangerous implications. In heterogeneous areas, as in our country, the productivity will decline. There will be no optimum resource utilization and the country suffers as we have to provide jobs for

[2]This will be discussed below. *Growth Centres in Regional Economic Development*, (ed) Niles M. Hansen, The Free Press, New York, 1972.

people wherever they are. Further, what is true to international trade theory may also be true for inter-regional trade, i.e. the advantage of comparative cost for an area with better endowment for producing a particular product will not have been respected.

LESSONS FROM EXPERIENCE

One of the lessons from attempts at developing backward areas in our country is the failure to understand their problems in the correct perspective. More often than not a problem area is tackled through a small project, may be with a big project, without impact on the area. The examples of Bhilai and Rourkela which have left hardly any impact on the surrounding areas make the point clear. There is no point in tackling the backward areas on an ad hoc basis; either do it wholly or not do anything at all. In this connection, it is necessary that a backward area be properly defined and demarcated where a special step or action is possible covering possible centres of growth. Even within a backward area it is necessary to choose only the centres with potential or otherwise any extraneous growth effort would end up in temporary activity, finally resulting in social disaster. It is also necessary to derive a proper size for effective growth centre and choose proper complementary activities for action. We may observe in passing an investment in highly sophisticated plant may not have any effect on the region, nor mere association of top experts solve problems. Further, we should avoid being lost in solving small problems. It is also necessary to consider minimum threshold requirements in the choice of growth centres and provide for a big push in terms of sizeable and proper investment. It should be such that an initial activity starts a chain of activity and keeps it going until it increases local expenditure, local export and reduces regional balance of payment deficits and provide for self-sustained growth.

THE ISSUES

An area for planning should be large enough to provide for efficient in-jrastructure facilities and small enough to organize and administer. It should also provide market for local small-scale produce and minor agricultural product. However, it would be futile to generalize on its type and size and apply them to all unequal parts of the country. The first step in this direction before adopting the backward area for development is resource survey (geological, physical, soil, rainfall, human etc.). On the basis of this survey develop a regional model with comparative advantages for development in one or the other direction. Having done this, it is necessary to concentrate in the area(s) with comparative advantage. In the selected area(s) it is necessary to provide for capital equipment and minimum infrastructure. Further, simultaneously an attempt should be made to provide for social infrastructure like education, health and also training system. Although it is claimed that all these are being done in our country, I am afraid there is neither a system nor a whole-hearted approach.

The acceptance of the need for the development of the backward area introduces a new dimension in the task of economic development as against earlier non-spatial economies which had completely ignored the complicated areal dimension. Now, an attempt is being made to think in terms of alternative geographically located places of production, i.e., a clear sign of the need for understanding geographical distribution of population, other resources and markets. It does even cover soils and mineral distributions. What is required is not a mathematical model of spatial economy, but an understanding of the complex geography of supply and demand.

Let us now turn to major issues concerning backward areas. In fact this revolves round the approach, selective or general, and the criteria to be adopted for identification of backward areas. As observed earlier, developed parts co-exist with backward areas and more often backward areas are inhabited by socially backward and tribal people.

The need for a choice of approach is mostly determined by financial and administrative constraints. While a proper development approach will have to be built on proper resource inventory, it will be difficult to wait until such a detailed study is completed. Yet another issue that should be observed is the need for development efforts to percolate to the adjoining backward or semi-backward areas. More often than not the issue of returns from investment in backward areas raises its head. It is argued that investment in backward areas do not bring social returns and perhaps many a backward area has zero development potential. This argument cannot be carried too far as the development of a nation should be complete and cover the human element as well. It is needless to say that the social justice and the economic development should not conflict, but would call for an appropriate strategy. In this connection, the desirability of selective investments on priority basis in backward areas deserves attention. As observed earlier this point can be better made by adopting a few growth centres with potential for investment. While development is one thing, yet another need is the compulsive element of providing minimum needs in the backward areas in the country. Thus, a distinction between development and minimum needs must be clearly made: the latter should be provided for, irrespective of development potential. All backward areas should be provided with basic amenities of living. In view of development potential differentials of backward areas, it is necessary to evolve a strategy wherein attempt should be made to bring about a balanced development, with investments in the regions where the returns are maximum. It is also necessary that care should be taken to provide proper income distribution or otherwise its effect would be lost. In this connection, an appropriate development subsidy pattern should be evolved. (It is already there in some form but without much effect.) The subsidy should be so patterned as to provide a maximum growth possibility to a sector which has a decided comparative advantage.

While the strategy of growth in most of the backward areas is closely linked with agriculture, the decided advantage for an industry should be taken care of. While agriculture may suffer from natural disadvantage, the difficulties faced by industry may be due to faulty location. In most of the situations the problems of backward areas are linked with the relationship between agriculture and industry and increasing scale of efforts, organization, and institutional facilities.

The immediate solution, though difficult, could be found in adoption of proper agro-industrial linkages where they have scope for growth. Further, proper strategy where both irrigated areas and non-irrigated areas receive attention may also be useful. It should be noted that more than the speed of development, the progressive transformation of the people is important.

In the promotion of industries there is a need for selective approach. In the backward areas, there is scope for two major groups of industry: establishing ancillary around industrial unit located in backward areas and agro-based and resource processing industries. In this connection, it is also necessary to develop appropriate technology for isolating industries or processes which are particularly suitable to backward areas. The development of the infrastructure should take care to encourage industrial development and develop technological skill through training. The provision of incentives, although necessary, is not sufficient to assure development unless the provision is made for infrastructure and technological development. In this connection suitable pricing policy can also play an important role.

The controversial issue is the adequacy of incentives. While the incentives have to be related to the advantage of the location in backward area, it is difficult to precisely measure its disadvantage as it varies from place to place and over time. Even so, the subsidy can be related to disadvantage of location, in the short run and at the point of establishing the unit. As of now, the emphasis is on capital subsidy and it may be desirable to examine the provision of labour subsidies and output subsidies.

In fine, the issue of backward areas deserves much more careful study before a last word is uttered on policy of backward area development. The problem becomes more acute in view of heterogeneity among the backward areas and no global solution can be thought of. This requires elaborate micro-level studies which should not result in inaction and in fact the present policies with suitable modification should be continued. The investment in the backward areas should be broadly governed by the cost and comparative advantages. It is also necessary that the state action should be in a package covering almost all the sectors through an integrated areal plan.[1] The implementation of the policy could be successful only if there is proper supporting staff trained by appropriate agencies. It is also necessary to restructure the existing organizations and if possible reduce the multiplicity

---

[1]Some attempts have been made to prepare such plans, particularly for command areas in Andhra Pradesh and Karnataka.

of institutions working in the area. Finally, the most important element in the development of a backward area is local leadership.

A STRATEGY FOR BACKWARD AREA: INTEGRATED DEVELOPMENT

The integrated development is seen essentially as an aspect of economic specialization (regional/sub-regional versus national) and provides for adjustments with the system. It also emphasizes the importance of looking at economic growth as integral part of total change engineered in all sectors of development simultaneously: while it considers expansion of the agricultural sector as a must for regional development, it provides for simultaneous growth of industrial and tertiary sectors. Further, the development of marketing and the market is considered essential for generating and sustaining higher income and employment. Thus, integrated development plan efforts are considered essential for uniform growth of all the sectors at a given related space. All in all, it also provides optimum employment, and growth of income, natural resources, infrastructure, social overheads and industry.

The systematic approach to backward area development is of recent origin. The broad objective is to provide for a rapid optimum utilization of resource potential in the region. This basically warrants co-ordinated development approach. It will be necessary to provide for infrastructure like roads, railways, markets, warehouses, electricity, education, animal husbandry and other facilities. All these are basically necessary to strengthen and stabilize the economic base.

GROWTH CENTRE APPROACH

Whereas the centres of economic development should be dispersed and their impact percolate to grassroots as widely as is feasible, it cannot b carried home to each and every settlement in a region: nor can it be confined only to already developed urban centres. An alternative and feasible compromise is the growth centre approach to areal development. The growth centres are the points/nodes around which the future development is most likely to cluster. The industrial concentration, particularly agro-industries, in such centres is desirable to minimize waste of scarce resources and to optimize the use of existing resources; this has particular relevance to the need for utilizing existing infrastructure facilities.

The growth centre approach as a rational instrument for regional planning is built on two principles; that growth concentration results in economies of scale, and that development, viewed as a process of innovation and growth, does not occur everywhere at the same time but originates only at certain points from where it percolates to other centres. The growth centre approach is a synthesis of concentration and decentralization. It is, in short, "decentralized" concentration of development of rural India.

The village is the lowest order settlement with certain population agglomeration with or without minimum facilities. In the hierarchy "centre settlements," occupying the lowest rung are the dependent settlements discharging some lower order functions. These settlements depend on the neighbouring higher order centres, "service settlements," for other services. The service settlements or market town discharges higher order functions to the hinterland consisting of central settlements along with their dependent settlements. The probability of one of these centres developing into a growth centre is higher than the claim of lower order centres as the latter possess nil or low potential for growth.

In a situation where all settlements cannot be developed and where impulses of development should not be allowed to concentrate in metropolitan areas, the logical step would be to identify the growth centres in a region to bring about decentralized concentrated development.

The central point is that the cluster of growth centres in a region would develop into a growth pole performing apex functions for larger areas.[4] Here a specialized activity (may be agro-processing units) which is normally performed by other centres (concentration of administrative and superior functions) is developed to aid economic changes.

While the uncoordinated development programmes tend to produce uneven impact on the hierarchy of settlements, a well-directed "growth centres" policy helps us in less unbalanced spatial development.[5]

The concept of "growth" is comprehensive enough to cover not only economic but geographical, social and cultural aspects. It takes in its stride the development of physical or human resources and helps integrated development of a backward area and its people. The growth manifests itself in a size-function hierarchy of settlements.

The first task is the identification of a hierarchy of central places and their hinterland. The structuring of the facilities should be functionally and spatially related providing for continuum and help optimizing the use of existing infrastructure. The evolution of growth centres should be based on the present development needs and cost of filling the chasm in infrastructure and complexity of management of available resources. The identification of a growth centre is based on factors such as geographical and functional centrality and resource potential. Spatial centre should possess good transport and communication links (critical distance) with its own hinterland settlements, and with the neighbouring higher or equal order centres on the other.

In case a settlement does not command certain facilities corresponding to its population size, such facility should be taken upon for development on a priority basis. Thus, supplying the gaps in infrastructure facilities will

[4]A. Kuklinski and R. Petrella Mouton (eds.), *Growth Poles and Regional Policies*, the Hague, Paris, 1972.

[5]The SIET Institute employed (present author along with T. Raghupathi and D.V. Rao, was associated with both the studies) the hierarchy technique for identifying growth centres in the Nagarjunasagar and Pocham pad Commands, sub-regions in the state of Andhra Pradesh.

help creating functional centrality. The larger the functions the settlement possesses the more would be the number of dependent villages. This should raise the functional status of the higher order centres. The effectiveness of the candidate geographical and functional central place would be more pronounced if it is buttressed by growth potential—agricultural, industrial, mineral, livestock forest, etc.[6] The synchronization of these three functions would facilitate optimum exploitation of resources through minimization of investment and maximization of returns. The juxtaposing of the three functions lead to creation of "effective centrality" or the "growth centre."[7]

An analysis of the tertiary sector should cover the existing net-work of transport and communications, markets, power, banking, education and medical facilities and also ways and means of strengthening and modifying the present structure.

The identification of the gap helps in visualizing the magnitude of the task ahead. With a view to exploiting the external economies created, a complex of agro-industries—processing, input, demand-based—may be suggested. Here the governing criterion would be the maximization of the value added by manufacture at the source of raw material.

Finally, the whole programme is viewed in the spatial context.[8] The spatial context needs identification of levels of settlement such as extension centres, central places, service centres and growth centres. This requires a careful assessment of the existing level of functions in each settlement. A review of projected development and identification of location and areal gaps in the availability of functions is made. There is a need not only for taking into consideration the population and area thresholds but also threshold requirements to sustain a particular level of activity. After estimating agricultural potential, the identification of candidate industries—type and number—are made.

The approach is to study the location of an industrial complex instead of any industry in isolation. Subsequently a plan for the number of units in each industry that could be sustained by the envisaged primary sector potential would be drawn.

CASE ILLUSTRATION

In the earlier two sections attempt is made to describe the general frame of, and an approach to, backward area development. This section illustrates a case where an integrated development plan for a backward area was prepared. The study area, a part of Karimnagar District in Andhra Pradesh,

[6]The optimization of location of small and medium industries will be plausible with the identification of central places and estimating the potential of hinterland.

[7]The growth centre is a central place: this has to be corrected to geographical centrality (pre-irrigation hierarchy) and be superimposed by potential (agricultural and other sources) on which depends pace and direction of growth.

[8]Rober D. Dean *et al.*, *Spatial Economic Theory*, The Free Press, New York, 1970.

comes under Pochampad Irrigation Project (Godavari River). The study was sponsored by the Government of Andhra Pradesh for the World Bank and the present author was the Director of the project executed by Small Industry Extension Training Institute, Hyderabad. Following is a brief review intended to focus on certain aspects of the development plan and does not purport to be the summary of the Report prepared and submitted in 1972.

Objectives of the Study
The objectives of the study were:

(i) Structural analysis of the secondary sector with particular reference to small and agro-industries arising out of development of the primary sector;

(ii) Assessment of agricultural growth potential, as a basis for future industrialization;

(iii) Location of growth centres and identification of candidate industries;

(iv) Infrastructure requirements including roads, power, location and construction of warehouses, marketing facilities, etc.

(v) Estimation of required processing facilities for new materials and their marketing; and

(vi) Financial and administrative implications of the programme.

Design of the Study
The study,[9] spread over 12 months was divided into two stages. In the first stage, lasting seven months (Part I of the report) the study confined to 0.1 million hectares of command, covered by IDA loan in the taluks of Armoor (Nizamabad District) benefiting 273 villages. According to 1971 Census half a million persons live in these 273 villages in the command. In the second stage (Part II of the report) the study area extended up to the end of the First Phase i.e. 0.23 million hectares of command in the same taluks.

It was not possible to visit all the villages to contact innumerable agriculturists, officials and local leaders.

However, to help matters regarding the plan of the study, a number of visits were made to the villages and towns in the command. An extensive tour of the command along with the senior officials connected with the project was undertaken to assess its requirements and to determine the scope of analysis. The objectives and aspects of the study were discussed at a series of meetings at the project site, Daroor Camp (Jagtial) and Alagnoor (Karimnagar).

[9]Sponsored by the Government of Andhra Pradesh for the World Bank (SIET Institute, Hyderabad).

The Setting

The geographical area benefiting from Pochampad Project, an important irrigation reservoir across the river Godavari, comprises (a small part of Armoor Taluk of Nizamabad District and Metapalli, Jagtial, Peddapalli, Karimnagar and Manthani taluks of Karimnagar District) 24 per cent of the area of Karimnagar District and 2 per cent of the area of Telengana. With the World Bank aid, 0.1 million hectares, net irrigable area, is planned to be irrigated.

Until recently the Godavari, skirting the Northern and Eastern boundaries of Karimnagar District, was not harnessed for irrigation in these parts. The Manjira traverses from West to East in the middle of the District and is an important source of irrigation except for Metapalli and Jagtial taluks. Peddavagu and Chinnavagu are the other rivers which join the Godavari in the District.

The atmosphere is mainly dry. The command exposed to both the monsoons, but the major portion of rainfall occurs during the South West Monsoon (83 per cent of total annual normal rainfall) and only nominal rainfall during the North East Monsoon. A comparison of these two districts (Karimnagar and Nizamabad) with other districts of the State reveals that Nizamabad and Karimnagar rank first and sixth, respectively, for the total annual normal rainfall during South West Monsoon and eleventh and eighteenth, respectively, for total annual normal rainfall. This emphasizes the urgent need for water conservation and optimum utilization.

The full utilization of the potential created by Pochampad reservoirs would transform the agricultural landscape of the command. That Karimnagar and Nizamabad districts are predominantly agricultural is evident from the fact that 85-90 per cent of the population lives in rural settlements and 70 per cent of the workers are engaged in agriculture. In other words agriculture has been the main source of livelihood for majority of the population. The prerequisite for development of the region does, therefore, lie in strengthening the agricultural base on which the future course of industrialization has to be anchored. Any development plan has to take into account the existing pattern of land use, mode of cultivation and scientific farming.

Pre-Irrigation Setting—Land

Of the total geographical area of the command settlements (283,000 hectares) 79,000 hectares (28.3 per cent) are not cultivable. The net area is 0.14 million hectares as against the gross area sown 0.15 million hectares (49.2 per cent). The area available for development, therefore, is 70,000 hectares (22.5 per cent). This consists of a large area of fallows, cultivable wastes, pastures and area under miscellaneous trees which is attributable to the poor irrigation and credit facilities as well as to the outmoded and uneconomic land use and cropping pattern. This state of under-utilization

[10]*Census of India 1977*, Govt. of India.

of available land is true of the entire Karimnagar District. The position is better in Telengana Region (20 per cent), than the State (19 per cent), and worse off compared to the country (25 per cent). Thus both in Karimnagar and Nizamabad there is considerable scope for extensive cultivation. This is particularly true of command taluks of Metapalli (39 per cent) and Peddapalli (27 per cent) which record higher returns.

As per the data available for the command 0.154 million hectares were under cultivation, of which 15,000 hectares were double-cropped (9.7 per cent). As against 12 per cent in the State, Telengana Region in general, Karimnagar (8.9 per cent) and Nizamabad in particular, have small area sown more than once.

Crop Pattern

With inadequate irrigation, cropping is bound to be biased towards dry crops. Food crops dominate with 85 per cent. Among the food crops[11] paddy accounts for 24,977 hectares (16.2 per cent) of the gross cropped area. Other irrigated crops are chillies and turmeric. Sesamum is also raised under dry cultivation.

This cropping pattern where food crops dominate and cash crops hardly have any status—2,845 hectares (1.8 per cent) of chillies and 2,605 hectares (1.7 per cent) of groundnut—reveals poor economic conditions of command agriculture.

Post-Irrigation

The programme of localization under Pochampad Project is for 0.1 million hectares by 1976 and 0.23 million hectares by 1979. It is noted that at present tanks serve as an important source of irrigation both in the command and the District. The position will be different when all the potential of envisaged irrigation projects are realized. Then canals will have a big role to play with 75 per cent in the command and 44 per cent of the gross irrigated area in the District.

The full exploitation of irrigation potential created depends on developing an optimum crop pattern. The crop pattern should be so visualized as to minimize cost of production, eliminate wastage and maximize returns. It is also inevitable that the pattern should suit the requirements of the soil, climate, current cultural practices and farmer's preparedness.

The agriculture department envisages ultimate crop intensity to reach 150 per cent in the localized area. The traditional cultural practice in the area is to sow rainfed dry crops during Kharif and wet crops during rabi. Thus the farmer, instead of remaining idle, is likely to continue cultivation in both seasons. In spite of all this, it is rather difficult to contend that the future crop pattern would actually confirm to the forecast. Certain factors operate effectively in influencing the choice of the crops:

[11]Other important crops are jowar (25%), maize (17.9%), greengram (17.1%), and other crops (23.7 %).

(*i*) The normal cultivation in the command is mostly confined to kharif season, while two-thirds of the area localized is for rabi and only one-third is kharif. The changes in the rhythm of work may have its impact;

(*ii*) Slow pace of land development in the command;

(*iii*) Inadequacy of credit facilities;

(*vi*) Illiteracy and lack of knowledge of scientific farming;

(*v*) Conservatism of the farmer and diehard tradition; and

(*vi*) Resistance to change from dry to wet and irrigated dry cultivation.

The area under new irrigation would increase four-fold, giving a great fillip to intensive cultivation. During the first few years of the project the area irrigated was mainly wet with hardly any provision for irrigated dry. By 1977, however, irrigated dry farming gained a dominant position.

This study was an attempt to identify problems and to suggest a way out. The problems are many and aspirations of the agriculturists are mounting. Suggestions and recommendations are made with a view to meeting them, at least partially.

The command has all along remained "traditional" with a large proportion of population depending on agriculture. This, in effect, has resulted in a poor industrial base. In a region where the density of population is high, cultivable land suitable for reclamation is small, soil is poor and rainfall low and unevenly spread, Pochampad Project brings new hopes for scientific farming and better water management.

An analysis of the impact of future crop pattern on secondary sector with particular reference to processing units were attempted. The main emphasis was perforce on buildingup of the secondary sector on the basis of the growth in agricultural potential. The scope for locating various services including warehouses and markets and industrial units in the command was examined both on the basis of the existing potential and its anticipated increase, due to an increase in the supply of agro-industrial raw materials. The technical co-efficient for determining the efficient operation of various services and industrial units were used for determining their optimum number. An attempt was made to suggest an optimum dispersal of the potential service and industrial units on the basis of hierarchy of settlements and on their hinterland potential. The study also estimated the requirements of infrastructure to aid the development process.

The study comprised, in the first instance, an analysis of the primary and secondary sectors in the pre-development period and of irrigation potential and the crop pattern envisaged in the command. After estimating the agricultural potential, identification of candidate industries—by type and number—was made. Emphasis was laid on the location of industrial complexes instead of any industry in isolation, preferably in the co-operative sector. A plan for the number of units in each industry over time and space that could be sustained by the estimated primary sector potential was consequently drawn.

An analysis of the tertiary sector covered the existing net-work of transport and commuications, marketing structure, power, banking, education and medical facilities and also ways and means of strengthening and modifying the present structure. Finally, identification of growth centres and cost of translation of all these into practice was made.

The Study

The optimization of dispersal of functions with multiple points of supply and or demand requires:

(*i*) Identification of central places;

(*ii*) Demarcation of settlements having communication with central places;

(*iii*) A rational ordering of central places in hierarchy reflecting the size of the area economically linked to the place and linkages between them; and

(*iv*) The supply/demand potential required by various industries at each of the places.

The identification of central places, their hierarchy and demarcation of the villages serviced by them require detailed field enquiry relating to services available in each settlement and interdependence of various settlements for various higher order services available at fewer places. This procedure of identifying central places and their dependent settlement could be followed only to a limited extent. Largely an alternative method was followed for identifying central places and their hierarchy using census data on workers in trade and commerce.

Central places up to a certain level were chosen for demarcating their service areas. The boundaries of the service areas of various central places for highest order services in the lowest order centre was demarcated half way between any two centres. The irrigation potential within the boundaries of each service area was taken as the index of potential increase in supply/demand for various economic activities at central places.

With the availability of vital irrigation input for agriculture, a command area experiences powerful push for economic development. The resulting increase in agricultural income creates potential for services and growth of small and medium industries. The requirement of service/industry cannot be met individually for each settlement but only to group(s) of them. Central places of these groups of settlements are optimum location for services and industries. However, not all central places could be optimum locations for all services and industries. These economic activities require minimum demand for or supply of raw material. If the area served by a central place satisfies this minimum requirement of a service or industrial unit, this minimum requirement of economic activities constitutes threshold requirements. Thecentral place becomes the location for at least one unit.

The threshold requirements of various economic or social activity could be expressed in terms of population or area, given the income and population distribution over the area. The activities are ordered according to threshold requirements. The highest rank is given to the activity requiring the highest threshold size expressed in common terms of population or area.

A place which satisfies the threshold requirements of a higher order service/industry is also likely to satisfy the lower orders, and here all the services/industries of lower orders are also likely to be located with the higher order ones. Hence, non-agricultural employment increases with the increase in the order of highest order service available at a place. The population density and non-agricultural employment of a place are, in a way, related to the highest order service available at a place. Hence, a marginally urban place has a minimum highest order service industry. If this can be identified it will be possible to define urban areas in terms of services/industries at the place. However, this is not possible because of lack of data on threshold requirements and employment potential of various service and industrial units. Although it is possible to forecast location of various services/industries at a place based on their threshold requirements of demand/supply and the potential demand/supply of the area served by it, it is not possible to forecast exactly whether or not a place can grow into an urban area. Further, forecasting employment in non-agricultural sectors and growth of population of a place with reasonable accuracy also encounters difficulty. Only a rough indication of these can be made by using multiplier method: relating growth in population and employment at a place to economic growth in the areas served by it. This is attempted in respect of trade and commerce. It could not be done for other urban functions due to difficulty involved in the collection of data.

Based on the forecast of employment in trade and commerce, and suggested dispersal of industries, certain places are identified as possible places for growth and therefore suggestion for providing certain urban facilities.

The study, although intended to be comprehensive, was, in terms of reference, confined to identification of centres for location of markets and warehouses and provision of infrastructure to facilitate their effective functioning. As a prelude to the identification of centres, an elaborate analysis of pre-irrigation hierarchy of the settlements in the command and the adjoining areas, within their orbit of influence, was undertaken. On the completion of pre-irrigation hierarchy model, the task was to estimate and project the future hierarchy and interaction of newly created irrigation potential with existing level/order/rank of settlement. This statistical exercise was essential to a scientific approach for identification of growth centres.

The study has revealed that there are one first order centre, 10 second order and 20 third order centres in the pre-irrigation hierarchy. In the post-

irrigation hierarchy, 3 towns, including Karimnagar, the District Headquarters stake their claim for first order, followed by 3 second order, 3
third order, 2 fourth order and the rest for the subsequent orders.

Population and Market Surplus

The planned infrastructure development in the command depends on the
quantity of production and ensuing marketable surplus of various crops.
The estimate of market and warehouse requirement depends on market
surplus which in turn is determined by total production, crop pattern[12]
and price behaviour. The estimated further production refers to the period
when irrigation potential is more or less fully utilized. The estimate is
based on the concept of minimum and maximum production likely at a
point when the irrigation potential is reasonably utilized.

The production estimate was based on the following assumptions:

(*i*) Area localized under paddy would be a net addition to the existing acreage under that crop;

(*ii*) The future cropping pattern in the localized areas of the command
settlements will be the same as visualized by the Agriculture Department; and

(*iii*) In the localized areas, as the water is let out during either kharif
or rabi season, the farmers will continue the traditional practice of sowing dry crops during other seasons.

The production is estimated on the basis of average yields of hybrid and
ordinary varieties assuming that 40 per cent of the area would be brought
under hybrid programme. The intensive cropping programme can be
realized through a liberal application of fertilizers.

The next step is to arrive at the market surplus, growth centrewise, for
important crops. This again is based on the experience in matured or
stabilized regions of the State. In other regions, intensification of agriculture, over time, has resulted in the increase of market surplus. Market
surplus is defined as a function of production, level of agricultural income
and changes in the structure of the economy. It is felt that, with development of agriculture and increased income, self-consumption requirement
of the farmers decreases (inverse relationship). Also change in food habits,
increase in market surplus and reallocation of labour from agriculture to
other sectors, reduce rural demand for food consumption. Although the
ratio of market surplus to production varies from region to region and
within a region from period to period, we have adopted the maximum
figure derived for the matured and stabilized command. This is because
action programme should provide for sufficient markets and warehousing
facilities for a point of time when the irrigation potential is realized to the

---

[12]Although the envisaged crop pattern is tested through opinion survey, the feasibility
of the programme was not examined by this study.

maximum. The market surplus was estimated on the basis of ratio of market surplus to production, derived through field investigation and established correlation in the developed neighbouring areas.

The prerequisite for utilization of waters is land development and water management. The central co-operative Land Mortgage Bank has formulated a phased programme for land development. However, the disquieting feature is that the progress made during the first two years was hardly 1,080 hectares (as against 20,234 hectares by 1975). Land development programme needs to be more dynamic with large coverage of agriculturists and farms. It may be necessary either to extend credit facility to non-members through block agency or increase the membership of primary societies to cover a larger number of command-farmers. The extension of activity should necessarily cover small and marginal farmers whose requirements are as great, if not more, as the middle level farmers.

The crop pattern, apart from helping to minimize cost of production and maximize returns, has to meet the chief requirements of soil/cultural practices and preparedness to take, on the part of agriculturists, to wet cultivation. As for the latter, it is seen that the command-farmers welcome the change and are prepared to adapt themselves to the new pattern envisaged by the Agriculture Department.

Although suitable for cultivation in the command, cotton and sugarcane are left out from the programme. These crops are likely to substitute paddy and other irrigated dry crops. The trend will, however, depend upon the relative prices of food and non-food crops. If the past behaviour is any indication, it would be difficult to keep cotton and sugarcane away from the command. Therefore, definite provision for their cultivation should be made. At least 10-15 per cent of the wet area should be earmarked for sugarcane cultivation. A sound price stabilization policy fixing minimum procurement price announced at least six months in advance of harvest is essential for a successful implementation of envisaged crop pattern. The Food Corporation of India should become more active in the area. It is also necessary to eliminate the middlemen whose role is not helpful to agriculturists.

Another important factor in the context of crop pattern stabilization is the availability of fertilizers.

In brief, the approach to the study was that of integrated and comprehensive area development where the agricultural potential for each growth centre becomes the base for future planning. The prime assumption for the estimate of agriculture potential was the probable crop pattern suggested by Agriculture Department and confirmed by the opinion survey conducted by the study team. On the determination of production level, as and when the command matures and stabilizes, the market surplus is estimated. The estimated market surplus was the basis for examining the adequacy of existing markets and warehouses and for suggesting new sub-markets and warehouses. The next step was to identify the gaps between the required and the

available infrastructure facilities—growth centre wise. The identification of
the gap helped in visualizing the magnitude of the task ahead. With a view to
exploiting the external economies created, a complex of agro-industries—
processing, input, demand-based—have been suggested. Here the governing
criterion was the maximization of the value added by manufacture at the
source of raw material. In fine, an aggregate cost, based on current prices,
with certain allowance for inflation, for all-round development of the ayacut
was estimated.

Markets/Warehouses

The present network of markets is not adequate to cover the entire
ayacut. The unserviced command would be around 1800 sq. kms. On the
basis of potential production and fertilizer requirements of the area, the
study suggested 6 new sub-markets and 17 warehouses with a total capacity
of 72,500 tonnes. This excludes existing and proposed warehouse capacity
of 50,000 tonnes.

Candidate Industries

While the type of envisaged crop pattern limits the extent and area of
agro-industrialization, it is necessary to exploit the agricultural resources to
the best advantage, to help reducing underemployment in agriculture and
transferring surplus agricultural labour to secondary and tertiary sectors.

The agro-based industries suggested by the study are rice mills (11),
groundnut oil mills (2), washing soap (2), maize starch (1), chillies and
turmeric (2), oleoresin (1), cattle and poultry feed (2), tanning (1), milk
chilling (2), fertilizer mixing (2), pesticides and insecticides (1), sprayers,
dusters and mist blowers (1), agroservicing centres (1), electric motor and
oil pump sets (1), agricultural implements and; (3), rice and oil mill parts
and servicing (1).

The Protein and Fisheries Development Plans of the State Government
are a necessary pre-condition for proper utilization of available ayacut
resources.

Infrastructure

The infrastructure facilities available in the command are inadequate for
the task of integrated development: the gap has to be plugged to create a
pre-condition for sustained development. The road links and a new railway
line are necessary for strengthening the existing infrastructure base. Establishment of a railway agency at Jagtial is necessary. Posts and telegraph
offices in all the identified growth centres and postal facilities for all the
settlements over 1,000 population are suggested.

As for co-operatives a liberal credit policy is called for. While the working capital of the societies should be strengthened, the present performance
(advance to agriculturists) is not encouraging. The co-operatives should go
all out to meet a large part of (Rs 52 millions) anticipated requirements of

farmers by 1978. Whereas co-operatives are expected to play a vital role, the commercial banks must service the needy command farmers with liberal credit. Bank branches should be opened at unbanked growth centres. A phased programme to cover all settlements with over 4,000 population by 1980, may be drawn up.

The settlements up to the fifth order in the hierarchy, uncovered at the moment, should be taken up for electrification immediately. All the villages with over 2,000 population should be electrified in phases. A Rural Electric Co-operative Society for the electrification of a group of command settlements may be established.

As regards education it is suggested that schooling facilities should be increased in the settlements depending upon population thresholds. Junior college may be started at all growth centres. Two Industrial Training Institutes should be established for upgrading and development of skills.

The available hospital facilities should be strengthened and new hospitals must be started in all the growth centres. The existing veterinary services require strengthening and new dispensaries are to be opened. Sufficient precaution may be taken to prevent the outbreak of new diseases, an off-shoot of wet cultivation. Fishing will be a supplementary source of income to the people in the command. While a nursery be established at Pochampad, there is a compelling need to erect a fish ladder at the reservoir.

The stupendous task of preparing an action programme on the lines suggested here, requires, the study felt, the right type of people and organization. In view of rich experience that Andhra Pradesh has, in implementing irrigation projects and development of the commands, the existing administrative set-up needs little change. As of now the State has a few command area authorities, including one for Pochampad. Yet in order to bring about effective co-ordination, "Godavari Development Authority," may be set up with wide powers on administrative and technical matters. This authority should be responsible for preparing blue-prints, implementation of development plan and their frequent evaluation. It should comprise all the development departments like agriculture, industry and public works and service departments, like education and health with full authority on these matters. With a senior officer at the top of the organization, the authority will serve as a top decision-making, co-ordinating and executive body. The strengthening of the agriculture department with full-fledged additional directorate at Jagtial is a first essential step towards effective implementation of agricultural programmes.

S. SUBBARAMAIAH AND K. NAGESWARA RAO

Economic Development of Rayalaseema Region

INTRODUCTION

Rayalaseema, a region of Andhra Pradesh is treated as one of the natural divisions of India. It is rated "low" by the experts in its level of socio-economic development and also in its capacity to direct rural population to industrial and urban nuclei.[1] As a "stalking ground of famines" it is too well-known and recently the World Bank has bestowed attention on this area under its Drought Prone Area Programme (DPAP).

The region, one of the three major divisions of Andhra Pradesh, includes the four southern districts of the State, Kurnool, Anantapur, Cuddapah and Chittoor besides the taluks of Giddalur and Markapur included in the district of Ongole. It extends over 28,000 square miles with a population of 8 million people according to 1971 Census.

Probably few regions in India have received so much public attention and so little benefit. The entry of the World Bank into this area perhaps reveals the gravity of the situation as well as the enormity of the problem and un-mistakably refers to the missed chances and the narrowing options for conservation and development.

In studying the region of Rayalaseema we have to keep in mind two factors. One, its peculiar physico-natural features described as drought prone conditions and the special circumstances relating to the formation and the consequent socio-political pulls and pushes in the State.[2]

The State of Andhra Pradesh (AP) was formed in two stages—the formation of an Andhra State and its expansion into the State of A.P., with the merger of the Telengana areas of the former State of Hyderabad. The new State had to pay a heavy price for this expansion and merger of all the Telugu-speaking areas of India. Not only was the merger on certain

---

[1]Sengupta and Galina Sdasyuk, *Economic Regionalisation of India—Problems and Approaches.*

[2]Socio-political conditions in Andhra Pradesh.

I Plan	There was no separate State of Andhra.
II Plan	Events leading to the formation of a separate State of Andhra. Problems of Integration.
III Plan	Normal conditions.
IV Plan beginning	Telengana Agitation
V Plan formulation	Recovering from the Andhra Agitation.

guarantees to the Telengana region and its people but the new State was regularly embarrassed and periodically threatened with agitations and attendant disturbances rendering the orderly functioning of the Government nearly impossible. Every action and policy of the State Government had to be judged and passed on the crucial test: does it ensure the guarantees given to the Telengana region and people? It was a very strange situation for few policies or persons seem to have survived this test and further the Telengana opinion assumed the extreme form of thinking that unless the Telengana region is separated from the State of A.P., Telengana would get no justice. As though to fully respond to these provocations, the rest of the State Andhra region comprising the Coastal Andhra and Rayalaseema organized a three-month agitation against a Chief Minister who happened to be from the Telengana region. The cabinet was split on this issue and the Ministers were parties to this agitation, culminating in the imposition of Presidents' Rule for the State.

These events were of immense consequence to the Rayalaseema region. There was not only another backward region in the State, namely Telengana, but a politically more powerful and legally elaborately armed with commitments and promises ensuring continued preferential government attention. The peculiar physico-natural disadvantages of the Rayalaseema region were ignored or if considered kept for residual attention. Instead of qualifying for unique and undivided attention, Rayalaseema had to seek a share as a minor partner with the backward Telengana. This approach shifted the focus from the drought prone features of the region to a mere regional allocation of public expenditure on some basis like the population or the geographical size of the region. But such allocation a region is entitled to even otherwise and with no extraordinary claims. What was evaded in the bargain was the special consideration (in quantum as much as in pattern) the region deserved because of its disadvantages.

RAYALASEEMA AS A DROUGHT PRONE REGION

Drought is a meterological concept and as such is amenable for several shades of meaning depending upon a variety of factors. The effect of drought on a particular place is not always determinate. In fact a great deal of controversy still persists in identifying a drought prone area. Each state government seems to have interpreted drought in its own way as the Irrigation Commission found to its surprise.

However, the term is basically related to the quantum and dependability of rainfall. An analysis of 77 years' rainfall in the Rayalaseema region showed that the occurrence of famine was traceable to failure of the South West Monsoon in 12 years and to the failure of North East Monsoon in 24 years. The period (1900-20) was identified as relatively free from famines.[3]

The rainfall data was analyzed on a taluk basis, for the 20 year period 1950-69. It showed that 31 taluks revealed a high coefficient variation as shown below:

Coefficient of Variation of Rainfall

| Name of the district | No. of Taluks | |
	Low: 20-30 per cent	High: 30-50 per cent
Anantapur	3	8
Chittoor	1	9
Cuddapah	3	6
Kurnool	5	8
Total	12	31

Source: Pitchi Reddy, *Planning and Development of Backward Areas*, p. 152.

Among the 4 Rayalaseema districts Anantapur was the most vulnerable.

Perhaps as a consequence of the poor rainfall, there are no major rivers in the region excepting Krishna and Tungabhadra. The average flow of all other minor rivers is confined to 20 days in a year.[4]

Since the last decade experts in agriculture and other sciences are making extensive studies to measure the consequences of drought on various crops. Their studies reveal that drought should be related to the moisture content in the soil and not to mere rainfall data. Efforts are also made to study the time of occurrence of the drought, its intensity vis a vis, the crop (aridity index) and the stage of the crop. However it is found that it is not possible to forecast the time of the occurrence of drought with any degree of

[3]**Famine calendar of Rayalaseema,**

Drought in consecutive years:

1875-'76
1896-'97
1899-'1900
1907-'08
1923-'24   In all these years Anantapur was the worst affected.
1900-'20
1921-'22
1924,
1931-'32
1934-'35   Value of crops affected—Rs 6.98 crores.
1937-'38
1941,
1942-'43   Unprecedented, very several, loss—Rs 9.74 crores.
1945-'46   Loss—Rs. 9.89 crores.
1951-'52

Source: Annexure II, Note on the Development of Rayalaseema, Y. Pitchi Reddy's report, *Planning and Development of Backward Regions*, p. 71

[4]*Ibid.*, Lakshmi Reddy, N., *Plan for Soil Conservation in Anantapur District*, p. 181.

reliability.[5]

The soil of the region is said to be highly porous, poor in organic matter and fertility possessing low holding (water) capacity. Some have found that the soils are not only being eroded, but they are also depreciating. It is estimated that an area of land in Cuddapah loses 5 lbs. of Nitrogen and 25 lbs of phosphorous pentoxide.[6] The soil of Anantapur is said to be deficient in zinc.[7]

Further the undulating terrain of the region is taking its own toll. As against an average slope of 1.5 per cent, the region's slope is said to vary between 2 per cent to 4 per cent thus promoting a fast run-off of rain water.[8] One estimate is that only 10 per cent of the rainfall is actually utilized for crop growth.[9] If the soil erosion continues in the same way there will be, says an expert, no soil left for cultivation in the next 50 years.[10] Another expert regretting the slow pace of soil conservation work in the region, says that if the present rate of soil conservation work is maintained, it takes 45 years to cover the Chittoor district.[11]

Referring to the physiography of the region, the following observation summarizes the situation.

No high mountain ranges, no thick forests, the paucity of perennial rivers, a low rainfall, an enervating climate—these are part of what nature has given to this land and no wonder its material progress is hampered.[12]

The assessment of the Perspective Plan is equally forthright.

. . . area can be described as one with no apparent substantial resource endowment and as one for which the potentialities for future development have to be carefully assessed and created with the help of necessary technological breakthrough.

The beginnings of a special policy for Rayalaseema may be traced back to the Famine Code Revision Committee constituted in 1938 to investigate and formulate measures for the prevention and recurrence of famines in Rayalaseema. The Committee recommended the construction of irrigation projects, (Tungabhadra Dam I Phase, and Pennar Kumudavathi Project)

[5]*Ibid.*, "Identifying Drought Affected Areas and Assessing Intensity of Drought."

[6]*Ibid.*, K. Ramalinga Reddy, "Plan for Soil Conservation in Cuddapah District," p. 188.

[7]*Ibid.*, Krishnamurthy, "Improved Agricultural production in Rainfed areas, Prospects and problems," p. 241.

[8]*Ibid.*, p. 188.

[9]*Ibid.*, p. 181.

[10]*Ibid.*, p. 188.

[11]*Ibid.*, P. Rajagopal Rao, "Plan for Soil Conservation in Chittoor District," p. 198.

[12]*Ibid.*, "Philosophy," p. 113.

geo-hydrological survey of the area, measures for the afforestation besides others relating to the supply of new seeds and fodder for cattle and live-stock. It also recommended the constitution of the Ceded Districts Econo-mic Development Board for planning the prosperity of these districts. But its most far-reaching recommendation was to amend the Famine Code to enlarge the functions of the State and make the Government responsible for the maintenance of its people in good health and prevent physical deterioration and dispiritedness.[13]

The recommendation for the formation of a Ceded Districts Economic Development Board was accepted and a Board was constituted in 1941.

Not much seems to have happened in the years that followed. With the termination of the Second World War the Government of India constituted Committees for the post-war reconstruction. The Madras Government deputed P.V. Subba Rao to make a quick survey of the region and recommend measures for the development of Rayalaseema, although the Ceded Districts Economic Development Board was functioning.[14]

With the short time and limited resources at his disposal Subba Rao made far-reaching proposals on the wide variety of issues affecting the economy of Rayalaseema. In fact it was he who successfully sponsored the name Rayalaseema for this region in the place of the colonial expression Ceded districts. His wish that the new name would be a reminder of past glories and pointer to future glories remains half fulfilled. Subba Rao's perceptive analysis and proposals form, so to say, the foundation on which later measures for the development of the region are made.

He made in all 96 proposals covering primarily soil conservation, agri-culture, irrigation and what is now referred to as extension forestry and social forestry. His proposals also include a separate section on the essen-tial and primary needs such as water supply, housing and education. A matter of particular significance is his special allotment of Rs 20 lakhs for Harijan housing schemes.

Subba Rao found that the Ceded Districts Economic Development Board (CDEDB) did not achieve much and as an advisory body with neither powers nor funds was inherently incapable of producing results. Keeping in mind the Tennessee Valley Authority and the Damodar Valley Corporation in India he recommended the reconstitution of the CDEDB as a Rayalaseema Development Board with powers to sanction individual proposals not exceeding Rs 5,000. For this purpose he wanted the Board to be granted Rs 5 lakhs annually. Subba Rao's proposals without much ado found their way into the archives.

But the Rayalaseema Development Board instead of the Ceded Districts Economic Development was constituted. It was a body of dignitaries and included 4 Ministers of the Madras Government including the one for

[13]Planning and Development of Backward Regions.

[14]*Ibid.*, "Proposals for the Economic Development of Rayalaseema," (P. V. Subba Rao's report) Annexure I, pp. 9-68.

Rayalaseema (Minister in change of Rayalaseema Development was the ex-officio chairman). It sat 14 times during a span of 5-6 years and made 142 proposals as it did not have any other powers.[15]

The 1953 famine caught the notice of Prime Minister Nehru who sent an expert committee under the leadership of P. C. Bhattacharya. The Committee recommended Rs 1.57 crores loan from the Central Government and Rs 17 lakhs subsidy for providing lasting and semipermanent relief measures. Also it recommended Rs 30 lakhs for soil conservation measures. Despite the total endorsement of this recommendation by the Rayalaseema Development Board, the Government remained unpursuaded to respond.

Not much seems to have happened in the 8-year interregnum, 1954-62.

In 1962 once again, Regions like Rayalaseema got a new recognition as "chronically drought affected areas." 40 of the 74 chronically drought affected talukas in India were identified in Rayalaseema. The State Government drew up a pilot plan to develop 12 chronically drought affected areas, 6 of them in Rayalaseema. It involved an expenditure of Rs 8.08 crores over a three year period. The Government did not approve this plan on the ground that most of the schemes have already been included in the Third Plan.[16]

Among the chronically drought affected areas Anantapur is one. The State Government envisaged an expenditure of Rs 17.71 crores. After an on the spot study of Anantapur district, the Government of India approved a plan of Rs 30.9 lakhs for the district. The draft outline of the Fourth Five Year Plan made a provision of Rs 52 crores for these chronically drought affected areas. In 1972, an Indo-French hydrological and hydro-geological survey was contemplated.

In 1969 once again the Government of Andhra Pradesh thought it fit to revive the Rayalaseema Development Board with a new name, the Rayalaseema Development and Planning Board. Its main function was to make proposals, review programmes relating to Rayalaseema and associate itself in the formulation of a 15 year-long-term plan for the region.[17]

Under the auspices of this body a Seminar on Regional Backwardness and Planning was held in 1970. This seminar brought out a veritable flood of information on the region.[18]

This was soon followed by a perspective plan for 1969-84, envisaging an outlay of Rs 1,124 crores, the details of which are shown below.[19] But as

[15]*Op. cit.*, "Note on Development of Rayalaseema," (Y. Pitchi Reddy's report) Annexure II, pp. 71-107.

[16]*Ibid.*, "Historical Perspective."

[17]*Select notes on Planning and Development Board for Rayalaseema*, Aug. 1972, p. 1.

[18]*Planning and Development of Backward Regions—A Case Study of Rayalaseema*, Volume I, Resource Inventory, 600 pages with maps, and charts excluded.

[19]Volume II of the same seminar proceedings : *Regional Development Plan for Rayalaseema, 1969-1984.*

a perspective plan it was too modest. For it promised to mitigate the suffering due to the recurrent drought and famine conditions, and sought to increase the per capita income of the region *as near as possible* the all India average by terminal year of the plan (*italics* ours). The perspective plan conceded rather unwittingly that there would be an investment gap of Rs 870 crores if the investment is to be raised sufficiently, to Rs 1,756 crores to reach the all India level of per capita income. A prominent feature of this plan was the special allocations made for the welfare of weaker sections.

The perspective plan spread over the fourth, fifth and sixth plan periods made some interesting priorities. The highest priority in overall expenditure was accorded to irrigation. But this was immediately followed by industry and mining. The expenditure on weaker sections earned a higher priority than agriculture and allied activities. The plan also showed large sums, Rs 229 crores under private investment.

The Drought Prone Areas Programmes (DPAP) is the successor to the earliest Rural Works Programme as well as the Minimum Needs Programme.[20] The distinguishing features of the DPAP is its reference to the ecological situation of the region and its plan to make the district the unit of planning enabling the linkage of sectors. The approach is novel in many aspects. The unit of project is a catchment area or a watershed rather than define it around administrative boundaries. The primary purpose of development is to recover and restore the ecological balance of the region. The priorities are accordingly rearranged to give the first place to animal husbandry rather than crop husbandry. Dairying, animal husbandry including sheep farming, pasture farming and afforestation, and soil conservation and minor irrigation and dry land farming is the order of projects. All

Drought Prone Area Programme, 1975-76 to 1979-80

	Outlays proposed in the World Bank Report (*in Rupees*)	
Irrigation	Rs 75.50	lakhs
Soil conservation	131.02	,,
Pasture development	74.65	,,
Forestry	45.82	,,
Dry land farming	29.43	,,
Sheep development	19.74	,,
Dairy development	301.52	,,
Project management	4.82	,,
District core funds	50.00	,,
Updating land records	39.00	,,
Total	771.49	
Add price contingency	497.83	
Grand total	1,269.32	

[20]General Report on Drought Prone Areas Programme (mimeographed).

these activities are treated as one integrated multi-dimensional programme. The five year budget of the DPAP for the district of Anantapur reveals these goals and priorities.

The first thing that strikes any observer is the multiplicity of studies, inquiries, reports of expert bodies on the region. If the Government was buying time or demonstrating its quick and alert response to a grave situation through these commissions, it is difficult to disapprove of such a practice. But in the case of Rayalaseema the tune was called too often to earn credibility.

This seems to have occurred right from the start. Even while the Ceded Districts Economic Development Board was functioning, Subba Rao was asked to make proposals only to be shelved later. Again another Committee was constituted whose proposals were either deferred or dropped. Bhattacharya's mission seems to have earned little to the region.

After a fairly long spell of 6-8 years, the Union Government began planning for the drought affected areas. Obviously these exercises brought perhaps more light than form to the region. Again the Rayalaseema Board was constituted. While its Chairman and experienced legislators demanded statutory powers and executive functions, the Government asked the Board to address itself to the highly skilled and technical task of plan formulation. The Board seems to have outwitted its sponsors by presenting a perspective plan with all the trappings of strategies, lead sectors, projections and models.

Alongside these plan exercises the Government of India was itself thinking of a massive programme of rural works to ensure minimum needs of the poor and the weaker sections of the society. The perspective plan for Rayalaseema which included a programme of Rs 100 crores for the weaker sections appears to have overlapped with the minimum need programme. Perhaps lack of coordination of this sort is not uncommon in a federal setup. However it is not clear which of the programmes was in operation during the latter part of the Fourth and the early part of the Fifth plans.

Obviously the dualism remained unsolved. In fact the sophisticated and magnificent policy making on the one hand and the traditional routinized functioning of the administration has continued to run parallel to each other.

RAYALASEEMA IN THE STATE OF ANDHRA PRADESH

We have already referred to the factors that led to Rayalaseema becoming a mere part of the State of A.P., claiming special consideration if any, only in the context of the backwardness of Telengana and in effect as a residuary claimant of privileges. Therefore the first thing to consider is whether at least the relative proportion of the region is maintained in some of the key sectors and activities of the economy.

Rayalaseema forms one quarter of the State of Andhra Pradesh in area and 18 per cent of the residents of the State are in this region. Portionality considerations demand that the region to be considered on par with the rest of the State and the other regions in it should at least possess 18 per cent of the productive capacities or income and employment benefits; or 24 per cent if area is the basis of reckoning.

As a drought prone region, the pattern of land utilization of Rayalaseema does not offer any surprises. A large percentage of forests, a sizeable area of uncultivable waste lands, besides the highly undulating terrain of the land requiring extensive soil conservation and reclamation is expected. Even the nature of forests, as described earlier, are yet to acquire value under the concept of social forestry. The Kurnool circle representing the region yielded the lowest revenue for any circle in the State. The area of reserved lands under forests was the smallest in Kurnool circle thus presenting no comparison with the other regions of the State.[21]

Within the region the forests of Kurnool alongside a portion of Cuddapah forests, referred as Nallamalai are by far the only valuable tract in the region. Both Chittoor and Cuddapah claim a third of their geographical area under forests.

Another prominent feature of the region is the inconspicuous size of the permanent pastures. While Telengana has nearly 4 per cent of the total area and Andhra has more than 3 per cent of its area, the respective share of Rayalaseema is slightly more than one per cent of its area. Paradoxically the region has more than its share of livestock derived mainly from the size of sheep and goat populations. An hectare of pasture land in Rayalaseema is burdened with 70 livestocks as against half the size in the other regions.

Among the Rayalaseema districts the position of Kurnool with about 4000 hectares under pasture lands is the lowest. Nearly 40 per cent of the pasture lands of the region are in Chittoor district.

The percentage of net area sown is the highest for any region in the state. This is a matter for alarm for the main problem of the region is the progressive extension of cultivation to marginal and submarginal lands. It is indicative of the high pressure the poor soils of the region are bearing.

Within the region, Kurnool and Anantapur claim the largest net sown area accounting for nearly half the geographical size of the respective districts. But the interdistrict differences in extensive cultivation get narrowed if we take into account the net geographical area—geographical area minus area under forest and barren lands. Yet the relative positions of the four districts remain unaltered.

If the intensity of cultivation is taken into account the last and low posi-

[21]*Statistical Abstract of Andhra Pradesh, 1975* issued by the Bureau of Economics and Statistics, Government of Andhra Pradesh, Hyderabad.

tion of Rayalaseema gets once again confirmed. Coastal Andhra claims 26 per cent of the net area sown under the second crop, while Telengana claims 12 per cent. Only 8 per cent of the sown area in Rayalaseema is brought under the second crop.

The cropping pattern of the region reveals a marked dispersion, indicating a reliance on a variety of crops. This is in contrast with that of Andhra where one single crop, rice, accounts for nearly 45 per cent of the cropped area. The reasons for dispersed cropping pattern are not difficult to seek. The vagaries of rainfall, its timing as well as quantum compel the farmer to seek a variety of crops to optimize his expected yields. If the onset of monsoon is early the farmer goes in for high valued long duration crops like cotton, groundnut and jowar. If the rains are delayed he will go in for *korra*. Even if the rains are early he develops a crop mix; his cultural practices are amenable for shifts in cropping patterns annually. Referring to the balanced pattern of cropping obtaining in Rayalaseema the Perspective Plan observes that the agricultural efficiency in Rayalaseema is "very very high."[22]

The uncertain monsoon conditions seem to have encouraged a variety of new crops under vegetables and fruits. Although the hectarage in Rayalaseema is too small, its relative position with other regions is high. In tomatoes, flowers, betel vines, coriander, mangoes, citrus fruits, grapes and onions, the hectarage in Rayalaseema is higher than either both or one of the other regions of the State. This once again demonstrates the flexible cultural operations of the region.

The open cropping list of Rayalaseema farmer is reflected in the higher proportion, 37 per cent of the sown area under non food crops. In the other regions the relative proportion is 19 per cent.

Within the region groundnut seems to be the most preferred crop in all the districts except Kurnool where jowar takes the pride of place. But among the four districts Chittoor is the only one where some sort of specialization seems to be emerging. In all others dispersion is still the rule as is shown by the table on the following page.[23]

Less than a quarter of the cropped area is irrigated in Rayalaseema. Though the position of Telengana is no better, this is in marked contrast with the Andhra region where more than half the sown area is irrigated. The higher intensity of irrigation in the region is however far below the levels of Telengana. Area irrigated more than once in Rayalaseema is 33 per cent as against 41 per cent recorded by Telengana.

The pattern of irrigation among the three regions reveals the vulnerable position of Rayalaseema.[24] Lift irrigation provides water for 41 per cent of

[22]*Perspective Plan for Rayalaseema, 1968-1984*, p. 27.

[23]Statistical Abstract, *op. cit.*

[24]The Perspective Plan warns "that the present utilisation of surface water is very much near the total dependable yield" P. 55. Another estimate: "If all the arable land of Rayalaseema, is to be cultivated the water requirement is 2000 TMC at an average of 18TMC for dry and wet crops. Whereas the actual availability is 200 TMC.

Chittoor	Groundunt	45	per cent of sown area	
	Rice	22	,,	,,
Cuddapah	Groundnut	25	,,	,,
	Jowar	22	,,	,,
	Rice	17	,,	,,
	Cereals and millets	10	,,	,,
Anantapur	Groundnut	30	.,	,,
	Jowar	15	,,	,,
	other cereals & millets	14	,,	,,
	Rice	10	,,	,,
Kurnool	Jowar	29	,,	,,
	Groundnut	19	,,	,,
	Cereals & millets	17	,,	,,
	Cotton	13	,,	,,
	Rice	8	,,	,,

the irrigated area. In Andhra nearly 60 per cent of the irrigated area is under canals whereas in Telengana, tanks are the foremost suppliers of water for irrigation. The density of wells and their intensive exploitation through electric energy is another distinguishing feature of irrigation in Rayalaseema.

Within the region too the predominance of well irrigation and the minor role of canals is easily seen. Chittoor is an outstanding example of total reliance on wells and tanks. At the other end is Kurnool depending largely on canals. The area irrigated more than once is the highest in Kurnool. The other two districts find themselves inside this range.

One of the most interesting changes suggested for the region is to re-arrange the priorities in farming—to raise animal husbandry to a place of importance and restrain indiscriminate and uneconomical expansion of crop husbandry. If animal husbandry is not an important activity it should be made so.[25]

Although the livestock population of the region is no less in size than that of the other regions, the size of pasture lands is a serious limiting factor rendering the livestock population a burden than a benefit. The combination of an extremely small size of pasture land and a sizeable livestock population can present a really distressing situation as shown below.[26]

An acre of pasture land in Rayalaseema has to support 72 heads of livestock including 37 heads of sheep and goat as against 29 and 10

[25]The DPAP report observes that livestock farming has a built in superiority over crop husbandry. DPAP General Report, op cit.

[26]Statistical Abstract, op. cit.

	Total livestock (in lakhs)	Total sheep & goats (in lakhs)	Pasture land (hectares)	Area under fodder crop (in tonnes)
Coastal Andhra	113.80	35.36	3.31	95,585
Telengana	143.94	54.74	5.59	13,923
Rayalaseema	72.89	37.10	1.03	3,084

in Telengana and 38 and 12 in Andhra respectively.

Within the region Anantapur and Chittoor have more livestocks than the others. More than half of the livestock in Anantapur are sheep and goats. Of the four districts Chittoor is perhaps the one endowed relatively with more resources to feed the animal population.

The position of Rayalaseema in respect of mineral resources is on an altogether different level. It occupies an important place in the State. The limestone deposits in Cuddapah district, estimated to be 12,000 million tonnes, at long last has attracted the Cement Corporation of India to instal a plant in the district. The deposits are supposed to be large enough to support another plant in Anantapur district also.

In an absolute sense the other mineral deposits of Rayalaseema do not seem to be either large or superior in quality to attract large-scale commercial exploitation.[27] The present output of ores from the various mines is too modest to promote setting up a plant in the region. Perhaps it is more profitable to export the minerals to other areas where water supply is not such a serious constraint, than processing them near the mines.

However, in at least two minerals the contribution of Rayalaseema to the State remains significant. Nearly all the iron ore mined in the State are from the mines of Anantapur as all the barytes of the State comes from Cuddapah, Kurnool is the second large producer of limestone in the State. Chittoor has no claims to mineral wealth.

Ahother area in which Rayalaseema's position is not the last one is in pisciculture. Inland fish production is more or less equal to that of Coastal Andhra where greater attention is paid to the production of marine fish. However compared with Telengana, Rayalaseema returns to its usual position of next best.

The fish farm at Kurnool is regarded as one of the best in the entire country. In an half acre farm with an expenditure of Rs 25,000 the farm is said to have produced 30 lakhs fish fry.[28]

If the agricultural position of the region is bad, worse are the conditions associated with industrial and manufacturing activity. In all there were 1011 industrial establishments under the Factories Act employing 20 persons on an average. Compared with the other two regions the scale and

[27]The Perspective Plan observed that several mineral occurrences were declared as uneconomical due to their relatively poor quality or *small* reserves (italics ours). Perspective Plan, *op cit.*, p. 97.

[28]Despite limitations "the area has now one of the best fish farms in the entire country." *Ibid.*, p. 79.

dimension of activity in the Rayalaseema region is far too small to be considered adequate. The H.T. electricity used by industries in the region was a quarter of Telengana's consumption and was less than a fifth of what Coastal Andhra used during the same period. In terms of L.T. electricity too the position of Rayalaseema did not show any improvement. The cottage industries of Rayalaseema seem to have used more electricity than their counterparts of Andhra. The record of Telengana in this category was far higher than either of the regions.

In respect of roads and communication the record of Rayalaseema cannot be considered inadequate. Two important railway lines run through the region—Madras and Bombay, and Bangalore, Secunderabad and the Dharmavaram-Pakala chord line. The railway line mileage for a standard unit of area is higher in Rayalaseema than the all India average and the average for the State.[29] Similarly the length of road mileage. While major portions of roads are black topped in this region only 70 per cent of Coastal Andhra roads and 60 per cent of Telengana roads are black topped. The higher record of road mileage of Rayalaseema may be traced to its strategic location in South India lying inside the triangle of three prominent towns and cities—Madras, Bangalore and Hyderabad. If one were to draw a circle of 200 miles radius from each one of these cities, they cover and intersect the Rayalaseema region. Also this reveals the limitations of Transport as a factor of economic development. By itself transport may not posses the potential to lift an economy or a region from its bootstraps particularly if the agricultural base is not strong.

Within the region Kurnool possesses the longest road mileage probably because of its location. Next comes Anantapur for similar reasons. But the position of Chittoor is significant. For the smallest district it has the longest mileage of black topped road. Cuddapah of course remaims at the last.

Not only is investment in industry very small but it is likely to be getting smaller and smaller. According to an official estimate the investment in the region during the First Plan period was Rs 182.78 lakhs as against seven fold this amount in the Andhra region and ten times this figure in Telengana. The position seems to have improved in favour of the region during the Second and Third plans. In the first three plan periods the gap in investment among the three regions decreased substantially. Investment in Rayalaseema was nearly half of that of Telengana and was a quarter of that of the Andhra regions. But this seems to have been only a short-term development. For the figures available for the years 1966-70, shows Rayalaseema receding to its earlier distance from other regions.[30]

[29]Rayalaseema has got 1. 97 route Km of railway line for 100 square Kilometres as against 1.65 Km for AP and 1.84 for India. Rayalaseema has 1331 Km of railway line.

[30]

	Investment in		(Rs in lakhs)
	Rayalaseema	Circars	Telengana
I plan	Rs 182.7	1347.72	1738.35
First 3 plans	1100.00	4600.00	2500.00
1966-1970	175.00	1500.00	6200.00 P. 110

We may now summarize the relative position of the region. Six indicators show that the development of Rayalaseema is sufficient on both the area and the population basis. Another seven indicators show sufficiency only on the population basis. If the items included under both bases are examined in some detail it will be clear how inadequate and incomplete are the foundations of sufficiency. It is indeed ironical to claim sufficiency in the matter of barren and uncultivable waste lands. Even the sufficiency in respect of the net sown area is secured at a very high cost to the region. The extension of agriculture as mentioned already to marginal and submarginal lands is one of the chief reasons for the ecological disequilibrium of the region.

But two of the items, the high percentage of well irrigation as well as the number of water pumps, reveal the resourcefulness of the people in exploiting whatever resources are made available. Also the region has demonstrated its agricultural efficiency by adopting a highly flexible cropping pattern and its relative strength in some of the crops. The high percentage of black topped roads will remain an infrastructure for future development.

Items in which the regional sufficiency is based only on the population basis are not of much significance either. Excepting certain crops under fruits, vegetables and flowers group all others relate to governmental services obtaining in this region. It is difficult to regard them as factors promoting the productive efficiency of the region. The rural bank is of course an exception. The area under forests may one day become an asset if the concept of social forestry is accepted and appropriate measures are taken to grow vegetation and pastures.

All other indicators remain to show how Rayalaseema exists without its proportional share in the economic life of the state.

Items which Indicate Sufficiency Both on the Fopulation and on the Area Basis

Barren and unculturable waste land.

Net sown area.

Pump sets and area under well irrigation.

Long-term loans distributed by the co-operatives.

Area under: groundnut, cotton, coriander, citrus Fruits, Tomatoes, flowers.

Black topped roads.

Items which Show Sufficiency only on the Population Basis

Forests.

Also the Perspective Plan observes: In the immediate future however the possibility of substantial change of the economy towards industrialization is very difficult.
Perspective Plan, *op cit.*, p. 117.

Area under: Mangoes, grapes, betel leaves.
          telephone exchanges, post offices.

No. of Hospitals, and
no. of Rural Banks.

RAYALASEEMA IN THE LAST TWO DECADES

All the eight indicators which have shown a decline during the 18 year
period are related to rural areas and agriculture. Among these the decline
in two indicators should be regarded as a favourable, and not as an
undesirable, development. A decline in the net area sown, however small,
deserved encouragement as the main problem of the region is the indiscriminate and uneconomic extension of cultivation to marginal and submarginal lands. Similarly the decline in the sheep and goat population is
again a welcome trend if it is one. The size of the bovine stock has been
far in excess of the capacity of the region. The decline will reduce soil
degradation taking place due to over grazing.

The decline in all other indicators is a matter of concern. The declining
size of forests seems to outweigh the advantages of the fall in the total
cropped area. It adds to the ecological disequilibrium of the area. The progressive fall in the area under permanent pastures and grazing lands is an
equally unfortunate development. It tends to show that the people and the
administration do not seem to have understood the problems of the region
or the importance of conservation as against indiscriminate exploitation.

The decline in area under cotton may be explained in terms of unfavourable market conditions besides the unhelpful climatic conditions which are
normal in any given year. But the decline in the area under flowers and
betel vines, is a trend which countervails the balancing cropping pattern
for which the region has earned a name.

Among the indicators showing an increase in the 18 year period is included all services of government departments like medical and veterinary,
public health and education. The increase in these services is taken for
granted although their significance is not discounted. But the increases in
such services do not directly affect the core problems of the region—the
capacity to survive the drought conditions, the incapacities and the inadequacies associated with the drought prone characteristics of the region.
Hence no further references will be made of them.

The increase in the size of barren and unculturable waste land is an
alarming development adding to the burdens of soil conservation and land
reclamation. The increasing size of livestock population again means a
further intensification of the problem of fodder, overgrazing and consequent
effect on soil. The increase in the area under fodder crops is nominal and
in terms of demand for fodder the direction of the indicator does not carry
much meaning.

The increase in the area under groundnut is perhaps the most encouraging signal from the region over the years. The region is in fact coming to be known for its specialization in groundnut. This may also provide an impetus for the establishment of the oil based units in the region, not excluding the transfer of some units from other areas under governmental subsidy.

The increase in the size of the irrigated area too deserves notice. The extension of canal irrigation in part, but mainly the expansion of lift irrigation facilities in the region, explains this trend. The region is also known for the high percentage of population covered under the rural electricity scheme. Intensive use of lift irrigation is another feature of this expansion. This is indicated by the large increase in the number of water pumps operated by motive power.

The increase in road length and the number of goods vehicles on road do not as yet seem to have made any impact in stimulating the spread of industrial and non-agricultural activity in the region.

INDICATORS SHOWING AN INCREASE BETWEEN 1956 AND 1974

1 Barren and unculturable waste land.
2 Area under crops: area under groundnuts.
3 Gross and net area irrigated and area irrigated more than once under wells. Area under canal irrigated under wells.
4 No. of water pumps.
5 Nos. of units under the Factories Act and employment in them.
6 Road length.
7 Goods vehicles on road.
8 Density of population and urban population.
9 All governmental facilities and services like education, health and medical facilities, including veterinary, and post and telegraphic services.

INDICATORS SHOWING A DECLINE BETWEEN 1956 AND 1975

1 No. of inhabited villages and towns.
2 Percentage of scheduled caste population.
3 Area under forests.
4 Area under permanent pastures and grazing lands.
5 Net area sown.
6 Area under cotton.
7 Area under flowers.
8 Area under betel leaves.
9 Size of sheep and goat population, cattle and buffaloes.

The increase in the number of units under the Factories Act and employment in them seem to have occurred more in the district of Kurnool. Over the years Kurnool is establishing itself as the industrial centre of the region probably because of the advantage in water facilities it enjoys over all others.

The other indicators showing an increase are the population and its density.

The several agitations in the State had made it necessary to show separately the plan expenditure incurred in the three different regions. The formulation of a plan for Rayalaseema helped the trifucation of public expenditure accounts of the State. Thus the government was compelled to announce the expenditure it had incurred in a given region. Thus during the 4 year period Rayalaseema's expenditure formed 20 per cent of the total plan expenditure of the State.

Securing some sort of a proportionality in the State expenditure was however an illusive gain. For the perspective plan for the region had contemplated an annual expenditure of Rs 44 crores. Against this the actual expenditure incurred was but half of the minimum needs. Again the region was caught up in the gap between the policy promises and the reality of allocations.

Share of Rayalaseema in State Plan Expenditure

	Plan exp. state Rs in crores	Rayalaseema exp.	Rayalaseema share
1969-70	96.94	12.18	12 %
1970-71	86.99	16.81	19.3%
1971-72	205.37	22.49	21.3%
1972-73	96.34	20.48	20.8%

Source: Select Notes an Planning and Development Board for Rayalaseema, p. 6.

In the last four years of the Fourth Five Year Plan Rs 1.40 crores were spent on the main programmes for the region: minor irrigation, afforestation, soil conservation and laying of roads. Nearly 40 per cent of this expenditure was on road laying the remaining 60 per cent being more or less equally distributed among the other three programmes. Among these soil conservation activity seems to have been confined to a single spurt of activity in the first year, 1970-71. More than 80 per cent of the total expenditure under this head was spent on that year, tapering off to less than Rs 50,000 by 1973-74.

Compared with the physical targets achieved during this period one realizes how deceptively small the financial targets are. Or from another point of view it shows how much more resources are to be diverted for these purposes if effective minimum physical improvements are to be achieved. Soil conservation may be cited as an illustration. The physical target achieved during the 4 year period does not even scratch the surface of the problem. The DPAP target for Anantapur district alone is 80,000 hectares, involving an expenditure of Rs 1.31 crores over the 5 year period.

As of now the region is covered by the well known DPAP. Among the four districts Anantapur has qualified for a programme approved by the

World Bank. The five year plan, commencing from 1975, involves an outlay of Rs 13 crores to be funded equally by the World Bank, the Government of India, and the Government of Andhra Pradesh. The 13 crore plan includes a large cushion of estimates to meet with the problem of price rise.

Nearly 50 per cent of the outlay is on dairy development. If functions ancillary to dairy development are also taken into account like pasture development and sheep development, this programme alone will be of the order of Rs 4 crores.

Next is soil conservation on which 16 per cent of the total outlays are budgeted. Nearly equal amounts are allocated for pasture development and minor irrigation. Rs 50 lakhs is shown against adopting village records. This is indicative of the priorities of the programme.

But even a programme like the DPAP with such international affiliations is bogged down by the not unusual delays in the bureaucratic system. The first progress report mentions several activities which are either yet to begin or yet to gain momentum. The following table gives details of the progress made in the first year of the programme in Anantapur district.

	Proposed outlay physical targets	*Expenditure/physical up to May 1976*
Wells programme	375 wells	143 sanctioned est. exp. Rs 8.33 lakhs
Minor irrigation	4 New works 8 spill over works	Rs 5.16 lakhs
Soil conservation	Rs 23 lakhs	Rs 10.12 lakhs
Forestry	Rs 18 lakhs	Rs 13.00 lakhs
Total	Rs 90.87 lakhs	Rs 55.10 lakhs

Source: Progress of DPAP in Anantapur District (unpublished).

Expenditure Incurred During the Fourth Plan (4 years)

	1970-71	*1971-72*	*1972-73*	*1973-74*	*Total*	*Physical Targets*
Minor irrigation	6.26	9.21	8.33	3.51	27.31	9966 hectares
Soil conservation	25.00	1.34	2.48	0.49	29.31	4711 ,,
Afforestation	9.07	9.58	7.41	2.03	28.09	1440 ,,
Roads laid	11.71	22.38	16.79	3.60	54.48	297 km
Total	52.04	42.41	35.01	9.63	139.19	

Source: DPAP General Report.

SUMMARY

The change in the description of the region as a stalking ground of famines into one of the drought prone areas is not a mere preference for euphemism. It also represents the emergence of a new culture in which the social commitment to rescue a poorly endowed region to a level on par with the others is accepted. Perhaps the most outstanding contribution of the various committees and expert bodies lay in facilitating the emergence of the new culture. While it was a great and crucial effort it was none the less inadequate. Commitment of resources to the Rayalaseema region have always fallen short of the minimum. The gap between the two is widening mainly because ignored problems cumulate and acquire new dimensions over time. What was essentially a problem of soil conservation and reclamation nearly 50 years ago has become a matter of ecological disequilibria within the region demanding concerted action and change in priorities. The needs of the region are conservation of the existing resources and not their indiscriminate exploitation in the conventional pattern of development. Except perhaps the experts few appreciate and receive the message of the DPAP. It is likely that the developmental programmes for the region may deviate from the strategy underlying the DPAP mainly because of popular demand and governmental convenience. It is said that a technological breakthrough is the only solution to the cumulative problems of the region. Undoubtedly it is necessary. But it is not sufficient. A break-through in the value system of the region specifically the acceptance and adherence to the priorities of the DPAP and not to deviate from it is a condition which the region can ill afford to ignore.

K. PUTTASWAMAIAH

An Appraisal of Irrigation Projects

INTRODUCTION

In a developing economy, full utilization of all the valuable resources at command, not only *capital* but also other factors of production viz., *land, labour* and *enterprise,* is important and the extent of utilization of the latter depends largely on how well the capital which is more scarce than other factors is put to maximum use. Three major tasks face the development planner, in this connection: to determine the changes in his country which most need to be speeded up, to design action or activities (development projects) of Government or other organizations which give most promise of bringing about the desired changes with the highest ratio of benefits to costs, and to administer projects as efficiently as possible. The expenditures both in the public and private sectors in the context of Five Year Plans have been large and the benefits accrued from certain sectors of the economy have not been commensurate with the investments made, partly due to the wrong choices of projects and partly due to the lumping of investments on specific projects which do not yield returns to the economy immediately. Investment choices should be guided by "clear-cut criterion of economic efficiency."[1] Efficiency does not call for one to choose the best alternative from a bad lot—that is, to ignore the utility of a search for better opinions.[2] Allocation of resources should be such that it should aim at more efficiency and attempt at a fair redistribution of wealth in a way desirable to correct the regional imbalances. A fundamental economic problem of individuals, firms and nations alike is, therefore, the allocation of resources. One such resource is *capital* which may be broadly defined as available funds. The funds available to an economic unit comprise those currently on hand plus those additional funds that can be raised in one manner or another. There are a wide variety of opportunities for the investment of the available funds. The nations must choose from among a myriad of possible fund uses. While choosing so, the well-being of all should be kept in mind. Agriculture is the main occupation of the majority

[1]Ronald N. McKean, *Efficiency in Government Through Analysis,* (Operations Research Society of America), Wiley, 1968, p. 32.

[2]Harvey Leibenstein, "Allocative Efficiency Vs. 'Ex-Efficiency',", *American Economic Review,* June 1966, pp. 392-415.

of the people in India; it accounts for the major share of the national product; it employs the bulk of the labour force; a domestic viable agricultural
sector offers the requisite market for the growth of manufacturing. In fact,
it is the agricultural sector which affords opportunities for experiments of
pushing the production possibility curve upward by means of exploitation
of resources with minimum cost. The expenditure in the context of planning havebecome so large that a calculative effort towards achievements
of "maximum additional benefits"[3] to as large a population as possible is
necessary. While applying this criterion in the investment of funds, the
basic objective should be to provide the best use or combination of uses,
of water and related land resources to meet all foreseeable short- and long-
term needs. Economic development of each region within a country, is essential to the maintenance of national strength and achievement of satisfactory
levels of living. Water and related land resources development and management are essential tools for the achievement of such satisfactory levels of
living and economic development and growth. It is apt to quote from an
American document:

. . . well being of all the people shall be over-riding determinant in considering the best use of water and related land resources. Hardship and
basic needs of particular groups within the general public shall be of
concern, but care shall be taken to avoid resource use and development
for the benefit of a few or the disadvantage of many. In particular,
policy requirements and guides established by the congress and aimed at
assuring that the use of natural resources, including water resources,
safe-guard the interests of all our people shall be observed.[4]

Agriculture, being the biggest sector of the Indian Economy providing
livelihood directly or indirectly, to nearly 70 per cent of the population,
provides opportunities for an even development, provided investments are
spread all over. The desirability of an even development all over the country
in the field of agriculture aiming at the well-being of all the people by
taking recourse to more minor irrigation works and provision for a larger
number of irrigation wells is explored in this paper. The pros and cons of
the economics of the major irrigation projects vis-a-vis the minor irrigation projects are outlined in the light of the empirical data available in the
Indian context. The progress achieved in various segments of agricultural
sector is analyzed after the criteria in appraising irrigation projects are
considered. The comparative advantages of minor well irrigation are

[3]Otto Eckstein, *Water Resource Development—The Economics of Project Evaluation*,
Harvard University Press, 1965, p. 4.
[4]*Policies, Standards, and Procedures in the Formulation, Evaluation and Review of
Plans for Use and Development of Water and Related Land Resources,*Document prepared
under the direction of the President's Water Resources Council, U.S. Senate, Document
No. 97, Washington, 1962, p. 4.

brought out. In the context of the national irrigation plan, which is in the offing in the country, this paper sets out policy direction to bring uniformity in the availability and use of water resources.

CRITERIA IN APPRAISING IRRIGATION PROJECTS

Efficient and correct choices are those that yield the most gain or benefit from available resources. Efficiency here does not mean miserliness or cost comparing regardless of the gains that might be produced; nor does it mean insistence on achieving particular gains regardless of the cost (i.e. sacrifice or other desirable things). It may be added that a familiar rule for deriving maximum benefits calls for the production of each good or service out to the point at which the marginal cost equals the marginal benefit. For any line of output this marginal gain is the worth of an extra unit of output, and the marginal cost is the benefit foregone by producing the extra unit of that output, that is, the value of alternative goods that could have been produced. So complex and pervasive is the problem of making forecasts in respect of these benefits that pales the efforts of a forecaster. The problem of forecasting the outcomes of certain kinds of investment opportunities is so difficult as to verge upon the impossible. Yet, attempts are being made since decades to forecast the benefits of major enterprises by application of sophisticated techniques of project appraisal. The cost-benefit analysis is a practical way of assessing the desirability of projects. Although the subject has come into prominence among economists only in recent years, it has quite a long history, especially in France, where Dupuit's classic paper on the utility of public works, one of the most original path-breaking writings in the whole history of economics, appeared as long ago as 1844. In the present century, the concept of cost-benefit analysis first came into prominence in the United States. Here, according to Hammond, it was "in origin and administrative device owing nothing to economic theory and adapted to a strictly limited type of Federal activity—the improvement of navigation."[5] Since then, a number of documents have been published by the U.S. Government to identify the benefits from cost on projects. It was considered that "if the benefits to whom-so-ever they accrue are in excess of the estimated costs" the project was considered worthwhile. This definition was later on broadened by bringing in to the benefit ambit the secondary and indirect benefits including intangibles. In 1950, an Inter Agency Committee produced the "Green Book,"[6] which was an attempt to qualify the general principles. Interest among economists in this technique has grown tremendously in the last few years. There seem to be several reasons

[5] R.J. Hammond, *Benefit-Cost Analysis and Water Pollution Control*, Standford, California University Press, 1958, p. 3.

[6] Inter-Agency River Basin Committee (Sub-Committee on Costs and Budgets), Proposed Practices for Economic Analysis of River Basin Projects, *The Green Book*, Washington D.C. 1950.

for this. One of the reasons has been the growth of large investment projects absorbing a large amount of resources, having repercussions over a long period of time or substantially affecting prices and outputs of other products etc. Another obvious reason is the growth of the public sector considerably compared to the earlier years. Thus, a technique which is explicitly concerned with the wide consequences of investment decisions is obviously of much more interest today than it was in the past. Of late, in addition to the cost-benefit technique of evaluation in determining the desirability of the projects, techniques such as operations research, system analysis etc., both in the public and private sectors of the economy, have come into vogue. Particular emphasis on these techniques is laid by McKean.[7]

It is always important, and perhaps especially so in economics, to avoid being swept off one's feet by the fashions of the moment. In the case of cost-benefit analysis one must recognize that it is a method which can be used inappropriately as well as appropriately. Therefore, two very clear general limitations of principles must be recognized. First, cost-benefit analysis as generally understood is only a technique for taking decisions within a framework which has to be decided upon in advance and which involves a wide range of considerations, many of them of a political or social character. Secondly, cost-benefit techniques as so far developed are least relevant and serviceable for what one might call large size investment decisions. "All decision making persons or groups attempt to economise, in the time sense of the word. That is, they try to make the 'mosts' as they conceive of the 'most' of whatever resources they have."[8] One of the major conceptual problems subjecting public investment decisions to economic analysis lies in defining the Government's utility function. Only when this has been been done is it possible to make our nation's benefits and costs sufficiently meaningfull that quantitative appraisal of economic alternatives can be expected to lead to a higher level of performance than more intricate methods of decision-making permit. Therefore, in the words of Marglin, "the goal of a programme choice can, in general, be stated as maximisation of utility subject to whatever constraints the economic and political environment imposes."[9] Cost-benefit analysis was thus introduced "as a means of project 'justification' alone, not as a tool for project planning . . . it often has served as window dressing for projects whose plans have already been formulated with little if any reference to economic criteria."[10] The strategy of growth embodied in the plans leaves many questions unresolved, and it is these tactical decisions that are the province of benefit-cost analysis.

[7]McKean, *op. cit.*

[8]*Ibid.*, pp. 3-4.

[9]Stephen A. Marglin, *Public Investment Criteria*, George Allen and Unwin Ltd., 1967, p. 15.

[10]*Ibid.*, p. 18.

AGRICULTURE IN THE INDIAN ECONOMY

In India, agriculture is the main occupation of majority of the people, 69.5 per cent (52.8 per cent cultivators and 16.7 per cent agricultural labourers) of the total population engaged in it in 1971. Broadly speaking, 45.6 per cent of our land area was under cultivation and only 21.5 per cent is under forest in 1971-72. As compared to many other countries, land under cultivation in India is very high. In the U.K., it is only 30 per cent, in the U.S.A. 20 per cent, in Japan 16 per cent, in the U.S.S.R. 10 per cent, in Australia 4 per cent, in the Canada, the granary of wheat, only 4 per cent. No other country in the world has such a large proportion of land under cultivation as India has and yet, other countries produce much higher yields than we do. One of the principal reasons for India's low productivity is the progressive deterioration of soils due to erosion and other natural calamities like flood hazard in some areas, alternating with protracted drought conditions in others.

Irrigation development in any country will have to be viewed in the context of climatic conditions obtaining in the country. It has been held that India is served by two monsoons viz., South-West and North-East monsoons. Most of the rainfall occurs during the South-West monsoon between June and October. The rainfall in the country is also to some extent unequal, irregular and quite often liable to complete failure. With such a wide difference in rainfall between one part of the country to another, and from year to year, famines have occurred several times in the past. The areas affected by these conditions are the regions of Punjab, U.P., a large part of Bihar and Tamil Nadu, some portions of Maharashtra and parts of Karnataka. It is for this reason that most of the irrigation works that were constructed in the olden days were mostly in these regions. Irrigation facilities are, therefore vital for the success of agriculture in almost all parts of the country. In order to ensure successful irrigated agriculture, it is essential that the available water resources should be conserved during years of good rainfall for utilization during lean years. In spite of the concerted efforts made during Plan periods, the irrigation aspects of Indian agriculture have not very much improved and the variations in the percentage of the irrigated areas among different States have remained as they were. Thus, the percentages of irrigation in various States at the end of March 1975 was as follows: Andhra Pradesh 29.9, Bihar 26.01, Gujarat 13.20, Jammu and Kashmir 38.30, Madhya Pradesh 8.20, Tamil Nadu 46.20, Maharashtra 9.00, Karnataka 14.50, Punjab 76.50 and Uttar Pradesh 35.10. The fluctuations in the irrigated areas in different parts of the country would result in an uneven development. This emphasizes the need for bringing in more area under irrigation.

The plan for agricultural development should be such as to aim at maximum benefit with minimum cost. It is a considered fact that irrigation facilities should be a vital need for the success of agriculture in almost all parts of the country. In order to ensure successful irrigated agriculture, it is

essential that the available water resources should be conserved during the
years of good rainfall for utilization during the lean periods instead of
making the country a victim of the vagaries of rainfall. The droughts
which occurred during the last two or three years, in fact, underline the
necessity for a change in our policy so far as investments for better agricultural production are concerned.

The country has enormous water potential. By 1951, only about 9,500
crore cu. m has been utilized by the irrigation projects of the pre-plan
representing 17 per cent of the estimated utilizable resources or 5.6 per
cent of the total annual flow. By the end of March 1970, various major,
medium and minor projects enabled the utilization of nearly 22,200 crore
cu. m of water i.e. 26 per cent of the utilizable resources. In addition to
these, it has been estimated that about 350 thousand million cu.m. (285
million acre ft.) sink into the soil and get stored underground. This emphasizes the need for digging a large number of wells to tap the underground
water.

The total water potential of India, by way of mean annual river flows,
is estimated at 1,88,100 crore cu.m. Of this, 87,000 crore cu.m. can be
utilized for irrigation development. This was assessed by the Irrigation
Commission in 1972. As against this, at the end of March 1975, the utilization was 34,300 crore cu.m. of water, i.e. 39 per cent of the utilizable
resources. A large number of storage reservoirs were constructed during
the plan periods. In spite of the increase in the irrigation potential, the
gross area under irrigation in 1960-61 and 1971-72 was 28 million hectares
and 38.60 million hectares respectively. It has been estimated that the
total area which could be brought under irrigation under all sources would
be 107 million hectares. Out of this, an area of 22.6 million hectares had
already been brought under irrigation during the pre-plan period. By the
end of 1974-75, the area under irrigation had gone up to 44.10 million
hectares. There is thus ample scope for extension of irrigation in the
country and a definite course of action is warranted during the Sixth and
subsequent Plan periods.

ROLE OF AGRICULTURE—DEMAND AND ACCOMPLISHMENT

The basic economic problems in India have their roots in food production
and agricultural development. Unless supreme efforts are economically
directed to these basic problems, the danger implied in the food crisis due
to population growth will inevitably lead to an acute food shortage and
thus stultify all planning for development and better standards of life. It
is here that the basic economic problems are really baffling in their variety
and content, largely because of their extreme contradictions, enlarging
complexities and enormous difficulties. It is evident even for a casual observer that Indian agriculture has not met the challenge of economic development in spite of the efforts through successive Five Year Plans to reach
the basic objective of self-sufficiency in food production. The effort

of planning should, therefore, be to nullify the oft-quoted metaphor of Malthus, the well-known population theorist, that "While population is supposed to increase at a hare's speed, food supply grows at a tortoise's speed." According to him, "If we can persuade the hare to go to sleep, the tortoise may have some chance of overtaking him." In spite of earnest endeavours of planners and huge investments on a number of major and minor irrigation projects in the country, it has not been able to belie the statement of Malthus. While the index of actual population increase by 1969 over the base year 1951 was 176.00, the index of paddy production rose by 7.7[11] pounds with high fluctuations during the intervening years. The demand for food created by the growth of population has not been commensurate with the food supply over the years with the result the objective of self-sufficiency in food supply enunciated by the policy makers and planners has remained a dream. This has forced to import foodgrain from other countries as is evident from Table 1.

TABLE 1[12]
Import of Cereals

(in thousand tonnes)

Cereals	1964	1965	1966	1967	1968	1969	1970	1971	1972	1973	1974
Rice	645	783	787	453	446	487	206	240	131	—	—
Wheat and wheat flour	5621	6583	8270	6400	4766	3090	3425	1814	314	2414	4203
Other cereals	—	96	1738	1819	482	295	—	—	—	1200	671
Total	6266	7462	10795	8672	5694	3872	3631	2054	445	3614	4874

The food imports have decreased substantially over the years from 1.07 crore tonnes in 1966 to 0.48 crore tonnes in 1974.

The compound rates of growth in agricultural production and productivity during 1949-50 to 1968-69 have not been attractive enough to claim self-sufficiency. If the standard of living of the rural masses have to improve to attain at least a tinge of the socialistic pattern of society, the income of the rural sector should improve and our approach in the allocation of funds to the agricultural sector vis-a-vis other sectors and in the agricultural sector, to minor irrigation vis-a-vis the major and medium irrigation should undergo a radical change. More than 70 per cent of the total population live in villages and agriculture is their main occupation. If these persons are to be benefited, investments on minor irrigation covering small tanks and wells should be increased.

Investment on Irrigation
It has been estimated that the overall irrigation potential in the country

[11]Paddy production is taken as a representative example.
[12]*India, 1977*, Publications Division, New Delhi, May 1976, p. 183.

is 107 million hectares of which 44.10 million hectares have been exploited by 1974-75. Exploitation of this huge potential requires large investments. Outlays on irrigation and flood control during the first three Plans, annual plans and Fourth Plan are contained in Table 2.

TABLE 2
Plan Outlays

Rs in crores

Particulars	First plan	Second plan	Third plan	65-67	67-68	68-69	Fourth plan
Total outlay	1,960	4,672	7,500	2,261	2,242	2,253	15,724
Outlay for irriga-tion	380*	380	580	130	133	183.7	16,160
Outlay for flood control	14	49	86.4	15.19	13.87	18.7	Actuals

*Includes Rs 80 crores of pre-plan expenditure.
Source: *INDIA, Year Books.*

It is clear from Table 2 that the outlays on irrigation have considerably increased and during the different plan periods, the increase has not been commensurate with the total increase in plan outlays.

Irrigation Potential and Utilization

India has the highest irrigation potential in the World but its utilization has been very slow. Table 3 explains the irrigation potential and its utilization source-wise and year-wise.

It may be seen from Table 3 that the ultimate potential of all sources would be 107 million hectares of which 22.6 million hectares was utilized

TABLE 3
Development of Irrigation Potential and its Utilization

(Million hectares)

Item	Ultimate poten-tial	1950-51		1968-69		1973-74		1974-75	
		Poten-tial	Utili-zation (created)	Poten-tial	Utili-zation (created)	Poten-tial	Utili-zation (created)	Poten-tial	Utili-zation (created)
Surface water	72	16.1	16.1	25.1	24.0	28.6	26.6	29.7	27.5
Major and Medium	57	9.7	9.7	18.1	17.0	21.1	19.1	22.0	19.8
Minor	15	6.4	6.4	7.0	7.0	7.5	7.5	7.7	7.7
Ground water	35	6.5	6.5	12.0	12.0	16.0	16.0	16.6	16.6
Total	107	22.6	22.6	37.1	36.0	44.6	42.6	46.3	44.1

Source: The Times of India Directory and Year Book, 1977, The Times of India Press, Bombay, p. 48.

before the First Plan. As a result of the efforts of the three Five Year Plans, Annual Plans and the Fourth Plan, the extent of utilization has increased from 22.6 million hectares to 44.10 million hectares. Thus, more than half of the country's irrigation potential is yet to be utilized. It may be further seen from Table 3 that there have been striking efforts towards utilization of potential in the major and minor irrigation sectors only and the utilization has gone up from 9.7 to 19.8 million hectares from 1950-51 to 1974-75. The utilization when compared to the ultimate potential has been very slow in the fields of minor irrigation and tapping of ground water and exploitation of surface water sources. The increases in these fields have been from 6.4 to 7.7 and 16.1 to 27.5 million hectares from 1950-51 to 1974-75 respectively though the ultimate potential in those fields is 15, 35 and 72 million hectares. Table 4 and Table 5 indicate the growth of irrigation in the major and medium fields over the plan periods and the area under irrigation source-wise from 1950-51 to 1971-72.

TABLE 4
Irrigation Potential Created and Utilization

At the end of	Gross area potential	in million hectares utilization
First Plan	2.6	1.3
Second Plan	4.6	3.4
Third Plan	6.9	5.5
1966-67	7.4	6.1
1967-68	8.2	6.8
1968-69	8.9	7.3
1969-70	9.6	7.6
Fourth Plan	11.2	9.1
Fifth Plan	17.4	14.3

Source: India 1976, Publications Division, New Delhi.

TABLE 5
Area Under Irrigation

(*In crore hectares*)

Sources of irrigation	1950-51	1971-72	Increase (+) or decrease (−)
Canals	0.83	1.28	(+) 0.45
Tanks	0.36	0.41	(+) 0.05
Wells	0.60	1.21	(+) 0.61
Other sources	0.30	0.26	(−) 0.04
Total	2.09	3.15	(+) 1.07

Source: India 1976, Publications Division, New Delhi. May 1976, p. 178.

It may be seen from Tables 4 and 5, that the area under irrigation under major and medium schemes have increased from 1.3 to 9.1 million hectares from the First Plan to the end of Fourth Plan respectively. It is expected that this would reach 14.3 million hectares by the end of the Fifth Plan. It has also to be confessed that the area utilized under irrigation indicated in the above Table do not represent the true picture and one-fourth of the total area indicated as utilized may be roughly taken as area intensively utilized. Though there has been steady increase both in respect of the potential created and the actual utilization from one plan period to another, the utilization of the irrigation potential has not been commensurate with the potential actually created during the period. While there has been an attempt to increase the area of the potential which is not substantial during the successive plans, efforts at their utilization have not been there. Increase of area under irrigation under wells and tanks has not been much.

Obstacles for Utilization of the Irrigation Potential Under Major and Medium Irrigation Projects

The problem of slow utilization of the irrigation potential under the major and medium projects has been engaging the attention of administrators for quite some time past. It is an accepted factor that many ambitious irrigation projects are completed sometimes according to schedule but not all the water that the project had made available are fully utilized by our farmers. Sometimes, only half of the stored waters are used. Non-utilization of water is not a particular phenomenon applicable to one project or other, but a general phenomenon all over the country which may at best differ in degrees. As analyzed previously, there have been attempts to invest tremendous amounts of money in large-scale projects but the returns to the economy have been almost nil due to the non-utilization of the potential which are due to various reasons.

Availability of sufficient water in time is an important factor in growing crops. It is especially so in the arid and semi-arid regions. In many pockets under the Tungabhadra ayacut, for example, a general complaint was being constantly heard in the initial stages[13] that there were either no field channels to serve the particular area or insufficient water supply due to various reasons including breaches in the distributaries and sub-distributaries and the consequent starving of field channels.

In this contest, it is relevant to mention that the first lesson the irrigation experts learnt from the Bhakra Dam was that the canal system should be completed before the main dam or at least the completion of the canal system should synchronize with the completion of the main dam. If the distributary system is not complete when the main dam is complete and if water cannot reach the fields it is like preparing ample food in an area where there are few people to eat. "The extension of irrigation

---

[13]The defects obtaining at the initial stages are now rectified. The construction of field channels till the last survey number has been treated as the responsibility of the Govt. which helped to a greater extent in the creation and utilization of the irrigation potential. The net-work of the water distributary system is now complete in all respects but this took little over 20 years after the water was first let out on 1 July 1953.

benefits from the Hirakud to the Tungabhadra had to be postponed because the canals were not ready in time."[14] This statement is still applicable in the context of many projects in the country which are incomplete after tremendous investments as it is said:

> Out of 72 major irrigation projects with a total command area of 13.4 million hectares started during 1951-65, by 1966 only 3.7 million hectares (28 per cent) have been irrigated, 4.2 million hectares (30 per cent) are in an advanced stage of construction, and 5.6 million hectares (42 per cent) are still in an early stage construction.[15]

The Nagarjuna Sagar Dam, the World's largest masonry gravity dam may be cited as another example where there has been lack of synchronization of the completion of the main dam and the canals and distributaries. This dam is expected to irrigate 1.4 million hectares from its 11 million cubic meters of stored water. The canals and distributaries built by the end of June 1967 can serve only 0.26 million hectares or 20 per cent of the whole area. It is estimated that the 1.4 million hectares cannot be irrigated until 1983. Proper allocation of costs between dam and canals at the very inception is, therefore, very vital in irrigation project planning so as to see that there would be synchronization in the completion of the dam and canals which would help in increasing the benefits.

There are several other reasons for the slow utilization of the irrigation potential. In the context of an irrigation project, it involves not only the construction of irrigation works like the dam and the canals, but also includes other items of land development like, levelling and bunding of the area, construction of water distributaries and the necessary roads and paths. This naturally disturbs the existing proprietary rights. In addition, the creation of other infrastructure facilities, like provision for marketing and storage would require huge sums of money. The cultivators may not be willing to have any change in the existing proprietary rights and it may be difficult to plan out for the investment of huge sums for creating proper infrastructure facilities. Further commencement of major projects involve a large amount of initial expenditure by way of preliminaries like roads, buildings, equipment and machinery. Such expenditure would be unremunerative if adequate progress is not maintained after commencement of work. At times, projects are likely to be dropped or postponed after incurring some initial expenditure for want of financial resources.

In instances where projects are completed, the operation and maintenance cost of irrigation facilities is a burden to the governments in underdeveloped and developing countries. In advanced countries, the water rate charged to the farmers is the same as the rate of operation and maintenance costs, while governments compensate all the operation and

[14]Vishnu Dutt, "What We Have Learnt from Bhakra—Full Use of Water Knowledge in Dam Building," *Yojana*, 14 December 1958, p. 7.

[15]*Asian Agricultural Survey*, Asian Development Bank, 1969, p. 531.

maintenance costs for farmers in underdeveloped and, to some extent, in developing countries. This increases the cost on major irrigation projects as the water rates are very low and the concept of betterment levy is a myth. The collection of betterment levy has no credits during the last few years anywhere in the country and in the case of Tungabhadra Project the collection has been almost nil.

Benefits of Irrigation Projects

In addition to the inherent bottle-necks which were discussed above, the experience has shown that the benefits from major and medium irrigation projects completed in all respects have been marginal if not minus. They have not brought sufficient returns to the economy from a cost-benefit angle in the short run. Projects of this kind would help the economy in the long run, provided the investments are made in the best potential areas and the selection of project should be on the basis of sophisticated techniques of project appraisal. It is, therefore, clear that the *lack of cost-consciousness in major sectors of the economy like the major and medium irrigation projects, among others are hindering* the economic progress of the country. This is proved by the fact that, in spite of huge investments and priorities on irrigation and agriculture in the Five Year Plans, the country is left still with huge irrigation potential and what is covered is only a small portion of the existing total. The lack of cost-consciousness is also evident in the public sector projects in the country. The Bell Commission which made a special study of some of the public sector projects in the country including the Russian built H.E.C. and coal mining and machinery plants made the following observations: "There seems to be insufficient cost-consciousness. This goes for the choice of projects, the design of projects and also for running of projects."[16] There has been lack of cost-consciousness in most of the public undertakings studied by the Bell Commission. Pearson is somewhat optimistic on the future of Indian prospects. In this report[17] to the World Bank, he has pointed that "India's performance during the last two decades has been mixed . . . India's future depends on the solution to a number of basic problems which are difficult and most pressing."[18] The problems which he has highlighted are those relating to the growth of population and shortage of food supply, the financial bottle-necks, particularly shortage of foreign exchange and the problem of making growth affect lives of the rural and urban poor. If the benefits of economic growth has to touch the poor and all, the investments in the agricultural sector in India should be spread all over which requires a cautious change in the policy of agricultural development and its allied fields.

[16]Text of Bell Commission Report appended in *The Hindu* of Madras and also quoted in the *Capital* dated 30 May 1968, p. 1061.

[17]The Report of the Pearson's Commission, officially known as Commission on International Development appointed by the World Bank, was released on 1 October 1969 at Washington.

[18]Quoted in *Economic Times*, Bombay, 2 October 1969.

Need for a Change in Policy

The above experience of the working of major and medium irrigation projects emphasizes the need for a radical change in the policy relating to investment of funds in agricultural sector if self-sufficiency in food has to be attained and the investment made has to yield immediate returns instead of returns at a distant future as "in the long run, we are all dead."[19] These projects which require large investments in selected places would be at the expense of the people all over for the benefit of a few. The investments will have to be thinly spread all over if all are to be benefited and regional economic imbalances have to be minimized. This is possible if the country could place highest priority for the irrigation under wells and other small works. The type of works that could be included here are:

1 Construction of new wells,
2 Restoration of old tanks,
3 Boring of wells,
4 Installation of Persian wheels,
5 Installation of electric pump sets on wells or streams,
6 Installation of diesel pump sets on wells or streams, and
7 Small drainage embankments.

The amount invested on such small works would begin to yield immediately and the loans sanctioned to farmers for digging irrigation wells etc., would be returned to the Government by them. Out of the total ultimate irrigation potential of 107 million hectares in the country, only 57 million hectares come under major and medium irrigation projects of which 19.8 million hectares of area has already been covered under projects now in various stages. Of the remaining potential area, 72 million hectares have to be brought under irrigation by using the existing surface water and 15 and 35 million hectares of area by minor works and tapping ground water respectively. Of the ultimate potential of 35 million hectares of area which has to be exploited by means of irrigation wells, only an area of 16.6 million hectares have been used. The exploitation of the surface water for irrigation purposes also requires small investments by farmers for installation of irrigation pump sets and other similar means. It is, therefore, necessary to place highest priority on irrigation wells and agricultural pump sets, etc., and the investment on major and medium projects should be minimized which would accentuate the regional imbalances and take away the finances of the State for the benefit of the people of a particular area at the cost of all in the State. This would also be against the "canon of equal welfare for all." "The nations are like a lot of children playing marbles. One is getting all the marbles, and the game cannot go on unless something is done to give some back to other children."[20] If the marbles (benefits

[19]J.M., Keynes, *General Theory of Employment, Interest and Money*, 1936.
[20]*The Indian Journal of Economics*, July 1947, Conference Number, p. 21.

from irrigation) are to reach all at a time when the magnitude of unemployment is so huge and baffling, the investment should be at the *low ebb* of the economy and the capital so invested should be of immediate and intensive use directed towards maximization of benefits. This would be possible only if major irrigation projects are taken up only when there would be surplus capital at the disposal of the Government's Exchequer and the policy on agricultural development is directed towards the intensive use of capital and investment at the *low ebb* for multiplying the number of irrigation wells and agricultural pump sets, construction of small tanks and pick-ups and restoration of the existing tanks which have been damaged and/or silted up. Thus, the future policy should have an accent on minor irrigation with a modification to the effect that the large and medium projects should also be taken up when the Exchequer is having a safe breathing. The economic development of the country is at present somewhat confused with many problems like the regional imbalances, shortage of finances, etc., which are the real constraints to the *velocity* of economic growth. In spite of huge investments over the plan periods, it has been observed that "both countries (India and Pakistan), despite appropriately worded paragraphs in their Five Year Plans assigning high priority to agriculture, neglected this overwhelmingly important sector."[21] There is some truth in this statement. The bulk of investment in the agricultural sector has gone to chosen places of irrigation projects thereby depriving the benefits to the majority of the Indian population who are dependent on agriculture. The benefits from these projects have also been not encouraging and the country should henceforth concentrate on small irrigation works. The nationalization of banks with the objective of increasing the standard of living of the masses would also give a helping hand in making available the necessary credit for agricultural development all over the country by providing facilities to the small landholders. The decision of the nationalized banks to declare "lead banks" for each district is a step in this direction.

Added to the above, minor irrigation works including the irrigation wells are advantageous in that (*i*) the initial outlay on them is small, (*ii*) they can be executed quickly, (*iii*) they yield quick results, (*iv*) they generally require no special assistance by way of foreign equipment or personnel, and (*v*) they can be executed with local resources with little incentive from the Government. Even in cases where loans are given for digging wells, the amount is completely repaid to the Government with interest. Minor irrigation works are the means for accelerating agricultural production and economic development. It may be quoted: "The fact of the matter is that we have in India literally a race between the hare and the hound. Since Independence our labour force has increased by 40 million but the registered factory employment has increased only by two to three millions. Even considering all the possible increases in secondary and tertiary employment, we have on hand many millions of people whom we must put to

[21]Edware Mason, quoted in *Commerce, Annual*, 1967, p. 15.

work by all means at our disposal."[22] Agriculture being the main sector which could absorb a large number of the unemployed, small irrigation works in place of major and medium ones would *help all as against a few at the cost of all* and the major and medium irrigation projects may be considered whenever there are surplus funds. But the locational decisions should be purely on economic criteria.

[22]"Productivity," editorial, *National Productivity Council Journal*, Vol.IX, No.2, monsoon 1968, p. 2.

S.M. VERRARAGHAVACHAR

The Seventh Finance Commission

The Union Government has announced the setting up of the Seventh Finance Commission under the Chairmanship of Shri J.M. Shelat, a former Judge of the Supreme Court. Besides the normal features a few specialities in the terms of reference may be noted. While formulating its recommendations, it has been asked to take into consideration the requirements of backward states to raise the level of their general administration and upgrade the standards in non-developmental sector and services to bring them to the level obtaining in the more advanced states over the period ending 1983-84. The earlier commissions had been asked to take into account the requirements of these states to raise the level of their administration not to the highest, but to the all-India average. The Commission has also been asked to take into account the scope for better fiscal management and economy in expenditure of the states consistent with efficiency and the need for ensuring reasonable returns on investments in irrigation and power projects, transport undertakings, other industrial and commercial establishments.

The Commission, while making its recommendations about the distribution of central taxes and excise duties to the states, has been specifically asked to take into account the requirements of revenue account of the states to meet the expenditure on administration and other non-plan commitment and liabilities keeping in view the national policies and priorities.

The Commission has also been asked to suggest changes, if any, to be made in the principles governing distribution among the states *inter se* of the net proceeds of estate duty on property other than agricultural land, additional excise duties in replacement of states' sales-tax levied and collected on cotton, woollen, rayon or artificial silk fabrics, sugar and tobacco.

In view of the new direction that the Janata Government proposes to give to economic policy during the Sixth Plan, the setting up of the Seventh Finance Commission has a special significance. The greater the emphasis on agriculture and social services the greater will be the rise in expenditure of the State Governments. The states' needs have been growing over the years and the states have succeeded in getting more and more from successive Finance Commissions. The Shelat Commission has to transfer more resources to the states because of the greater emphasis on agriculture, cottage and small-scale industries and also the need for raising the level of administration and social services of the backward states to the level of the advanced states.

At the outset, I would like to make certain general comments. I have pleaded often that the Finance Commission should be a permanent body. It should give representation to the State Governments. The Commission which is to be an arbiter between the Centre and the States is in a way dominated by the Centre. It is appointed by the centre and its terms of reference are determined by the Centre and its award is not binding on the centre. While the Commission can sit in judgement over the fiscal management and economy in expenditure in the State Governments, it cannot do the same thing with regard to the Union Government's fiscal management or economy in expenditure. The Commission also has no power to alter the heads of taxes to be included in the divisible pool. Of course, it may entail a Constitutional amendment; but if that is necessary it could be done. It cannot be denied that the states have inelastic sources of revenue and elastic functions. It is also a fact that there is a clear tendency towards centralization of finances, which goes against the spirit of federalism. On an average the states depend on the Centre for revenue transfers to the extent of 36 per cent and for capital transfers to the extent of 66 per cent of the total. Moreover, resources transferred through the statutory Finance Commission is declining compared to transfers made by the Planning Commission and other discretionary transfers made by the Centre. The following table illustrates this trend clearly:

(in crores of rupees)

| Years | Resources transferred through | | Other transfers | Total |
	Finance commission	Planning commission		
1951-56	447	880	104	1,431
1956-61	918	1,344	606	2,868
1961-66	1,590	2,738	1,272	5,600
1966-69	1,782	1,917	3,415	7,114
1969-74	5,316	4,230	5,307	14,853
Total 1951-74	10,053	11,109	10,704	31,866

In spite of a clear case for widening the tax-base of devolution, we do not find any significant change in the terms of reference to the Seventh Finance Commission. The exclusion of corporation tax from the tax-base of devolution cannot be defended. In fact the corporation tax which has become more elastic than income-tax should be legitimately shared with the states as it is income-tax paid by companies. The Sixth Finance Commission pleaded its inability to include corporation tax in the divisible pool on constitutional grounds. We can only hope that the Seventh Finance Commission will not put the same plea. In fact, the First Finance Commission included Union excise duties in the divisible pool even though it did not come under the mandatory sharing. Only the Parliament has to approve it. In fact, even customs duties could be included in the divisible pool as it is a tax on transaction and as such it is not fundamentally different from excise duties which are now being shared. As regards the percentage share, there is a clear case for increasing percentage share from Union Excise duties to at least 40 per cent. I would therefore suggest that the Seventh Finance Commission should widen the tax devolution base by including Corporation tax, customs duties and increase the share from Union excise duties to at least 40 per cent. The surcharge on income-tax also should be shared with the states. Coming to particular issues, the Sixth Finance Commission had distributed 90 per cent of the states' share of income-tax and 75 per cent of the states' share of union excise duties on the basis of population which goes to the advantage of the backward states. The Commission has also distributed 25 per cent of the states' share of union excise duties on the basis of the "distance" of a state's per capita income from that of the state with the highest per capita income multiplied by the population of the state concerned. It also allowed additional amounts for raising standards of administration in a state to the level of the all-India average.

The previous Finance Commissions have adopted different criteria for arriving at the states' share in each of the component of the divisible pool. While population has been given greater weightage, the other criteria adopted have been collection for income-tax, backwardness for excise duty, location for estate duty and mileage and density of population for railway passenger fares. We could suggest that a uniform principle should be applied by treating the entire divisible pool as one unit. Origin and collection, population, per capita income and degree of backwardness of development are the factors that could be given weightage. The collection criterion has been rightly rejected. In the case of income-tax, the Sixth Finance Commission has given 10 per cent weightage for collection. This is not justified as with increasing integration of the national economy the correlation between origin of income and collection of income tax has progressively weakened. Hence the principle of collection should be given no weightage.

With regard to population criterion, one may concede that it provides a broad measure of relative need, but it could be (non-discrimination) only if all the states are economically equal. This principle would mean equal per capita distribution irrespective of the advantages enjoyed by more advanced states both in terms of potential for mobilization of resources and development. A less developed state may not possess even the infrastructure as a base for development. Development could be measured in terms of the development of the different sectors like agriculture and irrigation, industries, power, transport and communications, education, health and employment. But the Finance Commissions which are temporary may really find it difficult to get up-to-date information on the various indicators and it may be even more difficult to get a common measure of agreement among the various states as to the weight to be given to the different indicators. One can at least suggest for a start that at least 20 per cent weightage could be given for development criterion and the rest being on the basis of population.

As regards grants-in-aid, the Sixth Finance Commission observes:

While we have made every effort to assure the states adequate resources to maintain budgetary equilibrium, we have not adopted the approach of mechanical filling up of the gap between receipts and expenditure on present levels of efficiency in the collection of revenues and management of public enterprises. Our proposals envisage determined and purposeful efforts on the part of the states at reduction of arrears of taxes and improvement of returns from investment in quasi-commercial and commercial projects. . . The Commission has also provided for grants for the backward states to come up to a certain national minimum.

While these observations are unexceptionable in principle, in practice it may create problems. For example, according to the Sixth Finance commission, the total non-plan gap for Karnataka as estimated by the State forecast was Rs 825.96 crores, whereas according to the Finance Commission's reassessed estimates it was only Rs 45.02 crores. The variation being Rs 780.94 crores. Does this mean that Karnataka had grossly underestimated its revenue or overestimated its expenditure? While one can concede that the game of underestimating revenue and overestimating expenditure may be played by each state, can there be such a difference? Could it not be that the states' forecast may be near the actuals rather than the Finance Commission's forecast? It would be really revealing if either the Seventh Finance Commission or some researcher could make a comparison between the states' forecast and the Commission's forecast for the period 1974-79 and see who was nearer the actuals. As regards grants to raise the level of administration the Seventh Finance Commission faces really a difficult problem as it has to raise the level not to a national average, but to that of the advanced state. But while this is welcome, the needs of other states which are relatively advanced but whose per capita incomes are still very low in absolute terms should not be ignored. Another relevant issue is, what is the reward for additional tax effort and what is the penalty for not utilizing the tax potential during the fifth plan period. While one can attribute to some extent the states' fiscal problems to the imbalance between sources of revenue and functions assigned to them under the Constitution, one cannot deny the fact that the tax efforts of the states is also inadequate. In spite of repeated exhortation of the Planning and Finance Commission, the states do not have the political will to tap agricultural income either directly or by charging economic rates for water and power. The states also are dragging their feet in implementing the agricultural holding tax which would make land taxation equitable and progressive. The Seventh Finance Commission has been asked in allocating grants to take into account expenditure economy and securing better returns from irrigation and power projects. The Seventh Finance Commission should device a scheme of incentives and penalties so that additional tax effort and economy in expenditure is not penalized.

While no attempt is made to go in depth to the problem of central loans to the states, one can make a few observations. In loan financing there are two factors: (*i*) the capacity of the borrower to repay and (*ii*) the capacity of the investment to yield direct money returns. The first is related to the over-all financial position of the state, whereas the second is related to the commercial viability of particular projects. A uniform grant-loan ratio for all the states is not justified. One can suggest that the grant-loan ratio should vary inversely to that of states' per capita income. For example, one can adopt a 70:30 grant-loan ratio for the per capita income states of say below Rs 400 and a ratio of 30:70 for states having more than Rs 800 per capita income. On this principle, one could plead that for a poorer state a larger period of repayment should be fixed compared to the richer states. Interest and repayment schedule should be matched with the repaying capacity of the projects or purpose for which the loan is given. Investments in social services like education, health services or even slum clearance or providing drinking water do not yield any direct monetary returns. They should be financed only by grants and not loans. Similarly with regard to drought relief either a loan finance should result in an asset or it should be financed by grants. With regard to other loans, the repayment schedule must be related to long or short gestation period, its productivity as well as the relative capacity of the borrowing states to repay.

In conclusion, I would once again plead for a permanent Finance Commission, which should take into consideration both plan and non-plan gap in recommending the transfer of resources from the centre to the states. A mere association of a member of the Planning Commission with the Finance Commission will not enhance the importance of the statutory Finance Commission. When one does not even know the final shape of the Sixth Five Year Plan and its financial implications, what coordination can be brought about between the Finance Commission—which will be out of existence even before the Sixth Plan is finally formulated—and the Planning Commission?

Index